AFTER THE TITANIC:
A LIFE OF DEREK MAHON

AFTER THE TITANIC: A LIFE OF DEREK MAHON

STEPHEN ENNISS

Gill & Macmillan

Gill & Macmillan
Hume Avenue, Park West, Dublin 12
www.gillmacmillanbooks.ie

© Stephen Enniss 2014
978 07171 6441 7

Index compiled by Grainne Farren
Typography design by Make Communication
Print origination by Síofra Murphy
Printed and bound by CPI Group (UK) Ltd, CR0 4YY

This book is typeset in Minion 11.5/14.5 pt.

The paper used in this book comes from the wood pulp
of managed forests. For every tree felled, at least one
tree is planted, thereby renewing natural resources.

A CIP catalogue record for this book is available from
the British Library.

5 4 3 2 1

For my mother and father

CONTENTS

ACKNOWLEDGMENTS

I am grateful to Derek Mahon first for the poems, and grateful to him as well for tolerating this reconstruction of his life story. I thank him for his friendship and trust, and for those enjoyable conversations over meals in Greenwich Village, Dublin, Soho and Kinsale.

I would like to thank the Leverhulme Trust for the fellowship that allowed me to take leave of my day-to-day duties and conduct the initial research for this book. Linda Matthews, Warwick Gould and Ron Schuchard were supportive from the beginning.

Numerous friends and literary associates shared memories and made letters and other documents available to me. Jill Schlesinger shared with me important early letters, and Richard Rooke, Mahon's former roommate from graduate school, gave me access to manuscripts which Mahon left behind when he abruptly left Canada for America in 1965. The late James O'Halloran collected Mahon's letters and manuscripts in the 1980s, and that collection proved an important resource for those years. After Jim's death, his wife, Gay, and son, Lawrence, continued to make his collection available to me.

Many of Mahon's friends granted interviews or responded to questions along the way, including Louis Asekoff, Eavan Boland, Terence Brown, Chris Cahill, Gerald Dawe, Serge Fauchereau, Eamon Grennan, the late Roy Harrison, Marie Heaney, the late Seamus Heaney, Aidan Higgins, Alannah Hopkin, the late Glyn Hughes, Kenneth Irvine, Dillon Johnston, Maurice and Sandra Leitch, Mary Leland, Jeremy Lewis, Michael and Edna Longley, Stella Lubsen, the late Samuel Menashe, Patricia Moynagh, Barry Murphy, Frank Ormsby, Richard Ryan and Sara Tolchin.

I want to thank as well Victor Blease, Rosita Boland, Robert Boyers, Ann Cremin, Seamus Deane, Eugene Dubnov, Douglas Dunn, John Dunne, Philip Edwards, Maurice Elliott, Roy Foster, Elgy Gillespie, Grey Gowrie, Nicholas Grene, the late David Hammond, Jock Houston, Paul Jackel, Harold Jackson, Jennifer Johnston, Paul Keegan, Brendan Kennelly, Tony Lacey, Reverend C.J. McCollum, Lucy McDiarmid, Kathleen McDowell, John Minihan, John Montague and Elizabeth Wassell, Letty Mooring, Piers Plowright, Jon Stallworthy and the late Bernard Stone.

Quotations from the work of Derek Mahon are used by kind permission of The Gallery Press, Loughcrew, Oldcastle, County Meath, Ireland. "Winter", by Samuel Menashe, is reprinted with permission of the Literary Classics of the United States, Inc., New York.

I could not have written this book without the archival and print collections held in libraries in the US and abroad, and I am grateful to the many librarians and archivists who provided valuable research support at the following: BBC Northern Ireland Sound Archive; BBC Written Archives Centre; Beinecke Rare Book and Manuscript Library, Yale; Belfast Central Library; British Library; Burns Library, Boston College; Castrum Peregrini, Amsterdam; Fales Library, New York University; Gotlieb Research Center, Boston University; Harry Ransom Center, University of Texas; Harvard University Archives; Houghton Library, Harvard; James Joyce Library, UCD; Library of Congress; McClay Library, Queen's University; National Library of Ireland; New York Public Library; Pennsylvania State University Libraries; Public Record Office of Northern Ireland; Tate Library and Archive, Tate Britain; Trinity College Library, Dublin; State University of New York Library (Buffalo); University College Dublin Archives; University of London Library; University of Rhode Island Library; University of St Andrews Library; Robert W. Woodruff Library, Emory (special thanks to Kathy Shoemaker, and to my former colleagues Donna Bradley, David Faulds and Susan McDonald).

Other privately held records proved helpful, including those at Oxford University Press, the American Irish Historical Society, the *Belfast Telegraph*, Church of Ireland House, Condé Nast, Raidió Telefís Éireann (RTÉ), the Royal Belfast Academical Institution, the Trinity College Student Record Office and the 92nd Street Y.

I want to thank my agent Jonathan Williams, one of the book's earliest readers. He believed in it and offered important editorial guidance and support. It has been a pleasure working with everyone at Gill & Macmillan. A special word of thanks to Conor Nagle and Deirdre Rennison Kunz.

This book is dedicated, with love, to my mother and father who brought poetry into my childhood home at an early age. My own children, Harris and Rebecca, were there at the start and grew up while this book was in the making. Finally, I thank my wife, Lucy, who has shared our household with this shade and, like Derek Mahon, always believed in the new life within our reach.

DEREK MAHON: A CHRONOLOGY

1941 Norman Mahon marries Maisie Harrison (14 January); German bombers strike Belfast (April–May); Norman Derek Mahon born (23 November).

1946–53 Attends Skegoneill Primary School.

1952 Takes class trip to England and Belgium.

1953 Begins attending the Royal Belfast Academical Institution ("Inst").

1954 Sings in Inst Easter concert; attends a church music course at the Rossall School, Lancashire.

1955 Publishes first poem ("I have been to England") in *School News*; participates in Junior Debating Society; sings in Easter concert.

1956 Family spends Easter vacation in Portrush; takes school trip to France (July); performs in School Players' production of *King Lear*.

1957 Performs in school production of *El Sordo* (The Deaf Man).

1958 Elected to the Literary Society Committee; works in the school library; wins the Forrest Reid Memorial Prize for best student poem ("The power that gives the waters breath").

1959 Acts in George Bernard Shaw's *Arms and the Man*; publishes poems in *School News*; participates in inter-school debate.

1960 Attends the funeral of William Harrison, the model for "My Wicked Uncle" (7 February); enters the May Morton

Memorial Prize competition; completes studies at Inst; enters Trinity College, Dublin; publishes "Subsidy Bungalows" in *Icarus.*

1961   Works part of the summer picking peas in East Anglia; hitchhikes around France, Germany and Belgium; begins seeing Letty Martin; addresses the Philosophical Society on Louis MacNeice.

1962   Throws himself into the River Liffey in a failed suicide attempt (22 January); meets Louis MacNeice and W.R. Rodgers; serves as editor for one issue of *Icarus* (December).

1963   Shares a flat in Merrion Square with Michael Longley; begins seeing Jill Schlesinger; suspended from Trinity for "unsatisfactory lecture attendance"; "An Unborn Child" wins third place in the Borestone Mountain Poetry Awards and is published in the *Best Poems of 1962*; works at the Belle Vue Hotel in Port Erin, Isle of Man, during the summer; moves to London with Jill; "End of Season" is published in *The Listener* (September); Jill returns to America; Mahon works at the Harrods department store stock room.

1964   Readmitted to Trinity; first poem published in *The Irish Times* ("In Memory"); begins seeing Eavan Boland; writing a novel; suspended from Trinity for a second time; travels to Paris where he audits lectures at the Sorbonne; visits Brittany; best man in Michael Longley and Edna Broderick's wedding (30 December).

1965   Readmitted to Trinity; visits grave of Louis MacNeice; shares Eric Gregory Award with Michael Longley, John Fuller and Norman Talbot (March); finishes courses at Trinity but skips commencement; visits the Aran Islands with Michael and Edna Longley (July); enters graduate school at the University of Western Ontario in London, Ontario; "In Carrowdore Churchyard" wins a Guinness Poetry Prize at the Cheltenham Literature Festival (October); *Twelve Poems* is published in Belfast.

1966   Visits Jill Schlesinger in Atlanta; abandons graduate school; moves to Cambridge, Massachusetts; *Design for a Grecian Urn* is published; moves to Toronto where he works in a bookstore, as a switchboard operator at the Canadian Broadcasting Corporation and later teaches English as a second language.

1967   Returns to Belfast (April); revisits the Aran Islands with Michael Longley (June); teaching at a Jordanstown grammar school; seeing Doreen Douglas; attends the funeral of Patrick Kavanagh with Seamus Heaney, Longley and David Hammond (December).

1968   Doreen moves to London; planned reunion with Jill at Easter falls through; *Night-Crossing*, a Poetry Book Society Choice, is published by Oxford University Press (September); sectarian violence erupts in Northern Ireland (October); moves to Monkstown, County Dublin.

1969   Teaches English as a second language; begins a play on Hugh O'Neill; works at the Trinity College Library; with Longley visits sites of rioting in Belfast (August).

1970   With Seamus Deane and W.J. McCormack founds *Atlantis* (1970–74); contributes to BBC schools programme "Books, Poems, Plays"; *Beyond Howth Head* is published by the Dolmen Press (June); moves to London; *Ecclesiastes* is published (October).

1971   Begins reviewing plays for *The Listener*; Doreen moves into Observatory Gardens with Mahon (August); Mahon protests Longley's "To Derek Mahon" (December).

1972   "Bloody Sunday" (30 January); publishes the *Sphere Book of Modern Irish Poetry* (March); *Lives* is published (25 May); Mahon and Doreen visit France in the summer; Derek and Doreen are married at St Mary Abbots Parish Church in Kensington (30 September).

1973   Working as an advertising copywriter for Masius, Wynne-Williams & D'Arcy-MacManus.

1974   Working as Features Editor for *Vogue*; James Simmons publishes "Flight of the Earls Now Leaving" in *The Irish Times* (4 June); Derek and Doreen visit Desmond O'Grady in Greece (August).

1975   In anticipation of the birth of their first child, Derek and Doreen move to Ford Manor outside Lingfield, Surrey; Rory born (May); Mahon is Henfield Writing Fellow at the University of East Anglia in the summer; meets Robert Lowell; publishes *The Snow Party* (31 July); lectures on Brian Moore at the Yeats Summer School (August).

1976   Working as a freelance writer and broadcaster.

1977   Katherine Jane Mahon ("Katie") born (13 February); publishes *Light Music* (March); undergoes treatment for alcoholism at the Epsom Hospital (March); Seamus Heaney and Mahon take part in an Arts Council reading tour of Northern Ireland, *In Their Element* (May); appointed Writer in Residence at the New University of Ulster; moves to Portstewart, Northern Ireland.

1978   Hospitalised for alcoholism at the Gransha Hospital, Derry; Derek and Doreen separate; Doreen and the children go to live with her mother in Portballintrae; spends summer staying with friends (Heaney, Eamon Grennan and John Montague); moves to Kinsale (late summer); resumes Coleraine appointment in the autumn; separated from Doreen and living at Craigvara House in Portrush; Katie christened in Cushendun (November).

1979   Hospitalised again; finishes Coleraine appointment (May); Andrew Waterman publishes "On the Mend" in *Encounter* (June); travels alone to America where he has a summer appointment at Wake Forest University; J.G. Farrell drowns in Bantry Bay; returns to London where he goes to work in the script unit of the BBC Radio Drama Department; living at the home of Walter Allen in Canonbury Square; publishes *The Sea in Winter* (November); publishes *Poems 1962–1978*

(29 November); working as a radio drama producer for the BBC Radio Drama Department; spends Christmas in North Antrim.

1980   Mahon declines to participate in A Sense of Ireland festival in London; his adaptation of Jennifer Johnston's *Shadows on Our Skin* airs on the BBC programme "Play for Today" (20 March); returns to Observatory Gardens (April); reunited with Doreen and the children (August).

1981   Mahon and Philip Haas collaborating on a film, *Gillespie*, based on the life of a Northern Irish evangelist; *Courtyards in Delft* published (March); Doreen and the children vacation without Mahon (summer); Mahon's Olivia Manning profile, "Never a Day", airs on BBC radio (July); visits Samuel Beckett in Paris; begins duties as poetry editor of the *New Statesman* (October); Wake Forest University Press becomes Mahon's American publisher.

1982   Mahon's adaptation of Jennifer Johnston's *How Many Miles to Babylon?* airs on BBC 2; profile of John Montague, "The Grafted Tongue", airs on BBC Radio 3; publishes *The Chimeras* (October); publishes *The Hunt by Night* (18 November).

1983   Visits America for *The Hunt by Night* reading tour; meets Patricia King; Mahon family vacations in west Cork (July); visits Paris and sees Beckett (October); quits editorial post with the *New Statesman*.

1984   Publishes *A Kensington Notebook* (March); Mahon's adaptation of John Montague's *The Cry* is broadcast on the BBC programme "Play for Today" (July); Field Day production of *High Time* tours (September); profile of Robert Lowell, "Pity the Planet", airs on Radio 3 (December); Norman, Mahon's father, dies (31 December).

1985   House hunting in Ireland; *Summer Lightning* broadcast on RTÉ (April); Derek and Doreen vacation apart (summer); attends European Festival of Poetry in Leuven, Belgium

(October); *Antarctica* published (November); Derek and Doreen separate (December); *The Death of the Heart* airs on ITV (December).

1986	Writer Fellow at Trinity College, Dublin; living openly with Jenneke; begins reviewing regularly for *The Irish Times*; participates in Trinity commencement where he retrospectively receives his bachelor's degree (June); Jenneke and Mahon separate (June); Mahon and Pat King in Kinsale for the summer.
1987	Breaks his relationship with Oxford University Press (March); publishes his translation of Philippe Jaccottet's *Selected Poems*; awarded a master's degree from Trinity College (June); begins drinking again (summer); publishes his translation of Raphaële Billetdoux's *Night Without Day* (November).
1989	Moves into 58 Fitzwilliam Square (June); receives the Scott Moncrieff Prize for translation; moves into 45 Fitzwilliam Square (November).
1990	One-month residency at Yaddo (April); reads at the 92nd Street Y (16 May); co-edits *Penguin Book of Contemporary Irish Poetry* (June); Doreen sells Observatory Gardens and seeks divorce settlement; *Selected Poems* published in Ireland (November).
1991	*Selected Poems* published in Britain and America; artist-in-residence at Villanova University (January–April); staying in a borrowed apartment on Washington Square (May–June); publishes translation of *The Bacchae* (August); Associate Professor of English at Queens College, CUNY (1991–3); treated for alcoholism at St Vincent's Hospital, New York (November); on disability leave from Queens College (11 November–31 January 1992); spends 50th birthday in St Vincent's Hospital.

1992   Living on West 12th Street in Greenwich Village; seeing a therapist and attending Alcoholics Anonymous; admitted to the Seafield Center; returns to Dublin where he is admitted to St Patrick's Hospital (14 August–20 October); publishes *The Yaddo Letter*; receives *The Irish Times*/Aer Lingus Poetry Prize from President Mary Robinson (20 November).

1993   Mahon's Queens College appointment not renewed (May).

1994   Teaching at Barnard College and at NYU.

1995   Teaching at Cooper Union; visits Key West with Pat King (June); returns to Dublin (June); Trinity College awards Mahon an honorary Doctorate in Letters (July); *The Hudson Letter* published (October); Seamus Heaney wins Nobel Prize for Literature (October).

1996   Publishes an adaptation of *Phaedra* (February) and the play opens at Dublin's Gate Theatre (February–March); Mahon's mother, Maisie, dies (13 October).

1997   Publishes *The Yellow Book* (October).

1998   Visits Monte Carlo and Switzerland (January); Belfast ("Good Friday") Agreement is signed (April); visits Italy.

1999   Publishes *Roman Script* (June) and *Collected Poems* (November); spends Christmas in Tangier.

2000   Pat King undergoes treatment for cancer; spends autumn in Paris.

2001   National University of Ireland, Galway, awards Mahon an honorary doctorate in literature; publishes *The Seaside Cemetery* (June) and *Resistance Days* (November).

2002   Moves to London; publishes *Birds* (October).

2003   Loses lease on Fitzwilliam Square flat (January); Maisie Rose Mahon is born (3 November); moves to Kinsale.

PHOTOGRAPHS

1. Derek Mahon, c. 1944. (*Emory*)

2. "A first rate chorister": Derek Mahon in St Peter's Church choir robe, c. 1954. (*Emory*)

3. Derek Mahon with his father, Norman Mahon, and mother, Maisie Harrison Mahon, 7 Glenwell Park, Newtownabbey, Co. Antrim, c. 1961. (*Emory*)

4. Alliance Française identity card for Jill Schlesinger, 1962–3. (*Courtesy of Jill Schlesinger*)

5. Peter Alscher, Ruth Grene and Derek Mahon, Co. Wicklow, c. 1964. (*Courtesy of Ruth Grene*)

6. Derek Mahon as best man at the wedding of Michael and Edna Longley, Dalkey, Co. Dublin, 30 December 1964. (*Courtesy of Michael and Edna Longley*)

7. "The Less Deceived": Derek Mahon and Michael Longley pose for a publicity photograph after sharing the Eric Gregory Award in March 1965. (*Emory*)

8. "The Poets Lie Where They Fell": Derek Mahon in Toronto, 1967. (*Courtesy of Paul Jackel*)

9. Derek Mahon, c. 1968. (*Courtesy of Gay O'Halloran*)

10. Derek Mahon reading at the Morden Tower, Newcastle upon Tyne, December 1970. (*Jeremy James/Morden Tower*)

11. Doreen Douglas, by A. Gascoigne, c. 1971. (*Emory*)

12. Derek and Doreen's wedding at St Mary Abbots Parish Church, Kensington, London, 30 September 1972. (*Courtesy of Glyn Hughes*)

13. Michael Longley, Seamus Heaney and Derek Mahon at Marie Heaney's parents' home in Ardboe, Co. Tyrone, 1977. (*Emory*)

14. Derek Mahon with Seamus Heaney, *In Their Element* reading tour, 1977. (*Emory*)

15. Craigvara House, Portrush, Co. Antrim. (*Emory*)

16. Derek Mahon on the set of *Summer Lightning* starring Paul Scofield, October 1984. (*RTÉ Stills Library*)

17. Derek Mahon with Cathal Ó Searcaigh and Pat King at Wake Forest University, North Carolina, 1984. (*Courtesy of Rachel Brown*)

18. Derek Mahon and Dillon Johnston at Wake Forest University, 1984. (*Courtesy of Rachel Brown*)

19. Derek Mahon with his son, Rory, and daughter Katie outside Doheny & Nesbitt in Baggot Street, Dublin, c. summer 1990, by Tony Gavin. (*Emory*)

20. Derek Mahon, c. 1995, by Bill Doyle. (*Emory*)

PREFACE

We are poor passing facts,
warned by that to give
each figure in the photograph
his living name.

Robert Lowell, "Epilogue"

Derek Mahon received author's copies of his first collection of poems, *Night-Crossing*, in September 1968, when he inscribed one to his future wife "Doreen, for the love that's in it".[1] The book had been selected as a Poetry Book Society Choice, and his publisher arranged for him to read from the new collection at the annual Cheltenham Festival in the first week of October.[2] When Mahon returned home to Belfast a few days later, he returned to a community suddenly in crisis.

The Royal Ulster Constabulary's (RUC) attack on civil rights marchers in Derry on 5 October marked an intensification of the long-simmering political crisis in Northern Ireland. The march had been organised by the recently formed Northern Ireland Civil Rights Association, but the Minister of Home Affairs, William Craig, had banned the gathering just two days before it was to be held. When marchers turned up to challenge the ban, they were met in Duke Street by a line of RUC policemen blocking their path. According to newspaper accounts at the time, a second group of police officers closed in behind the marchers, effectively trapping them. After a few minutes of tense speeches, the two police lines advanced on the marchers, wielding batons. Those who managed to get through the line and reach the Craigavon Bridge were met there with a water cannon. The entire confrontation, including images of bloodied marchers, was captured on film by an RTÉ cameraman and broadcast worldwide.[3]

That evening rioting erupted in Derry's Catholic Bogside, and in the following days demonstrations against the police response spread rapidly across the six Northern counties. On 9 October students at Queen's

University, Belfast organised a demonstration of solidarity with the Derry marchers. On 16 November—the same day *Night-Crossing* was reviewed in *The Irish Press*—thousands retraced the route of the Derry march, ending with a sit-down demonstration in Belfast city centre. Increasingly, however, demonstrators were met by violent counter-demonstrators, by members of the B-Specials (a reserve force of the Ulster Special Constabulary, with which Mahon's own Uncle Robert had served) or the overwhelmingly Protestant RUC, which often turned a blind eye to violent attacks on the demonstrators.

New Year's Day 1969 began with a march from Belfast to Derry that the People's Democracy organisers had patterned after Martin Luther King, Jr's march from Selma to Montgomery, Alabama. The four-day march became a test of resolve as the protesters were repeatedly attacked along the 75-mile route. Just seven miles outside Derry at the Burntollet Bridge, the marchers walked into an organised ambush by Loyalists, who attacked them with stones, bottles and clubs, all under the gaze of the RUC.

Two years into the Troubles, after Northern Ireland had become consumed by sectarian violence, the poet Eavan Boland interviewed Mahon and other writers from the North about their reactions to finding their own personal history "seeded with crisis".[4] At what point, she asked, did each become aware of the underlying conflict? Seamus Heaney pointed to "the IRA business of the late 1950s" as a moment of political awakening for him, and Brian Friel answered matter-of-factly, "I always knew that the burst was going to come".[5] In contrast, Mahon expressed shock at the eruption of violence. When Boland asked him when religious discrimination in the North had become a reality for him, he answered, "Last year [1969] for the first time".[6] Mahon was not being completely forthright. His Uncle Robert had served in the B-Specials throughout his childhood years, and with the outbreak of sectarian violence in the North had been deployed in street action. When Boland asked how the crisis revealed itself in his work, Mahon replied, "the thing must be translated into a personal sense of fracture, a sense of what might have been, of loss". He added, "I'm choosing to use my own personal dilemmas as metaphors for the Northern situation".[7] Mahon did not name those personal dilemmas, but his reference to moments of fracture and of loss in his own past merits our attention because Mahon is, more than any of his contemporaries, Ireland's laureate of loss.

A formative event in the development of Mahon's poetic personality was an early trauma that occurred nearly seven years before, in his second year at Trinity College, Dublin. In January of that year, the 21-year-old Mahon tried to take his own life, and the lingering effects of this emotional crisis led to his expulsion from college the following year. While he has never spoken directly of what occurred, his poetic response to that crisis was the major formative event in his young life and in his early development as a poet. From that point forward, poetry became a way to restore some of the wholeness that eluded him in life.

Mahon's statement to Eavan Boland that he was choosing to use his personal dilemmas as metaphors for the Northern situation establishes a correspondence between the personal and the historical which this biography takes as its starting point. With the outbreak of violence in the North within days of the publication of his first collection of poems, he revisited his own past of personal trauma for corollaries to the country's present crisis. "Although I've never been a motorist", he confided years later to fellow poet Eamon Grennan, "I felt perhaps as a hit-and-run driver must feel when he wakes up the next morning".[8] What is most remarkable about this statement to his friend is the degree of personal culpability it signals for Northern Ireland's sectarian crisis.

It is a critical commonplace to speak of Mahon's renunciation of history, but what has not been fully appreciated is the degree to which his poetry is rooted in the very past he renounces. Mahon's poems have more often been read impersonally, as commentaries on the "underlying spiritual desolation" of Ulster Protestant culture, as Edna Longley describes them,[9] or as ongoing quarrels with "a condition of modernity", as Hugh Haughton puts it.[10] As insightful as these readings are, both critics, and others who have followed, have been complicit in separating the poems from the life.

The early poem "After the Titanic"—first published under the title "As God is My Judge"—is the key poem for accessing the personal trauma in Mahon's past. The poem is most often read as a statement about man's hubris and folly, a critique of the early twentieth-century's faith in industrialisation, or, alternatively, as a poem about "the decline of Ulster Protestant political and economic power".[11] Before it was any of that, it was a poem through which Mahon expressed his own deeply felt guilt in the face of an unspeakable tragedy.

"After the Titanic" is not about the captain of the doomed passenger liner, but about the chairman of the White Star Line, Bruce Ismay, who is said to have escaped from the sinking ship in a lifeboat filled with women and children. Mahon's subject is less the sinking of the great liner than it is one man's shameful flight.

> They said I got away in a boat
> And humbled me at the inquiry. I tell you
>   I sank as far that night as any
> Hero. As I sat shivering on the dark water
>   I turned to ice to hear my costly
> Life go thundering down in a pandemonium of
>   Prams, pianos, sideboards, winches,
> Boilers bursting and shredded ragtime.[12]

Mahon's own grandfather had worked on the *Titanic*, and the poet has often referenced this family connection to evoke a vague and more generalised guilt. In fact, the poem is among the most personal of any he has written.

It is worth noting that, in this poem, Mahon does not use personal experience as a metaphor for the present state of Ireland; just the opposite, he uses history—the sinking of the *Titanic*—to evoke the enormity of his own guilt. We have had it exactly backwards. The correspondence Mahon speaks of in the Boland interview runs in the other direction, and we see this reversal of expectation reoccur repeatedly in his mature poetry.

During his second year at Trinity, Mahon experienced a personal crisis, and it was in that state that he threw himself into the Liffey, only to be pulled from the water by a rescue squad from the Tara Street Fire Station.[13] When he was later expelled from Trinity, he travelled first to the Isle of Man, where he found temporary work at the Belle Vue Hotel in Port Erin, before moving to London, where he stayed for the remainder of the year. Later, when his first collection of poems was about to be published, it was Edna Longley who suggested the title *Night-Crossing*, with its allusion to just such a sea passage—the "sleepless night-crossing" named in Mahon's poem "Jail Journal".[14] Mahon would repeat that flight to London in 1970 after the outbreak of violence in the North, and again after the calamitous time as Writer in Residence at the New University of Ulster in 1979. It was after the latter move that he resolved never to live in Northern Ireland again.

The personal crises that lie behind each of these relocations and resolutions have been in plain view all along. These moments of trauma are deeply embedded in Mahon's work. But it is the crisis in his second year at Trinity College Michael Longley had in mind when he noted in his review of *Night-Crossing* his friend's struggle with "extreme experience" and praised "his courageous excursions into chaos and nightmare".[15] Longley was not speaking metaphorically. Mahon's nightmares, ever-present in his early poems, have their origin in a long-suppressed personal history.

The fact that these events elicited a poetic response should come as no surprise. Mahon has been chronicling the formation of a poetic persona from the very beginning. Even the ordering of his *New Collected Poems* (2011) follows the arc of his own life and reminds us of a personality in the making: from the early, pre-Troubles poems "Spring in Belfast" and "Glengormley", through poems of early married life like "Ford Manor" and those of middle-age crisis, "Dawn at St. Patrick's", to "New York Time" and the later poem "Harbour Lights". For all his attempts to be free of history, the pattern traced in this body of work is in some ways more reflective of his time than is Heaney's more nostalgic gaze. Mahon is the poet of a broken Ireland.

Reading Mahon's work through the lens of his personal history reminds us, if we needed reminding, that the origin of his art is in suffering. Mahon's poetic project, however, was not merely to chronicle experience. Poetry offered him a way to reshape that experience and impose form on the formlessness of his own life. Mahon's best poems are those that put suffering to constructive use, those that probe his past of fracture and of loss while working through that human condition towards some longed-for recovery. The signature Mahon gesture is renewal—mushrooms bending towards light in a keyhole, in his most celebrated poem—and it is that hoped-for act of regeneration and renewal that animates his finest poems. The origin of that compensatory impulse in his own life is what *After the Titanic* makes its subject.

Chapter 1

"WASHING-LINES AND GREY SKIES"

Whatever then my inherited or acquired
Affinities, such remains my childhood's frame
Like a belated rock in the red Antrim clay
That cannot at this era change its pitch or name—
And the pre-natal mountain is far away.

Louis MacNeice, "Carrick Revisited"

On the night of 7 April 1941 six German bombers struck Belfast, inflicting damage to the docks, the Harland and Wolff shipyard, and the residential areas near the Lough. The Germans met no significant air defences, and eight days later more than a hundred enemy bombers returned, again targeting the lightly defended shipyard and other industrial sites in a prolonged and devastating strike on the city. Particularly hard hit were the residential areas north and west of the city centre. The neighbourhoods between York Street and the Antrim Road suffered heavy damage, perhaps owing to the German pilots mistaking the nearby waterworks for the River Lagan. On that one night alone, more than seven hundred people were killed and hundreds more injured. It was the greatest loss of life any British city would suffer for the remainder of the war, with the exception of London at the height of the Blitz.[1]

In the immediate aftermath of the bombing, over one hundred thousand residents fled the city to seek safety in the surrounding countryside. Norman Mahon, a fitter in the Harland and Wolff shipyard, was needed for the war effort and he and his new bride, Maisie, stayed behind and "lived it bomb by bomb", as their son would write years later of another conflict altogether. Norman and his wife had married the previous January and at the time of the April bombings Maisie was pregnant with the couple's first and only child.

On 4 May a large formation of German bombers again targeted Belfast. The raid caused scores of fires across the city and, when morning came, another 150 residents had been killed. A smaller raid the following night would be the last attack on the city, but the damage from the combined assaults had been staggering. Over fifty-six thousand homes had been damaged, more than three thousand were completely destroyed, over eight hundred people had lost their lives and many thousands of residents had been left homeless. It would take six months for the shipyard to resume full wartime production.[2] Some residents would never recover.

Norman Derek Mahon was born on 23 November 1941, like his father before him amidst a global world war. "Derek", as he was called to differentiate him from his father, could hardly have been aware of the war's progress. Nevertheless, the adult poet would be shaped by his own assumed posture as a survivor of our civilisation's barbarity, and his earliest memories of wartime Belfast would reappear in his poems for years to come. Many years later, he would imaginatively set his own birth against the background of global conflict: "While the frozen armies trembled / At the gates of Leningrad / They took me home in a taxi / And laid me in my cot, / And there I slept again / With siren and blackout …"[3] It was undoubtedly a frightening time for the new parents. St Paul's Church of Ireland in York Street had been badly damaged in the bombings, so the Reverend Lyndon visited the house and christened Norman Derek Mahon at home on 21 January 1942.[4]

Among Mahon's earliest memories were the sight of American warships in Belfast Lough and soldiers, sailors and airmen marching up the Antrim Road in a victory parade. As a child growing up in the post-war years, his first landscape—his own "pre-natal mountain", to use Louis MacNeice's memorable phrase—was the bombed-out city. He and his friends spent their days "roaming among the broken bricks and rubble".[5] The war had receded as an imminent threat, but in childhood Mahon often heard adults recite the names of those who had died in nearby streets.[6] His four uncles on his mother's side of the family had all served in the Royal Navy and provided escort for Atlantic convoys. They returned with stories of visiting the ports of Gibraltar and Casablanca. One uncle returned from sea with a lacquered cigarette case Mahon would speak of in talismanic terms well into adulthood. An air raid shelter remained in the back garden, and the recent war provided the plots for countless hours of imaginary play. Years later, reflecting on his childhood, Mahon noted with regret that there was "no real heroism in the family record". Other boys' fathers had flown with the RAF or served with "Monty" in North Africa, but Mahon's family had no such stories to share.[7]

The Mahon home was at 1 Kenbella Parade, just off Salisbury Avenue in a working-class neighbourhood north of the city, one of the areas that had been hard hit during the April bombings. Both parents were small of stature, as their only son would be. Mahon's father worked, like his father before him, in the Harland and Wolff shipyard, while his mother had worked, up until her marriage, for the York Street Flax Spinning Company. In later years, when Mahon would speak of his origins, he would often emphasise his parents' close ties to "the two Ulster industries, shipbuilding and linen".[8] Long into adulthood, he would identify his mother and father with industrial Belfast in a way he was never able to himself.

Over the years Mahon has given a number of different accounts of his family origins. In one, borrowed from Edmund Spenser's *A View of the Present State of Ireland*, the Mac-mahons were descended from the Norman line Fitz Urse.[9] Mahon's own father may have been named "Norman" in recognition of this distant and vaguely remembered history. According to this version, the Fitz Urse name, meaning "son of the bear", was later hibernicised as Mac Mahon, and then simply Mahon. In another account, the Mac Mahon line originated in County Fermanagh, but the family fled to France during the Flight of the Earls after the defeat of Hugh O'Neill by the English forces at Kinsale. In still another version, Mahon left out such heroism and explained that his ancestors simply "'took the soup' in famine times, turned protestant, dropped the 'Mac' & moved to Belfast where there were new jobs in linen & shipbuilding".[10]

Mahon has traced appearances of his family name through Spenser's *A View of the Present State of Ireland*, T.S. Eliot's *Murder in the Cathedral* and Joseph Conrad's *Youth*,[11] thus substituting a literary lineage for a strictly genealogical one.[12] That would all come later, however. Among the first books the young Derek enjoyed reading were the *Beano Annual*, the *Wonder Book for Boys* and the popular *Biggles* books, which related the exploits of a British pilot during World War II.

Mahon's father was originally apprenticed as a fitter in the shipyard and rose to become an inspector of engines, a job he held for 40 years "with some little promotions". He is not a figure who inhabits his son's later poetry; indeed, when asked about his father, Mahon speaks of him by his absence: "My father was usually out at work … the shipyard was his life".[13] On another occasion he described him as "a rather dim figure", and in a remarkable admission added "I have no clear definition of him at all", despite the fact that his father lived well into Mahon's own adulthood, dying at the age of 70 when his son was 43.[14]

As a boy Mahon lived in the figurative shadow of the shipyard if not its literal one. All the men in his family either worked in the shipyard or served as merchant seamen, and the lore of these vocations exerted a powerful pull on the young boy's imagination. His own maternal grandfather, Henry Harrison, had worked on the *Titanic*, a connection Mahon seems to have viewed with a combination of awe and shame. As a child, he pored over his Uncle Roy's copies of the *Marine Engineer* and memorised ship names, shipping lines and the features of the great liners. Many of these ships would remain distinct and vivid into adulthood; he recalled clearly a school trip on which he and his classmates sailed from Belfast to Liverpool on the *Ulster Monarch* and the sight the following morning of the River Mersey through a porthole window.

His grandfather Harrison had been a boilermaker and held "strongly socialist views". As a young man he had spent two years as a kind of hobo, as Mahon would himself, travelling around Canada and the United States. "I think the way they travelled in those days … was they took jobs in ships, sort of casual merchant seaman among other things, and got off at the other end," Mahon has explained. "He came back in the same way and went into the shipyard".[15] Mahon's grandfather wore a smoking cap and took to calling his grandson "Mahaffy". Years later he would serve as the model for the retired seaman in "A Refusal to Mourn". "I'm not long for this world", Mahon recalls him saying in that poem, "I'll not last the winter". The poem concludes with the seaman fading into the blankness of time, but Mahon insists on an afterlife in "other times and lives":

> In time the astringent rain
> Of those parts will clean
> The words from his gravestone
> In the crowded cemetery
> That overlooks the sea
> And his name be mud once again

And his boilers lie like tombs
In the mud of the sea bed
Till the next Ice Age comes
And the earth he inherited
Is gone like Neanderthal Man
And no records remain.

But the secret bred in the bone
On the dawn strand survives
In other times and lives,
Persisting for the unborn
Like a claw-print in concrete
After the bird has flown.[16]

The poem is significant for the close bond it describes between the child and his grandfather. Equally important is the absence of any similar poem about Mahon's own father.

Like others of her generation, Mahon's mother stopped working when she married, became a housewife, and grew "house-proud". Mahon's earliest memories are of her dusting and keeping "everything bright as a new penny".[17] Above all else, she embraced those traditional Protestant virtues of tidiness and thrift, and exhibited an obsessive concern with appearances, as her son would put it, "in a neighbourhood of bay windows".[18] It would have been her idea that her son take piano lessons from Mrs Hynes at the end of the street. In the elegy he wrote for his mother after her death, he recalls her moving through her daily chores humming "South of the Border", "On a Slow Boat to China" or "Beyond the Blue Horizon", all popular tunes that held the allure of distant places she would never visit.[19]

Mahon would sometimes remark that he was raised by women, by which he meant his mother and an extended circle of aunts. Among them was his great-Aunt Louise, on his mother's side of the family, whom he later wrote about visiting as a child. In the unpublished poem he recalls the dark house, the tick of a grandfather clock, and lemonade. His imagination takes him elsewhere, however, when he is handed a photograph album of his great-aunt's travels to France as a young woman when she was in service as a lady's maid:[20]

It was a dismal day,
The coal recalcitrant
And the skies grey;

But suddenly there was
An album in my hands
And you, Louise,

Were pointing out
The places you had been,
The cathedral cities

And watering places
Of a lost era preserved
In paint and literature.

And there among them
A young woman, you,
Not a day over thirty,

In white muslin
On the promenade at
Nice or Biarritz,

Holding a parasol
And a phrase-book, smiling
Into the camera.[21]

Mahon grew up aware of a larger world beyond his north Belfast neighbourhood, and from an early age France figured in his imagination as a place he might one day visit.

From the time he was four, Mahon attended the Skegoneill Primary School. Among the earliest family photographs is one of a child dressed in his school uniform wearing a cap bearing the school crest. Long into adulthood he retained a memory of dashing around the Skegoneill playground, arms outstretched, pretending to be an aeroplane.

Though Mahon was an only child, he lived just a few streets from his cousin Conacht Murphy, and the two boys, who were the same age, were for a time like brothers. Conacht appears as "Collie" in a children's story Mahon wrote for a BBC schools programme in the early 1970s. In that account Conacht lived in a bigger house than his own, full of mysterious rooms waiting to be discovered. "There was the cupboard under the stairs where the gas-meter was … there was the box-room, full of old rugs and tool-kits, and the garage … where the rabbit hutch was, and the bicycles, though there was no car. And then there was the cellar, with a bare light-bulb, and that's where the washboard and mangle were kept, and old bicycles without tyres, and empty lemonade bottles…."[22] In the back garden was a coal shed that would reappear years later in Mahon's poem of childhood, "Courtyards in Delft":

> I lived there as a boy and know the coal
> Glittering in its shed, late-afternoon
> Lambency informing the deal table,
> The ceiling cradled in a radiant spoon.[23]

When the weather was bad, "which it usually was", the two boys would play with a Hornby train set.[24] On nice days they would play cricket in the garden, making wickets on the air-raid shelter with chalk, cinders or pieces of slate. In Mahon's fictionalised account, the neighbourhood children once made a submarine out of dustbins and fashioned the conning tower out of a watering can.[25]

When the two boys were left alone in his cousin's house, as they sometimes were, they would creep upstairs to his uncle's wardrobe, which they were not supposed to open. In "A View from the Long Grass" Mahon recalls that it smelled "like pipes and peppermint and important things".[26] The boys would take out his uncle's dark green RUC uniform and, from the bottom drawer, his black, shiny belts and guns.[27] Actually Mahon's Uncle Robert was not in the RUC but in the B-Specials, an auxiliary civilian militia that would be responsible for some of the worst offences in the coming Troubles. As Mahon recounts, the guns were all "too heavy to hold for long", while two defused grenades felt "like big heavy eggs or stones all smooth from the sea".[28] Collie wanted to be a policeman like his father, while the first-person narrator longed to be a captain in the Navy and wear the uniform his own father had once worn.

For the young Mahon, his cousin's house retained associations of discovery and peril. "Being at home wasn't as good as being at his Aunt

Helen's and Uncle Tom's [fictional names for his Aunt Violet and Uncle Robert] because it wasn't as bright and there weren't so many dark places to find things". Besides, "the back garden was always short and empty and there weren't any trees like in Strathmore Avenue". Across the Shore Road, past the railway tracks and some prefabricated structures, was the beach, nothing more than "a bit of blue muck with stones and a couple of poles with sea-gulls on them". This was before the motorway was built, and from the muddy shore the ships seemed to the young Mahon "terribly big", and "I knew what I wanted to be when I grew up".[29]

Mahon's parents attended St Peter's Church on the nearby Antrim Road, and while they were not committed believers, the church, like the shipyard, served as one of the fixed points around which they ordered their days. The grey stone church had been completed in 1900, when the neighbourhoods were spreading north towards Cave Hill, the rocky outcrop that dominates the horizon. When the church building was enlarged in 1933, the Reverend J.F. MacNeice, father of the poet Louis MacNeice, officiated at the new church's first communion. Indeed, throughout its history, St Peter's has had numerous literary associations. Reverend Breene, the rector throughout Mahon's childhood, was himself a literary man who once published a volume of his own poems, *Songs of the Nativity and Other Verses.*

Mahon later said his parents attended services only "for the look of the thing".[30] His recollections of the church, whether expressed in poems or in interviews, often reveal this doubleness, which he first encountered in his own home. Despite this, Mahon's later posture as a poet would resemble, in some ways, those believers who stand up a headland bellowing into the wind, "Abide with Me".[31]

After joining the children's choir, Mahon attended regular Wednesday night choir practices and two Sunday services. Something about the hymns "invaded the mind", he has written. He would remember some of the words and tunes long into adulthood; in a 1991 interview, he confessed that he still hummed some of those hymns first learned as a small child:

From earth's wide bounds, from ocean's farthest coast,
Through gates of pearl streams the countless host,
Singing to Father, Son and Holy Ghost:
Hallelujah, Hallelujah!

These hymns expressed in aspirational language the desire for wholeness that would characterise the work of the mature poet. Asked years later whether he responded to the hymns as a believer, Mahon replied, "I believe in the words and in the tunes; that's quite enough for me".[32]

At the time Mahon's neighbourhood was mixed, and he and his cousin Conacht sometimes played with Catholic children who lived nearby. "I didn't really understand this stuff about Protestant and Catholic", he would later say. "We'd a family around the corner called Matthews, who were Catholic. And we—the Protestant kids—used to play with the Matthews kids. Probably other Catholic kids as well and there was absolutely no problem".[33] In an autobiographical magazine piece about his childhood, Mahon described much the same memory, but in that instance gave this Catholic family the name Kane.[34]

Still other childhood memories, however, suggest a precocious sensitivity to these invisible differences and divisions. The Matthews children would not play cricket, nor would they invite Mahon inside their house. Once he was playing with the Matthews boy when the boy's sister came to get her brother. When Mahon asked where they were going, she said to Confession. When he asked if he could come too, they said it was only for Catholics. "I said what are Catholics? What do you mean?"[35]

"The tribal conflict", as Mahon has called it, was most evident between his friends and "the Shore Roaders, tough monkeys from mean streets". About once a month, Mahon later recalled, "word went round that 'they' had come up in large numbers looking for trouble, and we quaked in our shoes".[36] Nothing ever came of these rumours of imminent violence, but the childhood fears were real.

In an unpublished version of the short story he wrote for a BBC schools programme, Mahon elaborated on the source of these anxieties and fears. In this account, a Catholic family, the McSorleys, lived on Salisbury Avenue. To the neighbourhood children, the family was mysterious; the McSorley children attended boarding school and were seldom seen. Their home was the largest in the area and had an equally large garden which abutted the unnamed narrator's own. In Mahon's fictional account, the children were always losing balls over the garden wall; in fact, the McSorley garden must have been full of balls children kicked over the wall and never had the courage to retrieve.[37]

Mahon recounts a day when the narrator, his cousin Collie, and a friend named Sammy were playing together, and Collie showed them the revolver he had taken from his father's house. The boys hid in the air-raid shelter where they took turns holding the gun. "It was dark and heavy and kind of smooth and rounded where the bullets came out, and when you looked down the barrel you couldn't see very far, even in the sunlight". When Collie pulled the trigger on the unloaded gun, "it made a slow noise like a car-door locking". As the boys grew bolder, they began playing with the gun in the back garden. During a struggle, it flew loose and, to their horror, dropped over the wall into the McSorleys' garden.

After debating what they should do and mustering their courage, the boys went together to the front door, knocked, and asked Dr McSorley if they could look for their ball. The doctor showed them the way through the house where "some kind of holy picture" was hanging. He joined them in their search, so when they spotted the gun in the long grass, they were unable to reclaim it. After a time, Dr McSorley called off the search and told them he would simply throw the ball over the wall when he found it.

The boys tossed cinders at the air-raid shelter to see who would climb over the wall and retrieve the gun. Collie gave the narrator a leg-up, and he climbed along the wall to where he could drop down into the garden. No sooner had he reached the gun and taken it in his hand, however, than he sensed someone else in the garden. He flattened himself in the tall grass, frozen with fear, as the person moved closer down the garden path. "I lay there not breathing, scared stiff and wishing to hell he'd go away, and I could feel myself wanting to cry with fear and frustration".[38] When the figure came into view, it was not Dr McSorley but a Catholic priest, and the sound the narrator had first heard was the sound of him reading softly to himself from a breviary. As Mahon wrote, "I suppose I knew all along he was going to look up and see me. He couldn't fail to. The grass was long but not that long … at the very minute I realized the mumbling wasn't in English at all but a foreign language, he stopped mumbling, raised his head sideways from the book with a kind of thinking look and looked straight at me. I was looking straight at him, the gun tight in my fist, and for a few seconds we stared right into each other's eyes". After a tense moment, the priest walked on. When the narrator heard the door to the house shut, he threw the gun over the wall and hurriedly climbed back over to safety. In the house, "Collie was dancing about, all happy to get his gun back, but I just knelt there in the entry, shaking and swallowing hard again and again".[39]

What brands a child may not be the extraordinary terrors of growing up, but the ordinary ones. Looking back on his childhood, Mahon gave this supposedly fictional story extended attention, though he stopped short of trying to explain its importance to him. What is clear, however, is that the young Mahon carried with him, long into adulthood, associations of guilt and fear embodied in a gun, a holy picture and a black-robed figure speaking in another tongue.

Chapter 2

ROYAL BELFAST ACADEMICAL INSTITUTION

O sages standing in God's holy fire
As in the gold mosaic of a wall,
Come from the holy fire, perne in a gyre,
And be the singing-masters of my soul.
Consume my heart away; sick with desire
And fastened to a dying animal
It knows not what it is; and gather me
Into the artifice of eternity.

W.B. Yeats, "Sailing to Byzantium"

For a time Mahon and his cousin Conacht were both members of the local Boy Scout troop which met in the basement of St Peter's Church. Their troop leader, Skipper, was a former RAF man who would take the boys on hikes and camping trips to nearby Cave Hill. Mahon would later set an early short story in an abandoned cottage on Cave Hill, one the main character knows well, "for he had spent many nights there as a Wolf Cub and Boy Scout".[1] Years later, looking back on his childhood, Mahon recalled that the Scout meetings could be frightening when Skipper was not there. "I have vague scary memories of things that went on", he said in a 2002 interview.[2] Mahon may well have had these childhood experiences in mind when he wrote more than fifty years later of "the dreams, vivid but short, / scaring us as they did when we were ten: / child murder in *Macbeth*, wolves at the door, / the dizzying height and the obscure disgrace, / indictments for a guilt we seldom face".[3] What we know with certainty is that Mahon's father suddenly took his son out of Boy Scouts and enrolled him in the Youth Cadet Corps, which was attached to the Royal Ulster Rifles.

In December 1952 Norman Mahon completed his 11-year-old son's application for admission to the Royal Belfast Academical Institution. "Inst", as it was known, had been founded early in the nineteenth century by Protestant businessmen who wished to provide greater educational opportunities to the "middling classes".[4] That mission expanded further with the Butler Act of 1944 and its counterpart in Northern Ireland, the Education Act of 1947. As part of these post-war reforms, the educational system was reorganised and an examination implemented at age 11 which directed a student's future study into an academic or non-academic track.

Mahon's school report from the Skegoneill Primary School indicates that he had consistent marks of "very good" in all categories: in "capacity to sustain effort", "promise", "conduct" and "background and goodwill". "A grand little boy", his teacher noted, "but small size tends to make him 'show-off' rather immaturely".[5]

On the strength of his school marks, Norman Mahon arranged for his son to sit for the Inst entrance exam in the hope he would qualify for one of four academic scholarships. He learned in the spring his son had done well, but "not quite well enough".[6] Despite that disappointment, his parents made what sacrifices were required, and Mahon entered Inst the following September at a time when the school was expanding rapidly and numbered close to a thousand students.

Inst occupied a large Georgian brick building in Belfast's city centre, just a short walk from City Hall and the nearby Gaumont cinema in Castle Lane. The school day began with assembly in the Common Hall where the boys were led in singing hymns and listened to the day's announcements.[7] It was around this time, when Mahon was 12, that his parents gave him a Raleigh bicycle for his birthday. With that his world expanded beyond the area bound by Cave Hill to the north and the muddy stretch of shore to the east. He was soon riding his bicycle to school, racing down the hillside on side streets and even overtaking the morning bus. The bicycle brought within reach his maternal grandparents' home, "Hilltop", in Glengormley, and the home of his Uncle Roy, who lived near them. Uncle Roy had served in the Merchant Navy, but during these years he worked in insurance. He owned a portable Imperial typewriter he used for preparing claims, and when Mahon visited, his uncle would let him type on it. When asked about that time, Roy Harrison recalled a day when Derek started typing the news reports he was listening to on the radio. When the announcer reported that King George VI's health was improving, he typed "the King's health is still increasing", much to his uncle's amusement.[8]

Mahon continued to be active in the church choir, and when he was 13 was invited to take part in a special course for choirboys held at the Rossall School near Blackpool in England. He performed exceedingly well, coming in third out of 170 students.[9] His housemaster, Mr Brice, noted that his voice was "clear & full, and of good range". His piano lessons had improved his sight-reading, and, Mr Brice added, he was "very well-mannered and well-behaved … a first rate chorister".[10]

Mahon's first exposure to metrical form was, in fact, the *Church Hymnal*, and the early praise he received in the St Peter's choir was an important influence in leading him to try his hand at writing verse. When Mahon was 13 or 14, the Rector at St Peter's, Reverend Breene, chose one of his poems for the annual Christmas card.[11] It was his very first publication and an important early acknowledgment of his gift for writing. Mahon sang in the Inst choir as well, first as a treble, then as an alto. When his voice broke at 14, his name disappeared from the choir roll.[12]

Mahon's Aunt Kathleen recalls her nephew was "always scribbling", a choice of words that conveys something of his family's incomprehension.[13] His mother took to calling her son "an oddity", a judgment Mahon would later repeat matter-of-factly, like one long reconciled to it.[14] More supportive was his independent-minded Uncle Roy, who read novels and subscribed to French cinema magazines. He also followed politics and read the London newspapers: the *Times* and the *Daily Telegraph* during the week and on the weekends the *Sunday Times* (Mahon would later publish in some of the newspapers first encountered in his uncle's home). The young Derek would often ride his bicycle to his uncle's house where he could read his newspapers and periodicals, and he has credited his Uncle Roy with the development of his earliest political awareness.[15]

Mahon's first surviving poem was published in the Easter 1955 *School News* when he was 13. The poem was prompted by a class assignment to read Hilaire Belloc's "The South Country", and Mahon's pastiche appears alongside a number of similarly formulaic contributions by his classmates:

I have been to England
　Far across the sea,
Where the towns are dull and drear
　And none appeal to me,
There the boys make fun of me,
　There the fields are mireland,
But I never see these things,
　Because I come from Ireland.

I have been to Scotland
　Where the food is bad,
There the weather, wind and rain,
　Nearly make you mad;
There the rivers are wide and deep
　(The streams are in the higher land)
But I never see these things
　Because I come from Ireland.

I have lived in Ireland
　From when I was born.
Here the people aren't unkind
　And the fields are full of corn;
Here the weather's very good
　Though England is a drier land,
And I always see these things
　Because I come from Ireland.[16]

In the original, Belloc contrasts thoughts of home in "the south country" with the sodden landscape of the British Midlands, the grey skies of the north of England and the brown water of the Severn to the west. Belloc's original is an expression of longing for both the landscape of the south and the friends he has left behind. Mahon sets up a similar set of contrasts between England, Scotland and Ireland. England is dull and drear and Scotland has wind, rain and bad food. The terms of this comparison, however, force him to describe an idyllic Ireland "full of corn" and a place where "the weather's very good". Of more interest than the conceit forced on him by Belloc's original, however, is his description of England as a place where "boys make fun of me", a reference to his recent time at the church music course at the Rossall School. When he tries to express the antithesis of this idea, however, it does not come out like Belloc's evocation of remembered friendship, but as a double negative; Ireland is a place where "the people aren't unkind".

Mahon's family would sometimes spend holidays in the picturesque coastal village of Cushendun on the Antrim coast, or, on one occasion, Portrush. He would later memorialise the latter in "The Last Resort", part of his 1978 poem sequence "Autobiographies". In the poem he recalls sandwiches on the strand, dead gulls on the beach and ice cream in the Arcadia Ballroom. He would also trace his own sexual awakening to one of these summer holidays: "One hot July fortnight / In the Strandmore Hotel / I watched the maid climb / The stairs, and went to my room / Quivering with excitement, / Aroused for the first time".[17] In another poetic reminiscence he recalls growing "frolicsome" on a summer holiday in Cushendun and "the first awakenings under a northern sky".[18] That was the summer they spent their holiday in a caravan park at Shane's Cairn, in the hills above Cushendun. The landscape painter Maurice Wilks, to whom Mahon would later dedicate "Cushendun in Winter", was spending the summer there as well, and his daughter was Mahon's age. "Girls watched the boys go by, the boys the girls, / the Lavery sisters and the postman's daughter; / later we'd flirt with them at Lynn's Café".[19]

As a Form II student, Mahon joined the Junior Debating Society, and at the March 1955 meeting he and his classmate J.F.R. McIlveen were picked to debate the proposition "This House would have supported Cromwell in the Civil War".[20] He was elected to the Society's organising committee the following December, and he stayed active in the club for the remainder of his time at Inst. The following summer he proposed for debate "the 'good old days' were not". On that occasion, he argued that nuclear annihilation was preferable to "the old-fashioned stab in the back".[21] The Debating Society's meetings were characterised by an equal mixture of levity and debate, an environment in which Mahon excelled. Among the more lighthearted motions was one that "Belfast should be towed out to sea and sunk".[22]

The following summer Mahon took part in the class trip to France. He and his classmates took in the Champs-Élysées at night and were impressed by the fountains, trees, open-air cafés and floodlit Arc de Triomphe—all sights that stood in sharp contrast to the Belfast they had left behind. A coach tour the following day included stops at the Place de la Concorde, the Sorbonne and the Eiffel Tower, followed, the next day, by a visit to the Louvre. They were in Paris for the annual Bastille Day parade and, that evening, fireworks. They took a boat ride on the Seine and completed their visit with a trip to the Palace of Versailles. From Paris the students travelled to the port city of Saint-Malo where they enjoyed five days of swimming, playing table tennis and eating French ice cream.[23] On their last day in Brittany some of the boys were enlisted as extras for a film crew that was shooting beach scenes for a new British comedy, *True as a Turtle*.[24] While the cameras rolled, the boys splashed about in the surf in the background. Although Mahon did not record his impressions of the trip, this was his first visit to a country that would, in time, become an adopted home.

Mahon took an active part in reviving the Inst Literary Society, which had grown rather moribund in recent years. Under new leadership the society sponsored talks on a variety of literary topics, including one on journalism from a former Instonian who wrote for the *Belfast Telegraph*, and one on modern poetry from the head of English, Mr Cowan.[25] That same year Mahon had supporting roles in two school plays. In December he played a courtier in *King Lear*, and the following February a Spanish bandit in *El Sordo*, written by members of the school staff.[26]

Mahon also remained active in the Youth Cadet Corps which took weekend outings to the Army base at Ballykinler, County Down, where the boys would practice shooting in the sand dunes.[27] Shooting appealed to him in a way team sports at Inst did not. Inst was a big rugby school, and for a time Mahon was expected to play scrum-half, but he neither excelled at it nor enjoyed it. His later descriptions of Inst and of school sports there suggest he felt keenly his small size. He recalls Inst was "a big boys' school, full of big tough boys who played rugby and fought. It was full of philistines and tough guys".[28]

While his parents were similarly small of stature, they seem to have been unable to provide much in the way of emotional support for their teenage son; indeed, Mahon has traced his dislike of team sports at Inst to "something in the way I was treated in my family situation". While he and Conacht had been, for a time, like brothers, "Conacht was a bit taller and he always was considered the more interesting and more manly, more able one. I was a bit of a dead loss in comparison. This was internalized, entirely, and gave me a lot of trouble at the time". Looking back, Mahon recalls that it was then he began to mope and brood.[29]

Mahon's English anthology at Inst was E.W. Parker's *A Pageant of English Verse*, which opened with the thirteenth-century song "Summer is icumen in" and concluded with Auden, MacNeice and Spender. "I think it was that book that did it for me ... the first poem that really turned me on—aside from the hymns—was 'The Stolen Child' ... that and early Dylan Thomas, things like 'Where once the rivers [*sic*] of your face'".[30]

When he was 16 or 17 Mahon began frequenting a coffee bar near Inst called the Piccolo. It was new and trendy (one of the first restaurants in Belfast to have an espresso machine), and popular with students.[31] Mahon and a small "clique of school aesthetes" would gather there in the afternoons and delay for as long as they could the bus ride home.[32] Later, he would associate those afternoons with the writers he and his friends were reading at the time: "the First World War poets, Yeats, Dylan Thomas, Eliot, MacNeice, Salinger, Orwell, and especially Graves".[33] Girls from the nearby Victoria College also frequented the Piccolo, and Mahon would recall, too, the sexual electricity in the air at the time. He was particularly attracted to a student named Kate Olivier, though he seems not to have made his feelings known to her. Years later, after his move to London, he would encounter her again and they would become friends.[34]

Just before Christmas 1958 Mahon learned he had won the Forrest Reid Memorial Prize for his poem "The power that gives the waters breath". The recently inaugurated annual prize was for the best poem of 80 lines or more from any boy in the school.[35] Mahon composed his poem explicitly for the competition, taking as his model Dylan Thomas's "Where once the waters of your face". His entry came in at 84 lines, the shortest it could be, given his choice of Thomas's six-line stanzas. The poem is an extended meditation on the soul, what Mahon calls the fused substance "that shall endure / When all my blood-beats die". This metaphysical self is tossed this way and that in a fantastic landscape of "howling sea", "earth-foam of the dawn", "phosphorescent rain" and "acid air": Mahon had adopted a romantic and archaic language straight out of Coleridge. When his poem was selected over those of several sixth-formers, he remembers thinking, "this was the thing for me".[36]

Mahon followed up his prize-winning poem with three additional poems published in the Easter issue of *School News*. One of these, "Children at Prayer", flies in the face of the season and offers evidence of the 17-year-old Mahon's growing disenchantment with the church. In the poem children kneeling at prayer experience only an "appalling silence" while the faithful are described as "numb" and "deaf". While they wear the "uniform of their rosy eyes", one cannot escape the suggestion that they have somehow failed to grasp the meaning of the "climatic twilight" where they live and where they will die.[37] "Resurrection", the second of the three new poems, offers a poetic response to the painting of that name by Stanley Spencer[38] (the first of Mahon's poems prompted by a painting). Here the resurrected return with curiosity to "the lost familiarity" of their former existence. The poem opens,

> Impromptu as the sun
> subtle between soil and stone,
> angular as the viviparous crucifix,
> casual as the discordant wall,
> full of harmonious bricks,
> in unison they sprawl
> upwards and transfix
> the bleary paradox of all.[39]

"Dancehall Impromptu" takes a more ordinary and less self-consciously literary subject. The first-person speaker in the poem crosses a deserted dance floor on "prosaic feet that he has not used tonight". His "undancing neighbour" defies the lights and risks failure on the now-empty floor as a sweeper enters to clean up the detritus of the evening.

> And he senses the grotesque bond
> and sorry fusion of pathos found
> and contentment lost in the years of unfulfillment
> and success outdreamt by an incorrigible ailment,
> for the sweeper drives a dog-eared brush
> and picks up fag ends
> for his flesh.

The poem resembles numerous later poems—"The Apotheosis of Tins", "A Refusal to Mourn", "A Disused Shed" or "A Garage in Co. Cork"—in which Mahon surveys the cast-off rubbish of some earlier, unfulfilled action.

That summer the *School News* reported that Mahon was "gravely concerned (as he so often has been) with the rotten state of society".

The writer offered a litany of complaint: "Society was falling apart" and "degenerate to the core". Above all, it was "unappreciative of the artist who was stifled by the oppression of its philistinism".[40]

The following October, Mahon and his classmate Seán Haldane took part in an inter-school debate for which they were assigned the difficult task of arguing that temperance is a virtue. The *School News* noted, "Mr. Mahon produced an assortment of quotations, of doubtful benefit to the point he was alleged to be supporting", among them quotations from Horace and Chesterton, and concluding with lines from Sigmund Romberg's rousing song from *The Student Prince*, "Drink! Drink! Drink!" The judges were so amused at the performance that Mahon and Haldane were advanced to the next round, despite having taken the opposing side from the one they had been assigned. Mahon had himself begun frequenting the local pubs, the Hercules and Kelly's Cellars, lingering with his friends as long as possible until "eventually we'd have to go home".[41]

Among the most important influences at Inst was his tutor John Boyle, who taught English, French and History. "Basher Boyle", as he was called by the students, was so named "not because he was physically violent but because … he had the large frame and great concave mug of one who could take care of himself in a tight corner".[42] Mahon read *A Short History of Ireland* in Boyle's class, which was unusual at the time; Irish history was not customarily taught in Protestant schools. Boyle took a particular interest in Irish labour history, and years later Mahon credited him, along with his Uncle Roy, with introducing him to a new political perspective.[43]

When Boyle began hosting a series of Radio Éireann broadcasts on literary and historical subjects, Mahon listened attentively, and in his final year at Inst he delivered several papers to the Literary Society that owed direct debt to Boyle's lectures. In the first of these—a paper on Synge—Mahon recounted Synge's interest in music, his time at Trinity and later in Paris. He noted approvingly Yeats's advice that Synge go to the Aran Islands and live among the people and hear their stories. Mahon might as well have been describing his own coming movements.

Mahon was making plans to enter Trinity College in the autumn of 1960, and over the Easter break he made the 100-mile trip to Dublin by bike to visit the college. His horizons were expanding in other ways too. When he saw an announcement for the May Morton Poetry Prize, he remembers thinking he would submit a poem since there was no one else writing in Ireland. Literary recognition had come easily to him at Inst, but the national competition proved an unexpected challenge. He was shocked when the award went to another poet—one he had never heard of, named John Montague. Mahon stood at the threshold of a bigger literary world than Belfast had to offer.

Chapter 3

| ICARUS

"We got our scholarships, drank a bottle of Guinness with John Boyle in the Crown Liquor Saloon, and went down to Trinity".[1] That is how Mahon remembered taking his leave of Belfast. He would later romanticise his Trinity years as "golden days". From the beginning, he cultivated the persona of a poet. Such behaviour attracted the ridicule of his more conventional classmates, who viewed his mannerisms as affectations, but Trinity was unquestionably a formative time for him. There he met teachers who would make a deep imprint on his intellectual development and his poetic taste; he formed life-long friendships (most notably with fellow poet Michael Longley); he fell in love (more than once); and it was while at Trinity that he committed himself to being a poet. These life-altering experiences came amid emotional blows that would shake his very sense of himself and leave scars that would shape—as much as the positive influences—the nature of his mature poetry.

Among the classmates going with him from Inst was Robbie Brown, with whom he roomed in his first year. As Mahon has explained, the strongest students from the North went to Oxford or Cambridge, the next best to Trinity and the weakest to Queen's University, Belfast. "Tells you a bit about self-esteem in the North", he once quipped.[2] In the 1960s Archbishop McQuaid maintained a ban on Catholics attending Trinity, prompting the ditty:

Our young men may shoot,
Plunder and loot
And even have carnal knowledge
But however depraved
They still may be saved
If they don't go to Trinity College.[3]

While Trinity was growing in the early sixties, the ban in the heavily Catholic south was a genuine threat to the college, and enrolment was maintained only by admitting Protestants from the North and English public school students who had failed to get into Oxford or Cambridge.[4] On arrival in Dublin, away from home for the first time, Mahon was struck by the sheer beauty of the city—by the trees, the handsome and imposing college buildings, and the girls. He had been admitted as a sizar (a student of limited means who had performed well in school-leaving exams) and was given rooms on the top floor of No. 1 Front Square, just inside the main gate. These rooms, which he shared with Brown and a classmate from Scotland, John ("Jock") Houston, had "a sitting-room, two bedrooms and a tiny kitchen consisting of a gas ring and a sink … the sets [of rooms] led off a staircase, at the bottom of which was a lavatory and a black notice board giving the names and floors of the various occupants".[5] Jock had the single room overlooking the Provost's Garden;[6] Derek and Robbie shared the double room overlooking the cobbled Front Square, which in the autumn of 1960 was crowded with Fiat runabouts, popular at the time.[7] Jeremy Lewis, a year behind Mahon, recalls:

> Trinity itself had the look of a rather large and agreeably coarse-grained Oxbridge college, which had commanded a large area in the middle of Dublin, within hailing distance of the river in one direction and Grafton Street in another. Designed by Sir William Chambers, the main frontage, which looked up Dame Street towards the Guinness brewery and Christ Church Cathedral, was massive, benign and grey, with a faded blue clock in the middle of its pediment; beneath the clock was the Front Gate, manned at all hours by the porters in jockey caps.[8]

From the beginning Mahon and his roommates revelled in their new-found freedom; one classmate recalls with nostalgia what a "den of iniquity" No. 1 Front Square was.[9] Pranks were common, including "water-throwing", the dowsing of unsuspecting passersby with buckets of water thrown from the upper windows of the college rooms. One drenched victim was moved to write a letter of complaint to the student paper in which he charged that "water-throwing seems to go hand-in-hand with scholarship and an inadequate sexual life" (twin insults by the code of the day). The anonymous letter writer signed himself "Young Northern Poet (Brutally drenched)".[10]

On the strength of the dozen poems he had published in the *School News*, Mahon arrived at Trinity with a budding sense of himself as a poet. Michael Longley, two years ahead of him, recalls the reaction among his more athletically oriented friends: "Thinks he's a poet", they would smirk among themselves, while Longley has admitted to feeling a combination of envy and resentment at the arrival of this precocious new college poet.[11]

In the evening Mahon and his roommates would don their commoners' gowns for dinner in the main hall. Lewis recalls dining beneath the "enormous portraits of well-fed eighteenth-century Church of Ireland bishops and weatherbeaten members of the Anglo-Irish Ascendancy". A typical meal included potatoes, Brussels sprouts and jugs of stout served by "purple-faced men in white jackets", one of whom they feared had spent his days unblocking lavatory drains.[12] The young men living in rooms were still called gentlemen—"without obvious irony", Mahon notes—by the college staff or "skips", as they were known.[13]

Mahon read English, French and Philosophy at Trinity, though "truth to tell", he later admitted, "I hardly did a hand's turn in four years". "Four years" is a bit misleading on his part; in fact, he would not finish for five. By his own account, the only classes in which he applied himself were those taught by Alec Reid, Owen Sheehy Skeffington and A.J. ("Con") Leventhal (though Mahon and Leventhal overlapped only briefly before his tutor retired and moved to Paris).

Alec Reid taught English and was popular among the students for his quick wit and vast store of humorous limericks. Reid had a round face, a warm and friendly demeanour, and an unruly shock of white hair that betrayed something of an undomesticated nature. Unlike many of his fellow professors, he enjoyed the company of his students as well as the camaraderie and banter of Dublin pub life, and on occasion was even known to hold informal tutorials in O'Neill's pub in Suffolk Street.

One of Mahon's classmates, Deborah de Vere White, recalls Reid pacing during class lectures: "What is poetry?" he would challenge his students. "Whatever lifts the hairs on the back of your neck while you're shaving? Sends shivers down your spine? Gets lost in translation?" As she recalls, he would answer his own rhetorical question by quoting lines from Hilaire Belloc's "Tarantella":

Do you remember an Inn,
Miranda?
Do you remember an Inn?
And the tending [sic] and the spreading
Of the straw for a bedding,
And the fleas that tease in the High Pyrenees,
And the wine that tasted of tar?

She recalls that this had a "hair-raising, spine-tingling" effect on her and her classmates.[14]

Reid had been responsible for founding the college literary magazine *Icarus* some ten years before, and for this too he was a favourite of the more literary-minded students. When Mahon attended his tutor's first lecture, he recalls Reid reciting a short poem which he had published in *Icarus* years before and of which he was still proud:

Remembering the eagle's high adventure
And eager to resume the ethereal search,
I sit in a suburban drawing-room,
A clever parrot on a polished perch.

This acceptance of one's own writing as an extension of one's literary studies came at an important moment in Mahon's schooling. Indeed, years later, looking back on his time at Trinity, Mahon would perform one of many acts of self-revision and claim that he and Michael Longley "began to write" under the influence and example of Alec Reid, such was Reid's importance in their early creative life.[15]

Reid's literary interests were broad and included the metaphysical poets, Keats, Yeats, MacNeice and Beckett (he later wrote a critical study of Beckett's plays entitled *All I Can Manage, More Than I Could*), as well as more recent drama which he reviewed for *The Irish Times*. That range of mind, that understanding of a canon not circumscribed by anything more limiting than one's own intellectual curiosity, was perhaps the most valuable lesson Reid taught Mahon. In just a few years, Mahon would join his tutor as a contributor to *The Irish Times*, and some of the most enduring figures in his own personal canon would closely mirror his former teacher's.[16]

Mahon read French under Owen Sheehy Skeffington, a more earnest figure than Reid but one who also took a particular interest in his students. Skeffington's father had been murdered by a British officer during the Easter Rising, and his son had grown up with a keen interest in politics and in resisting encroachment on the rights of the individual. While his public quarrels with the Church made him a well-known figure in Ireland, at Trinity he was admired for taking the students' side against the college authorities. His reputation was such that when the Literary and Historical Society at neighbouring University College Dublin invited him to speak on Beckett, the college authorities promptly cancelled the lecture.[17] Indeed, Skeffington seems to have taken some pride in his reputation as a fighter for lost causes, whether these were his anti-clerical opposition to the church, his campaign against corporal punishment in schools, his support for women's rights or his engagement with the censorship battles of the day. While Mahon found Skeffington a rather authoritarian figure,[18] he was attracted to his iconoclasm. In addition, Skeffington had a particular interest in Gide and Camus, writers Mahon felt were right up-to-the-minute.

Con Leventhal also had ties to that larger European world. He had lived in Paris in the 1930s and was a friend of Beckett. Unlike the sober-minded Skeffington, Leventhal was a cynic, with a dry wit Mahon found deeply appealing.

Soon after his arrival at Trinity, Mahon sought out Michael Longley. "Can I borrow your typewriter?" he asked when he ran into him in Front Square (in another version of the encounter, he shows up at Longley's rooms). Longley recognised Mahon's name from poems he had seen published in *School News* while he was still at Inst. His impression on now meeting his younger classmate for the first time was that he was "rather short and very cocky". Nevertheless, when Mahon submitted his poem "Subsidy Bungalows" to *Icarus*, Longley spoke up for the submission, despite his envy of this over-confident freshman.[19] Longley would have recognised the setting of the poem: Belfast's northern suburbs where new housing was expanding farther into the countryside and where Mahon's own parents would move in the coming year. Mahon and Longley soon became friends, and Mahon was a frequent visitor to Longley's rooms, No. 16 Botany Bay (so named because the buildings had originally enclosed the college vegetable garden, long since replaced by a tennis court).

Only a few months before, Mahon had imagined himself to be the only poet writing in Ireland, but at Trinity he discovered a community of fellow writers who shared his interest and ambition. They contributed regularly to *Icarus*, to its rival *T.C.D.: A College Miscellany* or to the student newspaper *Trinity News*. Brendan Kennelly and Rudi Holzapfel, both a few years ahead of Mahon, were the most celebrated of the campus poets at the time. Longley was also making a name for himself with his frequent contributions to the college magazines, as was his future wife, Edna Broderick, who contributed reviews. Deborah de Vere White, daughter of Terence, the literary editor of *The Irish Times*, was a regular contributor, as were Jeremy Lewis and Thomas Murtagh. Eavan Boland would join this group in a few years and begin contributing some of the poems later collected in her first volume, *New Territory* (1967). Indeed, here was a creative literary community that pre-dated the Belfast Group in the North. One searching for Mahon's literary origins will find them in these college rooms, in the streets around Trinity, in the Bailey or in O'Neill's in Suffolk Street.

Mahon soon joined Trinity's literary community as a regular contributor to the college publications, and in a brief essay in *Trinity News* in his first year one sees signs of his own evolving literary taste. He argues for the growing importance of the auditory and musical qualities of poetry, now available through long-play records and BBC Third Programme readings. Dylan Thomas, whom Mahon calls "the only contemporary poet to excite the popular imagination", owes much of his success to his public recitations which were available on Caedmon Records. "He may have been only a minor poet", Mahon writes, "but he was a great singer".[20]

In the spring of his first year Mahon published an article on the likely contenders to be the next Poet Laureate (in the end, John Masefield would not vacate the post for another six years). Among those he singled out as candidates were Siegfried Sassoon ("too old, and besides a Catholic and a pacifist"), Edmund Blunden (an ideal laureate "were he better known"),

John Betjeman (a "cheap versifier with a fan club"), Robert Graves (he would refuse the post, Mahon says), W.H. Auden (must be ruled out because of his American citizenship), Stephen Spender ("a dilettante socialist") and T.S. Eliot (an unlikely choice since "his particular brand of tradition is Continental rather than English"). Despite the flippant quality of these judgments, the article is revealing for what it suggests about the range of Mahon's reading and the direction of his own literary compass. That needle pointed unmistakably towards England, and the piece betrays a sensitivity to the politics of literary reputation. If nothing else, in 1961 the post of Poet Laureate was one the young Mahon imagined merited attention.

Equally significant, however, is the poet Mahon does not name. Louis MacNeice, who would play such an important role in his own creative development, does not make his list of candidates; indeed, Mahon's review of MacNeice's *Solstices*, published in *Icarus* a few weeks later, reads more like a rebuke that the poet of *Autumn Journal* was "writing now out of force of habit", with "sterile" results. Mahon's criticism betrays, in fact, a deep interest in the older, Belfast-born poet. Indeed, he chooses to criticise MacNeice precisely because he fails to live up to his own high expectation of him. In an interview years later, Mahon spoke of the importance of MacNeice's example when he was first beginning to write. As he explained, when "casting about for somewhere to put one's feet on solid ground, one started off with what was immediately in front of one's eyes, and in my sort of particular cultural, geographic situation—which was this Northern Irish Protestant thing—the poet immediately in front of one's eyes was Louis MacNeice".[21]

In other ways, too, Mahon was literally looking for a place to put his feet, but during his first year at Trinity that ground was shifting rapidly. "Subsidy Bungalows", the poem that marked his arrival at college, describes a landscape in transition. On one level the poem is about the erasure of his own childhood home. At the end of his first term, Mahon moved out of college rooms, a costly decision since, as a sizar, he had been paying no board at Trinity. He would move frequently in the coming year, staying for a time at the home of Mark Fisher, a junior lecturer in philosophy who was active in the Fabian Society, and later in a flat in North Great George's Street, north of the Liffey. He was eager, no doubt, to be on his own and free of college rules, though he also wanted, it seems, to get away from the "fops with silk scarves, cavalry twill trousers and snarling little red MG two-seaters".[22] He was also, in his own way, identifying himself with the working-class residents north of the river, who were similar to those he would celebrate in his early poem "Spring in Belfast".

At the end of term, Mahon and classmate Ronnie MacMillan got jobs canning peas in East Anglia. The canning factories in Britain were always looking for student workers in the summer, and according to a *Trinity News* report one could earn as much as £60 in a month and then set out for the Continent. Mahon did just that, spending several weeks hitchhiking across France, Belgium and Germany, a trip that would leave him with memories of a landscape still disfigured by World War II and the sight of people physically or emotionally maimed.[23] He would capture some of his impressions in an early, uncollected poem, "The Burnt Out Synagogue in Cologne".

Back at Trinity in the autumn, he tried his hand at short fiction, publishing one of his few completed short stories, "Lupercal", in *T.C.D.* The story's action centres on an abandoned gamekeeper's cottage on the side of Cave Hill, not far from Belfast Castle.[24] It opens with descriptions of the Belfast Castle estate and the main character's longing to escape his conventional suburban life for a more carnal one in the secluded cottage. One winter evening during a heavy snowfall, the protagonist leaves his sleeping wife, walks out of the house and down a path to the cottage where, like a latter-day Rip Van Winkle, he falls asleep. While the snow continues to fall and animals at the nearby Belfast Zoo howl in their cages, events take a more phantasmagorical turn. The roof of the cottage collapses under the weight of the snow, and the sleeping figure is encased in ice; the following morning children out playing are brutally attacked by a wolf, and a young girl is dragged away and never seen again.[25]

Mahon drew many of these elements from Cave Hill's long literary history and its reputation as a trysting place for lovers. The eighteenth-century ballad "Easter Monday for Ever; or the cobler [sic] at the Cave-Hill" recounts the tale of one Dick Awl who locks up his wife at Easter in order to steal away to Cave Hill; he sees men and women rolling "heels over head" and engaging in behaviour he dares not repeat. Similar associations appear in William Read's *Hill of Caves*, which also incorporates elements of human sacrifice, and Samuel Ferguson's story of doomed love "Corby Mac Gillmore". Much later, it is Cave Hill where Tusker in Brian Moore's *The Feast of Lupercal* goes to "pick up two dolls".[26]

Despite its flaws, this piece of juvenilia is important for its exploration of sexual repression and release. In contrast to the tame and ordered suburbs stands Cave Hill where, we are told, the "grounds swarmed with motorbikes and lovers all the weekend". The young girl killed at the story's close re-enacts the ritual sacrifice of the pagan festival of the Lupercalia. Years later, when asked to describe his own parents' marriage, Mahon replied, "bored with each other, timorous, [it] drove me away actually".[27] Whatever else this short story does, it gives expression to that wish to escape a similar condition of sexual barrenness which Mahon associated with his parents and with the Belfast suburbs of his childhood.

Mahon's early years at Trinity—living on his own, away from the scrutiny of parents—were a formative time in his own sexual development, as indeed they were for the culture at large. These were the years, Philip Larkin famously noted, when "sexual intercourse began ... between the end of the *Chatterly* ban / And the Beatles' first LP".[28] Mahon's own descriptions of his earliest sexual awakening are often expressed in terms of distance (the sight of a chambermaid climbing the stairs ahead of him, as described in "Autobiographies").[29] Trinity, however, threw the sexes together, despite rules aimed at limiting such contact (women did not have rooms in college and were to be out of male students' rooms by 7:30 p.m.). The college reading room was a favourite pick-up spot, and Mahon recalls distinctly the "sexual electricity" of the time. The college skips who looked after the students' rooms were a tolerant group by and large, and it was understood that a "modest emolument" would be left out if a female guest had spent the night.[30]

In his second year Mahon met Letty Martin, a first-year student reading philosophy, familiarly referred to as "Mental and Moral". Letty was from London and close friends with Louis MacNeice's daughter Corinna, and W.R. Rodgers's stepdaughter, Nina Gilliam. Letty often spent her breaks in Kinsale, County Cork, where she would help out at the Spinnaker restaurant Corinna's mother, Hedli, had opened after she and MacNeice had separated.[31] When Corinna had to deliver the family's Afghan Hound to her mother in Kinsale, Mahon leapt at the chance to accompany her and Letty, only to be met with some coolness by Hedli, who was being protective of the two girls. Though Mahon would come to know Hedli better in later years, he recalls this first meeting was "not a success".[32]

In June 1961 Corinna's father, Louis MacNeice, took a flat in Regent's Park Terrace with the actress Mary Wimbush, and Corinna was staying with him in anticipation of the start of art classes at the Slade School. It was there, on a visit to London, that Mahon first met MacNeice, though it was hardly a meeting. The older poet was absorbed in a rugby match on television, and Mahon later noted "the curtains were closed" on any conversation. "He was tired of words, of which he'd written a great many".[33]

Letty would certainly have attended the talk Mahon gave on MacNeice to the College Philosophical Society, "The Phil", that November. Mahon had already moved out of rooms at Trinity by then, and, Letty recalls, he was living at Mark Fisher's place. She and Mahon were soon seeing one another, often meeting at O'Neill's or in the coffee shops around Trinity.[34] On the strength of these friendships, Mahon invited Nina's stepfather, the poet W.R. Rodgers, to attend his November talk and to say a few words about MacNeice.[35] Rodgers had trained for the ministry but had given up his pastorate years before in order to devote himself to a second career as a poet and broadcaster. He had worked with MacNeice at the BBC and the two men remained close. Mahon had admired Rodgers's *Awake! And Other Poems* and *Europa and the Bull*, and was delighted when Rodgers not only accepted the invitation but attended the talk with Hedli. The visit was an important occasion for Mahon, who once described Rodgers, along with MacNeice, as "the only other poet of Ulster birth alive today who commands a more than purely regional interest".[36] Michael Longley recalls Rodgers had drunk a good bit that evening, but "he spoke brightly about MacNeice the poet and MacNeice the broadcaster".[37] Mahon thanked Rodgers afterwards for a "very enjoyable and exciting three days". It had been a particular honour to see Hedli, with whom he intended to stay in touch.[38] Through these friendships with Corinna and Nina, Mahon felt "somehow remotely in touch, in a personal kind of way, with people whose work I knew through books, that is to say, MacNeice and Rodgers".[39]

In his second year in Trinity Mahon took an active part in the revival of the Modern Languages Society. A series of talks was planned, as well as a new magazine entitled simply *Review*. As Mahon and his classmates planned it, the magazine would serve as an outlet for poetry in translation and thus avoid direct competition with *Icarus*.[40] Mahon himself was writing at a fast pace. Each issue of *Icarus* contained two or more of his latest poems, and within Trinity's literary circle he was coming to be known as one of the college's most talented poets. It was around this time that Mahon and Longley attended a meeting of a Catholic student group, the Laurentian Society, where Brendan Kennelly and Rudi Holzapfel were to read. They were both surprised when Kennelly graciously asked if they would each like to read something. Longley recalls racing back to his room to retrieve his folder of poems. It was the first public reading for each of them, and an important rite of passage.[41]

Among Mahon's recent poems was one intertwined with the Belfast shipyards and his own family mythology. "The Titanic" recounts the promise of the great liner—"Had all the best stars in her trees"—and its subsequent sinking while all nature watches its end unmoved:

> Meanwhile the sea had eaten ice and basked
> In the cool backdrop no true god could sink,
> The enormous night sky formed into a ring
> To see the end and know the matter clinched.[42]

The "true god" triumphs over man-made artifice, and the poem closes with the ocean rising up, swallowing the *Titanic* like a pint, and belching. Mahon was proud of the poem and disappointed when Terence de Vere White turned it down for *The Irish Times*.

———

Recalling his time at Trinity many years later, Mahon once described an incident when he "nearly smashed up a friend's car driving back to Dublin from an all-night party in the Wicklow hills". Ever since, he explained, he had been a non-driver.[43] While the fact that Mahon does not drive is well known to his friends, he had never before explained the reasons in print, nor would he ever again. A party in County Wicklow would have likely been at Ruth Grene's parents' farmhouse in Ballinaclash (Ruth was a classmate, and at the time she and Robbie Brown were close). The incident Mahon refers to so fleetingly is distant and indistinct, but what is surprising about his memory of it is that nothing presumably happened. The near-accident was averted, or so Mahon insisted when he wrote about it years after the fact. Why, one might ask, would he retain such a persistent memory of a non-event, and why would something that didn't happen lead to a life-long resolve never to drive again?

A classmate remembers Robbie and Derek both being deeply depressed in their second year and "not handling things well". Robbie could hardly stir from his bed.[44] Only a few weeks after the car incident, Mahon showed up at Longley's rooms after heavy drinking and the two friends quarrelled. When Longley said it might be best if Mahon were to leave, he remembers Derek saying with emphasis, "Alright, Mike, goodbye". In an effort to lighten the tone, Longley answered "Cheerio", but Mahon replied, "No, Mike, *goodbye*". Later that evening, he threw himself into the Liffey, a drunken gesture Longley describes as "partly theatrical, partly suicidal".[45] Depending on the currents and the tides, such a gesture could indeed have been quite dangerous.

The following morning *The Irish Times* ran a front-page story about a man who had drowned in the Liffey the previous evening. The account concludes with a brief reference to a near-drowning that had also occurred on the same night: "Meanwhile an unknown passer-by rescued 20-year-old Norman Mahon of North Great George's Street who had fallen in. The young man was taken by Fire Brigade ambulance in [*sic*] Mercer's Hospital where he recovered".[46] The reporter for *The Irish Press* provided a few more details. Mahon was first seen in the water near Butt Bridge, one of the last bridges before the river would have carried him past the ferry docks and into the open harbour beyond. A rescue squad from the Tara Street Fire Station was called and, according to the *Irish Press* account, resuscitated Mahon at the scene before taking him to the hospital, where he was detained (attempted suicide would not be decriminalised in Ireland until 1993).[47]

Longley remembers he and Edna visited Mahon in the hospital, but the incident seems to have passed quietly; some later heard he had simply gone swimming in the river.[48] An unpublished poem from the time, "A Bender", describes Mahon's experience waking up in hospital:

On the third day he rose, in sheer terror—
What has the world been up to while he was away?
His eyes rebuke him from a hospital mirror,
Unnatural in the familiar light of day.

The doctor makes his rounds, a seminar
Of students looking on from either side.
Him they ignore, and his painful avatar.
(He saw his card later—
attempted suicide …)

In late morning,
Friends and acquaintances arrive,
Faces in formal mourning
But scavenging, acquisitive—
Fresh clothes, cigarettes, and
An excellent pretext for an immediate hooley!

No one, really,
Seems to have acted on his absence.
The clocks are still going (twelve-thirty now)
And the office girls
Clicking past on high heels.
He is briefly aware of two worlds of sense—
Presence, and presence.[49]

Absent from these accounts, however, is any underlying explanation for his suicidal action or for the terror named in the opening line of this discarded poem.

Whether prompted by his family's ties to the sea, or perhaps associations with Shelley, references to drowning reappear frequently in Mahon's early poems, including one he would later dedicate to Longley, "Brahms Trio": "time is running out fast, I shall soon be drowned—".[50] Allusions to an automobile accident recur as well; in another unpublished poem called "Second Childhood" he writes cryptically, "I shall re-enact the disasters I have known, / Sitting in bare rooms after my collisions".[51] Another, "Never Otherwise", offers a series of reflections on two opposing halves of life experience, love and death, which Mahon compresses into a single word, "lovedeath". Mahon casts this subject in motoring terms, contrasting "Love's lay-bys" with "the roundabouts of death". The first-person speaker of the poem states defiantly "I will not be / Hauled all this distance merely to be thrown / Into a ditch through dangerous driving". It is revealing language for one who may himself have been in an accident, or have nearly averted an accident, just weeks before. The first-person speaker returns home to his lover where they keep the window fast against the encroaching cold, "although Death drift upon the pane".[52] "Never Otherwise" is a syntactically confused poem, and that confusion may itself be a strategy of evasion even as Mahon incorporates into the poem direct references to his own recent experience. After its publication in *Icarus*, Mahon would never again allow the poem to be reprinted. Instead, it joins that growing number of poems he cast off as either unsuccessful or (possibly) too personally revealing.

The psychological repercussions of these events would only reinforce Mahon's embrace of the pose and persona of a *poète maudit*, Longley's most common way of describing his friend during their Trinity years. Mahon's translations of Villon, Baudelaire and Rimbaud would all come later, but these particular figures would appeal to him for their own manner of addressing the artist's outsider, even criminal, status.

Mahon has never acknowledged such an accident (there is only the one published reference to an accident narrowly averted), but the traces of tragedy and Mahon's feelings of guilt appear frequently in the early poems. "After the Titanic" did not appear in print until after Mahon had left Trinity, but the poem, written from a confessional first-person perspective, offers his most powerful depiction of internalised guilt, and differs dramatically from his treatment of the *Titanic* penned just a few months before his suicide attempt. In the poem Mahon adopts the voice of Bruce Ismay, the chairman of the White Star Line, who ordered the captain of the *Titanic* to increase speed through the dangerous waters of the North Atlantic. At the inquiry following the disaster, it was revealed that Ismay himself had escaped with his life only by slipping into a lifeboat with women and children, a cowardly act for which he was vilified by the public. The poem is not so much about the sinking of the great liner as it is about that personal fall and its consequences in the years that follow. Bruce Ismay spent his final years living in a house by the sea where, as Mahon imagines it, the tide left daily reminders of the lost ship and his own cowardice. "Include me in your lamentations", Mahon writes. Allusions to a secret and shameful tragedy would echo through his mature poetry for years to come.

In February 1962, following Mahon's plunge in the Liffey, Longley learned that Terence de Vere White had accepted his poem "The Flying Fish" for *The Irish Times*.[53] This was something different from publication in the college magazines, and while Mahon would have been happy for his friend, that happiness would have been tempered by no small measure of envy. Mahon had taken note when de Vere White became literary editor some months before; he had himself been submitting poems to *The Irish Times* and at least one angry letter of complaint to de Vere White when one of his submissions was rejected. Perhaps to make up for that

ill-tempered outburst, Mahon published an admiring profile of him in
T.C.D. in which he named him the "No. 1 Adjudicator of Irish Writing",
adding, "our literary life is now in his hands".[54] Mahon would not publish
a poem in *The Irish Times* for two more years.

In the spring and early summer of 1962 Mahon immersed himself
in French poetry and began publishing translations in the new Modern
Languages Society magazine, *Review*. In February he contributed a
translation of Corbière's "Le Poète Contumace" and later a version of
Villon's "Ballad of the Hanged",[55] another poem in which he adopts the
persona of the guilty and the condemned. He indulges in this kind of
role-playing most fully in his poem "Poète Maudit":

> It will mean living in a slum, always
> Drinking spirits, even when I want tea,
> Wasting money in brothels, throwing out
> The one girl who ever really loves me,
> Hunting in transference the perfect mother
> From one psycho-anaylst to another,
> Feeling at home with lice and the fox-mange,
> Scrawling immortal verse in every lavatory,
> Paying 'a friend of mine' for snow and strange
> Mercurial ointments, getting myself hurt
> In legendary fights in fun-palaces,
> Sleeping on prison mattresses and, worst
> Of all, perhaps, letting it get about
> That I have a slight homosexual tendency ...
> Yet it will be my one source of comfort
> To know myself irrevocably accursed.[56]

Alec Reid had criticised what he saw as affectation in some of Mahon's
and Longley's poems, suggesting in the pages of the student newspaper
there were times when "the business of being a writer seems to matter
more than using writing as a mode of communicating experience".[57]
The criticism was put in a more pointed way by a fellow student[58] who
predicted that the way Longley was headed would "probably lead to a
privately printed unsaleable 'slim volume' by the age of thirty and an
interest in geraniums at the age of forty". As for Mahon, the writer noted,
his poetry "is perhaps the most promising in the College", but "the only

tragedy will be if he goes the way of most writers in Dublin and decides that looking like a writer is enough".[59]

Mahon was indeed cultivating an image of the poet as outcast. It was around this time he moved into a room above The Brazen Head in Bridge Street, where he could often be found in the bar looking "like a young Shelley" in a long scarf, as Louis Asekoff later remembered.[60] Asekoff was two years older than Mahon and had recently graduated from Bowdoin College in Brunswick, Maine. He met and became friends with Mahon when he came to Dublin for a year of postgraduate study at Trinity.

The Brazen Head is described in Joyce's *Ulysses* as a "dosshouse" where one can find a cheap room for a night. It was still that in the 1960s. Jeremy Lewis lived there for a time, and he later wrote it was inhabited almost entirely by "elderly gentlemen who appeared to have come down in the world". Lewis recalls "none of the floors were straight, the beds tilted at disconcerting angles; the lavatories had no locks...."[61] Mahon was drawn, however, to the picturesque qualities of urban squalor. Just a few months earlier his former teacher at Inst, John Boyle, had noted in a special issue of *Threshold* that "Irish literature, with a few striking exceptions, is not at home on city pavements".[62] Boyle objected to the disproportionate emphasis in Irish writing on rural experience, a point to which Mahon would have been receptive. Increasingly he was making his subject the lives of the working-class urban poor.

As June approached, Dublin began preparations to celebrate Bloomsday by opening the Martello tower in Sandycove as a museum. Mahon had already visited the tower, and once spent a night on its roof after a late-night party nearby. Among those visiting Dublin for the celebrations were MacNeice and Rodgers (whom Mahon was now calling "Bertie"). MacNeice had been asked to cover the Bloomsday events for the *New Statesman*, but when his account was published a couple of weeks later, it proved to be more a celebration of Dublin pub life than a tribute to James Joyce. MacNeice described the Dublin pub as a "temple of talk", though he also noted the city's pubs could be terribly crowded and one might well find oneself "drinking cheek by jowl with teenagers".[63] Mahon recognised this as a reference to himself.

When Mahon heard that MacNeice had been seen at McDaid's, he tried to persuade Longley to go with him to meet the poet. Longley begged off, but Mahon and a couple of other friends went anyway. When they arrived, they found MacNeice at a table with Bill Webb, the literary editor of the *Manchester Guardian*.[64] Mahon approached the two men, hoping to engage MacNeice in conversation, only to be met by "a polite snarl" and "a sidelong flash of the horsy teeth". "Both were on the whiskey", Mahon later wrote of the meeting, "the effect being to make Webb witty and MacNeice morose".[65] As he noted many years later, it was "not exactly Keats and Coleridge". Despite that cool reception, Mahon would embrace MacNeice as a literary father figure whose footsteps he would follow for years to come.

Mahon had a more successful encounter with Rodgers, who promised him a new poem for the upcoming issue of *Icarus* Mahon was editing (the editorship of *Icarus* changed with each issue).[66] When Rodgers promptly followed up and sent him a new poem, "Visitation", Mahon was not shy about offering his critique. "I liked it immensely, and was not a little surprised to find it was in free verse. I think your best work has been in a stricter form, but I like the Visitation none the less for that".[67] Mahon was grateful to have a poet of Rodgers's stature in *Icarus*, and when the issue appeared the following December, he extended a special welcome to the older poet in his opening editorial.

As circumstances would have it, Mahon was putting the issue together in the immediate aftermath of the Cuban missile crisis, and he used his editorial to address the poet's responsibility in the face of such events (a subject that would take on added importance after the outbreak of violence in the North). "As we go to press", Mahon wrote, "the threat of a third world war has very recently been averted—at least for the time being". What is one's responsibility at such a time? "Should a poet remain uncommitted, exploring first principles of experience … or should he align his talent with a militant political ideology (in effect, the Left), contributing his voice to the furtherance of its aims?" Mahon considered a range of responses to the question, from the apolitical "softness" of the young Indian poet Dom Moraes[68] to the "windy shrillness" of Christopher Logue. While either position can be taken too far, he suggested, it was clear Mahon looked with suspicion on any poet "unresponsive to the human climate of his time". Noteworthy here, given the seasonal and climatic imagery in his own poetry, is the way he absorbs the political into a natural landscape. Mahon argues not for explicit political statement but for a depth of awareness to the conditions in which people live which incorporates the economic and the political. "These conditions", he writes, "are as much a part of the natural landscape as a thunderstorm, a full moon, or the seasonal habits of trees and birds".[69]

Early in the new year Mahon and Longley moved into a basement flat in Merrion Square. The squalor of the flat and the toothless housekeeper made the whole scene resemble something out of Beckett or O'Casey, Longley has recalled. As the ashtrays overflowed, Longley filled the flat with jazz and classical music on his Dansette record player.

> We inhaled with our untipped Sweet Afton cigarettes MacNeice, Crane, Dylan Thomas, Yeats, Larkin, Lawrence, Graves, Ted Hughes, Stevens, Cummings, Richard Wilbur, Robert Lowell, as well as Rimbaud, Baudelaire, Brecht, Rilke—higgledepiggledy [sic], in any order. We scanned the journals and newspapers for poems written yesterday.[70]

Sharing rooms, however, also posed something of a "poetic challenge". The two friends were pacing one another in their reading, in their critical judgments and in their own writing. Longley recalls Mahon defending Larkin's "The Whitsun Weddings", which they first read in *Encounter*, and that Mahon introduced him to George Herbert "as though he were a brilliant contemporary published that very week by the Dolmen Press".[71] Longley recalls something of the rivalry and has added, "our friendship and our abilities were often stretched as far as they could go".[72] "Brahms Trio" captures something of the spirit of the time:

> Naturalistic, cerebral
> And existential; with each record played
> We wrestled with your temperamental turntable,
> Its pilot light and roving arm—
> I scarcely noticed at the time,
> What an impression that fluffy needle made.
>
> With winter it all stopped; you chose to spend
> Your late nights listening to the Symphonies,
> And I drawn on by raw material noise,
> Struck out for a new kind of 'experience',
> (And of course, found it in the end)
> No deathless melodies have reached me since.[73]

Mahon soon introduced into this domestic scene an attractive young American named Jill Schlesinger whom he had met at a party. Jill had graduated from Emory University in Atlanta, Georgia and was spending a year travelling in Europe. Mahon was immediately attracted to her and her American ways, which set her apart from the young women with whom he had, up to then, been most familiar.

That spring Mahon and Longley learned the poet and editor Howard Sergeant had selected Longley's "Day of Dancing" and Mahon's "An Unborn Child" for publication in the Borestone Mountain Poetry Award anthology, *Best Poems of 1962*. Modest cash prizes were to be given to the three poems judged to be the best of the year, and when the anthology was published early in the new year Mahon's "An Unborn Child" had received third place, ahead of poems by Elizabeth Bishop, James Dickey, Donald Hall, Ted Hughes and Sylvia Plath, as well as Longley. The prize, which brought with it a cheque for $100, was Mahon's first anthologised publication, and it was a great boost for the 22-year-old. This personal success, however, would have been cause for wider celebration among the *Icarus* group, for the name of their college magazine was listed alongside such publications as *Harpers*, the *New Statesman*, *The New Yorker* and many of the leading literary quarterlies.

Though "An Unborn Child" would undergo revision in the years ahead, it would remain one of Mahon's most anthologised poems. The poem, which owes a debt to MacNeice's "Prayer Before Birth", had first been published in the December 1961 *Icarus* where it bore a dedication to Wendy Puxon, a former flatmate of Letty's who was separated from her husband and pregnant at the time.[74] By May, word of Mahon's and Longley's literary success had reached them in Dublin, and *Trinity News* ran a celebratory story under the headline "Poets honoured". The author of the piece could not help but note the irony of the timing: "Derek Mahon, who was an entrance Sizar and generally regarded as one of the most promising students to enter Trinity in recent years, failed his Junior Fresh English and has just been sent down for unsatisfactory lecture attendance".[75]

The expulsion was a blow to someone who had been admitted to Trinity just three years earlier with such high expectations. What had happened? Mahon had moved out of rooms at the earliest opportunity and rebelled, in his own way, against the lifestyle of his more conventional and more privileged classmates, whose sports cars filled Front Square.

College life had encouraged heavy drinking, which he did not always manage well, and he had applied himself only in the classes taught by tutors he respected. It could not have helped matters that Jill was not enrolled in Trinity and had no studies herself.

Mahon's parents had taken pride in their son's early school achievements and had hoped he would become a schoolteacher or take up some other, similarly respectable vocation. Their response to his being expelled was one of "incomprehension and dismay". Recalling these events years later, however, Mahon remembered caring little about their feelings, because "I had reached the hardened stage where I didn't give a damn what they thought".[76] Even at a distance of many years, the statement is startling for its bluntness. As he would later put it in "Late-Night Walk": "I am man self-made, self-made man, / No small-talk now for those who ran / In and out of my earthly childhood. / We have grown up as best we could … / They would gnaw my body to the bone…." What lies behind the anger of these lines and what is obscured by these ellipses has a deeper origin than a common adolescent breach with one's parents.

On some level Mahon may well have invited the crisis. In his two and a half years at Trinity he had broken from his parents and their ordinary lives, formed friendships that would prove to be life-long, confirmed his resolve to be a poet, and been touched by a personal tragedy so shameful he would suppress any mention of it for years to come. Writing in the mid-1980s about his time at Trinity, Mahon quoted F. Scott Fitzgerald's *The Crack-Up*:

> All life is a process of breaking down, but the blows that do the dramatic side of the work—the big, sudden blows that come, or seem to come, from outside—don't show their effects all at once. There is another sort of blow that comes from within—that you don't feel until it's too late to do anything about it, until you realize with finality that in some regard you will never be as good a man again.[77]

Mahon felt an affinity with Fitzgerald's portrayal of wasted youth and a particular fondness for Jay Gatsby, who towards the end of Fitzgerald's most famous novel is implicated in a fatal automobile accident. While Mahon deleted this passage in the published version of his essay, the reference remains in his working draft as a reminder of the trauma of his college years. With the Borestone prize fresh in his mind, he and Jill left Dublin for the Isle of Man, a destination with a pun on his own name that would have amused him. There, the two found summer jobs working at the Belle Vue Hotel in Port Erin.

Chapter 4

| THE LOST YEARS, 1963–5

"I'm reading a dirty book called *Moll Flanders* [and] catching up on my education after a 3-year convalescence at Trinity", Mahon wrote his friend Louis Asekoff in June.[1]
The Belle Vue Hotel was a faded Victorian hotel overlooking the Port Erin harbour. Jill got a job as a waitress and Mahon as a barman.[2] It was only a short walk to Bradda Head, where on a clear day one could see the Mourne Mountains to the west. "Flora & fauna very interesting", Mahon reported; "some lichen, the odd cormorant, a colony of little green flying penguins, and an almost extinct tribe of 'Yorkshire holidaymakers' (a kind of graceless flamingo)".[3] One particularly memorable day he and Jill took a boat around the bird sanctuary on the nearby Calf of Man.[4] When he memorialised these summer months in "Bird Sanctuary", dedicated to Jill, he took up the ornithological theme: "I expect great things / Of these angels of wind, / Females, males and fledglings. / The sudden whirring of their wings / Disturbs the noon, and midnight rings / With echoes of their island".[5]

That summer Mahon's "Girls in their Seasons" appeared in *The Dubliner* alongside three poems by another young poet named Jon Stallworthy. It was fortunate placement. Stallworthy was as an editor at Oxford University Press, and he wrote to Mahon in care of the magazine to say "how very good I think your poem. Immeasurably better (I'm sorry to have to admit!) than its companions", a reference to his own poems on the opposite page.[6] Stallworthy and Mahon had not yet met, but on the strength of "Girls in their Seasons" he invited Mahon to send him more of his work. It was the start of a publishing relationship that would last for more than twenty years.

"Girls in their Seasons" describes a series of former lovers the first-person speaker has left and "consigned to fate". Yet for all his resolve, he finds he still encounters them—or thinks he does—in unexpected places. He sees one standing under a lamp-post, another in a train window. One went away only recently, a victim "of cerebral adulthood", while another is intent on reminding him "Of a trip I made last winter / From dream into bad dream" (a veiled reference to the events of the winter of 1961/62). The final two stanzas bring the speaker into the present and anticipate the end of his latest love:

> Now we are running out of light and love,
> Having left far behind
> By-pass and fly-over.
> The moon is not there
> And matches go out in the wind.
> Now all we have
>
> Is the flinty chink of Orion and the Plough
> And the incubators of a nearby farm
> To light us through to the Land of Never-Never.
> Girls all, be with me now
> And keep me warm
> Before we go plunging into the dark forever.[7]

Mahon would come to regret the sexist tone of the poem, and he would omit it from his *Collected Poems*, but it is true to its time and reveals his resistance to the kind of commitments demanded by a world of adult responsibility. Never-Never Land, that imaginary place where boys do not grow up, remained deeply appealing to Mahon in the summer of 1963.

At the end of the holiday season, he and Jill took their summer earnings and travelled to London where they found a flat in Bayswater, not far from where he would live when he returned to the city in a few years' time. In order to share the flat as a couple, they had to pretend to be married, and they bought an inexpensive ring for that purpose.[8]

Though no longer at Trinity, Mahon continued to submit poems to the familiar college publications and to *The Dubliner*, a new journal that hoped to revive something of the spirit of Seamus O'Sullivan's defunct *Dublin Magazine*. He had an important breakthrough, however, when Anthony Thwaite published "End of Season" in the London-based weekly *The Listener* that September; this was something bigger than publication in *Icarus* or *The Dubliner*, and it brought him closer to MacNeice and Rodgers and their BBC circle. The news of MacNeice's death on 3 September came as a shock. MacNeice was only 55, but he had suddenly taken ill after being caught in a summer storm in Yorkshire. His chronic bronchitis from a lifetime of heavy smoking rapidly turned acute, and within days advanced to pneumonia. A funeral service was held in St John's Wood the following Saturday; a few weeks later a memorial service followed at All Souls Church adjacent to Broadcasting House.[9] Mahon did not attend either service, but he would have registered the death and read the newspaper tributes from Eliot and Auden.

Mahon was giving thought to other subjects of commemoration; that autumn he visited Yeats's former house in Woburn Walk, only to find that renovation to an adjacent building had destroyed the back rooms. The unpublished poem the visit inspired takes up familiar themes of time and decay and the hoped-for endurance of the artist: "When the walls crumble and the winds deprive / The roof of meaning, measure time by this— / But call it timeless if their names survive".[10] The poem takes a Keatsian stance towards the inevitability of decay, while poetry, it suggests, offers the only chance of survival.

Mahon was torn between whether to return to Trinity and finish his studies or find some casual work that would allow him to travel and write. He imagined his poetic subject was the lives of the working classes, and an uncollected poem begun in these months, "La Condition Ouvrière", shows him striving to make this identification even as he recoils from such a life himself:

November. Before dawn it starts again—
Alarm-clocks pealing in the flats above,
And uncomplaining men and women
Rising once more to the occasion. When,

Oh when, if ever, will this not remain
The only way to stay alive?

Maker and fitter, warehouseman and clerk,
Possessed by the unbeatable abstractions,
Lie down in darkness, rise up in the dark.
Inanimate matter waits … The early ones
Are there already, turning hands to work
Monotonous miracles—blood from stones.

It is this gives rise to the God we thank each night
And curse all day—and to the alluring Siren
Who meets us with reproach, unmanning doubt,
On winter mornings in the deliberate rain—
Shadows of that five-thirty we clock out
For ever, and never rise again.[11]

Another uncollected poem written during these months, "An Irishman in London", also addresses this theme and expresses directly Mahon's uncertainty about his own plans. He knows, "… Sooner / Or later I shall have to get up and go, / Inspect the darkness, make a course for home—", yet no sooner does he state that resolution than he rejects it: "… I do not intend / Lurching back seaward to that backward land / Which was mine once, not even one week-end— / For that would wreck a dream…." That dream included a commitment to his own "expected songs", which were linked, in his mind, with "white birds wheeling over western harbours". As the bar in which the speaker reflects fills with labourers from a nearby building site, he speculates, "These are my people coming into the light". This identification, however, is hardly a convincing one, and the poem reverts to a swirl of directionless movement: "… But now I see / I must go forward to go back, and back / In order to go forward…." Any identification with his people is abandoned; in its closing lines, the poem holds out as an ideal a quality of repose utterly disassociated from place.

An early version of the poem included the line "Odysseus may take no cheap night-crossing into Ithaca".[12] It was that linkage of Mahon's and Odysseus' travels Michael and Edna Longley had in mind when they later suggested "Night-Crossing" as the title for his first collection (when the poem was cut from *Night-Crossing*, he worked this title reference into "Jail Journal").

In November 1963, Mahon mailed a selection of his best poems to Stallworthy, and saw Jill sail from Southampton for America; she had finally grown weary of their impoverished living arrangements, and for some time her parents had been urging her to return home.[13] As for Mahon, their "six months as man and wife" had frightened him, as he made clear when he tried to capture something of this time in an unpublished poem, "True Romance". "I have been incumbent of the fireside chair / And charge-hand at the kitchen sink / Before my time", he wrote.[14] Still, it was a painful parting. "Bird Sanctuary", with its dedication to Jill, would be one of the few poems from this period he would retain in his *Collected Poems*.

After Jill's departure, a friend, Mike Jessel, moved in to share the Queensborough Terrace flat, and Mahon got a job working in the Harrods stock room. Many years later he recounted the time an American couple visiting Harrods addressed a black co-worker there as "boy". As he remembered it, the young black man turned to him and said, "You see why I will never be president—I'm too young".[15] The story sounds apocryphal, but Mahon was indeed following the news of the Civil Rights movement in America. That August Martin Luther King, Jr had delivered his "I Have a Dream" speech on the steps of the Lincoln Memorial in Washington, and a couple of weeks after that, a bomb planted by members of the Ku Klux Klan killed four young girls in a Birmingham, Alabama church. In November, the world registered with shock the assassination of President Kennedy. Through Jill, Mahon felt remotely connected to America and to these historic events.

When Mahon learned in December that his father was ill, he returned to Belfast despite his recent resolutions not to go back. It was likely then, in the weeks before Christmas, that he first met Seamus Heaney. No one has recorded the first meeting, but as Heaney has written, he met Edna and Michael first and then, through them, Mahon.[16] Edna had graduated from Trinity while Mahon was away and had secured a teaching appointment at Queen's. Heaney was teaching at St Joseph's Training College on the Stewartstown Road and he met Edna and Michael through a writing group they began attending that autumn. James Simmons was also in Belfast at the time and would have been among the group of new friends. Eight years older than Mahon, Simmons had edited a poetry anthology during his final year at the University of Leeds and had recently self-published a chapbook of his own poems, *Thoughts from the Mind.*

It was a formative time for these young poets. Heaney had stepped out from behind his early pseudonym and was publishing under his own name, and increasingly in larger-circulation magazines and quarterlies. Mahon too had ambitions for his writing; back in Belfast, he typed up a selection of his best poems and mailed them to Jon Stallworthy at OUP. He was casting about for work, and he had hopes that Bertie Rodgers would be able to help secure him a position at the BBC. Instead, the Head of English at Trinity, Professor Philip Edwards, intervened and got him readmitted in time for the start of Hilary term in January. Edwards had read Mahon's poems with admiration, and some months before had written in the pages of *T.C.D.* that his poems were "as good as anyone's in Ireland".[17] It was extravagant praise coming from one's professor, noteworthy too because the scope of the remark was all Ireland. Terence de Vere White marked Mahon's return by publishing his newest poem, "In Memory", in the pages of *The Irish Times* on 4 January. It was his first poem to appear in the newspaper.

The poem, reminiscent of "Girls in their Seasons", marks the passing of his and Jill's relationship. He recalls a nose, an eye, an ear and "that fall of hair", but these parts "form no human whole to which I could put your name".[18] He sent Jill a copy of the poem with the explanation that it "is about a beautiful American girl I used to know, & tells how the precise image of her face has blurred in my mind—as so often happens when you part from someone particularly close to you".[19] While the poem itself may be an act of resistance against forgetting, Mahon seems reconciled to the passing of former loves. As with his recent Yeats poem, what interested him was poetry's commemorative function.

In late January Stallworthy declined Mahon's latest manuscript. It was the gentlest of rejections, however, one that kept the door open for future publication. "We have kept your poems rather a long time I'm afraid; longer than is normal, in fact, because they are so much better than normal.... Several of us have read them, and we believe that you have here the nucleus of an impressive and exciting collection". The entire manuscript, however, added up to only 26 printed pages, "a little more than half the length of a normal volume" Stallworthy noted, and "While we cannot offer you publication as it stands, we hope we can persuade you to resubmit it when it is a little longer. Good as it is now, my feeling is that six months to a year it will be a great deal better and you would not, in the long run, regret the delay".[20] It was as encouraging a rejection as one could receive, and Mahon would begin speaking of his pending publication by OUP as a certainty.

Back in Dublin, Mahon participated in a poetry programme held in the Fellows Garden where he met a new student Eavan Boland for the first time. Her father, F.H. Boland, had been ambassador to Britain and more recently had served as president of the UN General Assembly during the U2 spy plane crisis and the construction of the Berlin Wall. In the course of her father's assignments, Boland had lived in London and New York, and on the family's return to Ireland had enrolled at Trinity because there was no Irish language requirement as there was at University College Dublin (UCD). She arrived with a strong interest in poetry. When she and Mahon first met, she had already published two chapbooks with the short-lived Gallagher Press. Boland recalls being utterly charmed by Mahon's reading in the Fellows Garden.[21] When they saw one another again a week later, he was similarly taken with her. He wrote Longley, describing her as a "fiery redhead", and a "Maud Gonne figure".[22] She had an assurance beyond her 19 years and, as Mahon later wrote, "she cut a striking figure wherever she went, with her flashing eyes, tawny hair and sometimes imperious manner".[23] Mahon found her attractive if "a little unnerving".[24]

For the next six months he and Boland met often in O'Neill's pub in Suffolk Street, Jammet's back bar or the lounge of the Royal Hibernian Hotel, for what Mahon would jokingly describe as "epistemological conversation".[25] Their talk ranged widely over writers important to each of them. For Boland, that meant Yeats and the Celtic twilight, while for Mahon it was MacNeice, Auden, Camus and Beckett. There were frequent disagreements, "dramatic scenes in O'Neill's".[26] Boland has admitted to being in awe of Mahon, who was already well known for the poems he was publishing in *Icarus* and in *The Dubliner*. In her memories of these months, he has a cigarette in his hand "like a votive lamp". She remembers her pleasure when, on showing him a poem of her own, "On Sandymount Strand", he announced, "It's a cat's breakfast".[27]

On his return to Dublin Mahon met another aspiring poet, Richard Ryan, who was studying at UCD. He and Ryan would remain life-long friends, even after Ryan later gave up poetry for a career in the diplomatic service.

Despite these new friendships, Mahon was finding college life intolerable. He was more eager than ever to graduate, but was unsure of what he might do once he had finished at Trinity. His friend Asekoff had returned to America after his one-year course, and Mahon wrote him he might teach English in France, followed by "a Poetastry Residentship … in some nice little city built on natural gas in Wyoming, Nebraska or some such pullulating [*sic*] hub of intellectual dynamism—but not a dry state".[28] He enclosed in the letter a new poem, "Homage to Malcolm Lowry", another in a series of tribute pieces he was writing during these months and another figure whose example pointed abroad.

Mahon submitted a selection of his poems to the Society of Authors for the Eric Gregory Award, an annual competition recognising the most promising young poets under 30. Unbeknownst to him, one of the judges that year was Ted Hughes, who had published two prize-winning collections of poems, *The Hawk in the Rain* and *Lupercal*. In his confidential reader's report, Hughes wrote:

> I found these poems extremely likeable, and at bottom full of interesting imagination of a rather visionary sort. If he has the temperament to do something with all of that, I wouldn't be surprised what he'll do. The main thing against him seem[s] to be a sort of facility, a youthful glibness about everything, though charmingly done.[29]

The 1964 Gregory Awards were shared by Robert Nye, Ken Smith, Jean Symons and Ted Walker.

When Mahon showed up for exams at the end of Trinity term, he carried with him a large block of concrete which he proceeded to drop with a loud crash on the exam room floor—a not-so-subtle expression of his view of the proceedings.[30] Others remember it differently. Edna Broderick heard that he had smashed a pair of cymbals in the exam hall.[31] Regardless of the specifics, Mahon once again left Trinity. He told Asekoff he had started work again on his novel, adding "I always do when I get thrown out".[32] While the manuscript of this novel has not survived, Mahon described it as being "about this student who drinks too much and has a heart of gold…. The women all love him, of course, but their finances are not inexhaustible" (a detail that points to the strains in his and Jill's relationship during their months together in London). "All the time the avenging forces are closing in", he adds, "the tall grey men who just don't know come shuffling up with their brief-cases full of badness and croak horrible distorted everythings in his ear". He added, "It's meant to out-Gingerman the Ginger Man".[33] Mahon's reading provided him with an abundance of role models, while his writing remained an important means of self-projection. He was trying to "out-Gingerman the Ginger Man" in other ways too; he reported getting "uncontainably tanked" at a party at Deborah de Vere White's house, where he broke a piano, and had to be put to bed.[34]

Edna Broderick was still teaching at Queen's, and after what Longley would describe as "some detours" he followed her there and got a job teaching at his former grammar school, Inst. Michael and Edna's absence made Dublin even more intolerable for Mahon, and he began making more regular weekend trips to Belfast, at least one with Eavan Boland.[35] When Boland later composed a poem about their relationship, "Belfast vs. Dublin", she identified him with Belfast and herself with Dublin, and in that opposition hinted at irreconcilable differences in their backgrounds and upbringing.[36]

Michael and Edna were attending the writing group organised the previous year by a new lecturer at Queen's, Philip Hobsbaum. Mahon, however, was still in Dublin during the week when the group met, and he was about to put even more distance between himself and these meetings. When his classmate Tommy Murtagh announced his plans to study in Paris, Mahon impulsively decided to go along. He had not been admitted to any programme of study, however, and Murtagh remembers wondering just what he was going to do there. Nevertheless, that September the two friends flew to Paris together in time for Murtagh to report for classes.[37] Mahon checked into the Hôtel du Lys in the Latin Quarter where he stayed until his money began to run low. At that point he moved in with a former classmate, Robert Walmsley, who had a flat on the Quai de Tournelle near George Whitman's bookshop, across the Seine from Nôtre Dame.[38] He called on his former French professor, Con Leventhal, recently retired from Trinity, and Jean-Paul Pittion—also in Paris at the time—whom Mahon had known as an assistant in Trinity's French Department.

He had hoped to get into the Sorbonne, but as he wrote Longley soon after his arrival, "my half-hearted attempts to enrol have become enmeshed in red tape". The university was terribly overcrowded, one of the conditions that contributed to the student protests a few years later, and Mahon reported one had to queue for an hour to get a seat in the most popular lectures. "Maybe I'll just sit up here & read books".[39] While it seems he did in the end receive a pass to audit classes, it is less clear that he ever made any use of it. As he said later, he had never been one to queue for lectures. Instead, he immersed himself in French literature, including Sartre's *Baudelaire* and Camus's *Le Mythe de Sisyphe*.[40] During the day, he would often visit George Whitman's bookshop and in the evenings would meet Walmsley, Murtagh or Pittion at the Café au Départ on the Boulevard St Michel.

An unpublished poem composed during these weeks, "Negroes on the Right Bank", reveals his awareness of the political events of the day. The Civil Rights Act of 1964 had been passed in America just weeks before Mahon wrote of seeing expatriate African Americans on the streets of Paris "far from the tedious prohibitions of home". He observes the black men's poise and bearing and notes "they are utterly self-possessed / And, in that sense, have surely overcome", a reference to the Civil Rights anthem of the day.[41] In time, Mahon too would come to see emigration as a way to escape the oppressions of home.

Without any formal academic standing, or, more importantly, any source of income, remaining in Paris for any length of time was proving difficult. He wrote a number of his Trinity friends asking for loans: Boland received an urgent appeal asking for a cheque to be sent immediately "thereby saving from the abattoir of his amour proper the priceless bacon of yours truly";[42] Brendan Kennelly sent him what he could spare. After only a few weeks of café life, Murtagh suggested he visit a writer friend, Alain Guel, who had a big country house in Brittany. The cost of living would not be as high there, and Guel was known to keep an open door for an odd assortment of hippies, eccentrics and oddballs, most of whom, Mahon later recalled, were "queer as cooks".[43] Mahon took the train to Saint-Brieuc and spent the remainder of the autumn there, where he wrote the series of poems "November Notes in Brittany" (after much revision the sequence would be collected under the title "Breton Walks").

In December he wrote Asekoff to update him on his plans: "At Christmas I return, jet-set, to the Emerald Isle, don a grey topper & swallow-tail coat, buy a second-hand L.P. of Miles Davis or Monteverdi, & present myself, with a certain ring, in the aisle of Dalkey Church on Dec. 28th to watch Longley and Edna join their hands in Holy Matrimony". His description has an air of resignation about it. He added, "Then I shall be completely alone in the world".[44] A home movie of the occasion captured the celebratory affair and Mahon putting on a brave face. Afterwards the wedding party, including Kennelly and Heaney, celebrated the occasion at Jammet's.[45]

In later years Mahon would attach great importance to his time in France and to his brief affiliation with the Sorbonne. Indeed, for the next 40 years he would include a reference to his studies there in any mention of his formal education. This account of his French education served a number of useful purposes. It provided him with a convenient explanation for why it took him five years to gain a degree, while references to his studies at Trinity and the Sorbonne would lead others to assume he had undertaken a postgraduate course of study.

Mahon the undergraduate was back at Trinity in time for the start of Hilary term in January 1965. He moved into a flat in Lower Mount Street where he planned to slip into "a cocoon of study" in preparation for his final exams in June.[46] The student paper took note of his return, commenting, "every university faculty must have a Wild Man to provide thrills and to shock crowded lecture rooms".[47] Boland remembers his sudden reappearance, and him reading to her "Four Walks in the Country".[48] He included the poem sequence in a new selection he sent to Stallworthy under the working title *Sisyphus*. The title poem was prompted by his recent reading of Camus and recounts the story of Sisyphus, who is condemned to roll a boulder up a hill, only to have it roll back down again, in a futile and unending cycle.[49] This view of life as a wheel of suffering appealed to Mahon, and captured something of his feelings for Trinity at the time.

On his return Mahon and Boland took up their relationship where they had left off, but over the spring differences that had been present from the beginning began to re-emerge more forcefully. "He came from Belfast … I was middle-class, with an address in Dublin", Boland later explained; "I had spent years in London and New York, while Derek had stayed in the North".[50] With the start of classes, she increasingly began sequestering herself in a "purdah" of isolation.[51]

Boland would later frame these differences as poetic oppositions.[52] He was looking for authentic experience among the working classes, and when he read for her another new poem, "Suburban Walk", he must have known that its depiction of ordered suburban life carried with it an implicit criticism of Boland's own middle-class upbringing. Mahon expresses in this poem his open contempt for those whose lives are bound by suburban hedges. He borrowed its opening line from Sophocles' *Antigone*, which he had recently encountered as the epigraph to Malcolm Lowry's *Under the Volcano*:

> Wonders are many and none is more wonderful than man
> Who has tamed the terrier, trimmed the hedge
> And grasped the principle of the watering can.[53]

Boland remembers, "I was admiring and hesitant". Only later did she come to see the poem expressed "the plight of a poet caught between definitions".[54] Over the spring Mahon's reports to the Longleys grew increasingly pointed. "She's in bed, on a more or less permanent basis reading Oblomov and *Vogue*", he joked.[55] Little did he know that he would one day work for *Vogue*.

A few weeks after his return to Dublin, he attended a programme at the Lantern Theatre where Hedli MacNeice and Thomas Kinsella read MacNeice's poems. Hedli opened the evening with "Dublin"; in her comment on the poem, she traced the origin of her late husband's interest in poetry to childhood insecurities, an interpretation Mahon would adopt also when, years later, he proposed a film on MacNeice. The programme printed Rodgers's poem "Tribute to Louis MacNeice", and it is likely Mahon was already thinking about what form his own tribute might take.

Mahon was visiting Belfast most weekends, staying with the Longleys, and it was during one of these spring visits that he, Longley and Heaney crowded into Heaney's Volkswagen and drove to Carrowdore in County Down to visit the MacNeice grave.[56] They signed the visitors' book in the church vestibule and searched the churchyard for the grave (it remained unmarked at the time). Longley recalls that each of them was contemplating an elegy, and when the friends met again a few weeks later, Mahon read for them "In Carrowdore Churchyard":

> This, you implied, is how we ought to live—
> The ironical, loving crush of roses against snow,
> Each fragile, solving ambiguity. So
> From the pneumonia of the ditch, from the ague

Of the blind poet and the bombed-out town you bring
The all-clear to the empty holes of spring,
Rinsing the choked mud, keeping the colours new.

The moment has been much mythologised, and Longley later recalled, "Seamus started to read his and scrapped it because he knew Derek had written the definitive elegy.... I knew as well and decided then and there not to make the attempt".[57] Heaney downplayed the poetic rivalry, and conceded that MacNeice was Mahon's poet from the beginning.[58] Years later, when asked what his first real poem was, his "Digging" or his "Thought-Fox", Mahon answered, "Carrowdore Churchyard" and "I knew it at the time".[59] He would later signal the poem's importance in his early development by choosing it to open his *Selected Poems* (1990).

On one of his Belfast visits Mahon accompanied the Longleys to a meeting of the Belfast Group. Philip Hobsbaum had come to Queen's from London, where he had developed a reputation as the organiser of a literary group that had once included Edward Lucie-Smith, Peter Redgrove, Peter Porter and, for a time, Ted Hughes.[60] Hobsbaum had set out to recreate a similar community in Belfast. The Group met regularly during term at his and his wife's home near the university. In the early years, the Group was directly shaped by Hobsbaum, who invited university colleagues or others from the community whom he thought would be interested. Among early members were Michael Allen; Seamus and Marie Heaney (Devlin at the time); Joan Newmann; Arthur Terry, a professor of Spanish at Queen's; James Simmons; and Hobsbaum's new colleague Edna Longley and her husband. Typically, the featured writer would give Hobsbaum a selection of his or her recent work and Hobsbaum would have copies run off on the English Department's Roneo duplicator, to be distributed before the upcoming meeting. The featured writer would read during the first half of the evening (usually poetry, but sometimes a short story or a play) and discussion from the group would follow. Participants would break for coffee and biscuits before reconvening for an open session. Hobsbaum recalls Arthur Terry reading Robert Lowell in the second half of one Group gathering; Michael Allen remembers Marie Devlin reading some of her own poems.

Looking back from a distance of only a few years, Mahon would note, "The Hobsbaum seminar ... was probably first to crystalise [*sic*] the sense of a new Northern poetry. Here was this man from London, people thought, whose name and whose friends' names appeared in leading journals, and he's actually taking us *seriously*."[61] Mahon would later come to regret this statement, since it has been taken as evidence of his own ties to the Belfast Group, but it nevertheless expresses something of Hobsbaum's reception at the time. Mahon would later go to great pains to separate himself from the growing myth of the Group—"Hogsbum", he would call him in a later letter—and, in fact, he only attended a meeting once.[62]

In March Mahon and Longley learned they were to share that year's Eric Gregory Award with John Fuller and Norman Talbot, and they were invited to London to meet Philip Larkin, the chair of the selection committee (Heaney would receive the prize the following year). The two friends whose literary successes had been so intertwined posed for a joint photograph in which Longley held a copy of Larkin's *The Less Deceived*. Mahon wrote to Stallworthy to let him know of the award, adding "I hope, quite unashamedly, that this will help sway your fellow-editors towards an affirmative decision on my poems. Also", he added, "I shall be able to pay for the drinks when we next meet".[63]

To Mahon's dismay, OUP declined his manuscript a second time. "We cannot, I'm afraid, offer to publish this as it stands: but while we feel it's possible that you could place it elsewhere, we hope you will decide to work on it—pruning in some places, adding in others—and give us another opportunity to consider it, say in a year's time".[64]

For some months Mahon had been making plans to follow his cousin Conacht to Canada when he graduated. Contributing to this decision would have been the example of his maternal grandfather, Henry Harrison, who had travelled in North America as a young man and had been "virtually a hobo at one time".[65] Equally important would have been the literary precedents. Brian Moore, who had achieved early fame for his chronicling of Belfast life in *The Lonely Passion of Judith Hearne* (1955) and *The Feast of Lupercal* (1958), would have been in Mahon's mind as he contemplated going to Canada, as would Malcolm Lowry, whose work Mahon had been reading. The previous June he had written an appreciative essay on Lowry for *Icarus* in which he praised Lowry's "itinerant and exposed style of life". Mahon too would have been drawn to the "fishermen, boat-builders and transient hoboes" Lowry had lived among on the Vancouver waterfront. With such precedents in his mind,

Mahon applied to the graduate programme at the University of Western Ontario, in London, Ontario.

The decision to go to Canada, however, was also a considered decision to leave Ireland. The months in London and France had interrupted Mahon's studies and stretched a typical four-year course to five, which, with the departure of friends, seemed interminable. While Trinity was "fine for a three-year course, four years is too long, and five is absolute hell!" he was quoted saying in a *Trinity News* profile shortly before the end of term.[66] Boland took her leave in a poem she dedicated to him:

> We have had time to talk and strongly
> Disagree about the living out
> Of life. There was no need to shout.
> Rightly or else quite wrongly
> We have run out of time, if not of talk.
> Let us then cavalierly fork
> Our ways since we, and all unknown,
> Have called into question one another's own.[67]

The poem's title, "Belfast vs. Dublin", highlights the oppositional nature of their relationship, while her reference to running out of time alludes to Mahon's "now we are running out of light and love" from "Girls in their Seasons".

While Mahon graduated from Trinity without distinction, more surprising may be that he graduated at all. He passed his finals but had no interest in going through the motions of commencement in order to receive his degree. As he later explained, "The ceremony would have involved hiring white tie and tails from Ging's, putting on a furry gown, queueing [sic] up on a platform to shake hands with the Provost, and receiving a parchment scroll in Latin signed by God saying Rodericus Mahon had scraped through. Then one would have introduced one's proud parents to everyone and forced a smile for various cameras, the sort of smile you smile when you're trying hard not to scream. Instead I fled to Canada, where they couldn't find me."[68] Just before the end of term he published a farewell poem in *Icarus*, "Dublin Evening":

> This kind of walk you take the last evening before
> Leaving a place forever—if not quite

Getting the hell out, at least getting out.
It is now that familiar things one had thought a bore
Take on their last dimension—
Rain on the wind, the dust-shower in a shaft of sunlight,
And an old man, drunk, lurching from door
To eighteenth-century door, thick shoulders hunched
Into the overcoat of his rejection.
Look, he can hardly stand. He must have started before lunch.

God help him, he cannot help himself. But two
Red eyes he rolls up to the western sky.
There is no shame now, no nothing—only
A voice saying 'Man, think on, and I shall exist for you'.[69]

Mahon left Dublin in search of new experiences, hoping to be the poet who would speak for those without voice.

Chapter 5

THE YOUNG IRISH POET ABROAD

Out of some subway scuttle, cell or loft
A bedlamite speeds to thy parapets,
Tilting there momently, shrill shirt ballooning,
A jest falls from the speechless caravan.

Hart Crane, "The Bridge"

Mahon spent the remainder of the summer of 1965 in Belfast, but rather than return to his parents' home in Glengormley, he often stayed overnight with the Longleys. In July the three friends visited the Aran Islands for a final holiday before he left for Canada. Both he and Longley would later memorialise the trip in poems published together in *The Dublin Magazine*. While Synge had famously written about the lives of the islanders, Mahon, in "Recalling Aran", describes an island populated only by gulls:

A dream of limestone in sea-light
Where gulls have placed their perfect prints.
Reflection in that final sky
Shames vision into simple sight—
Into pure sense, experience.
Three thousand miles away tonight,
Conceived beyond such innocence,
I clutch the memory still, and I
Have measured everything with it sense.[1]

The poem takes an increasingly familiar stance. Mahon looks back to a former time—his "dream of limestone in sea-light"—with longing and regret. Much of the poem's power stems from the implied difference between that former innocence and the present, though the nature of the speaker's intervening experience remains unspoken.

In September Mahon flew to Toronto without having made further progress towards publication of his first collection. He stayed briefly with his cousin Conacht before travelling to London, Ontario, halfway between Detroit and Toronto. He had been accepted as a teaching fellow in the graduate programme at the University of Western Ontario, though it is unclear if he was truly committed to the programme or if graduate school simply served as a pretext for getting out of Belfast. His former roommate, Robbie Brown, was in New Brunswick, but whether the two friends made their plans together or this was mere coincidence, no one can now recall. John Boyle suggested Mahon look up Professor Paul Fleck, who had done graduate work at Queen's, but otherwise he was on his own.

Mahon's frequent letters to Michael and Edna Longley offer the fullest account of his time in Canada. In his first, he recorded his impressions of London and its people:

> The town itself is, I suppose, like any other North American town with a population of 200,000 (i.e. just under half the size of Belfast). Topographically it is completely flat, with a dozen or so modest skyscrapers in the centre & the rest mostly nondescript one-storey buildings advertising 'Drugs' (!), 'Hi-Fi Campus (We're Glad You're Back)' 'Eats' or 'John McConkey, Chiropractor'. Life here is slower than in Toronto … for this is what Canadians call 'the sticks' (= the bogs). A transcontinental train goes through once a day, holding up traffic on Richmond Street for about ten minutes while it passes—otherwise you might be in Cookstown or Ballymena.

As for the townspeople, Mahon found them simple and plain: "If I were to walk into the bar downstairs, tap a man on the shoulder and say 'I'm a poet,' he would probably say, in a friendly, vacuous kind of way, 'I'm a sanitary engineer' and lose interest". The campus buildings were all ivy-less grey stone: "a drunk man on a dark night might think he was in Cambridge".[2]

When Mahon showed up at the English Department the following Monday, he found he had been assigned to teach General Literature and Composition, beginning with Chaucer. "The whole thing is quite hilarious", he wrote Longley, but, he added, "I managed to pull the wool over their eyes". The class soon moved on to Shakespeare's sonnets, Donne and *Paradise Lost* ("I shall have to read it at last"). He found the students "just about literate and no more", but more disappointing was that his class of 27 included "only one good-lookin' girl".[3]

Mahon was more fortunate, however, in the roommates he found: Ian Morrison and Richard Rooke.[4] Rooke too was in the English programme and, it turned out, writing a dissertation on Malcolm Lowry. He also wrote poetry, and had a car.[5] Their mutual regard for Lowry was an immediate point of connection. In his *Icarus* essay published a year before, Mahon had admired Lowry's depiction of man's fall in *Under the Volcano*. Geoffrey Firmin, the central character of the novel, is "bewildered by the failure of reason and the inadequacy of his own liberal sentiments". The temptation, Mahon wrote, is to see him as a representation of a kind of Sophoclean man, "'excellent in wit' … but knowing too much and lacking goodness commensurate with his knowledge".[6] The theme resembles what he hoped to explore in the novel he himself was writing at the time.

His letters to the Longleys over the autumn convey a growing sense of loneliness. When he suggested that Michael write to Robbie, who might be feeling "a bit lonely", he was, indirectly, expressing his own feelings. His letters soon became more straightforward: "God damn you, man, are you never going to write? Three months away & I only get one letter.… Life must be very full in Belfast".[7]

During these first months in Canada, Mahon was keeping pace with his students' required reading, sometimes reading the work for the first time himself, while also preparing for the seminars he was taking from Professor David Kaula (tragedy from Aeschylus to Lorca) and from Professor Herbert Berry (the Elizabethan lyric). He nevertheless found time to read Brian Moore's latest novel, *The Emperor of Ice Cream*, with its depiction of wartime Belfast, and Lowry's poems, which Rooke shared with him. While the latter were hardly Lowry's best work, he forwarded his favourites to Longley along with two new poems of his own, "Toronto" and "Exit Molloy". Mahon had produced little since the lauded "In Carrowdore Churchyard", which Terence de Vere White had published in *The Irish Times* the previous April. While he had doubts about his two new poems, he confessed, "it's a pleasure to be writing again at all".[8]

"Toronto" describes a "city of constant movement" reminiscent of "An Irishman in London". In the new poem, however, the city is characterised not as a maelstrom of movement but as a revolving orb: "... centre and circumference, / You are revolving round the sun...." That circular patterning, which brings to mind Mahon's use of circles, wheels and globes in later poems, has not yet taken definite shape; one gets neither a sense of a particular city nor an overall design. The second of the new poems he sent to Longley, "Exit Molloy", describes Beckett's anti-hero awaiting his death in a ditch. Molloy joins that growing line of criminal figures who appear in Mahon's early poems. The poem's title seems to promise an account of Molloy's final exit, but Mahon adopts Beckett's pattern of self-contradiction—"Now at the end I smell the smells of spring",—and there is no exit after all. "Strictly speaking I am already dead / But still I can hear the birds sing on over my head".[9] These singing birds, however, do not offer release, but signal a new start to the whole painful cycle. Mahon would come to see this repetition as the logical conclusion to "November Notes in Brittany", eventually expanded and re-entitled "Four Walks in the Country near St. Brieuc". It is the first of his extended multi-part poems that follows the action of a single figure over the course of a day.

Mahon had also resumed work on his novel, and he began to have hopes he would actually complete it. As he explained to Longley, "the nearest pub is a mile and a half away, so what can one do but sit at home & write?" By late autumn he had an outline of the entire book, and the characters had taken definite shape in his mind. The theme, he explained to Longley, was "innocence, experience, greater innocence", a progression that follows the patterning of some of his best poems. He thought he could finish the novel by May or June, which he knew would mean "letting the graduate work slide", but, as he explained, "I know I could never be an academic, so why try? Like you, I'm essentially unemployable & would probably do best as a school teacher".[10]

Meanwhile, 3,000 miles away, Mahon's first published collection was issued in a modest stapled pamphlet as the third in the Belfast Festival's new poetry series. Jon Stallworthy had suggested he consider issuing a selection in such a form while he continued to assemble a full-length collection for OUP. Longley's *Ten Poems* had been the first to appear in the series in October, followed by Heaney's *Eleven Poems* in November and Mahon's *Twelve Poems* in December. It was the first published collection for each of the three friends. The fact that they took this step together is evidence of their shared ambition and shows something of their respective rivalries: each pamphlet surpasses the previous one in the number of poems. Mahon opened his selection with "In Carrowdore Churchyard", which had been chosen for a Guinness Poetry Prize at the recent Cheltenham Festival. Seven of the 12 poems would eventually appear in *Night-Crossing* and would survive later pruning and be included in his *Collected Poems* 30 years later. In addition to "Carrowdore", the pamphlet included two of his Belfast poems ("Poem in Belfast" and "Glengormley"), two of his "Four Walks" ("Morning in Brittany" and "Man and Bird"), the family poem "A Grandfather" and "Day Trip to Donegal".

On weekends Mahon would sometimes get a ride into Toronto with Rooke, and on one occasion he went sailing on Lake Erie with a fellow graduate student. After the weather turned cold, he and Rooke organised a campus poetry reading, and he gave a talk on MacNeice for the Graduate English Society. Despite these efforts, Mahon had formed no ties to replace the close friendships left behind. Increasingly his thoughts turned to the upcoming winter break when he would take the train to Buffalo and meet his friend Asekoff for the drive to "the land of the bean and the cod". Asekoff was completing an MA at Brandeis University and living in Cambridge.

Mahon's plans took a sudden turn when he received an unexpected reply to a letter he had mailed to his last known address for Jill. "STOP EVERYTHING! STOP THE WORLD, I WANT TO GET ON! SPECIAL NEWS FLASH!", he wrote Longley. "I have just received a letter from beyond the tomb—from Miss Jill Schlesinger. My immediate reaction is to take a train to Georgia, knock her out, marry her, & carry her off to Inishmore". He began making plans to meet Jill over the winter break. "Who says there's no such thing as miracles? Now I believe in Santa Claus. I am overcome, I can't continue".[11] He replied to Jill's letter immediately, noting it had been "two whole years since the splitting of the atom" and asking about the possibility of them meeting.[12] His excitement was still at a high pitch when he wrote Longley again: "I knew you'd be thrilled about Jill. Fantastic isn't it? … When I'm quite sure the hook is in place I shall get out my net & land her gently but firmly. This time she isn't going to get away".[13] Mahon captured the moment of his discovery of Jill's letter in "Spring Letter in Winter": "there it is, coy paradigm— / Alone, a swallow back from the warm south, / Pleading there mutely to be opened. / My hands are tearing the white folds. Perhaps / There is still time, perhaps there is still time.…" Rarely in his poetry would Mahon recount his own experience so directly; that he chose this moment of second chances to do so says a great deal about his feelings at the time. "Water is flowing where no river was" he wrote in the closing lines, "I have come early to the sea in spring".[14]

Just before the winter break Eavan Boland published an appreciative review of *Twelve Poems* in which she identified for the first time a number of those qualities of Mahon's poetry that would become hallmarks of his later work: his wit, his mastery of metrical form and his humane sympathy. The latter she describes as "a quality of insight poised between charity and flippancy, a sympathy for all working conditions which sometimes becomes a radiant understanding of the point of rest". Boland, who had engaged Mahon in critical disputes many times, acknowledged shortcomings in some of the poems but added, "these are eclipsed by the beauty, force and charity of his work".[15]

With the arrival of winter break Mahon met Asekoff in Buffalo, and the two drove to Cambridge, where they showed up at the door of Eamon Grennan and his housemate Dara McCormack. Mahon was immediately taken with the university community. "Harvard is beautiful & Cambridge delightful.… People blithely jay-walk and the cars <u>stop</u> for them. There is drunkenness, indolence, humour, & <u>Joy</u>, dammit".[16] It was the presence of friends, however, which made the greatest difference. Mahon moved into Grennan and McCormack's house on Cambridge Street, just a few doors from Asekoff's apartment. Robert Lowell was a visiting professor at Harvard that semester, commuting from New York for classes two days a week. Grey Gowrie, an Irish earl whom Mahon would befriend, was working as Lowell's assistant for the term. Soon after Mahon's arrival, Jack and Marie Sweeney invited him to dinner. Jack was curator of the Woodbury Poetry Room; Mahon had met him on his summer trips to Ireland. In the mornings Mahon would visit the Grolier Bookshop on Plympton Street where he would lounge and read, and be introduced to visitors as "the young Irish poet". There were regular poetry readings and, given the times, pot parties in the evenings. He had already decided not to return to Canada. "I don't think the university really expects me to", he wrote Longley, "although the Canadian Immigration Office & the Bank of Montreal might have other ideas".[17] Longley was concerned that he was abandoning his graduate studies, and appealed to Sweeney to intercede and urge Mahon to reconsider. Sweeney reported back "Derek had already detached himself from Canada".[18] Mahon was hoping to find a job, "anything at all", either in Boston or in Atlanta, near Jill. In hindsight he began imposing a new design on the last few months of his life and on his recent moves. Jill was "why I crossed the Big Sea Water", he confided to Longley in stage-Indian (never mind that Ontario was nowhere near Atlanta).[19]

After a "riotous" Christmas in Cambridge, Asekoff and Mahon went down to New York City for several days. It was unseasonably warm that week, and they were able to walk down Fifth Avenue on New Year's Eve in their shirtsleeves.[20] As he did with any new place, Mahon viewed the city through its literary associations; in Brooklyn Heights, he paused to recall Hart Crane's lines from *The Bridge*, "Thy cables breathe the North Atlantic still". On New Year's Day 1966 Mahon boarded a bus for the 24-hour ride to Atlanta.

He had not seen Jill since their emotional goodbye when he put her on the train for Southampton two years earlier. "We didn't, of course, fall into each other's arms in dizzy resolution of two years' absence", he wrote Longley; "we came slowly & circumspectly into each other's arms, exploring possibilities. This will have to be recreated—it will take time". He added, "I would willingly devote my life to making her happy".[21] At the end of the week, he returned to Cambridge more deeply in love than ever, and depressed. Grennan remembers him sitting in the bay window of the Cambridge Street house on his return "meticulously knitting and sewing and turning a poem together".[22] His description captures something of the domestic quality of those months in Cambridge. When Mahon mailed the poem to Jill, he enclosed the following explanation:

"Preface to a Love Poem" is addressed, of course, to you ("the soul of silence", & of bone-idleness). It's about the impossibility of making a statement in language, the limitations & distortions inherent in the very nature of language, because words are only inadequate symbols for inexpressibly complex concepts. Thus, my saying "I love you" is "a form of words"—a gross, woman's magazine oversimplification of an extremely complex battery of feelings & responses which can, nonetheless, be rendered only in these words, language being what it is. The distortion is not total—a certain limited perception is achieved, so that while there isn't a noon-time blaze or a completely shuttered darkness, there is the intermediate stage represented by "a blind with sunlight filtering through". And so on. The words "I love you" urge me to them, & I do.[23]

"Preface to a Love Poem" would appear in *The Dublin Magazine* the following autumn. Years later, when it was republished in his *Collected Poems*, Mahon dispensed with this chronology and placed it just before "Bird Sanctuary", written during his and Jill's idyllic summer together two years earlier. There it appears under the title "First Love", a revision that quietly passes over Letty and Eavan and gives primacy to his relationship with Jill.

In January he was inquiring about teaching openings at a local prep school, Cambridge Academy, and at Boston University, despite the fact that he did not have a work visa. "Ever since I've been here I've felt just slightly unbalanced. I've felt criminal", he confessed to Longley.[24] He and Jill were staying in touch by phone, and he was considering whether or not he could live permanently in America. "An *affaire* conducted through Bell Telephone is peculiarly frustrating. I can't begin to predict the future".[25] We see Mahon turning over these questions in his mind in the letters he wrote to Michael Longley that winter:

> Is America the sort of place one could settle in permanently? Answer: No, not if one is a poet because this is a foreign culture—as foreign as France. One would have to start all over again, repeating to oneself 'In 15 [*sic*] hundred & 92 Columbus sailed the ocean blue' and reading Cotton Mather, Cooper, Hawthorne & Bret Harte till you knew them as well as Jane Austen & Dickens & Yeats.[26]

There was also a public and political dimension to these personal and literary questions. Despite keeping his distance from the anti-war demonstrations, he was troubled by America's actions in Vietnam. President Lyndon Johnson had recently announced a troop increase, and opposition to the war at Harvard and at Boston University was growing. "I WISH TO HELL THE STATES WOULD GET OUT OF VIETNAM", he wrote Longley in January.

> Those who aren't stupid or infantile wear the nightmare face of Lady Macbeth—not all the perfumes of Arabia … there is blood on every hand you shake. It comes away on your own. It stains the snow in

Harvard Yard. Jack Sweeney dilutes your whiskey with it, smiling urbanely. Oh, let me not go mad, not mad, sweet heaven! Out of your massive rooted normality, write to me.[27]

Despite his disapproval of America's intensification of the war, he thought no better of the student protestors. There was a self-righteousness in the American character he wanted no part of. "Even the so-called 'campus rebels,' the 'vietniks' & draft-card burners are, I suspect, not so much concerned with the welfare of the Vietnamese as with the moral righteousness of America.... The draft card burner is likely to be simply a Barry Goldwater in reverse".[28]

Through the efforts of one of Eamon Grennan's friends, Ruth Knutson, Mahon got a job at a Xerox shop on Massachusetts Avenue across from Harvard.[29] While he spent his days photocopying other people's dissertations, he was pursuing his own publication plans. He was hoping *Twelve Poems* would force OUP's hand or, failing that, attract the attention of another publisher willing to publish a full-length collection. Heaney had achieved just such a breakthrough after his poems had been noticed by Karl Miller at the *New Statesman* and subsequently picked up by Charles Monteith at Faber and Faber. *Death of a Naturalist* was to be published later that spring, and Mahon admitted he was "black in the face with envy & resentment".[30] Heaney's success was all the more difficult to bear because Monteith was a fellow Instonian with whom Mahon felt a school attachment. He still remembered the copy of Eliot's poems Monteith had presented to the Inst library, where Mahon had worked as a student.

Not long after Mahon arrived in Cambridge, he met an aspiring publisher, Jim Randall, whom he described as "sort of the Liam Miller of Boston". Liam Miller was the publisher of Ireland's Dolmen Press which, since the early 1950s, had been an important outlet for new poetry, including work by Austin Clarke, Thomas Kinsella and John Montague. Randall was hoping to publish a collection of Irish poetry in America, and Mahon immediately suggested Longley, Boland, Kennelly, Heaney and himself. While Randall did publish *Three American Poets*, his Irish project never came to pass. Mahon had better luck, however, with another young would-be publisher, John Cowles, who succeeded in bringing out his second chapbook, *Design for a Grecian Urn*, in a limited edition of 75 copies. Of the 12 poems collected there, six made up the poem sequence he would continue to revise as "Breton Walks". Only two other poems from the collection ("Canadian Pacific" and "Recalling Aran") would survive later pruning, to be collected in *Night-Crossing*. As he later reported to the Longleys, "The poems are printed on rough light-grey paper, very pop-arty, and the cover, at my request, is of the 'Greek blue' Joyce wanted for the cover of *Ulysses*, if you see the connection (between me and Joyce, that is)—I think it's the same blue as the clock-faces in Trinity".[31]

Mahon had decided not to return to the University of Western Ontario. That spring he got a job at Lee Academy, a boarding school for boys who had experienced difficulty in traditional schools. The Academy was located in the small town of Lee, Massachusetts, in the westernmost part of the state.[32] Grennan recalls he and McCormack breathed "a sigh of mixed relief and regret" when their house guest finally departed.[33] As it turned out, however, Mahon was not gone long. There was little in the town of Lee to hold his interest, and it seems the boys, some of whom had behavioural problems, were rather hard on him. As he explained to Edna Longley, "I like children better the more like adults they are. I would have made a good Victorian father".[34] Not long after Mahon left Cambridge, Grennan recalls that he and McCormack were in Cronin's Bar, off Harvard Square, when Derek walked in "like a prodigal son", muttering "fuck it, fuck it".[35]

Mahon attended the annual St Patrick's Day parade in south Boston, but skipped the anti-war demonstration on Boston Common a week later. As he explained to Asekoff, there were advantages to not being American, among them "peace and quiet, dilettantism, the easy life if you want it, and a good conscience".[36] He was invited to read his poems on a Boston radio station, along with X. J. Kennedy, and later gave a reading with several other campus poets (though he was not, properly speaking, a campus poet). There were other readings that spring, including a "read-in" for peace held by writers in Harvard's Memorial Hall, which featured X. J. Kennedy, Adrienne Rich and Susan Sontag.

Preoccupying Mahon and his friends that spring was Eamon Grennan's and Eavan Boland's upcoming marriage. Eamon and Eavan had begun seeing one another when Grennan was studying at University College Dublin and Boland, at Trinity. When Grennan entered graduate school at Harvard, they had remained in touch and were planning to marry the following summer, once Boland graduated. Mahon and Longley grew increasingly worried for Eamon as the date drew closer; both were aware of the intensity Boland brought to relationships (Longley set out to capture something of her irrepressible force in his poem "The Hebrides", which he dedicated to her).[37] Mahon confided to Longley there was a difference between "need" and "love", but felt unable to warn Eamon of his apprehensions. "The man who suggests to him the least reservation about their marriage will be a very tactless man indeed".[38] They were greatly relieved when the marriage was called off.

As summer approached, Mahon was, as usual, looking for work. He had been offered a job teaching creative writing at Boston University in the fall—"night classes, 2 hours every Thursday, poetry and short stories, do what you like, no questions asked, $500 a semester"—but he would have to return to Canada to obtain the proper visa. Poetry is a condition, not a profession, he complained to Longley, quoting Frost.[39]

Over the summer Mahon travelled to Brunswick, Maine, where he met Nicholas Grene, whose mother was organising a conference at Bowdoin College. Robbie Brown joined them there. Mahon was still unsure of his own plans, but, after the BU teaching position fell through, he decided he would indeed return to Canada, though not to the University of Western Ontario. Instead, he made his way to Toronto, where he stayed with Robbie while he looked for work and a place to live. His decision to return to Canada was also an admission that his and Jill's relationship was indeed over, that the life he had dreamed of sharing with her would not come to pass. Despite his pleadings, she had not visited him in Cambridge, and reviving their relationship via telephone and letter-writing had not worked. He marked this new resolution with a final poem for Jill, "What Would You Say If I Were to Tell You, Darling". It is "my last, I swear to God my very last poem for Jill".[40]

His reunion with his former roommate may have prompted Mahon to return to that shadowy incident in his second year at Trinity, now more than five years distant. "As God is My Judge", as it was named before Mahon changed it to "After the Titanic", is a powerful depiction of the lingering effects of suppressed guilt. Bruce Ismay, the first-person speaker in the poem, looks back on his shameful actions some years later, his life forever altered by the sinking of the *Titanic* and the manner of his escape. In this poem Mahon found a way to approach his own recent past that he would adopt in numerous other poems: the speaker, having undergone some profound experience, looks back with regret to the moment of his failing and to a former innocence he cannot regain.

Soon after his arrival in Toronto, Mahon met Paul Jackel, who had just returned from summer work gold mining in Canada's Northwest Territories. He and Jackel decided to share an apartment on Church Street, not far from the university.[41] As Mahon described it to Michael and Edna, "It's a great flat—six rooms, bar, telephone, two minutes from downtown, and inexpensive".[42] He found a temporary job at the University of Toronto bookstore, where he soon met an "amorous" co-worker named Sandra, whom he began seeing before she left abruptly for South America, "leaving a considerable affective gap in the life".[43] He took a second job as a night switchboard operator at the Canadian Broadcasting Corporation where he met Allen Ginsberg when the Beat poet visited Toronto for a reading: "definitely in the top six younger Jewish poets from Paterson, New Jersey", he wrote sarcastically.[44]

During these months Jackel was experimenting with a 16 mm camera, and Mahon picked up something of his roommate's interest in film. Soon after moving to Church Street he wrote the Longleys about Robert Flaherty's films, and sent them a copy of *The Innocent Eye*, a recent biography of the filmmaker he had enjoyed.[45] Flaherty was remembered for his documentaries *Nanook of the North* and, of more interest to Mahon, *Man of Aran*. Inspired by the Flaherty biography and Jackel's influence, the roommates began shooting a film around Toronto based on a now lost script Mahon wrote. "It's about an eighteenth-century British soldier who walks out of his case in the Royal Ontario Museum and spends a day chasing a girl round the city", he explained to Longley.[46]

Mahon was continuing to revise existing poems and compose new ones for his anticipated first collection. In a rare reference to his father, he confided to Longley, "the old man is worried, I know—he had reckoned on the poetry-nonsense all being knocked out of me by now".[47] That autumn he mailed Longley the latest version of the manuscript for his comment. While Longley's reply has not survived, Mahon's response hints at its character: "Your exposé of my inadequacies as a reviser and self-critic ('tin ear' was good) was startling". In the following letter he proceeded to defend his changes and revisions. He worried that "My Wicked Uncle" was too derivative of Lowell's *Life Studies*, while the line "It was my first funeral" carried a meaning he had not intended. "It is his first awareness of loss", he explained to Longley, "his first encounter with mortality, his first erosion of innocence which will be gradually stripped from him in his own successive deaths". Mahon proceeded to defend other cuts and revisions he had made in the *Night Train Journey* manuscript, as *Night-Crossing* was called at the time.

> As for your comment about my distrust of my 'former selves', let's just get one thing straight. I am not trying to keep a record of my psychic life (not that only, though of course it comes into it), but to make good poems—and if that means tinkering with old ones until I'm satisfied, I see no harm in that. This 'former selves' thing is nothing to do with it.

He enclosed with his reply a new poem, "In Dublin Hospital", written for their Trinity classmate Eugene Lambe, whom he heard had been hospitalised in St Patrick's with "a bad case of the wheels within wheels".[48] The poem, never collected, anticipates Mahon's own slide into alcoholism in coming years and his own St Patrick's hospitalisation more than twenty years later.

With Heaney's first collection out and being reviewed favourably, Mahon and Longley were even more impatient to see their own books into print. Longley was circulating his typescript for *No Continuing City* to London publishers, and Mahon was going through back issues of *Icarus*, hoping to fill out his collection with older work. In a letter to Longley at the time, he expressed his frustration with a sophomoric parody of Heaney's subject matter:

> Does your da drink stout?
> Does your mammy throw him out?
> Does your granny wheel the mangle round the yard?

"That image (the grandmother, in the serene sunset glow of her declining years, a tear in her eye and a smile flickering on her lips as she brushes back a silver lock, still dutifully wheeling a mangle round a yard, from toilet-shed to coal-bath and back again) has stuck in my mind's eye (it's hell in there) down the years and helped sustain me", he added in a deadpan tone.[49] Mahon had 37 poems which he thought publishable. "When I resurrect a few oldies and perhaps write another one or two, I'll be in a position to approach Jon Stallworthy again", he told Longley. "If he says no this time I'm going to start my own printing press".[50]

Mahon spent Christmas Day 1966 alone. As he reported to Michael and Edna, "I did a Scrooge and sat at home conducting an intimate dialogue with a bottle of Teacher's".[51] Over the winter he landed a job teaching new Canadians in a suburban high school five nights a week. The class was made up of French, Germans, Greeks, Mexicans and Chinese, all of them older students with whom he got on well.[52] He found the work and regular schedule restorative and reported to Jim Randall he was "a new man, active, industrious, sober and writing like it was going out of style, as indeed (says Marshall McLuhan) it may be".[53]

Mahon had decided to return to Ireland once his class ended in April, and he began writing to schools in Belfast inquiring about openings. In early March he made a trip to Montreal, which was deep into preparations for Expo '67. He took a ferry out on the St Lawrence River to see the site of the World's Fair and climbed nearby Mount Royal, which reminded him of Belfast's Cave Hill. That evening he dined at a crêperie in the French Quarter and imagined he was back in Brittany.[54] Each new setting reminded him of some other place he would rather be. Later that month he published an article on Canada's cultural life in the *Belfast Telegraph*, in which he wrote about how Canadian culture was dominated by a bland, academic Americanism that levelled all creativity to one form—words that seem to have a bearing on his own situation at the time. "Unless [the Canadian artist] is from Quebec, and has access to the lives of the farmers and fishermen, his world is the modern Canadian city (scarcely distinguishable from its American counterpart)". Both Malcolm Lowry and Brian Moore had made Canada their adopted home, Mahon concedes, but Moore's actions were a rejection of Northern Ireland rather than an expression of love for Canada. "His Canadian citizenship", Mahon notes, "is a negative thing—it makes him a citizen of nowhere".[55]

Mahon was continuing to send poems back to Ireland for publication, a sign of his failure to integrate with his adopted culture. When Harry Chambers revived the literary magazine *Phoenix* in March 1967, Mahon sent him a generous selection, including "Bird Sanctuary" (with its dedication to Jill), "Boise, Idaho", "As God is My Judge", "Poem to the Memory of Louis-Ferdinand Céline" and "Winter Song for the Rivers of New England". Though the Festival pamphlets had been out for more than a year, Chambers included in the first issue a retrospective review of the previous year's pamphlets, in which he described Longley, Heaney and Mahon as "three of the best poets in the whole of Ireland". Chambers added that Mahon was currently in Canada, "but more than any other poet in the series, his poems belong to Belfast".[56] Mahon was coming to feel the same way. In the spring he had a joint letter from *Threshold*'s editors, John Boyd and Sam Hanna Bell, asking to include "In Carrowdore Churchyard" in a special issue devoted to Ulster writing— more confirmation that Belfast was "where it's happening, baby".[57]

This sense of a burgeoning literary life in Belfast, combined with his lingering homesickness, was drawing Mahon home. He too thought of Belfast as his city, one inextricably linked to his life as a poet. "The homing urge is on me", he wrote that spring; "I ache with yearning for the wet streets, the horse manure, the shipyard sirens and the cracked and cobwebbed light-shades in a hundred musty little offices in Great Victoria Street and the Dublin Road.... I've lived on the margin of my culture for long enough".[58] In his last letter to the Longleys before his return, he wrote, "Starting on Friday week, my movements will be swift and inscrutable, surrounded by a cloud of dust, but you can expect me on your doorstep, *et dona ferentes*, on the 25th approx, grinning like a fool, a little bit disoriented by crossing the time-zones, scarcely a day older in wisdom, and very slightly drunk.... And if it's raining when I get to Belfast, so much the better. I'll go out and suck it off the streets".[59]

Chapter 6

| "THE DEDALUS OF BELFAST"

I'd like to get away from earth awhile
And then come back to it and begin over.

Robert Frost, "Birches"

With the arrival of spring, Mahon wrote a final Canadian poem, "April on Toronto Island". In the poem passengers who have disembarked from the ferry gather on the bank of Lake Ontario and watch the big ships passing in the seaway, much as Mahon had watched them move down Belfast Lough in years past. With their faces turned to the water, they "dream of other islands, / Clear cliffs and saltwater, / Fields brighter than paradise in the first week of creation...."[1] This poem of seasonal renewal anticipates the spring thaw and the new start Mahon was hoping for on his return to Ireland, and after a week with friends in Boston, he caught a plane home.

On his return, Mahon and Longley went to the Aran Islands hoping to recapture something of the experience they had had there two years before (Edna was carrying hers and Michael's first child and stayed in Belfast). The islands had grown into an idealised place in the two friends' imaginations. Longley's elegy for their first holiday had noted that they had left too soon, while Mahon, in "Recalling Aran", had transformed the rocky islands into a vision of innocence and light. En route to Inishmore, Mahon and Longley's boat stopped at Inisheer, and the two stepped ashore to get a look at the island. There they happened upon Tom Mac Intyre, whose work they had read in *The Dublin Magazine*. The chance meeting seemed fortuitous, and when Mac Intyre offered to find them a place to stay on Inisheer, they agreed. They spent the holiday in a stone cottage living on cabbage and rum, as Longley recalls. He remembers it was an "incandescent time", picking up on the same quality of light Mahon had described two years before in "Recalling Aran".[2]

Mahon would memorialise the holiday in a new poem, "In the Aran Islands" (later, simply "Aran"), which was first published in *The Irish Press* alongside MacIntyre's short story "Gunning's Word". The poem is a celebration of island traditions. "He is earthed to his girl, one hand fastened / In hers, and with his free hand listens, / An earphone, to his own rendition / Singing the darkness into the light". The first-person speaker in the poem—Mahon himself—steps out of the pub and out of earshot of the singing. A gull on the tin roof overhead cries out, and Mahon thinks: "I dream myself to that tradition / Fifty winters off the land— / One hand to an ear for the vibration, / The far wires, the reverberation / Down light-years of the imagination / And, in the other hand, your hand".[3] He would later change that reference to "your hand" (a direct reference to Jill) to something less specific: "And a loved hand in the other hand".[4]

Back in Belfast, Mahon took a flat in Eglantine Avenue near the university, not far from the Longleys. He would have been pleased by the address, which brought to mind Keats's "Ode to a Nightingale", a good omen to be sure. Mahon took a post in a school in Jordanstown, which Longley had found for him while he was away. As he explained in a letter to Jill, "I will be a respectable schoolteacher at the Belfast High School, which is not, curiously enough, in Belfast but in a little town ten miles up the north shore of Belfast Lough".[5] Mahon was glad to be back among friends, and soon he was spending evenings "sitting up with Longley and the lads in the Arts Club on Elmwood Avenue".

Not long after his return, he began seeing Doreen Douglas, an attractive young woman from the North who had been in his class at Trinity. Doreen had been active in the Drama Society, and when she and Mahon began going together, she was working as a news announcer for Ulster Television. Like him, she came from a family with close ties to the sea. Her father had been a sea captain and during her childhood had often been away from home. When she was only 12 he drowned tragically while in port in Durban, South Africa. She and her two sisters grew up without a father, but in her memories of him he cut a striking figure in his captain's uniform. When Jill Schlesinger unexpectedly wrote in August and suggested she visit him in Belfast, Mahon's reply lacked some of his former enthusiasm: "I don't know when you were thinking of, but I would recommend next spring, as being climatically & spiritually the best time of year".[6] While Jill still occupied a place in his heart, his hopes for a future together had been dashed by their failed efforts to reunite in America.

On hearing Mahon was back in Belfast, Jon Stallworthy wrote a welcoming letter: "The voice of rumour from across the Irish Sea whispers that you have turned your back on Expo '67 and returned to the land of plaster saints. Should this be so, I hope we shall see you in London soon (perhaps with some new poems)".[7] Stallworthy soon learned that Mahon, having grown frustrated by the protracted negotiations with OUP, had signed with a literary agent, Deborah Rogers, to find a publisher for his first collection. Internal memos at OUP make clear this development was cause for some concern. As Stallworthy reported to his colleagues, Mahon's typescript "comes via an agent who should have little trouble in placing it elsewhere if we do turn it down".[8] Stallworthy still had reservations about the selection, but any further delay on OUP's part would send Mahon to another publisher.

Stallworthy hoped to meet Mahon to discuss the collection when he visited Dublin in October, but Mahon was unable to get away from teaching during the week. Instead, Stallworthy put his thoughts in a long letter: "We remain convinced that there are some excellent poems here and would like to publish it for you next September/October, if you can prune it a little more; and if you should have a new poem or two to add, so much the better".[9] Stallworthy presented him with three lists: "unquestionably good poems, those less good but worthy of inclusion, and those that should perhaps be dropped".[10] The poems from the first two lists, however, would make a book of only 43 pages, and Stallworthy made clear he would welcome any new poems, even as he invited Mahon to consider the arrangement of the collection as a whole.

Mahon replied it was "great to be a (prospective) Oxford poet", but he also argued for retaining three poems Stallworthy had suggested he discard: "Glengormley", "Dowson & Co" and "Van Gogh". Of these, Mahon wrote "Glengormly is vital", and in an effort to win over his editor he submitted a revised version of the poem with new opening lines: "Clothes-pegs litter the window-ledge / And the long ships lie in clover; washing lines / Shake out white linen over the chalk thanes".[11] He also enclosed with his letter a just-completed poem, one of his finest, entitled

"The Forger". As the contents of the volume continued to be revised over the autumn, Mahon was also struggling with the arrangement of the selection, which he confessed he found harder than writing the poems in the first place. "I have no fixed idea about what the order should be, except that 'An Unborn Child' should be first". He was still proud of that prize-winning poem and considered it one of his best. The collection would, in fact, open with "Girls in their Seasons", the poem Stallworthy had first noticed opposite his own in *The Dubliner* some years before. In early December, OUP's offer of acceptance finally reached Mahon.

These negotiations coincided with the annual Belfast Festival, a two-week series of concerts, plays, exhibitions, lectures and readings, including that year a performance by the young guitarist Jimi Hendrix. Heaney, Longley and Mahon read for a programme devoted to "Ulster Poets" in the Student Union Bar on 22 November, and their three Festival pamphlets were reprinted for the occasion. Richard Murphy and John Montague were both in Belfast for the events, as was Thomas Kinsella, who flew in from America to lecture on "Poetry in Ireland since Yeats". One evening over drinks, Mahon was overheard boasting that Heaney, Longley, Simmons and himself were the four best poets in Ireland. Simmons thought it a naïve comment, but what he did not appreciate at the time was that Mahon had only expanded the number to four for his benefit.[12]

When the three friends learned of Patrick Kavanagh's death in the final days of the festival, they decided to attend his funeral together. Though Longley and Mahon had argued over the merits of Kavanagh's poetry in the past, both felt it important to be present, and on the day of the funeral they rode with David Hammond and Heaney to Inniskeen. Each of them was considering how to pay tribute to the older poet. In later years Heaney would speak about the moment of recognition when he discovered in Kavanagh's work subjects and forms of speech that were his own. "In his books there was the life I had lived in the yard and on the farm, and I was surprised to find that books could give me something of my own life. I got a kind of trust, if you like, in what I had lived myself and I began to put things down in words and I began to use my own words".[13]

Mahon experienced no such recognition. He had come to Kavanagh's poetry late: "A Northern Protestant by upbringing, cut off from the imaginative life of the rest of the country ... I had read Robert Graves,

Louis MacNeice and Dylan Thomas from cover to cover before I even heard the name of Patrick Kavanagh". What he admired in Kavanagh, however, was the way his poetry was tuned to ordinary life. "He kept no distance between himself and life", Mahon wrote in a special Kavanagh issue of *The Dublin Magazine*, adding, "it is a great and enviable thing, and the sure guarantee of immortality. It is the sign that a writer is earthed".[14]

Mahon had used that word "earthed" before, in his poem "In the Aran Islands", and in both instances it serves as a marker for some quality or condition he himself lacked. The rootedness he praises in Kavanagh would, in time, become Heaney's inheritance, but, as early as the autumn of 1967, those features of the friends' poetic personalities were already becoming clear. *The Dublin Magazine* published Mahon's essay the following spring alongside an elegy:

> November. The Sun went down
> And his friends kept on talking
> Under the feverish pub ceilings
> While the lights came on in London—
> But he lies without his glasses
> In the hungry soil of Monaghan,
> Bicycles squealing into the wind,
> February sleet-clouds rising blind
> A hundred miles from the sea, man
> And manure, inspiration of clay,
> At night dreams of a summer day
> He leaned alone on a haggard gate
> With the round world at his feet.[15]

In Mahon's poem, Kavanagh is drawn back into earth's elemental cycles, "man and manure". There is an erasure of the individual that runs counter to the memorialising occasion of the poem. In fact, it is less a poem about Kavanagh than it is about man's return to clay. Mahon himself makes an oblique appearance in the allusion to his own bicycle rides into the Irish countryside as a teenager, but his encounter with that bucolic world is a fleeting one. In the end the poem underscores his own remoteness from Kavanagh's rural ways, and he chose not to reprint it.

In his accompanying essay Mahon noted that the poet's power was potentially as great as that of evangelical religion,[16] an aspect of Kavanagh's writing he would elaborate on years later, when asked to review *Lough Derg*. Kavanagh possessed a religious sensibility, he later wrote, adding "the poetic act, certainly as he understood it, is itself a form of devotion". It is an important and revealing linkage. Elaborating on the idea, he added, "although there is a sense in which 'religion' is pure bunkum, there is also a sense in which religion is nothing of the sort". Kavanagh is like "a sceptic who experiences a revelation".[17]

This feature of Kavanagh's writing is of particular interest because at the time Mahon attended his funeral he was also exploring the relationship of poetry and evangelical religion in a new poem called "Ecclesiastes":

> God, you could grow to love it, God-fearing, God-
>   chosen purist little puritan that,
> for all your wiles and smiles, you are (the
>   dank churches, the empty streets,
> the shipyard silence, the tied-up swings) and
>   shelter your old heart from the heat
> of the world, from woman-inquisition, from the
>   bright eyes of children. Yes, you could
> wear black, drink water, nourish a fierce zeal
>   with locusts and wild honey, and not
> feel called upon to understand and forgive
>   but only to speak with a bleak
> afflatus, and love the January rains when they
>   darken the dark doors and sink hard
> into the Antrim hills, the bog meadows, the heaped
>   graves of your fathers. Bury that red
> bandana and stick, that banjo; this is your
>   country, close one eye and be king.
> Your people await you in the housing estates—
>   flaps for you in the housing estates—
> a credulous people. God, you could do it, God
>   help you, stand on a corner stiff
> with rhetoric, promising nothing under the sun.

The poem is an important one in the early canon, and depicts a typical Mahon scene of dereliction and abandonment—"the / dank churches, the empty streets, / the shipyard silence, the tied-up swings"—almost devoid of human life.[18] The only figure present in the poem is the second-person "you", standing on a street corner proselytising to his people. Whether this second-person pronoun points accusingly to a nameless figure or whether it is a generalised "I" remains unclear. The overpowering sense of rhetorical bluster invites one to think of this figure as a Paisley-like preacher; however, the reference to burying that red bandana and stick suggests the recently returned poet himself. But if this is Mahon, then what kind of temptation does he describe? "God, you could grow to love it, God-fearing, God- / chosen purist little puritan that, / for all your wiles and smiles, you are…." The second-person pronoun, the broken syntax of these opening lines and the poem's many elisions all seem aimed at putting the reader off the more declarative: *I, god-fearing, god-chosen puritan that I am, could grow to love this country.*

The tension of the poem lies in its resistance to the declarative statement, its own wish to slip out from under such certainties. The speaker's utter rejection of this alternative life comes home with greatest power at the poem's close: "God, you could do it, God / help you, stand on a corner stiff / with rhetoric, promising nothing under the sun". The harmonies evoked by the poem's title ("to every thing there is a season …") are absent, and that too becomes one of the false promises the poem holds out to the reader. "Ecclesiastes" is a poem of rhetorical betrayal which, in that light, seems to be a poem about Mahon's own choice of an alternative life committed to poetry.

It was becoming increasingly clear to Mahon he was not suited to being a teacher. Years later he would confess: "I was late every morning. Turned up in a taxi, the whole school looking out the big windows—looking out from morning prayers—at me getting out of the taxi, still half-drunk from the night before".[19] One of his students recalls him "sitting feet on his desk reading the morning paper, while his young charges did pretty much their own thing".[20] In an uncollected poem, "Teaching in February", he recreates just such a scene: "I think I have been sitting here all my life / Feet on desk, drumming a confiscated penknife / On the *Times Educational Supplement*…." The poem closes with Mahon dreaming of flight, driving away with "Deirdre Thompson of 5A" down through the midland counties to Galway through a landscape "bathed in sunlight and in rain".[21] The imagined dream flight, as he would call it many years later, was already becoming a characteristic Mahon response to boredom and feelings of entrapment.

Mahon had received Jill's unexpected letter soon after his return, and over the winter they began planning a spring reunion. However Mahon was seeing Doreen at the time, and without telling Jill of this complication, he did his best to dampen her expectations of the upcoming visit:

I don't think you'll like Belfast very much. Most people don't. It's a cold, wet, depressed, puritanical place with a high level of unemployment, sectarian prejudice & inefficiency. The working people are (justifiably) bitter, the Unionist government cynical & corrupt. The pubs close at ten, & all day Sunday.... Its good points are the Victorian-rococo Crown Liquor Saloon, Lavery's, & Kelly's Cellars. You're not likely to see much more than that.[22]

He promised, however, to introduce her to his Belfast friends, including Seamus Heaney, whom he was now describing as "the Third Man". Their plans were to meet in Belfast, hire a car for a driving tour of the west, including Galway and a trip to Inishmore, before returning to Dublin "for a sustained period of dissipation in familiar haunts".[23]

Mahon was making frequent weekend trips to Dublin, and on St Patrick's Day 1968 he, Longley and Heaney gave a joint reading at the Lantern Theatre in Merrion Square. On another occasion he helped sell copies of Hayden Murphy's poetry broadsheet at Trinity's Front Gate. Murphy remembers he and Mahon later went to O'Neill's for pints, where they joked about the dignity of art. Mahon was considering returning to school for an MA and writing a thesis on Louis MacNeice.

Just days before the planned Easter break with Jill, he received a letter from her saying she had decided not to make the trip after all. He posted two special delivery letters trying to salvage their plans. "Make no hasty decisions", he urged her in the first; "you could come for a holiday & go back in a couple of months if you feel so inclined".[24] Jill understood, however, that the visit would mean more than a holiday. It would also be a commitment to a future together, and at the last moment she hesitated. Mahon followed his first letter with a second. "By simply coming here you commit yourself to nothing", he argued:

If you decide to stay at home, what will you do? Go back to your job? Find, in time, an 'ordinary man' and grow towards fantasy-free middle-age secure in the knowledge that you have acted in violation of your own nature at the behest of one-dimensional textbook psychology? All life is a weave of illusions (each one as real as the next); you pays your money & you takes your choice. Please be sure yours is the right one.[25]

In the end, Jill did not make the trip, and when his school break arrived, a dejected Mahon returned to the Aran Islands alone.

Just before the end of spring term, he learned that *Night-Crossing* had been selected over new collections by Geoffrey Hill and Richard Murphy as the autumn Poetry Book Society Choice. It was an important affirmation, one that ensured a larger sale for the book and that it would be reviewed widely. In the rush of these events, he was also considering marriage, not to Jill, but to Doreen. "I'm not drinking & not married, although the second is beginning to look like a real possibility", he confided to Jill in a letter that summer. "Does that make you sad?" he asked her. "It makes me sad".[26] If he was still hoping to change Jill's mind and persuade her to come to Ireland, it was too late. The letter marked the end of their correspondence—they would not see each other again for more than ten years.

When Stallworthy invited him to read at the Cheltenham Festival, Mahon asked whether the Poetry Book Society, which was paying his expenses, could also cover those of his fiancé.[27] In the short statement he prepared for the Poetry Book Society *Bulletin*, Mahon wrote that the poems had already "begun to seem like the work, not of myself but of an old friend, perhaps, who emigrated and from whom I receive only the occasional postcard at longer and longer intervals".[28] Longley had already noted his friend's pattern of reinvention in comments that seem prescient, but the form that refashioning takes here is revealing. Former selves are linked to physical movement, to emigration: in a few months Mahon would perform another such metamorphosis, when he left Belfast for the last time. He added, "Owing, perhaps, to the peculiar circumstances of life in Northern Ireland, where I was born, brought up, and now live, I have always felt something that might be described as 'dispossession'—a cultural dislocation, a nostalgic (and slightly guilty) independence of community, and a resulting self-consciousness". There are doubtless multiple sources for Mahon's "dispossession"; however, it is worth noting he had been part of a post-war generation that had gone to college during a period of expanding opportunities for the young, and as a result had not taken up the kind of work that had been customary in Belfast for generations. In an unexpected turn, he linked his sense of disconnection from his community to uncertainty about the merit of his own writing. "I have never been quite sure of the value, if any, of my own poems. To have them the choice now of the Poetry Book Society is, firstly, a delightful surprise and, secondly, an important kind of reassurance."[29]

He received his author's copies of *Night-Crossing* in early September when he inscribed one for Doreen, though Jill had been the inspiration for many of the poems. He dedicated the collection not to his parents—his father was still hoping his son would get over the "poetry nonsense"—but to Michael and Edna Longley. The first review to appear was Longley's, under the headline "A Poet of Power", in *The Irish Times* on 1 October. "The bleak complexities of Belfast have had to wait all this time for their laureate. What Seamus Heaney has done for the rural hinterland of Ulster, Mahon does for the shipyards and backstreets".[30] Heaney, Longley and Mahon were laying claim to their respective subject matter, and positioning themselves and their work in relation to one another.

When Mahon returned from the Cheltenham Festival in early October, Northern Ireland was in turmoil. The timing of the publication of his first book could hardly have been worse. In an interview for BBC radio nearly nine years later, he would speak of his early poem "Glengormley" as a "historical footnote". As he put it then, "so much has happened since that much of the poem seems terribly dated".[31] While Mahon may have once longed to escape the "terrier-taming, garden-watering days" described in that poem, he had not foreseen what was now unfolding in the North. Despite favourable reviews, he would come to feel the entire collection dated. Many of the poems had been written years earlier in a different time altogether. His feelings of estrangement from Belfast would only deepen as the North sank into sectarian violence.

While rioting spread across the Northern counties, Mahon and Hayden Murphy gave a joint reading at Trinity; their friend, Jack Rogers, accompanied them on a Greek bouzouki. A few days later Mahon was in London for a reading with Stallworthy at the Poetry Book Society, and at the invitation of Walter Allen, he lectured on Louis MacNeice at the recently opened New University of Ulster in Coleraine.[32] He was unsure about returning to school but was having difficulty committing to steady employment. In a *Belfast Telegraph* feature on Belfast's young poets, he stated: "the job is not important; writing is the priority".[33] No doubt he had been emboldened by the publication of his first book, but the comment was nevertheless not one to open employers' doors. Belfast's laureate or not, he left the city for the last time in December 1968.

"Two days after I left the stones started flying," Mahon wrote Asekoff on his arrival in Dublin. "I felt distinctly like a rat leaving a sinking ship." Mahon moved in with friends Eugene Lambe and Chris Ramsden, who shared a garden flat in Monkstown in a house overlooking Dublin Bay and the Hill of Howth beyond. Lambe too was from Belfast and at the time was half-heartedly studying law at Trinity. Mahon was unemployed, "largely by choice" he told Asekoff, but he was writing. Without a steady income, he was off the drink and "cultivating a withdrawn, contemplative persona in keeping with my status as a 27-year-old has-been, recently scared off at the brink of provincial matrimony and studiously rethinking self and works from attic to cellar."[34]

It was soon after his arrival in Dublin that Mahon met Bill McCormack, who was in his final year at Trinity. McCormack had recently published a collection of poems under the pseudonym Hugh Maxton, and it was he who helped get Mahon a temporary job at the Trinity College Library. After days moving books in the Long Room, they would go to the pub or to McCormack's cousin's flat in North Frederick Street. After a few weeks of this temporary work, Mahon got a teaching job at the Language Centre of Ireland, which offered secretarial and language courses to foreign students seeking jobs in Ireland. In a discarded manuscript draft from the time he describes the work dismissively as "teaching Eng. Lit. to au-pair girls".[35] Mahon's heart was not in it, and McCormack remembers he would amuse himself by taking liberties with English idioms: if one was fooling you in a light-hearted, friendly way, he explained to his students on one occasion, you would say "you're pulling my legs".[36]

McCormack was a member of the Trinity Archaeological Society, a group of amateur enthusiasts who spent their weekends visiting ancient sites around Ireland. He also had a hand in organising an exhibition of photographs of the Newgrange excavation, which was then underway. No one in the Society took the weekend outings too seriously, and McCormack has described them as excuses to get out of Dublin and enjoy a few pints in a country pub. Through this group Mahon met a student named Clare, whom he began seeing, and the relationship became serious enough for her to accompany him on a weekend trip to Belfast.[37] The most lasting thing to come out of these months, however, was his poem "A Stone-Age Figure Far Below", dedicated to McCormack, which Heaney included in a special issue of *Threshold* he edited that summer. It is an important early poem, and as Hugh Haughton has noted, the first to take such a long historical view.[38] When interviewed by the Trinity newspaper that October Mahon emphasised the importance of a historical sense "through which one finds one's bearings in life".[39] "In spite of everything", he added, "I still belong to my Belfast Protestant working-class background".[40]

As the sectarian violence worsened, writers from the North were increasingly asked to speak on the unfolding crisis, but it was difficult to know what form their responses should take. The challenge was perhaps greatest for Mahon, who felt personally implicated because of his family background, and, specifically, by an uncle who had served in the B-Specials. It was this family history Mahon had in mind when he spoke of feeling "a personal sense of fracture". For him, the political crisis had a familial dimension, which contributed to his estrangement from his mother and father, and coincided with his commitment to become a poet.

Initially the outbreak of violence in the North had the effect of propelling Mahon into historical drama, and during these months he began working on a verse play based on the life of Hugh O'Neill. While Heaney was delving into tribal violence in *Wintering Out*, Mahon sought a historical corollary for the present troubles in 1602, that moment in Irish history when O'Neill's uprising failed and the seeds were sown for the future division of Ireland. In the summer, John Montague published a brief excerpt from the play in a special issue of *Threshold* devoted to the Northern crisis. That excerpt focuses not on the rout of O'Neill's forces at the Battle of Kinsale, but on the moment when O'Neill meets James I and is forced to acquiesce to conditions that will ensure Ireland's future partition. The climax, in Mahon's retelling, comes when James explains his plans for "a Scottish settlement of the North", to which O'Neill objects, "That way you would create two nations; / Think of the future generations".[41] Over the summer and early autumn Mahon filled a couple of notebooks with notes and drafts, but ultimately the subject proved too unwieldy and he abandoned the play. Years later he said it would have taken "a fat historical novel" to do the subject justice.[42]

In June Mahon joined Heaney and Longley in Cushendall, County Antrim, for the launch of John Hewitt's *The Day of the Corncrake*. Hewitt flew over from Coventry for the occasion, and later expressed great pleasure that "the young poets" had been there.[43] Mahon was travelling back and forth between Dublin and Belfast frequently, and on another weekend visit that summer, he and Longley went to see at first-hand the burned-out homes and shops along the heavily Catholic Falls Road, the site of intense rioting in previous weeks. The sectarian fault lines of the city were hardening and Longley and Mahon were defying those invisible boundaries in making such a visit.

Back in Dublin, Mahon and McCormack attended a poetry reading by Seamus Deane, who had recently returned to Ireland from teaching at the University of California at Berkeley.[44] They discovered they had much in common, including a dim view of Dublin's literary culture, and over the coming weeks the three friends met regularly. It was over conversation in the pub one evening that they hatched the idea of starting a new journal of literature, politics and commentary.[45] They hoped they could avoid the parochialism of the Dublin-based journals and place Ireland in a larger cultural and political context. The inaugural issue of *Atlantis* informed the reader, "The magazine will be published in Dublin, but not exclusively for Dublin".[46] Gus Martin, who was teaching at UCD, joined the three editors, and Michael Gill, of the firm Gill and Macmillan, was recruited for his publishing experience. As these plans took more definite shape, they began soliciting financial contributions for the new venture, and the list of contributors reads like a Who's Who of Ireland's literary community, north and south. Hewitt sent a contribution, as did Austin Clarke and John Montague. Mahon solicited support from his former tutors Alec Reid and Owen Sheehy Skeffington. When Samuel Beckett sent a cheque, Mahon was so delighted he considered keeping it, but in the end the editors gave in to necessity and cashed it.[47] Beckett would receive the Nobel Prize for Literature later that year, and *The Listener* and *Hibernia* both rushed to publish Mahon's poem "An Image from Beckett" within days of the announcement on 23 October.[48]

It was McCormack's idea to invite Conor Cruise O'Brien to contribute to the first issue of *Atlantis*, and O'Brien sent an essay on Edmund Burke which examined Burke's Irishness in light of recent political events. Mahon would have found much to identify with in the piece, including O'Brien's description of Burke as one cut off from Ireland by education and by taste, "if never entirely in feeling".[49] It was precisely the kind of critique of Irish identity that the editors—each with his own diverse background—sought to illuminate. Mahon solicited poems from a friend, Paul Hannigan, whom he had known in Cambridge, and Brian Moore agreed to contribute an excerpt from his new novel, *Fergus*. Over the autumn the three friends planned the first issue in the Monkstown flat.[50]

In October, Longley's first collection of poems, *No Continuing City*, was published by Macmillan, and a few weeks later Mahon, Heaney and David Hammond joined him for a reading in Derry in support of the Itinerant Settlement Committee, a group campaigning for better treatment of Ireland's travellers. The reading was part of a nation-wide campaign to improve the travellers' living conditions before the onset of winter. Local communities across Ireland mounted exhibitions, organised concerts and held charity auctions. The Derry reading was arranged by Brian Friel who published an impassioned appeal for community support in *The Irish Press*:

> This is a desperate appeal for immediate help for 78 Derry people, 25 adults and 53 children…. They live in hovels along the hedges at the outskirts of the city. The children sleep on wet straw. They are our itinerants. And if the Derry Itinerant Settlement Committee cannot get these 12 families out of the sodden ditches and on to a caravan site before winter sets in, there will be more deaths from exposure before the year ends.[51]

For many the treatment of the travellers amounted to a form of cultural apartheid; others observed that conditions in the camps were even harsher than those found in the Bogside.[52]

Some months before, Mahon had seen on television gardaí expel a group of travellers from a caravan site. It was becoming increasingly necessary to understand the nature of the poet's responsibility in light of such injustice, and indeed, in light of the spreading violence in the North. "We live in the sickly light of TV screens, with a pane of selfishness between ourselves and the suffering," Heaney would later write.[53] In "Gipsies", published a few months before he took part in the Derry reading, Mahon abruptly shifts the reader's attention from the particular circumstances of the travellers to a more universal one: "The fate you have so long endured is ours also". The conceit is not an entirely successful one (certainly not from the travellers' point of view), but the theme of man's essential homelessness is a recurring one in Mahon's work, one that would get its fullest treatment in *The Hudson Letter* more than twenty years later. Despite its shortcomings, Mahon was pleased with the poem, and for a while he adopted the poem's closing reference to a growing pile of "scrap metal" as a working title for the new collection he was assembling.

In the autumn Longley published a newspaper piece on "Strife and the Ulster Poet" in which he attempted to trace the fault lines of the present political crisis among his fellow poets. "Mahon is the most 'Ulster' of the Ulster poets, just as Seamus Heaney is the most Irish", he wrote. Each had available to him a familial hinterland to give him a firmer grounding in the present crisis, and, Longley added, "they help me to define myself".[54] With his own first collection out, Longley suddenly found himself creatively blocked, and in an effort to shake that malaise he took a holiday cottage in County Wicklow, where he hoped he would be able to resume writing. Mahon visited him there, and in an attempt to help him escape his writer's block—and with Auden's and MacNeice's *Letters from Iceland* in mind—suggested they exchange letters in verse. "We agreed on Marvellian octosyllabic rhyming couplets", Longley recalls, "and that he would start the ball rolling".[55] Mahon's opening verse letter began:

> I wonder why
> we felt the impulse, you and I,
> to start on this verse-dialogue
> of tail-chasing and dog-feed-dog.
> A ten-year friendship, rain or shine,
> calls for some celebration—fine;
> but something else a crying need
> in that dark cave which is indeed
>
> the heart of the artistic life
> unfilled by mistress or wife,
> a need for being on the trot
> while standing still at the same spot,
> imaginatively at least, demands
> we move on from the settled lands ...

Mahon embraced the exercise, and the regularity of the couplet form came easily to him. Longley too found the challenge liberating and would publish his response to Mahon's verse letter in the *New Statesman* the following year. While there is a convivial, light-hearted quality to the exchange, Mahon would soon put the form to more serious purpose when he began another verse letter to his friend Jeremy Lewis.

The critical success of Heaney's *Death of a Naturalist* and Mahon's *Night-Crossing*, followed by the publication of Longley's *No Continuing City*, solidified the idea of the three friends as a poetic group, and Stuart Evans, a producer of educational programming for BBC Radio 4, invited each of them to participate in a broadcast, "Books, Plays, Poems".[56] Mahon's work would become a semi-regular feature of the series in the coming years, generating some modest income. He was back in Belfast in February to record the programme with Longley, Heaney and Hammond, who often added a musical element to their readings. "We've met today in the BBC studio in Belfast, although we've known one another for a long time before today", Heaney opened the broadcast. "We'll be reading between ourselves, and hoping to share with you poems that we've written ourselves and poems by other poets that all of us here in the studio value and enjoy".[57] The first of the three broadcasts took the theme "Home and Heroes", and Heaney introduced the subject by directing the listening audience to consider not "the public heroes, the official heroes, those statesmen and soldiers commemorated in bronze statues" but the ones held privately in one's heart.

Mahon began with a reading of Wilfred Owen's "The Send Off". "It's not necessarily the brave world-shattering acts of courage in war that make us admire a man and love him," Heaney commented. "It can be endurance, an ability to bear up, a long-suffering capacity to accumulate and stand up to experience. Such a man grows like a tree, ring upon ring of memory and achievement hidden inside the strong bark of his body". The programme continued with readings of poems by Ted Hughes and Philip Larkin before turning to family heroes. Mahon, never one to celebrate family connectedness, was no doubt challenged by this change of direction, and passed over his mother and father to read instead "Grandfather" and "My Wicked Uncle". Heaney and Longley, on the other hand, followed with poems about their fathers. If Mahon's parents noted their absence when the programme was broadcast, their reactions have gone unrecorded. The friends were back in the studio the next day to record programmes on "Love and Loneliness" and "Work and Worry".[58]

Early in the new year Mahon added his name to a letter of protest opposing an upcoming visit to Ireland by the all white South African rugby team. Other signatories to the letter published in *The Irish Times* included Austen Clarke, Eiléan Ní Chuilleanáin, Seamus Deane, Pearse Hutchinson, Brendan Kennelly, Tom Mac Intyre, Bill McCormack, Hayden Murphy and Frances Stuart:

> Sir,
>
> As writers, aware of the urgency of fostering human dignity ... we detest the philosophy, practice and propagation of racism. Apartheid is more than a remediable social evil as found in Harlem, Moscow and Dublin. It is an assault on the definition of mankind, denying the reflection of ourselves that we see in each man's eyes. For that reason we cannot remain silent at a time when representatives of this inhumanity present themselves as sportsmen.[59]

It was a rare act of political protest on Mahon's part.

He continued to reflect on the social responsibility of the poet and had not yet recoiled—as he soon would—from overt political statement. In an essay he was writing at the time, he argued that the poet must have a "historical sense",[60] that he must be sensitive to the "weather of the world",[61] as he and his co-editors put it in the first issue of *Atlantis*. One must look hard, however, for points of historical reference in the poems of 1969, which raises important questions: what form does this historical sense take in Mahon's own work? What use would he make of his recent reading of Irish history and, more importantly, of the unfolding political crisis in the North? Answers may be found in the verse letter he began that spring to his friend Jeremy Lewis. Mahon had often stayed with Lewis when he was in London, and, as he explained when he shared an early draft of the poem with him, "It is ... addressed to your good self ... because you are conveniently located at the spinning hub of things, which suits my imaginative purpose".[62]

Originally entitled "Calor Gas", the poem was an extension of the verse form he and Longley had adopted for their verse letters just a few months before. When it was later published by the Dolmen Press under the title *Beyond Howth Head*, it would be longer than any he had written. The poem was modelled partly after Auden's *New Year Letter*, written in the early months of World War II, and partly after MacNeice's *Autumn Journal*, written against the background of the 1938 Munich Crisis; it shares with these poems a historical awareness not previously present in Mahon's work.

"Beyond Howth Head" opens with a typical Mahon scene of dereliction and decay. Winds blow in off the sea, hammering the doors of houses. The men have mostly already left (as Mahon himself would soon do), while the young girls exhange their innocence for "a little learning in a parked Volkswagen".[63] Of interest to Mahon are cyclical patterns—whether reflected in the repetitive motion of the sea or in each generation's succeeding coming of age. "For girls must kiss and then must kiss / and by this declension fall / to write the writing on the wall".[64] There is a fatalism in these patterns which Mahon juxtaposes against the larger movement of historical events.

Mahon turns from this opening tableau to a larger historical frame of reference, shifting from youthful discovery of sexual freedom to Edmund Spenser's sixteenth-century condemnation of Ireland's "lewde liberte". Spenser had taken particular pains to condemn Irish poets for their role in insurrection and rebellion. Drawing on his recent reading of Irish history, Mahon takes the reader back to 1598, when Hugh O'Neill and his forces burned Kilcolman Castle in County Cork, where Spenser had written *A View of the Present State of Ireland*.

'Lewde libertie', whose midnight work
disturbed the peace of Co. Cork

and fired Kilcolman's windows when
the flower of Ireland looked to Spain,
come back and be with us again![65]

The poem is full of contemporary references—the BBC, Volkswagen, the CIA, Dick Van Dyke—and draws upon the cyclical movement of Irish history as it appeared in the spring of 1970. Again Mahon emphasises the repetition of human history by using present events to echo earlier conflicts: "The writing on the wall, we know, / elsewhere was written long ago".[66] Though Mahon had abandoned his play on O'Neill, he salvaged its historical background for this poetic critique of Ireland's present conflict. "Beyond Howth Head" offers an updated view on the then present state of Ireland.

Trapped as they were in this repetitive cycle, Mahon and Lewis—both "bent victims of our linear thought"—could do nothing but flip the pages of an empty book "where the 'outdated futures' lie", or idly "spin celestial globes of words / over a foaming pint in Ward's".[67] Mahon and Lewis would meet at Ward's Irish House, just off Piccadilly, when Mahon was in London. Mahon's reference to an already outdated future alludes to Daniel Cohn-Bendit's recent book, *Obsolete Communism*, about the 1968 student riots in Paris. This and the poem's later reference to Norman Mailer's *The Armies of the Night* make clear that the violence that was gripping Ireland had contemporary corollaries, and Mahon draws on an ever-widening circle of historical reference throughout the poem.

One can find some clue to the patterning of "Beyond Howth Head" in a poem of Mahon's published the previous summer in *Phoenix*. "Straight Lines Breaking Becoming Circles" is a play of lines and circles in which two opposing forces clash. The speaker's wish "to define lifespace as line" confronts forces that bend that line into cycles of repetition, replaying personal and human history in a continuous loop. The speaker—himself a "Dedalus redivivus"—knows that his own "lines went hay- / wire long ago / and most diverged / in a ditch where / mind winked at / body's massacre / and circles buckl- / ed in a wood / so far from, yet / so near, the road." With this tortured syntax and broken speech, Mahon has concealed a personal referent he does not wish to name, but the more transparent allusion—one repeated in "Beyond Howth Head"—is to Beckett's Molloy looking up from the ditch where he has fallen. By the close of the poem, Mahon has conceded that his is not a forward movement. Rather, it is "forged from the nonchalant particles of time past", destined to be repeated in the future as certainly as dawn–dusk, spring–winter cycles.[68]

Such fatalism permeates the early stanzas of "Beyond Howth Head". The poem does not move progressively forward, but repeats. No human utterance or intervention can break the cycles of violence: "Meanwhile, for a word's sake, the plast- / ic bombs go off around Belfast"; the Greek poet and composer Mikis Theodorakis, who had been imprisoned for his opposition to Greece's dictatorship, remains confined in a prison cell, and the CIA has begun operations in Cambodia.[69] One reviewer called the poem "a self-portrait of a trenchant, up-to-the-microsecond sensibility looping the loop between irreconcilables—involvement or retreat".[70] The question for Mahon in the spring of 1970 is a familiar one: can poetry act as a force for good in the world, or was Auden correct when he famously said that poetry makes nothing happen? This, the central question of "Beyond Howth Head", is posed against the background of Ireland's deepening troubles.

To Mahon, the future remained bleak as long as Ireland remained caught in a repetitive cycle without prospect of forward movement. That idea is reinforced by Molloy's despairing loss of movement and by a sign posted in County Clare which instructs the visitor: "stop here and see the sun go down." The seasonal patterning of "Night-Crossing" no longer offers any comfort; instead,

> Spring lights the country: from a thous-
> and dusty corners, house by house,
> from under beds and vacuum cleaners,
> empty Kosangas containers,
> bread bins, car seats, crates of stout,
> the first flies cry to be let out;
> to cruise a kitchen, find a door
> and die clean in the open air.... [71]

Mahon contemplates his own response, and confesses he sometimes resolves to exchange his "forkful of the general mess" for the hazelnuts and watercress diet of some old hermit who withdrew long ago to a small island in a lake.

> Centripetal, the hot world draws
> its children in with loving claws
> from rock and heather, rain and sleet
> with only Kosangas for heat
> and spins them at the centre where
> they have no time to know despair[72]

At the last moment, however, when light itself seems to have left the poet in darkness, Mahon suddenly reverses the movement of the poem and punctuates the turn with an exclamation:

> ....look! the watch-
> ful Baily winks beyond Howth Head,
> my cailín bán lies snug in bed
> and the moon rattles her lost stones
> among the rocks and the strict bones
> of the drowned as I put out the light
> on Mailer's *Armies of the Night*.[73]

Or, as he would express it in a later revision:

> And here I close; for look, across
> dark waves where bell-buoys dimly toss
> the Baily winks beyond Howth Head
> and sleep calls from the silent bed;
> while the moon drags her kindred stones
> among the rocks and the strict bones
> of the drowned, and I put out the light
> on shadows of the encroaching night.[74]

In the end, Mahon's answer to the despairing movement of human history comes in a lyrical acceptance of nature's healing cycles.

While the poem is filled with contemporary references, more important is the circular movement Mahon works to achieve in the brief space of the poem. It is a movement he recycles in many later poems, including "The Sea in Winter", "The Hudson Letter" and "St. Patrick's Day", the poem with which he closed his *Collected Poems*. We see such patterning, too, in the circles and wheels that appear throughout his later poems. Time and time again, the narrative line of Mahon's poems bends, and the poem enacts a ritualistic and restorative circular movement.

"Beyond Howth Head" expresses more than any other poem Mahon's anguish over the worsening violence in the North, and speaks to his faith in art in a time of violence. Mahon came through the political and personal crises of 1968/69 with a renewed commitment to poetry. The following year he left Ireland for London, explaining the move not as a new direction, but as a repetition: "I had to do what MacNeice had done".[75]

Chapter 7

| THE ROUND TOWER

It must have been spring, a morning in spring.
I thought I heard birds, skylarks perhaps.

Samuel Beckett, *Molloy*

The publication of *Night-Crossing* and its selection as a Poetry Book Society Choice introduced Mahon to a larger readership, and on the strength of that success, he began to imagine "a larger audience than Ireland provides".[1] Karl Miller began publishing his poems in *The Listener* on a semi-regular basis, and London increasingly grew in his imagination as a city where one might live by one's writing. He knew he was not cut out for teaching, and was eager for a change in his life. As he later explained it, "I went to live in London in 1970 because I simply couldn't find work in Dublin".[2] His move to London coincided with Heaney's appointment at the University of California, Berkeley, and both would later be criticised for turning their backs on the violence of their respective communities and fleeing the worsening conflict. There was, however, ample precedent for their decisions. Thomas Kinsella was teaching in America at the time; Desmond O'Grady was in Rome; John Montague had made Paris his adopted home. For his part, Mahon would insist his decision was practical: "I couldn't live by writing in Dublin".[3]

He was following a long line of writers who had found it necessary to leave Ireland. George Bernard Shaw had famously defended his leaving on the grounds that an artist "must have a metropolitan domicile and an international culture", a point of view Mahon shared. The artist's "first business", according to Shaw, "was to get out of Ireland". Mahon would later assert, "there are at most three poets in Ireland who are up to anything worthwhile". Though not stated explicitly, it is clear from the context that he had in mind Heaney, Longley and himself. "It doesn't do to have an Irish writer judged by Dublin standards, I think you should be judged by London, New York standards, and most of them simply couldn't stand up to it".[4] His comments were published in the pages of *The Irish Times*. Mahon was burning his bridges.

When a selection of his poems was included in a new anthology, *Young British Poets*, he complained to Louis Asekoff, "<u>British</u> poets, for Chrissake—but the 'young' compensates".[5] Michael Hartnett saw the matter in a harsher light: "The inclusion of Derek Mahon, Michael Longley and Seamus Heaney I find disturbing", he began his review in *The Irish Press*.

> Spiritually speaking there can be no hedging: poets belong to their own countries; no arbitrary borders should confuse them. Perhaps those three poets have opted for Britain—which would explain their silence about oppression and brutality in the Six Counties: perhaps they are riding two horses, hoping to double their speed to whatever unpoetic goals they have set themselves. I believe that at the present time there should be no room for ambiguity: poets from the Six Counties should specifically declare themselves for one side or another.[6]

Mahon's feelings for Ireland were, in fact, more complicated than that. Unlike Hartnett, he understood that the Northern Irish poet was the inheritor of a dual tradition. To choose one over another could only be done at enormous psychological cost. Reviewing Edna O'Brien's novel *A Pagan Place* in *The Listener* that April, he identified with O'Brien's own conflicted feelings towards her homeland. "Her passionate love-hate for the place rings bells of memory and self-recognition for a great number of people, in Earl's Court or wherever", he wrote in a self-referential aside.[7]

Doreen Douglas had left her job at Ulster Television and preceded Mahon to London, and her presence there was added reason to move to the city. On arrival, Jeremy Lewis's sister helped Mahon find an upper-floor flat in Observatory Gardens in Earl's Court.[8] From its high windows he had rooftop views. The previous tenant had been a photographer, and one of the rooms had served as a darkroom and was painted completely black. The row of homes was called Observatory Gardens for the astronomer Sir James South, whose observatory had been located on the site in the early nineteenth century. In later years, the area had been home to Ford Madox Ford (around the corner at 80 Campden Hill Road) and Ezra Pound (down the hill in Church Walk). In time, Mahon would write poems to both former residents, and would incorporate astronomical references suggested by his new home into numerous poems.

Among his neighbours was Alexander Trocchi, the heroin-addled author of *Young Adam* and *Cain's Book*. "In 1970, the sixties were still there", Mahon later noted.[9] Maurice Leitch, from County Antrim, author of *Liberty Lad* and *Poor Lazarus*, was working as a BBC producer and also living nearby. Leitch and his future wife, Sandra, would become close friends. Patricia Moynagh, a friend of Doreen's with whom she had worked as a waitress, moved to the area around this time and shared a flat with Kate Olivier, whom Mahon had met at the Piccolo back in Inst days. Both women would soon become a part of Derek and Doreen's circle of London friends. Down the hill was Bernard Stone's bookshop, Turret Books, which specialised in poetry and served as a kind of social club for writers and artists on Saturday afternoons, when wine flowed freely.[10] Mahon would later describe the bookshop as "my headquarters in those years".[11] Regulars included Edward Lucie-Smith, John Heath-Stubbs and Eddie Linden. "The Churchill", in nearby Kensington Church Street, would become Mahon's local.

Mahon and Lewis would often meet at Ward's Irish House in Piccadilly, where Mahon could reclaim his Irishness on his own terms. The bar was below street level and was made up of separate alcoves, each of which had the name of an Irish province spelled out in green tiles on the wall.[12] Brendan Behan had been a regular there in the 1950s; Eamon Scully (who went by the pseudonym Alan C. Breeze) was a regular in Mahon's day. Scully had once been connected to the BBC crowd who frequented the pubs around Broadcasting House, and had known Louis MacNeice. According to Mahon and Leitch, Scully's greatest claim to fame was when his picture was printed in *The Times* with what he contended were T.S. Eliot's dentures.[13]

Mahon was reading and reviewing a novel a week, though *The Listener* typically bundled these into a single review essay once a month. Among the books he reviewed soon after his arrival were new novels by Iris Murdoch, John Banville, Isaac Bashevis Singer, Ray Bradbury and James Dickey, as well as a volume of short stories by his friend

Tom Mac Intyre, *Dance the Dance*. Edna O'Brien and Patrick White received more extended treatment. "Excepting *Ulysses*, the best Irish novels are about escape", Mahon opened his review of O'Brien's *A Pagan Place*, before going on to itemise Ireland's ills: its "poverty, superstition, bigotry, and ignorance".[14] White's *The Vivisector* he judged completely successful. He was attracted to the novel's depiction of the artist, or, as he phrased it, "the psychopathology of artistic creation".[15] He reported to Longley that he was making £25 a week, hardly enough to cover his living expenses.

While his reviews often reveal an Irish orientation, Mahon was not engaging with the current sectarian crisis in any direct way. On the contrary, in December 1970 he reviewed a tourist guide devoted to the "Wonders of Ireland" which was chosen for ironic effect or was a tin-eared measure of his disengagement from current events.[16] We are a long way from "One part of my mind must learn to know its place", his youthful poem about discovering his poetic subject among Belfast's working classes.

In fact, Mahon was deeply torn over what form his response to the Troubles should take. In the autumn he was drawn away from his usual mode—poetry and the book review—to address the subject in an essay for a special Irish issue of *20th Century Studies*. He opened the piece with a taxonomy of the "new Northern Irish group of poets", before rejecting the familiar sectarian labels and arguing that the subject was not so simple. "Seamus Deane, a Bogsider, suggested to me not long ago that a plebiscite taken among Northern Catholics before the place blew up would have revealed a slight majority in favour of what genteel Unionists smugly call 'the British connection'". Mahon added, "only the most insanely unyielding Protestant would deny that he is, in some sense (if not in every sense), Irish".[17] The essay rejects these confining notions of Irish identity and argues that what accounts for the resurgence of poetry in the North is a recognition on the part of Mahon's contemporaries that they are no longer writing, as a previous generation would have had it, for "the plain people of Ireland". Rather, they are writing for a larger "court of appeal" informed by American and British models, as well as Irish.

Mahon argued in the essay that a historical sense was necessary for a poet, and, as he had done with Hugh O'Neill, he was looking for parallels to the present conflict. The only trouble was these parallels were not always recognisable to his readers. His poem "Edvard Munch" was, he later insisted, "a political poem ... about the situation of the artist in a situation of violent political upheaval". Yet the poem makes no explicit reference to upheaval, only a veiled reference to "so much going on outside". What the poem does do is bind two distinct spaces, the interior space of the artist and an outside space of violence. One space is indeed a register of the other, but there should be no mistake: Mahon's interest is the interior space of the private self. When the poem was first published in *The Listener*, it bore the title "On a Photograph of Edvard Munch's Room in Oslo", even further distancing himself from events outside Munch's studio window. Mahon later explained "the poem became a refusal to write a war poem ... an assertion of the necessary private nature of a certain kind of artistic activity".[18]

For several years Mahon had been publishing poems in Harry Chambers's little magazine, *Phoenix*, and before his move to London he and Chambers had made plans to publish a selection of his poems in a limited edition. Longley and Heaney had both published in Chambers's series, as had a new friend, Glyn Hughes, author of the recent poetry collection *Love on the Moor*, which Mahon had reviewed for *The Listener*. While Mahon now had a major publisher in OUP, interim publication of this kind allowed him to get new work into print quickly and keep his poems circulating between books. Chambers had planned to publish *Ecclesiastes* in January 1970, but delays typical of small press publication pushed the date back to the following October, and the hardcover copies were not delivered until close to Christmas. By the time the selection finally appeared, Mahon felt it was hopelessly outdated, as he made clear in his brief introduction: "Most of the poems in this pamphlet were written between January and December 1968 ... the poems constitute, in some measure, the poetic record of an attempt by an uprooted Ulsterman to come to terms with his background".[19] Mahon was making clear that the poems preceded the outbreak of violence in the North, but his epigraph from *Ecclesiastes* 4:1 attempted to cast the poems in light of the recent political violence. "So I returned, and considered all the oppressions that are done under the sun; and behold the tears of such as were oppressed, and they had no comforter; and on the side of their oppressors there was power; but they had no comforter".[20] He added a second epigraph from the poet George Seferis, "We who had nothing will teach them peace".

Near the end of the year Mahon reviewed J.G. Farrell's novel *Troubles*. He found its depiction of "the dying rhythms of the Anglo-Irish minuet" highly appealing, and was drawn to the soporific setting: a once-grand, now run-down hotel in County Wexford with the ironic name The Majestic.[21] Farrell's novel dramatises not merely the inevitability of decay but the end of an imperial way of life. Over the course of the novel, the "M" of "Majestic" falls from the hotel signboard, a wash-basin breaks loose from the wall and foliage pushes up through the floorboards, all potent symbols of a larger process of breaking down. After Mahon's review ran in *The Times*, he received an appreciative note from Farrell; a short time later their mutual agent, Deborah Rogers, had them to dinner, where they met for the first time.[22] Farrell was living nearby in Egerton Gardens, and in the coming years the two writers would become close friends.

In December Mahon took the train to Newcastle upon Tyne for a reading with James Simmons at the Morden Tower, and a few weeks later Stewart Parker selected four poems from *Ecclesiastes* for a Radio 4 feature, "New Writing from Ireland".[23] Though it had taken years to assemble his first collection for Oxford, Mahon was writing at a fast pace, and in the spring he sent Stallworthy a new typescript he was tentatively calling "Scrap Metal". He had first considered "A Dark Country", but rejected it as being too similar to Heaney's second collection, *Door into the Dark*.[24] As Stallworthy noted in an internal OUP memo, *Night-Crossing* had done quite well for the Press. It had been well reviewed and had sold more than two thousand copies, a strong showing for a first collection. While he did not care for "the junk-heap-remainder-table associations" of the working title, he was enthusiastic about the new manuscript, which he described as "a distinct advance on *Night-Crossing*, more assured, more mature, more penetrating in its insights into man and society".[25]

That spring Mahon became the regular theatre reviewer for *The Listener*, which required that he attend plays two or sometimes three nights a week. Among the first shows he reviewed were revivals of Beckett's *Krapp's Last Tape* and *Endgame*, and Harold Pinter's new play about the distortions of memory, *Old Times*. "The past is what you remember, imagine you remember, convince yourself you remember, or pretend you remember", Pinter famously asserts. Mahon was himself grappling with the past and the poet's own role as maker, issues he explored in "Rage for Order", inspired by Wallace Stevens's "The Idea of Order at Key West". There the poet "… far / From his people" looks out of his high window and indulges his "Wretched rage for order". In the distance is the devastation of recent rioting: a scorched gable and burnt-out buses. Far from the destruction, the poet labours over words like Nero playing the lyre while Rome burns. The poem expresses Mahon's own ambivalence and even confusion in the face of recent events. The image of the poet at his window suggests Mahon himself, except the speaker of the poem aligns himself not with the poet but with those in the streets among the broken glass.

> He is far
> From his people,
> And the fitful glare
> Of his high window is as
> Nothing to our scattered glass.

From that street view, the first-person speaker condemns the distant poet and his grandiloquent rhetoric. In the poem's final lines, the two figures merge, and the speaker acknowledges his need for the poet's "germinal ironies" (a phrasing he later changed to "terminal ironies").[26]

As summer approached, Doreen was making plans to holiday in Greece. A former boyfriend had been Greek, and the country still held a special place in her heart.[27] Mahon planned to paint and furnish the Observatory Gardens flat in preparation for her return. "A hard summer stretches ahead", he told Longley. Tom Mac Intyre provided a welcome interruption from his labours when he visited for a week with "his dramatically sexy girlfriend". Louis Asekoff and his wife also visited, "a Korean cellist, I swear to God".[28] His friends were all of an age where they were marrying or settling into some other form of domestic arrangement. At the end of the summer Doreen returned and moved into the newly painted flat. Other friends continued to pass through London on a regular basis. John Montague came from Paris for a reading with Richard Ryan at the Poetry Society, and John Hewitt was down from Coventry to read with Mahon at the Irish Club.

Longley again proposed that he and Derek undertake an exchange of verse letters.[29] Mahon declined this time, explaining he was "much absorbed in sonnets", but encouraged Longley to go ahead without him— "a verse letter from you to me".[30] The resulting poem, "To Derek Mahon", appeared in the *New Statesman* in early December, alongside another, "To Seamus Heaney". The poem opens by recalling the two friends' visit to the Shankill and Falls Road areas of Belfast two years earlier:

And did we come into our own
When, minus muse and lexicon,
We traced in August sixty-nine
Our imaginary Peace Line
Around the burnt-out houses of
The Catholics we scarcely loved,
Two Sisyphuses come to budge
The sticks and stones of an old grudge,

Two poetic conservatives
In the city of guns and long knives.
Our ears receiving then and there
The stereophonic nightmare
Of The Shankill and The Falls,
Our matches struck on crumbling walls
To light us as we moved at last
Through the back alleys of Belfast?[31]

The poem recounts an earlier attempt to cross the sectarian divide when
the friends visited the Aran Islands the Easter after Mahon's return from
Canada. We were, he writes,

Eavesdroppers on conversations
With a Jesus who spoke Irish—
We were strangers in that parish,
Black tea with bacon and cabbage
For our sacraments and potage.[32]

Mahon was stung by the poem. He was not comfortable having his
own recent experiences exposed in this way, and he took a particular
exception to Longley's reference to "Catholics we scarcely loved" and to
the phrase "Two poetic conservatives". As he explained, "'The Catholics
we scarcely loved' still reads to me too much like 'The Catholics we didn't
much like and hadn't any time for'". "When?" he asked, "as we were
walking up the Shankill?"[33] Mahon felt compelled to reply with a letter of
protest published in the *New Statesman* the following week.

Sir,

A casual reader of 'Two Letters' by my friend Michael Longley might be forgiven for drawing one or two erroneous conclusions. Mr. Longley, with the best will in the world, appears to attribute to me attitudes to which I do not, in fact, subscribe. I refer to lines 6 and 9 of 'To Derek Mahon'—'The Catholics we scarcely loved' and 'Two poetic conservatives'. The implications of line 6, as it stands, are frankly untrue, not to say damaging, and the overtones of line 9 tendentious and misleading. No one likes to see his views misrepresented, however innocently. Mr. Longley may speak for himself; he doesn't necessarily speak for me.[34]

Mahon also asked Longley to revise the offensive lines before the poem reappeared in an anthology or in his next collection. When he refused and offered instead to include an explanatory note with the poem, Mahon reacted angrily. "Let's be quite clear about the letter/poem business. The reason I wrote the letter to NS was because I felt my feelings/attitudes had been misrepresented in yr. poem. I still think that". Both friends were hurt by the quarrel. "I would be happy to see the whole thing finished with so that we can get back to normal relations—and so, I know, would you", Mahon wrote Longley. But he had no intention of adding a note to Longley's poem. Nothing would do but that the offending lines be changed. When Mahon saw Heaney in London, he sought his support in the matter. "This is not a matter of censorship", he insisted in another letter to Longley: "Seamus, here last week, put it like this: by dedicating a poem to someone you make him in a sense co-author of the poem; you associate him, will he nill he [sic], with the contents of the poem, thus giving him some measure of, yes, proprietary right". The closeness between the two poet friends—the blending of their two poetic personae into a collective "we"—compelled them to make sharper distinctions. "You say 'we seem to be feeling differently and going, for a while, our separate ways'. Well of course we are, with the proviso that one knows where the heart lies. If we felt the same at every point and went the same way we'd be the same person and write the same poems. Poetically, the only ways are separate ways".

When the poem eventually appeared in Longley's *An Exploded View* alongside poems to Simmons and Heaney, the first of the offending lines was only slightly changed. The offence was now cast into the past perfect tense—"The Catholics we'd scarcely loved"—suggesting as it does some intervening change in feeling.[35] Longley elaborated on the point in an autobiographical essay on his Protestant upbringing published in the *New Statesman* a couple of years later. He wrote, "invisible apartheid operated so efficiently on both sides that I was 24 before I could count Catholics among my close friends, and unable until then to register the loss".[36] While Longley probed this condition through poetry, Mahon found himself unable to address it.

Mahon's distress over the incident became even more acute when British troops opened fire on Civil Rights demonstrators in Derry on 30 January 1972. Twenty-seven protesters were shot and 13 killed. Again, images of the violence spread around the world. The next day Westminster established a tribunal to conduct an inquiry into the loss of life, and the following week a large protest was held in Newry. Developments on the streets of Derry were being watched closely, and increasingly those in the arts community were asking themselves and one another what the responsibility of the artist was in a time of crisis. The release of the Widgery Report two months later, which absolved British troops from any wrongdoing, was greeted with widespread derision among Catholics. Thomas Kinsella responded to the provocation with his angriest and most direct political statement to date, the powerful long poem "Butcher's Dozen". The violence seemed to demand that positions be taken, yet Mahon felt unable to embrace a cause that would link him even remotely to the warring parties. The latest events only confirmed his conviction that Ireland was a benighted place, or, borrowing from Matthew Arnold in a letter to Asekoff, "a land of darkness, where ignorant armies clash by night. Catholic fascists versus Protestant fascists with British fascists on every street corner—there is no side to take".[37]

Heaney later noted: "it was an awkward time for anybody who wanted to stand apart from both sides".[38] Early in the new year when Heaney was invited to read his poems and discuss the recent events at London's Institute of Contemporary Arts (ICA), he suggested Mahon be asked to join him. The organiser, Lindy Dufferin, was descended from the Guinness family and her Holland Park home was at the centre of London's fashionable social world. Her sister-in-law, Caroline Blackwood, had once been married to Lucian Freud and was seeing Robert Lowell, who was in England for a visiting professorship at All Souls College, Oxford. After the *New Statesman* debacle, Mahon agreed to take part, but when the programme was printed, only Heaney was mentioned by name. "There appears to be some confusion about the proposed ICA Irish programme on the 25th of this month", Mahon wrote Dufferin. "Your assistant has phoned me to ask if I would be willing to take part in this, and I've said I would, but the ICA brochure lists only Seamus Heaney as taking part. Can you clarify this for me?"[39] In the end the programme took place without Mahon.

Dufferin tried to mend Mahon's hurt feelings by inviting him to participate in another programme a few months later, "No Man's Land", part of a week-long series of events leading up to Poetry International 1972. The programme was to feature Heaney, Mahon, Hammond and, at Derek's suggestion, Maurice Leitch. However, the advance notices for the programme were hardly reassuring: Mahon read that Heaney, Hammond, Leitch and himself would "read, talk and sing about the Belfast situation". The whole affair had an odour of opportunism about it, and when the day arrived, he and Leitch did not show up. A reporter covering the event noted, "a promised descent of Irish poets almost failed to materialize, but at last Seamus Heaney was discovered writing notes about Belfast in a corner, and carried the reading easily on his own, a stalwart, fuzzy, smiling figure who talked gently about the murderous divisions between Gaelic and Planter".[40]

In not appearing for these events, Mahon was acting out the central gesture of the poem he was composing at the time, "Fire-King". The poem would not be published for two more years, but he mailed a copy to Glyn Hughes at the end of March.

I want to be
Like the man who descends
At two milk-churns

With a bulging
String bag & vanishes
Where the lane turns,

Or the man
Who drops at night
From a moving train

And strikes out over the fields
Where fireflies glow
Not knowing a word of the language.

Either way, I am
Through with history –
Who lives by the sword

Dies by the sword.
Last of the fire-kings, I shall
Break with tradition and

Die by my own hand
Rather than perpetuate
The barbarous cycle.[41]

It was Mahon's most explicit statement to date of his ambivalence over the violence afflicting Northern Ireland.

Even as he was keeping his distance from these events, Mahon was framing an account of an unpartitioned tradition of Irish poetry which would serve as the introduction for a new anthology, the *Sphere Book of Modern Irish Poetry*. He passed quickly over the first 100 years of Irish poetry in English in order to get to Yeats, "with whom any discussion of modern Irish poetry necessarily begins". While he praises the poems themselves as the proof of Yeats's greatness, Mahon devotes considerable attention to Yeats's extra-poetical activities. "In his middle and later years", he writes, "he conducted, from a position of Olympian detachment, a continuous and unyielding arbitration in all matters relating to Irish literature and drama".[42] Editing the Sphere anthology was an attempt to assume a similar role as just such an arbiter. He notes that at least three writers "of international stature (Joyce, George Moore, O'Casey) refused to recognize the Yeatsian court", but the poets, he adds, largely "stayed at home and toed the line". The comment is revealing, coming so soon after Mahon's own move from Dublin to London. Where one chooses to live and work reveals something about one's position within a literary tradition.

Following the founding of the Irish Free State, Austin Clarke and Patrick Kavanagh contributed greatly to "the secularization and demystification of Irish poetry". They embraced "a rougher, terrestrial idiom" that was stylistically liberating for the younger poets to follow. Both contributed as well to the erosion of what Mahon calls a "residual Anglocentricity"—that English tradition that has held such a powerful sway over each generation of Irish writers. Most interesting about Mahon's survey of modern Irish poetry is his description of Longley and himself: "Protestant products of an English educational system, with little or no knowledge of the Irish language and an inherited duality of cultural reference". Mahon acknowledges the presence of that cultural apartheid that Longley had probed in a more direct way. While Mahon's introduction offers a helpful taxonomy of some of the main currents of Irish literary culture, noticeably absent from his account is any tradition of writing by Irish women.[43] Instead, Mahon defines his own origins, and gives extended attention to his adopted literary father, Louis MacNeice.

> For a long time it seemed that Louis MacNeice was Irish only by an accident of birth, but in recent years his reputation, never at the highest in Britain, has come to rest in the country he could never quite bring himself to disown. This is particularly the case in the North, where his example has provided a frame of reference for a number of younger poets in much the same way as Kavanagh's has done in the South. There is now, what there never was before, a vital and original body of work issuing from that once birdless, if still benighted province.[44]

A "still benighted province" is a surprising description of Ulster, coming from one who had set out to anthologise the best of Irish poetry from the North and the south. Mahon's ambivalence about his task reveals itself in other ways too. He concludes his brief introduction with the less-than-reassuring statement, "I don't think there is an absolutely bad poem in the book". One can only wonder what his editor at Sphere was thinking when he or she let that deflating comment stand.

Mahon chose to represent his own contribution to the Northern revival with three previously published poems: "A Dying Art", "An Image from Beckett" and "I am Raftery". The first of these offers a catalogue of the traditional arts and is a kind of relic of Ireland's ancestral past and the folkways of the poet's grandmother. Lamplighters and sailmakers have all but vanished, he reminds us, like native Manx speakers. In "An

Image from Beckett" Mahon shifts his gaze outwards to a wider European landscape, while "I Am Raftery" offers a glimpse of the poet himself as an inheritor of these dual traditions. When the anthology appeared in the spring of 1972, "An Image from Beckett" bore the dedication "for Doreen Douglas", his first to his future wife.

Mahon was thinking a great deal about poetry's relationship to the past and to present events, a subject he took up in the sleeve notes for an album by his friend Richard Ryan. Mahon and Ryan had first met in Dublin in 1969, but Ryan had only recently returned to Ireland after a period of travelling in Europe and America. "For a long time Irish poets worked within a deliberately narrow focus", Mahon wrote, introducing Ryan's poems. "The proper study of the Irish poet, according to this tradition, is the parish pump". As an example, he cited Kavanagh's "Epic", a poem that insists on keeping its gaze squarely on County Monaghan, despite the world-shattering events of 1938. "But now", Mahon continued, "the more adventurous younger poets are opening new ground".[45] While ostensibly commenting on Ryan's poems, Mahon was also talking about his own. Ryan's work, he continued, "is a living reproach to the parish-pumpery and intellectual inadequacy of Irish literary life".[46]

In April, John Hewitt, a poet of the parish pump, thanked Mahon for including his poems in the Sphere anthology.[47] He also heard from an annoyed Austin Clarke, who apparently had not been consulted about the publication of his poems. Similarly, the publisher Peter Fallon noted that Brendan Kennelly's poem "Bread" had appeared in the anthology without acknowledgment and, more to the point, without payment. Mahon wrote to Fallon to set things right. It was an inauspicious introduction to his future publisher.[48] In April he received advance copies of his new collection, now entitled *Lives*, and he asked OUP to send copies to Philip Larkin, Liam Miller and John Hewitt.[49] The new collection, with its cover image of workers leaving the Harland and Wolff shipyard at the end of their shift, was dedicated to his mother and father. The *Titanic* is just visible in the background, and Mahon's own grandfather might well be one of the indistinct figures captured in the photograph. At the time, his father was working at the shipyard still, and the book and its cover image make a claim for an alternative life in the manner of Heaney's "Digging". Indeed, manual work was his parents' measure of value, and to call someone "a worker", as his mother sometimes would, was an expression of great approval.

Despite his steady reviewing, he and Doreen were struggling to make ends meet, and Mahon turned to his friend Robin Skelton at the University of Victoria in British Columbia for help selling his manuscript drafts of *Beyond Howth Head*.[50] American and Canadian libraries were actively buying the working drafts of British and Irish authors, and Mahon hoped his own work might attract such interest. He and Skelton also began working on a film adaptation of Oscar Wilde's *The Picture of Dorian Gray*, hoping to tap into the lucrative film business.[51] Doreen, too, was doing her part to improve the couple's finances. It was around this time that she took a job as Harold Pinter's personal assistant. Though only in his early forties, Pinter was already a successful playwright, and at the time he was working on a screenplay for Aidan Higgins's novel *Langrishe, Go Down*, which would later be adapted for television and star Jeremy Irons and Judi Dench.

Doreen may have misunderstood just what Pinter's expectations were. Her friend Sandra Leitch spoke to Doreen almost daily during this period, and recalls that Doreen thought the job "was going to be her and Harold out all over London for wonderful lunches every day". In fact, Pinter needed someone to bring order and efficiency to his life. Doreen was ill-suited for a position with such vague duties, however, and she may have sensed that she was auditioning for some other role altogether. Pinter's relationship with his first wife, Vivien Merchant, was a strained one, and Pinter had only recently broken off a long-term affair with the BBC television presenter Joan Bakewell. He would base his 1978 play, *Betrayal*, on this recent experience. Sandra Leitch recalls that after much hesitation and worry, Doreen summoned up her courage and told Pinter that the job was not working out.[52]

In the summer, Derek and Doreen took the train north to visit Glyn Hughes, who had recently purchased a run-down cottage near Sowerby Bridge in Yorkshire.[53] Mahon later thanked Hughes for his hospitality by sending him a version of the fourteenth-century Welsh poet Dafydd ap Gwilym's poem "Yr Adfail" ("The Ruin"), which he reworked as "Runes",[54] another poem he would leave uncollected. Following this visit, he and Doreen embarked on a holiday in France where they stayed for a week with Douglas Dunn and his wife, Lesley, in Tursac, a small town in the Dordogne, before moving on to Provence to visit Eugene Lambe. Dunn had recently won the Somerset Maugham Award, the proceeds of which allowed the couple to spend a few months in rural France. They had established a comfortable routine of turning in early and rising early, but that schedule was disrupted by Derek and Doreen's arrival. To secure fresh fish or meat, Dunn had to rise early and walk to the main road to flag down the fishmonger or butcher in the early morning. "A bit of a slog if you'd got to bed at 2 in the morning full of booze and poetical conversation", he later recalled.[55]

During the visit the two couples heard disturbing news reports from Belfast. Intimidation of families living in "mixed" neighbourhoods had been on the rise as 12 July approached. Barricades had gone up in many parts of the city, and tensions were already high when the IRA called off its ceasefire and Belfast erupted in violent clashes. Eleven people were killed over the course of the weekend, including a priest and a 13-year-old girl. A bomb exploded outside the Belfast office of *The Irish Times*, and a hooded corpse was found off the Antrim Road, Mahon's own route into the city from his childhood home.

Dunn later incorporated the experience into his poem "Realisms", which he dedicated to Mahon.

> Its echo reached us here,
>
> Far down in France, the thud
> That hits the citizens who die
> For random's cause—
>
> The cause of being them,
> Of being there, blown to pieces
> As they drink their tea.[56]

Dunn described the visit in a letter to Longley in which he noted that "Doreen seemed remarkably insensitive to it all—a Constance Markievicz of the Blues". Mahon, on the other hand, became noticeably depressed. "I think Derek's solution is the best", Dunn added; "I think it's tremendously brave of him to have renounced the whole business and cleared off".[57] Longley replied two days later: "I'm glad you said that about Mahon, courage is one of his qualities, and doesn't it come through in his poetry? Those swift, finely poised, almost cavalier, lightning gestures against the dark".[58] He added, "Seamus [Heaney] says that Mahon is the Stephen Dedalus of our group: he left Ireland a long, long time ago".[59]

A few days later the crisis reached a new low when the IRA detonated more than twenty bombs across Belfast within a two-hour period. Nine people were killed in the synchronised attack, and more than a hundred and thirty wounded. With the increase of violence, Mahon's move to London was coming to be seen in a new light. James Simmons, reviewing *Lives* in the Belfast-based magazine *Fortnight*, used the occasion to take him to task. "The last time I saw Derek Mahon I said 'You shouldn't be going to London. Go back to Belfast and live with your own people'", to which Mahon replied, "'What do you think I've been doing up to now?'" Simmons asserted Mahon's talent was in danger, adding: "Perhaps it does matter where you live and how you earn your bread. I have no doubt that MacNeice and Rodgers suffered for their easy choice of London and the BBC, and perhaps London and *The Listener* may not be what Derek Mahon needs".[60] It was a harsh attack, though Mahon was not helping his cause by reviewing guidebooks for an idealised Ireland as the bombing intensified.[61] Early in the new year he reviewed *The Companion Guide to Ireland* for *The Times*, noting that it managed to fit in "just about everything of interest to the tourist".[62]

After leaving Tursac, Derek and Doreen travelled to the Côte d'Azur, stopping in Trets for a few days, just off the Marseille-Nice road.[63] They were back in London by the end of the month, in time to finalise wedding preparations.[64] On Saturday, 30 September, they were married in St Mary Abbots, the local parish church of Kensington, a short walk from their Observatory Gardens home. Mahon's parents came over from Belfast, and Doreen's mother, Greta Douglas, also attended. Derek had been best man in the Longleys' wedding eight years before, and this time Michael, in jeans according to the dress code of the day, stood in and gave Doreen away. Among the small group of friends who attended were Maurice and Sandra Leitch, J.G. Farrell and Aidan Higgins and his wife Jill. Glyn Hughes, down from Yorkshire for the occasion, met his future wife, Roya Liakopouls, at the wedding.[65] Derek had not wanted to hire a wedding photographer, but Glyn sat in the back of the church and snapped pictures of the occasion. Afterwards family and friends returned to Observatory Gardens for a champagne party in their flat. Soon Mahon began sharing the news with more distant friends. "Doreen & I got ourselves married on Sept. 30th", he wrote to Asekoff; "You should have seen the sardonic gaze of God as the faithless Mahooon bent the knee in His consecrated house. No bolts of lightning, however. Merely an embarrassed silence".[66]

Chapter 8

| LONDON AND FORD MANOR

Derek and Doreen spent their first Christmas as a married couple visiting Belfast, Portrush and Dublin, during which time he inscribed a copy of *Lives* for Michael Longley with the acknowledgment "reflecting an old gratitude". Back in London after the holiday, Mahon began the new year and married life by giving up theatre reviewing. As he confided to Asekoff, he had "jacked in the theatre job out of sheer pique/exasperation and am casting about for crumbs of labour".[1] Doreen was teaching at a nearby school, but her pay was hardly sufficient for the couple to live on, and their finances were "grim".[2] Mahon was pinning his hopes on the screenplay of *The Picture of Dorian Gray*. After two years of theatre reviewing, he knew something about what made a successful play, and he thought scriptwriting might be a way to make a living.

In January Peter Orr interviewed Mahon for a BBC radio broadcast, during the course of which he asked whether he or his fellow poets had anything particularly valuable to say about the situation in the North. "I think possibly yes", Mahon replied, "but he should not try to say it in the course of a radio interview or in a newspaper. It should come through the poetry somehow, when it comes".[3] Mahon had mailed Longley a new poem a few days earlier entitled "A Disused Shed in Co. Wexford".[4] The poem was initially turned down by the *TLS* and would not be published until the following autumn, but he had finished it in January in time for it to be included as the final poem on a Claddagh Records LP he recorded that month. When the new poem finally appeared in print, it bore a dedication to his friend J.G. Farrell.

Mahon's "Disused Shed" roams widely over historical time but springs from Farrell's depiction in *Troubles* of Ireland in the midst of civil war. Writing 50 years on, Mahon links that historical crisis with the present violence and with moments of apocalypse throughout history, ranging from the destruction of Pompeii to the atrocities of the Nazi death camps. As Heaney later noted, the poem gives voice to "a whole Lethe full of doomed generations and tribes, whispering their unfulfilment and perplexed hopes in a trickle of masonry."[5] The still point of the poem is a derelict shed where lime deposits grow on a rain barrel, masonry crumbles and mushrooms strain towards a keyhole's dim light.

> Deep in the grounds of a burnt-out hotel,
> Among the bathtubs and the washbasins
> A thousand mushrooms crowd to a keyhole.
> This is the one star in their firmament
> Or frames a star within a star.
> What should they do there but desire?
> So many days beyond the rhododendrons
> With the world waltzing in its bowl of cloud,
> They have learnt patience and silence
> Listening to the rooks querulous in the high wood.

While the poem was partly inspired by the garden shed on the grounds of the Hotel Majestic in Farrell's novel, Mahon would also, eventually, cite his friend's novel *The Lung* as another source. In that novel the central character, Sands, like Farrell himself, experiences the first symptoms of polio. "Good heavens, you're bleeding. And you look so pale", a house guest says to him.

> He remembered the door of a disused potting-shed he had once opened and the long, sickly white shoots racing each other interminably across the earth floor towards the minute bead of light

from the keyhole. Tulips, or seed potatoes, or merely anonymous weeds, it was impossible to tell. Perhaps by now one of them had reached the keyhole and, obstructing it, had condemned the others to death in the darkness, only to expire itself in an unaccustomed blaze of sunshine.

"I'm a pale fungus growing towards the light", Sands replies.[6]

Mahon's reworking of Farrell's text was quickly recognised as one of his finest poems. In the familiar images of utensils and crockery that have outlived their useful lives, Mahon captured a universal condition of struggle in a disinterested and unresponsive world. Mahon closes the poem by giving voice to these inanimate objects, and through their cry, expresses man's common hope for deliverance:

> 'Save us, save us,' they seem to say,
> 'Let the god not abandon us
> Who have come so far in darkness and in pain.
> We too had our lives to live.
> You with your light meter and relaxed itinerary,
> Let not our naive labours have been in vain!'[7]

The poem is a rarity in Mahon's body of work in that it would remain unrevised and unaltered in all later reprintings.

With no relief from the couple's financial difficulties in sight, Mahon contacted Skelton to see if anything could be done about the manuscripts of *Beyond Howth Head*, which Philobiblion Books in Victoria, British Columbia, had been unable to sell. Skelton did what he could to help: he offered $50 for a review of Montague's new collection *The Rough Field*, and, at his urging, Philobiblion came through with $150 to buy the manuscripts for stock, since there was still no immediate buyer. Mahon was circulating the screenplay of *The Picture of Dorian Gray* among London agents but also without success. "The Wilde play is not getting the kind of reception I think it deserves", he wrote Skelton in February. "The fault lies with one Osborne who is known to have completed his own version".[8] John Osborne's screenplay would in fact be picked up by the BBC, killing any prospects for Mahon's and Skelton's adaptation.

In March Mahon and Douglas Dunn gave a joint reading for the Poetry Society at the Mermaid Theatre in Blackfriars. As was typical,

Mahon's payment for the reading was modest, a mere £15 plus "a meal and a drink".[9] Book reviews paid little more than that, and in an effort to bring in extra money Doreen began a feature article on "the arts in Ulster in a time of crisis", which she hoped to sell to *The Observer*. She asked John Hewitt for help, and put to him a series of questions she planned to work into the piece: "Are you conscious of your work having been affected by the crisis?" she asked.[10] It was the kind of question her husband loathed. Despite Hewitt's cooperation, the *Observer* piece came to nothing, and it was during this time of financial extremity that a friend of Doreen's interceded and helped Mahon get a job as an advertising copywriter with Masius, Wynne-Williams & D'Arcy-MacManus. Mahon's heart was not in the work, or the nine to half-past five schedule, and he confided to Skelton it was "a purely temporary expedient".[11] In later years he would skip over his brief time as an advertising copywriter without comment.

Despite his day job, Mahon was writing well, and in April he published a new poem, "The Snow Party", which had been prompted by his reading of the Japanese poet Matsuo Bashō's *The Narrow Road to the Deep North*. In the Penguin translation Bashō recounts a pilgrimage to the Shinto shrines of Ise, Nagoya and Kyōto, during which he is invited to a snow-viewing party. Mahon juxtaposes this exercise in contemplation with the violence of Japan's ancestral past, and finds in that contrast a parallel to Ireland's present state.

Elsewhere they are burning
Witches and heretics
In the boiling squares,

Thousands have died since noon
In the service
Of barbarous kings;

But there is silence
In the houses of Nagoya
And the hills of Ise.[12]

Bashō offered Mahon a model of composure in the face of atrocity that increasingly was his public posture in response to violence.

In the spring Mahon made a weekend trip to Cardiff for a reading with Montague and Heaney. He had recently finished his review of *The Rough Field*, in which he compared his friend's work to that of Patrick Kavanagh and called him "the best Irish poet of his generation". What impressed Mahon was the way the local and highly specific subject matter had been given wider historical meaning: "Montague is telescoping 360 years of local history in order to point up a recurrent pattern; for the psychological reality is the same today as it was in 1603". In both the creation of the plantations and the present influx of foreign capital into the country, Mahon saw history repeating itself, with disastrous consequences for the local inhabitants. *The Rough Field* made plain these historical patterns and did so through "the subtly orchestrated music of the verse".[13] Mahon took further note of his friend's success that July when more than seven hundred and fifty people attended a special reading of the poem by Montague, Heaney and Benedict Kiely, with musical accompaniment by The Chieftains.[14]

Mahon's Observatory Gardens flat was becoming a regular resting place for travelling poets and academics, and, despite his new work schedule, these visits were often boozy affairs. Montague and Longley were regular visitors whenever they were in London, and that spring and summer house guests included Tom Mac Intyre, Robin Skelton, Louis Asekoff and a professor of Irish drama from Toronto, D.E.S. Maxwell. On one occasion, after a night of particularly hard drinking, Mahon and Maxwell collapsed in the same bed. "No need to apologize, ould hand", Mahon wrote after Maxwell's departure. "I don't think any arrangement made in the state we had achieved on that memorable evening could be considered by any reasonable man to be either substantial or binding".[15] Professor Lester Conner, from Chestnut Hill College in Philadelphia, recalls an evening drinking with Mahon and Maxwell at a bar near Leicester Square (which he chose for the pun on his friend's name). At one point in the evening Mahon collapsed and sank to the floor. His friends left him there undisturbed, and after 15 or 20 minutes "he popped up into his seat and resumed his drink".[16]

In September "A Disused Shed", with its dedication to Farrell, finally appeared in print, and a few weeks later it was announced that Farrell had won that year's Booker Prize for the second novel of his Empire Trilogy, *The Siege of Krishnapur*. On accepting his prize money at the award dinner, Farrell took the podium and proceeded to denounce capitalism and, by association, the prize's sponsor Booker McConnell, Ltd. The *Evening Standard* ran a story the next day: "Booker winner bites the hand that gives £5,000". Farrell had seized on the occasion to lash out "against privilege, public schools, the Royal Family, over-priced company chairmen and tycoons generally".[17] It was just the kind of behaviour Mahon delighted in, and when he wrote a magazine profile of his friend a few months later, he would take up Farrell's theme himself.

Mahon was having his own quarrel with capitalism, and in the autumn he decided he had had enough of steady employment, and abruptly quit his advertising job. As he explained to Bill McCormack, "there is only so much one can say about nappies".[18] With his final pay he made a trip to Spain, where he met Aidan Higgins on the Costa del Sol; Doreen was working and unable to get away. After a few days drinking with Higgins in Málaga, he visited Torremolinos, but the hotels along the coast left him unimpressed. He returned home to find his mother-in-law visiting, an unfortunate constraint on both his writing and his drinking.[19] Despite advertising work, it had been a creative period; towards the end of the year, he told Longley he thought he had enough poems for a new collection, which he was tentatively calling "The Snow Party".[20]

In search of more agreeable work, Mahon applied for the post of Features Editor at *Vogue*, and in January 1974 learned that the position was his. He told friends that he would be responsible for "the serious bits between the clothes".[21] Before taking up his new duties, he flew to Toronto for the Canadian Association for Irish Studies conference at York University. D.E.S. Maxwell had assembled as convivial a group as Mahon could have hoped for. In addition to Montague, Heaney and Longley, other participants included Walter Allen, Brian Friel, David Hammond, Maurice Leitch, Tom Mac Intyre, Brian Moore, James Simmons and Robin Skelton. Toronto was bitterly cold, snow covered the ground, and, as Leitch later recalled, "we all got the flu".[22] Nevertheless it was an enjoyable gathering of friends, and Mahon was particularly glad to renew his acquaintance with Brian Moore, whose work he would lecture on in a few months time.

Mahon was paired with Montague for a discussion moderated by Professor Eugene Benson of York's English Department. Asked to comment on influences on his own work, Mahon gave a rambling reply that vacillated between accepting and rejecting the familiar labels. "Well, I'm from the other side of the political fence, of the religious fence, in origin that is, from Montague here", he began. "I don't consider myself a Protestant in fact; I consider myself some kind of pagan—but for a Northern Irish Protestant poet there is a tendency to think of Louis MacNeice very much as a background figure". The sectarian labels in Ireland posed a greater challenge for Mahon than they did for Montague. The Anglo-Irish MacNeice was a familiar lifeline in such circumstances, but on this occasion Mahon downplayed the connection. "I worked for several years to get MacNeice out of my system", he said, adding, "I think perhaps it's happened now".[23]

En route home, Mahon passed through New York where he spent several days at Asekoff's East Village apartment. He prepared himself for the long flight by borrowing freely from his friend's poetry books and, on his return to London, reported in a letter to Asekoff that Doreen was "displeased that I had such a good time without her".[24] Once back, he took up his duties at *Vogue* (or "Vague" as he called it) and, writing to friends on his new stationery, would cross out the Hanover Square address and replace it with "Hangover Square". He would later describe himself as the worst-dressed staffer at the magazine. Despite the ill-fit of his new job, he had wide latitude to pursue stories that interested him, and among the first he took up was a profile of J.G. Farrell, who was still riding the wave of his Booker success.

Despite Farrell's recent harsh words about the royal family, the magazine assigned Lord Snowdon as the photographer for the piece. The day of the shoot the light was poor in Farrell's flat, so the three men stepped outside; Snowdon snapped Farrell in front of a shop window where two cats were sunning themselves. Afterwards the trio went to the Bunch of Grapes pub in Brompton Road, where Snowdon was immediately recognised, despite of, or perhaps because of, his dark glasses. There they chatted over drinks as other patrons in the pub tried to look inconspicuous while stealing glances at the famous photographer and member of the royal family.[25]

Mahon used the magazine profile to expand on the theme Farrell had taken up in his Booker Prize remarks. "One devotes too much time to giving satisfaction to one's ego, time which could be better spent in fruitful speculation or in the service of one of the senses", he quoted Farrell. "Owning things which you don't need ... has gone clean out of fashion". Mahon took mischievous delight in these jabs at the *Vogue* culture and seems only to have encouraged his friend further in this direction. Farrell concluded, "I'm sorry to have to break this news of the death of materialism so bluntly. I'm afraid it will come as a shock to some readers".[26] It may be the only time consumerism has been denounced so roundly in the pages of *Vogue*.

Mahon's unsuitability for his work revealed itself in other ways too. At the time, he was arguing for more space in the magazine for poetry, and he quarrelled with his editor over his insistence that a forthcoming poetry feature would have room for only one poem by each of the six poets profiled. He had led Douglas Dunn to expect something more expansive, and signed his note of apology to Dunn: "from the man in the Ladies' loo with his head in his hand".[27] When Mahon's "Spotlight on Poets" appeared, however, it ran to a substantial six pages and included especially commissioned photographs of each of the poets. Mahon used the piece to counter the notion of the sterility of British poetry (what he calls "the one-damn-thing-after-another school of English poets").[28] "The average poem published in Britain today is a sorry looking object", he began, "small, colourless and apologetic, as if it really wanted to be prose, but lacked resolution to decide".[29] Mahon proceeded to introduce an eclectic choice of younger voices: Brian Patten ("a kind of poetic analogue of the Beatles"), Douglas Dunn ("the archetypal 'provincial' poet"), Paul Muldoon ("genuine myth-making of a high order"), Jeni Couzyn ("a child spirit") and Hugo Williams ("a delicate elegiac lyricism"). Indirectly he was also countering criticism of himself and the view that he had cut himself off from his poetic roots by moving to London.

In early summer Mahon was in Dublin staying with the Heaneys when James Simmons' poem "Flight of the Earls Now Leaving" was published in *The Irish Times*.

> The famous nest of singing birds has flown
> across the border or across the foam.
> Mahon was too fastidious for Belfast,
> he fled to Dublin, but that didn't last,
> onward and upward, the ambitious rogue
> rests now in London, on the staff of *Vogue*.
> And Heaney's hiding in some quaint retreat
> in Wicklow or at large in Baggot Street,
> talking with editors in Dublin bars
> far from his students and his seminars.[30]

The charge was not merely that Mahon and Heaney had left the North, but that they had done so for self-serving reasons; in Mahon's case, in order to break into commercial journalism. Edna Longley recognised the personal nature of the decision and the untenable position Mahon occupied because of his Ulster Protestant background. Writing in the pages of the *Honest Ulsterman*, she noted lightedheartedly:

> Derek Mahon
> Is doing all he can
> To rid his imagination
> Of the Northern Irish situation[31]

Mahon's *Vogue* feature on young British poets had in some measure been a defensive piece, an assertion that there was indeed poetic life abroad. But Simmons's attack was too direct and too personal to be shrugged off as a humorous jab. Mahon felt its sting, and he chose to reply in kind—in verse—not in the pages of *The Irish Times*, but in the London-based *New Statesman*.

"Afterlives" is a poem about going home and the remembrance of a former life, a poem in which place acts as a marker for change in the speaker. It opens with a characteristic Mahon moment: morning after a shower of rain, a first-person speaker looking out of a high window:

> I wake in a dark flat
> To the soft roar of the world.
> Pigeons neck on the white
> Roofs as I draw the curtains
> And look out over London
> Rain-fresh in the morning light.
>
> This is our element, the bright
> Reason on which we rely
> For the long-term solutions.
> The orators yap, and guns
> Go off in a back street;
> But the faith does not die

That in our times these things
Will amaze the literate children
In their non-sectarian schools
And the dark places be
Ablaze with love and poetry
When the power of good prevails.

In the fourth stanza Mahon abruptly shatters this vision of the benevolent influence of love and poetry.

What middle-class cunts we are
To imagine for one second
That our privileged ideals
Are divine wisdom, and the dim
Forms that kneel at noon
In the city not ourselves.[32]

When the poem ran in the *New Statesman*, it was dedicated to Simmons, but to make sure the point was not lost on him, Mahon wrote him to explain his intentions:

The fourth stanza may repel you because it seems to reject the love and poetry posited earlier. It doesn't really do this, or only in one sense. What I'm saying is, the liberal position is untenable in the face of human nature, the evidence of history; although I grant you no other position is tenable either, or not for long. The dim forms may be shooting … or praying over the dead, as I prefer to think, or perhaps dying themselves. The point is that they are about some ancient, symbolic business, something that belongs to the dark side of life; and the fact of (liberal) daylight does not dispel them, it makes their outline clearer.[33]

The second half of the poem recounts Mahon's recent return to Belfast ("For the first time in years") and the shuddering of the ship as it moves up Belfast Lough. "The 'home' I'm talking about is not something I admire", Mahon explained to Simmons. "The ship 'trembles' and 'shudders' as it approaches, and so do I". The poem concludes with two of Mahon's most quoted stanzas:

And I step ashore in a fine rain
To a city so changed
By five years of war
I scarcely recognize
The places I grew up in,
The faces that try to explain.

But the hills are still the same
Grey-blue above Belfast.
Perhaps if I'd stayed behind
And lived it bomb by bomb
I might have grown up at last
And learnt what is meant by home.

Mahon tries to imagine how his perceptions might be different if he had stayed in Northern Ireland, as Longley and Simmons had done. Revealingly, he describes such an imagined scenario as staying "behind". When *The Snow Party* appeared the following year, Mahon opened the collection with "Afterlives".

That summer Derek and Doreen flew to Athens, "a sort of smaller, quieter Paris", where they saw Glyn Hughes and "his Greek missus", Roya. The friends drank the local Retsina, and visited the Parthenon at night.[34] From there Derek and Doreen took a boat to the islands of Patmos and Paros where they stayed with Desmond O'Grady, whom Doreen met for the first time. There was a thriving summer community on the island, and among the visitors that summer was Philip Haas, who would later become well known for directing *Angels and Insects* and other films.[35] O'Grady introduced Derek and Doreen to his friend Gisèle d'Ailly, a Dutch artist, who lived in an eleventh-century monastery on the island. Gisèle, in her sixties at the time, was a remarkable woman who had sheltered Jews from the Nazis during the German occupation of Holland. Staying with her for the summer was an archaeology student from Amsterdam, Stella Lubsen, who joined the small circle of friends. In the evening they would gather in the café. There was much impromptu reciting of poems under the stars and, one night, a reading in a local shop. During the Paniyiri Festival, hundreds of people descended on the monastery and, following a Greek Orthodox service, the small town overflowed with revellers eating, drinking and dancing in the streets late into the night.[36] Writing home,

Doreen reported all activity was "eating, swimming, and sleeping, and body and soul are slowly mending. Can't imagine London really exists".[37]

For Mahon, travel often entailed some form of literary assimilation, and while in Greece he read Cavafy and worked on a poem inspired by the Greek poet's personal history and his ambiguous relationship to his homeland. Born in Greece but raised in Liverpool, Cavafy was, on his return to Alexandria, an English subject in the city of his birth.

> There is no new country, no new sea.
> Only the same old city
> Shadows you night and day.
> You will spend your life
> In the same dim suburb,
> In the same house grow grey.

Mahon saw in Cavafy's personal history parallels with his own Anglo-Irish inheritance, but the poem is also a statement about the impossibility of escaping one's origins and one's past.

> In this city of homecomings
> Where all voyages end
> There is no way out.
> Your failure here
> Was a failure everywhere
> In the world at large, as if talked about.[38]

Soon after their return to London, Doreen discovered she was pregnant. When Mahon wrote O'Grady a note of thanks for his hospitality, he shared the news: "You may recall that on the day Mrs. Mahon and I arrived in Naoussa you put us to sleep for the afternoon in the bed in your front room", he wrote; "I'm afraid we didn't sleep straight away, as a result of which there will be another black Proddy in the world about mid-May".[39]

The approaching birth of their first child led the couple to take stock of their finances and their living arrangements. Mahon had turned in the typescript of *The Snow Party* and was actively exploring teaching opportunities abroad. When Robin Skelton passed through London, they discussed the possibility of an appointment at the University of Victoria.

He also sought advice from Walter Allen, Eamon Grennan and Brian Moore, and went so far as to solicit a letter of recommendation from D.E.S. Maxwell: "Perhaps you could say that you have seen me dealing with students and let them draw their own conclusions", he helpfully suggested.[40]

In the end none of these plans came to fruition, and when Doreen learned of an inexpensive flat on a nineteenth-century estate in Surrey, that seemed an attractive option. Their expenses would be less there, she would not have to climb stairs with a new baby and a move to the country would take her husband away from the alcohol-fuelled literary life of the city. "Ford Manor", as it had originally been named, was located just outside Lingfield, in the flight path for planes coming into nearby Gatwick Airport and only 50 minutes by train from Victoria Station. The estate had been built in the 1860s by the owner of the Bass Brewery. During World War I it had been used as a convalescent home for American soldiers, and during World War II had been occupied by the Canadian army. The once imposing home included a block of service buildings that had been converted into flats. There was a derelict greenhouse on the property with its glass smashed out, and "a disused garden shed where gas-masks from the war decayed".[41] More promising was the presence of a comfortable pub just beyond the estate's main gate, the walls of which were painted with murals left behind by the Canadian soldiers billeted there during the war.[42]

In November Mahon joined Heaney and Montague for a reading at the annual Cheltenham Festival, and the following month, when Doreen's school term ended, the couple began preparing for the move to Ford Manor. He reported to Longley, "we are now motorized, with a small black Ford Prefect which cost £25 and goes like a wet dream".[43] He submitted to *Vogue* a profile of Lord Grey Gowrie, whom he had first met at Harvard in 1966, when Gowrie was working as Robert Lowell's teaching assistant. He was planning to write another feature on Anthony Burgess when he was suddenly replaced at the magazine. As he explained it to Longley: "Deeko, rather to his relief in one respect, has been sacked as Features Ed ... and made literary editor instead, a less onerous post which consists largely of book-reviewing".[44] The downside, however, was that he was no longer on salary, but instead working on a modest retainer of only £1,500 a year. To make matters worse, his contract prevented him from signing with any other publication, and he again found himself in financial trouble.[45] This time Farrell came to his aid and gave him a loan from his Booker Prize money.[46]

In moving from London to Surrey, Derek and Doreen were, consciously or not, following the example of the Heaneys, who had recently moved from Belfast to rural Wicklow. The change had been liberating for Heaney. It had ushered in a period of creativity, and Mahon was no doubt hoping for similar results. For Heaney, however, the move had marked a reconnection to his rural roots; Mahon's move was a radical dislocation for a poet whose subject was most at home on city pavements. As he would later observe, "Seamus is very sure of his place. I've never been sure of mine".[47]

With his change of duties at *Vogue*, Mahon's editor declined to pay his travel expenses to Rome to interview Burgess. He told Desmond O'Grady the magazine was reluctant "to finance boozy binges abroad if they can be avoided", but when an Arts Council grant came through, he decided to make the trip at his own expense.[48] He spent several days in Rome, and O'Grady went with him to his lunch meeting with Burgess. The whole trip was a "very unsober time", and O'Grady caused something of a scene when he broke his plate during lunch.[49] Mahon's account of the visit would run in *Vogue* a few weeks later. Despite a transport strike, he was back in London in time to move house. They had sublet the Observatory Gardens flat, and Mahon was speaking of the move as permanent.

Although the poem would not appear in print for a couple of years, it was soon after the move to Surrey, during Doreen's first pregnancy, that Mahon wrote "Ford Manor", with its glimpse of their new life:

Even on the quietest days the distant
Growl of cars remains persistent,
Reaching us in this airy box
We share with the fieldmouse and the fox;
But she drifts in maternity blouses
Among crack-paned greenhouses—
A smiling Muse come back to life,
Part child, part mother, and part wife.[50]

Maurice Leitch visited them in their new home and recalls waking to the sound of a typewriter and thinking this was the way a writer should live. Only later did he learn that Mahon was not composing new poems but typing up job and fellowship applications.[51] That spring one of his letters paid off: he learned he had received the Henfield Writing Fellowship at the University of East Anglia. The three-month appointment was to run from April to June, an inconvenient time since Doreen was expecting in May. But the pay was not to be turned down, and Mahon could remain in Lingfield and commute by train to Norwich when he had to make one of his occasional appearances.

Mahon reported to Longley that the university had the appearance of "a light engineering works built on a golf course".[52] He was given a room with a view of the Careers Office (prompting numerous jokes) and he met with creative writing students in "a Hobsbaum-like session" once a week. He was responsible for organising a university reading series, and among those he invited to read was Andrew Waterman, whom he had known in London. On the day of Waterman's reading, he and Mahon met at Liverpool Street Station and, as he later recalled, they spent the trip to Norwich drinking in the buffet car.[53]

In May Doreen gave birth to a son at the Crawley Hospital in Surrey. "The infant duly appeared, a manchild of wondrous aspect, and is called Rory", Mahon reported to O'Grady in biblical tones.[54] Rory is an anglicised form of the ancient Gaelic name "Ruaidhri" or "the red-haired king". Mahon had turned to Irish history, rather than the King James Bible, for a name. He was having difficulty adjusting to the introduction of "Roarin' Rory" into his and Doreen's life together, and by all accounts the couple struggled to establish a new pattern to their lives.[55] Doreen's friend Patricia Moynagh came from London to offer what help she could, but for his part Mahon was glad to slip away from parental responsibilities at any opportunity.

A few weeks after Rory's birth he and Doreen were invited to a Claddagh Records party in London, attended by Robert Graves and William Empson, where he met Robert Lowell for the first time. He and Lowell chatted about Belfast, which Lowell had recently visited, and the older poet invited Derek and Doreen to visit him and Caroline Blackwood at their country home in Kent.[56] Mahon was thinking about proposing a magazine feature on Lowell, but following the recent changes at *Vogue*, that came to nothing.

When his East Anglia fellowship ended, Mahon seized the opportunity to escape from domestic life and go to Ireland for the annual Yeats Summer School, where he had been invited to lecture on the novels of Brian Moore.

From there he attended the Kilkenny Arts Week events where Heaney had arranged the poetry programme and where Lowell and Richard Murphy also read. *The Snow Party* had just been published, and Edna Longley's review ran in *The Irish Times* at the start of the week-long series of concerts, exhibitions and readings. "Launched without the ballyhoo of *North*, signalling less obviously its relevance to the present conflict, it equally speaks for a representative Northern Irish (Irish) imagination", she opened her review. Heaney's *North* had been published just a few weeks before, and Longley continued with the inevitable comparisons: "Whereas *North* by its very title opts for involvement, however qualified, the title poem of *The Snow Party* apparently opts or even drops out".[57] She noted the way "The Snow Party" and "The Last of the Fire Kings", poems she picked out for particular praise, betrayed Mahon's own wish "to be through with history". Though less strident in her remarks than Simmons, Longley too took Mahon to task for his tendency towards flight, noting, "the poet faces the plausible charge that he has opted too far out".[58]

Despite this criticism, she closed the review on a high note, calling "A Disused Shed in Co. Wexford" "an extraordinary tour de force".[59] All in all it was a perceptive and appreciative piece, but not without barbs. When she reviewed the collection a second time in *The Honest Ulsterman*, she was even more direct: "We must hope that [the collection's] author continues to fight the temptations of silence, exile and shunning".[60] Poets were being judged by how they engaged with the subject of political violence; appearing alongside this second review was Ciaran Carson's infamous review of *North*, in which he called Heaney "the laureate of violence".[61]

The poets invited to Kilkenny were housed at the home of the painter Barrie Cooke and his partner Sonja Landweer, just outside the town. Heaney had warned Lowell that sleep might be difficult because of the cries of peacocks in the couple's garden.[62] Meeting Lowell for only the second time, Mahon thought he seemed on the verge of an "episode", but Lowell might well have said the same about him.[63] Mahon was drinking heavily that week; Elgy Gillespie, an *Irish Times* reporter, recalls with embarrassment a scene at Kyteler's Inn when Mahon lunged for her as he toppled to the floor, pulling her down with him. Lowell and Richard Murphy could only look on helplessly.[64] The festival was plagued by other mishaps too: on the evening of Lowell's reading, the van that was to have brought the poets into town wouldn't start, and they had to push it down the drive in a futile effort to jump start the dead vehicle. When they finally reached Kyteler's, the microphone wasn't working and Lowell had to read without it.[65] Despite these difficulties, Mahon's own reading went well, and his bad behaviour on the opening night was forgiven when, despite being hungover, he got up and gave a strong reading from his new collection. "White-faced, he sat upon a window-ledge and accepted the succor of Heaney's arm and a jar," Gillespie later wrote of the evening.[66]

By that autumn Mahon was able to report to Douglas Dunn that he and Doreen were "slowly clambering out of the distraught insomniac condition pertaining to earliest parenthood".[67] His parents visited that Christmas to see their grandson and their son and daughter-in-law in their new home, but it seems Mahon was already thinking of another move. He was inquiring about possible teaching posts, or any steady employment, and was disappointed when Michael Longley hired an assistant at the Arts Council of Northern Ireland without mentioning the opening to him. In January, however, he learned through Jim Randall that one of his inquiries had panned out. The position of poet-in-residence at Emerson College in downtown Boston was his for the asking. Mahon mailed a set of his latest poems—part of his *Light Music* sequence—to Emerson's literary journal in anticipation of a move to America later in the year.

Mahon had accepted an invitation to participate in the Festival of Ulster Poetry to be held at London's Institute of Contemporary Arts in February. Ted Little had approached Longley to help organise the events and Longley had written with a list of "Group A" and "Group B" poets who should be included. Among the Group A poets was John Hewitt, "the spiritual daddy of most of us"; John Montague, "a sort of bridge figure between Hewitt & Co. and my own generation"; James Simmons, "the troubadour in our midst"; and Seamus Deane, "more of a critic than a poet, but … our only fully.fledged egghead". Seamus Heaney "requires no introduction". Longley added, "I grew up, poetically speaking, with Heaney and Mahon and don't think one is better than the other", but he reserved his most extravagant praise for Mahon, naming him

… the Stephen Dedalus of Ulster poetry! One of the most gifted poets I know and the successor, in my opinion, of Louis MacNeice whose view of Ireland Mahon extends and deepens. *The Snow Party*, his latest collection, reflects the Ulster tumult with more subtlety and complexity than Heaney's *North*, and his long poem, "A Disused Shed in Co. Wexford", is the best poem any of us have written.[68]

Longley also included a B list of younger poets and outlined for Little's benefit some of the perils of such an event. "I write at such length because the Ulster crisis has to be taken with absolute seriousness, and because only the best poetry which has coincided with, and occasionally grown out of, it should be celebrated", he wrote Little. All the poets he recommended

> … have reservations if not serious regrets about the emphasis of an anthology such as *The Wearing of the Black*, and most, I know, would prefer not to take part in an event which attempted to sell itself through the Northern Irish tragedy. This is why I must have appeared rather jaundiced to [Derek] Bailey when we met in Belfast recently: I had just refused to take part in a symposium with a title like "The Artist and the Troubles" or "The Embattled Arts". Life and art just aren't like that, though of course during a week of Ulster poetry the troubles would loom large, directly and, in much of the best work, indirectly. Neurotic ragbags like some recent anthologies only make a shallow mockery of Ulster's complexities and corrosions and of the imaginative efforts of artists to come to terms with them.[69]

Longley was referring to a recent meeting with the jazz guitarist Derek Bailey and to Padraic Fiacc's 1974 anthology *The Wearing of the Black*, in which a generous selection of Mahon's poems, as well as his own, had appeared. The view he took such pains to explain was one Mahon shared.

When the final schedule was announced, Longley was surprised to see listed with the poets he had recommended Paul Yates, a young poet from Belfast whose forthcoming collection *Sky Made of Stone: War and Other Poems* would violate all the sensitivities Longley had gone to such lengths to explain. Longley wrote to Little to express his displeasure at Yates's inclusion on the programme and added "one member of the team feels strongly enough about Yates to contemplate withdrawal".[70] That person was Mahon, who did indeed pull out of the programme, resulting in some last-minute reshuffling of the schedule. When the ICA released a revised schedule, the programme included pairs of readers composed of a Group A and a Group B poet. John Montague was paired with Tom Paulin, John

Hewitt with William Peskett, Michael Longley with Paul Muldoon, James Simmons with Michael Foley, and Seamus Heaney with Frank Ormsby. Paul Yates—the odd one out—joined Hewitt and Peskett. The press release added, "Derek Mahon's poems will also be read", without further explanation.[71]

A photograph taken in the spring shows Mahon with Rory in a baby carrier on his back, and Doreen—the former Trinity acting student—posing for the camera with a daffodil in her teeth. This image of bucolic family life was misleading. Mahon would often slip away to London where he would meet friends in one or another of the pubs around Broadcasting House. Maurice Leitch recalls drinking in the George in Mortimer Street until the pubs closed for the afternoon at 3:00. At that point he and Mahon would move to the rather dingy Marie Lloyd Club (the "ML", as it was known), where one could continue drinking without interruption. When the pubs reopened, they would retrace their steps back to the George.[72]

Mahon had begun carrying a Gladstone bag in which he kept a bottle at the ready, and his friends grew increasingly worried about his drinking. Montague shared his concerns with Heaney, "He doesn't drink for pleasure like us, but extinction", he wrote, "as if he can't stand the dishonesties of our world".[73] Montague was perhaps over-theorising matters, but his concerns were real. When Mahon visited Belfast for a reading in March, the student paper noted his drunken condition. When Louis Asekoff visited Derek and Doreen in Surrey, he found himself in the midst of a family crisis. Doreen met him at Lingfield railway station, and in the car she broke down and confessed, "I just can't do it anymore. He drinks and he's not there".[74] It was in this state that Doreen came up with a desperate plan. She would go away for a week, and Derek would have to stay sober for the baby's benefit. It was a crazy idea, but her friend Sandra Leitch encouraged her—not so much for Derek's sake as for her own emotional well-being. As Sandra recalls, Doreen was no sooner out of the house than Derek rang up asking her husband, Maurice, to come stay with him and help with the baby. Maurice was an experienced father, and Sandra recalls the two men and baby had quite an enjoyable week. Doreen, however, was furious—so much for her ideas about "Derek shaping up for the week".[75]

Mahon's drinking was also taking a toll on his writing. He had begun a long poem, which he jokingly was calling "The Long Poem", but was having difficulty giving it sustained attention.[76] As he explained to Frank Ormsby, editor of *The Honest Ulsterman*, "Since the onset of paternity last year I haven't been able to think straight for more than a few minutes at a time, with the result that all recent poems are of great brevity".[77] He was referring to a new poem sequence called "Light Music", made up of brief vignettes. Many of the pieces read like fragments of what might have been fully formed poems under different circumstances, and indeed a number of them contain images or phrasing that would eventually reappear in other work. Mahon began to publish the first of these in magazines and journals in the spring of 1976, and in August he sent O'Grady a set of 15 of the new poems, including one whose origin lies close to "The Apotheosis of Tins":

The terminal light of beaches,
pebbles speckled with oil,
old tins at the tide-line
where a gull blinks on a pole.

Readers were divided about this new direction in Mahon's work, and he confided to Ormsby, "Big Mike [Longley] considers them trivial, I fear".[78]

In the summer Derek and Doreen learned they were expecting their second child. Mahon had precipitately—too precipitately, it turned out—resigned his *Vogue* post in anticipation of the move to America, but with a second child on the way they abruptly abandoned these plans and decided to remain in Lingfield. Once again Mahon found himself looking for work, preferably something with light responsibilities and good pay. In this state of extremity, he put his name forward for a Writer in Residence post at the New University of Ulster in Coleraine.

The arrival of a daughter on 13 February 1977 only compounded Mahon's anxiety. "Katherine Mahon safely delivered yesterday and resting in hospital with a copy of *Finnegans Wake*", he wrote the Longleys.[79] Either at Doreen's urging, or possibly of his own resolve, Mahon was trying to moderate his drinking. His friend Reggie Smith referred him to a doctor who had helped him through similar difficulties. There was a wait for treatment, however, and a hospital opening did not become available until three weeks after Katie's birth—the most inconvenient time. Mahon was admitted to Epsom Hospital, and Patricia Moynagh again came down from London to help out with Rory and the new baby in this time of emergency. The doctors prescribed valium for Mahon's anxiety and a regimen of vitamin B injections. In his second week he started group therapy. From the hospital he reported he was "a new man in the making, clear-eyed & rarin' to go as husband, father, &, one hopes, salaried employee".[80] Secretly, he knew he would drink again.

In this fragile state, Mahon was eager for some word about the Coleraine appointment, and he wrote to Simmons, "I've been really quite anxious about that Coleraine job, especially since the birth of my daughter Katherine two weeks ago. Full-time salaried employment now an urgent necessity".[81] Mahon admitted to Douglas Dunn how little new work he had been able to complete, something he attributed to "the oppressions of paternity—a hard graft let me tell you". As for his new daughter, "let us hope she marries a rich man".[82]

Over this difficult spring Mahon was in touch with Dillon Johnston, who had proposed that Wake Forest University Press publish a selection of his poems in the United States. Mahon was unhappy with the New York office of OUP and its lack of effort on behalf of his books. Nevertheless, Oxford was not prepared to hand his work over to another press, and Stallworthy wrote in March to say OUP could not accept the Wake Forest proposal. The idea of a selected Mahon now appealed to him, however, and he wrote to ask "would the Press consider the possibility that my next book—in, say, 1979—would be a bringing together of the poems in *Night-Crossing*, *Lives*, and *The Snow Party*". Having refused to allow Wake Forest to produce such an edition, OUP could hardly now refuse to publish it. "The reason I'd like to do it this way is that I think 'A Disused Shed in Co. Wexford' marks the end of one stage in my verse-scribbling progress, and constitutes a natural turning point. The other, more mundane, reason is that since the onset of paternity two years ago I've completed very little in the way of poetry and will not be able to offer you a new collection for, I imagine, quite some time".[83]

In March Mahon received the welcome news that he had indeed been appointed Writer in Residence at the New University of Ulster, and he and Doreen began rearranging their affairs for the move to Coleraine. It was the end of his "attempt at English country life".[84]

Chapter 9

| POET IN RESIDENCE

A few years later still the Majestic itself followed the boats and preceded the pines into oblivion.

J.G. Farrell, *Troubles*

Long before any thought of Coleraine, Mahon and Heaney had agreed to take part in a reading tour Longley had proposed two years earlier. The Arts Council of Northern Ireland had expanded its support for the literary arts and in recent years had sponsored a series of joint readings: Heaney, Longley and David Hammond had toured together in 1968 as part of a programme called "Room to Rhyme"; John Hewitt and John Montague had appeared together in "The Planter and the Gael" in 1970; and Paul Muldoon and James Simmons read together in "Out of the Blue" in 1974. From the beginning, the aim had been to link Northern Ireland's Catholic and Protestant traditions and "by weaving the two cultural traditions together to try and contribute to [a] community of enlightenment".[1] Longley proposed a similar tour featuring Heaney and Mahon which he suggested calling "In Their Element". "Since both refer frequently in their work to the four elements", he explained, "a comparison might be pursued by granting Heaney water and earth, Mahon fire and air".[2] Among themselves the friends dubbed the upcoming tour the "Heaney/Mahon Road Show".[3]

As the date approached, however, sectarian tensions in the North were running high. The Arts Council had been forced to cancel a traditional music programme in April, and in early May the United Unionist Action

Council (UUAC) called a strike. Barricades were erected on roads in an effort to enforce the strike, and businesses that remained open risked being targeted with violence. On the fifth Longley reassured Heaney "if there is any risk by the end of the month, we shall of course postpone 'In Their Element'".[4] The strike, however, was called off on the 13th and the week-long tour opened 10 days later at the Ulster Museum, during the annual Belfast Festival. Katie was only 12 weeks old, so Doreen remained in Lingfield with the two children; Patricia Moynagh again came to help out in Derek's absence.

Longley had arranged for a special publication of his two friends' work which featured an attractive graphic representation of the four elements on a silver reflective cover. Paul Muldoon was working for BBC Northern Ireland at the time, and he gave the tour a lift by producing an accompanying radio programme in which Mahon and Heaney spoke about their poetry. Although his chapbook *Light Music* had just been published, Mahon passed over those new pieces and chose to read instead some, by now, familiar choices: "Glengormley", "In Carrowdore Churchyard" and "The Snow Party". He added "Ford Manor" and "Penshurst Place", two new poems written during his time in Surrey.

The three friends visited a different venue each night: Irvinestown (where they read at the aptly named Mahon's Hotel), Omagh, Derry, Magherafelt, Banbridge and Ballycastle. Despite Mahon's recent hospitalisation and resolutions, the tour turned into a week-long drinking session.[5] Touring together invited comparisons, and Mahon offered his own perspective on these in his remarks for the BBC broadcast. "Seamus has had the good fortune to grow up in a rural setting.... I had the misfortune to grow up in a rather more suburban setting", he began. Heaney's rootedness in rural traditions had been an enabling influence for his poetry, but Mahon's own experiment at country life had not had the same effect. There is a marked contrast between Heaney's poems of rural life and Mahon's recent Surrey poems. The two friends were emphasising these differences, but Mahon seems to have felt disadvantaged by the role this cast for him. "One can only deal with one's origins as one finds them", he commented.[6] At the end of the week, sectarian tensions were still running high, and Longley made sure he saw Heaney safely onto his train in Ballycastle following the final reading.[7]

When Peter Fallon asked Mahon to contribute to an anthology of Irish poetry he was planning, Mahon sent him "Ford Manor" and "Penshurst

Place".[8] Relocation required a kind of creative recalibration for Mahon, and he was struggling with the consequences of his upcoming move to Coleraine. His ambivalence reveals itself in the new poem he was writing at the time which he would dedicate to John Hewitt, that poet of the home ground. "A Departure" (later entitled "Going Home") is neatly balanced with five stanzas about Lingfield and five about Coleraine, and it betrays something of Mahon's uncertainty over his own proper place:

> I am saying goodbye to the trees,
> The beech, the cedar, the elm,
> The mild woods of these parts
> Misted with car exhaust
> And sawdust, and the last
> Gasps of the poisoned nymphs.
>
> I have watched girls walking
> And children playing under
> Lilac and rhododendron,
> And me flicking my ash
> Into the rose bushes
> As if I owned the place;[9]

Here, Mahon's capacity for role-playing and mimicry is on full display. He strolls the grounds as if he owned the place, "as if I belonged here too", he puts it in a later stanza. His sense of ownership reveals itself, however, not in some form of rural husbandry but in a display of defilement. Flicking his cigarette into the rose bushes betrays his resentment, as does his more pointed statement from the sequence "Surrey Poems": "I have a right to be here too".[10]

The upcoming move seems to have shaken his sense of self, and the title changes the poem underwent underscore his uncertainty over whether he was leaving or arriving. "A Departure" also appeared under the titles "Goodbye to the Trees", "The Return" and "Going Home". So what was his point of orientation? In its earliest forms the poem included the place-specific tag "Lingfield-Coleraine, 1977", reflecting its dual position as a poem of both departure and arrival, yet when Mahon describes the place he is going to in the final five stanzas, he depicts it as a series of absences:

> But where I am going the trees
> Are few and far between.
> No richly forested slopes,
> Not for a long time,
> And few winking woodlands.
> There are no nymphs to be seen.

Despite his relief over the Coleraine appointment, "A Departure" reveals a deep anxiety about the move he was making.

Coleraine is located at the mouth of the River Bann, not far from the towns of Portstewart and Portrush. Its seaside location satisfied one of Mahon's criteria for a hospitable place to live, and it was close to Doreen's mother, in nearby Portballintrae. The New University of Ulster had been created in 1969 when it had been decided that Northern Ireland needed a second university. The selection of Coleraine as the site had been a controversial one, however, since it was widely viewed, as Mahon would later explain, as "a deliberate slap in the face" to the Catholic community of the city of Derry 30 miles to the west. Mahon would later come to view that "original error" as one of the direct causes of the outbreak of violence in the North. "The Civil Rights movement had been active for some time, concentrating its attention on such issues as jobs and housing; but the decision to choose Coleraine (a market town with no intellectual tradition) over Derry created a quantum change in the 'minority' perception of Unionist arrogance and complacency".[11]

When Mahon wrote that harsh assessment, his feelings towards the town had hardened, but at the end of 1977 the move seemed to offer some release from financial worries, a certain modest academic recognition and, for Doreen, help with the two children. Whatever hopes he and Doreen may have had for this new chapter in their lives, however, were dashed almost immediately. He had not been successful controlling his drinking, and the strains in their marriage followed them to Coleraine.

Doreen reported to a friend that winter that they had attended a party where Derek had been rationed to a single pint of ale. She added, "he needs to stop all drinking whatsoever, as he still seems to be dependent on it at moments of crisis".[12] By the spring, however, these efforts were again failing, and with no end to the destructive cycle in sight, the couple separated. Doreen and the children went to stay with her mother, and Derek took a room in the Northern Counties Hotel in Portrush. Sandra

Leitch, Doreen's friend in London, recalls "it was quite an organized split up". Life changes "as it should" when there is a baby involved.[13]

The Northern Counties Hotel makes a brief appearance in "The Chinese Restaurant in Portrush", where we glimpse the newly homeless Mahon eating out on prawn chow mein in the early spring ("the doors that were shut all winter / Against the north wind and the sea-mist / Lie open to the street"). The poem, an oblique treatment of Mahon's new circumstances, anticipates one of his later work's recurring preoccupations: the loss of a former home—either a place or a state of mind—and the impossibility of return. It anticipates by more than fifteen years "Chinatown", another poem in which a Chinese restaurant serves as a substitute for the lost home.

> While I sit with my paper and prawn chow mein
> Under a framed photograph of Hong Kong
> The proprietor of the Chinese restaurant
> Stands at the door as if the world were young,
> Watching the first yacht hoist a sail
> —An ideogram on sea-cloud—and the light
> Of heaven upon the hills of Donegal;
> And whistles a little tune, dreaming of home.[14]

A persistent theme of Mahon's poetry is the longing look back to a time and condition of former innocence. On this spring morning, it is "as if the world were young". That oblique "as if" recalls the "as if" of "A Departure". Both, in fact, remind us otherwise. The upheavals and displacements that have brought this restaurant proprietor to this northern shore are not named, but that prehistory haunts the poem. The sunlight on the hills of Donegal and the sight of "the first yacht" hoisting sail signal a new beginning, even as the restaurant proprietor dreams of his past life, represented by a framed photograph of Hong Kong.

Mahon found in this vignette an ideogram for his own circumstances and, more broadly, for a universal condition of homelessness. A colleague recalls that he was a "forlorn figure" in the days and weeks after his separation from Doreen, and that he could often be found drinking alone in the Senior Common Room or at his hotel.[15] When his condition worsened in the spring, he was admitted to the Gransha Hospital in Derry, where he spent several weeks drying out and undergoing aversion therapy.

Up until his hospitalisation, he had managed to continue reviewing regularly for the *New Statesman*, but his reviews ceased between March and May. A planned reading in Hull with Douglas Dunn and Andrew Motion came and went without Mahon showing up, and days later he wrote to the organiser to ask that he "forgive this shambles".[16]

It was while Mahon was in this fragile state that his colleague at Coleraine, Andrew Waterman, penned a harsh portrait of him in Gransha Hospital, "On the Mend":

> And also in the Male Ward, there's our friend
> the alcoholic artist. Visiting
> you he scatters litter, yanks a door
>
> to wrench a Lucozade-top off so gouts
> splatter annoying the cleaners. Insufferable
> the suffering can be: by turns he fawns,
> insults, all nerve-ends frayed; once, turkey-faced
>
> accused we'd swayed his never-worn estranged wife,
> then waddled huffing down the corridor.
>
> Well, outside, in a Belfast pub they'd smash
> his face for less … But, 'He needs help', we say.[17]

This attack was provoked, in part, by Mahon's accusation that Waterman had made advances towards Doreen. Certainly Mahon harboured such suspicions, and expressed them in early drafts of a new poem called "The Old Snaps", which he originally intended to dedicate to Doreen. "Women are born mistresses or wives", he wrote in lines later dropped from that poem:

> You, love, were a born mistress
> But who can relive their lives?
> Now, in our problematical distress,
> You know where the old snaps are—
> Framed for ever in your heart and mine
> Where no hands can twist or tear.[18]

The lines would be rewritten before the poem appeared in print and the compromising dedication dropped. "We have never known a worse winter", he wrote in the published version, but, in its earliest draft form, it is a peculiar love poem that betrays a still-fresh hurt.[19]

The novelist Jennifer Johnston lived nearby and visited Mahon in the hospital, which she recalls was more "like a terrible prison".[20] By late May, though, Mahon was able to report to Longley that the cure had worked. "I take one antabuse every morning (one drink and I collapse) and a sleeping pill every night, and I feel better than I've done for ages".[21] In this state he looked back on the wreckage of the past months with remorse and anguish. Writing to D.E.S. Maxwell, he confessed: "Ford Manor is now a thing of the past, except for the last electricity bill and the few remaining lettuces, to which you are welcome should you find yourself making a nostalgic pilgrimage".[22] He was memorialising not only Ford Manor but also Coleraine, his hopes for his university appointment and the idyll of his own marriage.

Mahon resumed book reviewing in June with a review of Craig Raine's first collection, *The Onion, Memory*. He praised the title poem, which describes a visit between Raine and his ex-wife: "Divorced, but friends again at last, / we walk old ground together". The subject of an estranged couple who have achieved a new relationship was particularly appealing to him at the time, and Mahon described it as "the one moving poem in the book, and the most achieved".[23]

At the end of the spring term he was still without a home, and he threw himself on the hospitality of friends. "I am leaving this benighted province to tour the south and write sycophantic articles about authors willing to put me up for a few nights", he wrote Maxwell.[24] With the end of the term he also drew no university pay, and was hoping to get by on the modest income he received from reviewing and writing the occasional journalistic piece. He planned to write a profile of Jennifer Johnston for *Vogue* or possibly one on Montague.[25]

Friends were doing what they could to help him through this time, and as a result of Johnston's efforts he was commissioned to write the television screenplay for her novel *Shadows on Our Skin*, which had been shortlisted for the Booker Prize the previous year. The new work proved a good fit. Mahon would have seen something of himself in the protagonist of Johnston's novel, a young boy with an interest in poetry growing up amid violence and bigotry. One of the novel's key scenes lays bare the young Joe's fear when he conceals his older brother's handgun during a search of his family's home by British soldiers. The scene is reminiscent of Mahon's similar probing of childhood fear, also centred on a gun, in his autobiographical children's story "A View from the Long Grass". In both stories a child discovers an inherited link to ancestral violence, though in adapting Johnston's novel Mahon assumed a Catholic persona.

With the arrival of summer Mahon went to Dublin, where he spent a week with the Heaneys. O'Grady passed through en route to Limerick, but their visit lacked its usual lightheartedness. Mahon later apologised for his sombre mood, attributing it to "the peculiar mechanics of withdrawal from the demon drink. I don't expect to be liked very much at this stage". He assured O'Grady he was "off the drink (for good, I hope) and beginning to do, in absentia, what I should have been doing from the beginning—my best for Doreen, whom I love above all persons and whom I have signally failed to make happy and at peace. If she gives me a second chance I shall grasp it with both hands and this time it will work".[26]

The following Sunday, Richard Ryan drove Mahon to Ballymoney, County Wexford, where Eamon Grennan was living in a tower house on the coast. He and Grennan walked along the beach and Mahon confided to his friend what a terrible year he had had in Coleraine.[27] Grennan recalls he was "running away from drink" and "deeply depressed".[28] Mahon had hoped to stay a couple of weeks, but Grennan was expecting his parents the following weekend, so on Friday they drove into Wexford and a dejected Mahon boarded the bus for Cork, where John and Evelyn Montague were expecting him. Two surviving poems from this summer—"The Attic" and "Everything Is Going To Be All Right"—offer glimpses of Mahon in the Montagues' attic room.

> At work in your attic
>   Up here under the roof—
> Listen, can you hear me
>   Turning over a new leaf?
>
> Silent by ticking lamplight
>   I stare at the blank spaces,
> Reflecting the composure
>   Of patient surfaces—

I who know nothing
   Scribbling on the off-chance,
Darkening the white page,
   Cultivating my ignorance.

It had been his Aunt Kathleen who had described his childhood writing as "scribbling", but in his fragile condition he adopted the disparaging word himself.

During the summer, while living with the Montagues, Mahon met the journalist Mary Leland, a regular contributor to *The Irish Times* and the *Cork Examiner*. She had recently separated from her husband and their similar circumstances and need for companionship brought them together. They began seeing each other regularly, either meeting at the Montagues' home or going for walks or drives. Mary would later base the character Dan Hackett on Mahon in her short story "Passing the Curragh". In this loosely autobiographical story, Hackett is remote and emotionally unreachable. "I know when the stage is too small for me", he says to Louise in the story. "I move as soon as I can see the place I want to get to".[29] To Mary, Mahon seemed "something of a refugee", fleeing drink, depression and what she called "active suffering". Recalling the summer years later, she would admit "we really were no great help to each other".[30]

Evelyn Montague saw Mahon daily during the summer and thought he was making good progress. He was writing again, and the BBC was moving forward with plans to produce his adaptation of *Shadows on Our Skin*. By the end of July she reported, "we have succeeded in healing Derek". Much to her alarm, however, he showed no sign of leaving, and she warned her husband that her generosity wasn't endless.[31] And so in August, Mahon relocated to the nearby harbour town of Kinsale, either at Evelyn's insistence or on his own volition. There he took an attic flat on Denis's Quay, across the road from the Kinsale Yacht Club. He spent the last weeks of summer strolling the streets of the picturesque town with the last of the holiday visitors, listening to the screeching of gulls and the clink of sailboat riggings.

On his return to Coleraine, he moved into another temporary residence—a Georgian house in Portrush overlooking the West Strand and the Arcadia Ballroom. In the distance, on a clear day, he could see Dunluce Castle, Fair Head and, just offshore, the chain of islands called the Skerries. Doreen and the children were still at her mother's in Portballintrae, but Derek was seeing them regularly and he confided to Longley he was hopeful of a reunion. Soon after his return, Mahon received word of a £4,000 grant from the Arts Council: a welcome—if temporary—release from financial worries. Money had been one of the many strains on his and Doreen's marriage, and Mahon shared with Montague that Doreen had taken note of his improved circumstances. "I think a reconciliation may be possible, though it will take a little time", he reported. "She seems to be very well, and looks younger and brighter than she did earlier in the year ... in fact, she looks bloody marvellous, and I want to marry her all over again".[32]

Mahon was making a real effort to avoid alcohol, and he boasted to Leitch, "I am so sober now that I'm thinking of becoming a Presbyterian minister". Leitch visited him at his new residence, and found the set-up depressing. The rooms were cold and empty except for a table, a chair and a bare bulb hanging from the ceiling.[33] Mahon would later describe the scene and offer a portrait of his mental state at the time in the poem "Craigvara House": "That was the year / of the black nights and clear / mornings, a mild elation touched with fear", he would write.

> I slowly came
> to treasure my ashram
> (a flat with a sea view, the living room
>
> furnished with frayed
> chintz, cane chairs and faded
> watercolours of Slemish and Fair Head);
>
> and it was there,
> choosing my words with care,
> I sat down and began to write once more.
>
> When snowflakes
> wandered on to the rocks
> I thought, home is where the heart breaks—
>
> the lost domain
> of week-ends in the rain,
> the Sunday sundae and the sexual pain.

I stared each night
at a glow of orange light
over the water where the interned sat tight,

I in my own prison
envying their fierce reason,
their solidarity and extroversion,

and during storms
imagined the clenched farms
with dreadful faces thronged and fiery arms.[34]

In an effort to divert him from his troubles, Peter Fallon proposed publishing a selection of Mahon's poems paired with those of another poet of his choosing. Mahon suggested instead a single long poem, "The Sea in Winter", which he had been working on intermittently for the last couple of years and had taken up again in Portrush.[35] He was also retyping his early poems—and revising some of them—for "a sort of interim collected poems".

The multiple crises of recent months heightened the importance of the book in his mind, and he took an unusual degree of interest in the details of its publication. Writing to Jacqueline ("Jacky") Simms, his editor at OUP, he requested that the new book appear in hardback, "my first hardback", and the cover feature Botticelli's *Primavera* or *The Allegory of Spring*. He wanted the three graces to appear on the back of the dust jacket and "the Flora figure, modelled on my wife" to be placed "slap bang in the centre of the front cover".[36]

These plans took on new importance for OUP when it learned that Heaney was leaving the Press as his US publisher to go over to Farrar, Straus and Giroux. OUP New York had planned to market Mahon's selected and Heaney's new collection together, and had hoped the joint reviews would boost sales of Mahon's book. With the departure of Heaney, OUP New York was less confident about a Mahon selected and was reconsidering their earlier refusal to allow Wake Forest to publish such a volume. James Raimes wrote his counterparts in London to suggest that OUP let Wake Forest proceed with a selection after all.[37] Simms was stunned by the reversal and replied with dismay:

The most amazing part of it was really the terrible news that we have allowed Seamus Heaney to go off to Farrar, Straus and Giroux. This is really disastrous, in the longest of contexts. He is the greatest Irish poet now writing, better thought of than Yeats at the equivalent period of his life, and a poet who will reap dividends in the future, in subsidiary rights. He is an investment as well as a great poet! It is surely a great blow to the English Lit. list in the States, and really to us here too, since we would give our eye teeth to publish Heaney, and at least you had him. What can have been the reasoning behind letting him go? Did you fight to retain him? We can't understand how you could calmly allow this to happen to your list?[38]

Simms was troubled, too, by what this meant for Mahon's own selected.

The extraordinary volte-face over Derek Mahon's work seems comparatively minor in this context. But surely you re-read your correspondence with us of a year or so ago, when we firmly assured Wake Forest and Derek himself that the Press could do so very much better than another US publisher for him. Of course it would have been convenient to publish Heaney and Mahon together, but it was not one of the main considerations when we discussed matters a year ago. What then has happened to your 'best efforts'?[39]

Heaney's decision to move to Farrar, Straus and Giroux had wide repercussions in the small world of poetry publishing.

In November Elgy Gillespie visited Mahon in Portrush to interview him for a "Saturday Profile" she was writing for *The Irish Times*. They met at "his gloomy seaside house", where Mahon put on a brave face under the circumstances.[40] He spoke of Doreen without acknowledging they were in fact separated at the time. "Doreen is from Portballintrae", Gillespie later wrote, "and he claims his only real outings at the moment are teaching his three-year-old Rory how to swim in the North County Baths".[41] Mahon was less than forthright, too, about his reasons for returning to Northern Ireland, saying mysteriously, "I came back for very complex reasons".[42]

He was still unsure about his and Doreen's future, but the couple was together in November when they presented Katherine Jane Mahon, "Katie", for baptism in the church in Cushendun where Rory and Doreen herself had been christened. Reporting on the events to Louis Asekoff,

Mahon explained that "for technical reasons you couldn't be a godfather, as we wished, but the witch-doctor extemporized a formula whereby you are 'associated with the moral and spiritual welfare' of the dripping, bawling star of the occasion".[43] Patricia Moynagh, who had helped so much in the days following Katie's birth, served as a second godparent.

Over the winter Mahon experienced a relapse. Michael Longley recalls him travelling by taxi from Portrush to Belfast where he was admitted to the Shaftesbury Square Hospital. He had been unable to turn to Doreen in this latest crisis—his most reliable support was still Longley, more than fifty miles away. That winter he again found himself back in Gransha Hospital. He missed a planned reading at Trinity College, and the whole painful cycle was repeated. On his release, he spent the weekend at Jennifer Johnston's home, and it was there he wrote "Derry Morning".[44] The poem describes that riot-ravaged city, with its helicopters whopping overhead, and equates the uncertain progress towards peace in the North with his personal struggle towards recovery. "A strangely pastoral silence rules / The shining roofs and murmuring schools; / For this is how the centuries work— / Two steps forward, one step back".[45] He marked the new year by mailing to Simms his selected poems, unaware of the transatlantic quarrel that had broken out between his British and American publishers.

Despite his continuing struggle to break the cycle of addiction, Mahon was writing well, and he followed "Derry Morning" with "North Wind" and "An Old Lady". The latter would eventually be retitled "Greta", after Doreen's mother, Greta Douglas. It forms part of a group of poems from this time, including "Father-in-Law", that reconstitutes a family centred not on his own parents but on Doreen's. In "North Wind" he takes the harsh climate of the northern coast as a corollary for his own psychic state:

I shall never forget the wind
On this benighted coast.
It works itself into the mind
Like the high keen of a lost
Lear-spirit in agony
Condemned for eternity

To wander cliff and cove
Without comfort, without love.

Against this meteorological and psychological background, he sets the townspeople's reassuring and familiar routines:

> But the shops open at nine
> As they have always done,
> The wrapped-up bourgeoisie
> Hardened by wind and sea.
> The newspapers are late
> But the milk shines in its crate.
>
> Everything swept so clean
> By tempest, wind and rain!
> Elated, you might believe
> That this was the first day—
> A false sense of reprieve,
> For the climate is here to stay.[46]

These cleansing moments appear so frequently in Mahon's work, they constitute a poetic signature. This is his moment. Despite history, genetic predisposition, addiction and other forms of determinism, perhaps, the poem suggests, one really can start anew.

Over the spring of 1979 Mahon was continuing to rework the manuscript of *Poems 1962–1978*: revising some, changing the titles of others, adding new poems and reordering the sequence as a whole. He added new stanzas to "The Sea in Winter", including one that questions the value of poetry ("And all the time I have my doubts / About this verse making …")[47] and inserted the line *"No tengo más que dar te"* ("I have no more to give you"), a late addition directed to Doreen. As he explained to Simms, "The Spanish phrase is engraved on a gold ring found near the wreck of the Armada ship *Girona* at Portballintrae near here, and suits my purpose admirably".[48]

The collection was to go to proof in May, and Simms was becoming increasingly concerned about Mahon's continued revisions. "My opinion as an editor is of no interest to me—only I do care about your poems", she wrote him early in the month. "I almost feel, but I suppose you would adamantly disagree, that your poems as they were first published exist now whether you like it or not".[49] Unable to dissuade him from further changes herself, she urged him to talk to Michael Longley. Aware of the difficulty he was causing, Mahon wrote in mid-May, "Tell me to stop this!", to which Simms replied, "Stop this!"[50] In the end, he was only able to stop revising when the time came for him to leave for America. Through the efforts of Dillon Johnston, whom he had met two years before, he had secured a one-month appointment at Wake Forest University in Winston-Salem, North Carolina. He had just left for America when Andrew Waterman's harsh portrait of him in hospital ran in *Encounter*. Looking back on his time in Coleraine, Mahon began telling friends the university should be pulled down, with Waterman beneath it.[51]

Mahon flew first to Boston and spent a week with the Heaneys, who were wrapping up the spring term at Harvard. Johnston had planned to attend a six-week summer seminar at Yale taught by John Hollander, and he and Mahon had arranged to meet in New Haven. There Mahon caused an awkward scene when he sat in on one of the seminars. He arrived late, and, on taking a seat, placed the remainder of a six pack of beer on the seminar table. It was reminiscent of the kind of behaviour he had engaged in as a Trinity undergraduate. Mahon took the train from New Haven to New York and spent the last two weeks before his Wake Forest appointment with Louis Asekoff.

Johnston accompanied Mahon to Winston-Salem ("Wakeful Forest", Mahon called it)[52] where he got him installed in a campus apartment sublet from a faculty member who was away for the summer. When Johnston returned to New Haven, Mahon was left on the deserted campus under a scorching summer sun. "This is a very odd place, smelling strongly of tobacco", he reported to Simms soon after his arrival. "The campus is way out of town—a small town in itself".[53] With temperatures in the nineties every day, Mahon sought relief from the heat at the university pool. He spent his evenings reading and smoking in the half-darkness of his apartment, surrounded by reproduction prints from Audubon's *Birds of America*.

A reporter for the local newspaper sat in on one of Mahon's classes and wrote a frank assessment of the new visiting writer-in-residence. "It is 9:30 on a sultry summer morning, and the dozen or so students seated around the table in a Wake Forest classroom are attentive but quiet.... Derek Mahon, a visiting Irish poet who is teaching a summer school course at the university, surveys the class from behind a small pile of books at the head of the table. His previous experience teaching at the New University of Ulster has left him unprepared for an American classroom". The reporter proceeded to describe Mahon's efforts to draw out his students. What did they know about W.H. Auden? When Mahon was met with silence, he plunged ahead, describing one episode after another of Auden's outrageous conduct during his years of alcoholic decline. When one particularly bold student interrupted, wanting to know if she could ask a question, Mahon bellowed, YES! "Alternately soliciting and rebuffing participation", the reporter wrote, "Mahon is perhaps not the most consistent of individuals. He may be by turns polite or abrupt, attentive to a conversation or lost in some private corner of his mind".[54] The newspaper account was as perceptive as it was disheartening. Any number of close friends and family—Doreen first among them—were familiar with this anxious and erratic behaviour.

Mahon's interest in Auden during his years of alcoholic crisis suggests a degree of self-awareness of his own precarious state. There was in his actions a strong element of mimicry. Mahon first met the female reporter at his faculty apartment wearing only "red, white, and blue underpants", as she noted in her newspaper account. Actually, it was a Speedo swimsuit, but Mahon was no Mark Spitz. He was, again, drinking heavily. Lee Potter, a colleague from the English Department, and his wife, Edith, intervened to get him into the university hospital. One student who had looked forward to the summer course reluctantly dropped the class, having decided "I wasn't interested in getting to know Derek Mahon".[55]

"Astronomy in North Carolina" (later entitled "The Globe in Carolina") offers a picture of the poet during this summer crisis. He later explained the background of the poem for a BBC interviewer: "I was there for a month, rather lonely, with my wife and children back home on this side of the water". He was maintaining the fiction that his separation from Doreen was simply a summer expediency forced on him by his temporary teaching appointment. "In the evenings I would generally sit reading, or smoking in the half-darkness, in the faculty apartment I'd been provided with.... On a table near the window stood a large terrestrial globe".[56] This globe set off a train of associations for Mahon, all of which emphasised his remoteness from Doreen. "It's the author who is out in space contemplating the Earth like an astronaut", he later explained to Dillon Johnston. The poem "switches suddenly to address, not the globe, but Mrs. Mahon, substantial embodiment of the female principle of which the globe is a symbol".[57]

... You lie, an ocean to the east,
Your limbs composed, your mind at rest,
Asleep in a sunrise which will be
Your midday when it reaches me;
And what misgivings I might have
About the true importance of
The 'merely human' pale before
The mere fact of your being there.[58]

In its earliest version, the poem contained an entomological mistake, a reference to chirping lightning bugs, which he corrected in later printings.[59] His successive revisions, however, went beyond corrections of fact and underscore the importance of the poem to him. He would expand the poem in the coming years from its original five stanzas to seven.

At the end of the summer, Mahon returned to Belfast to the news that his friend J.G. Farrell had drowned while fishing near his home on Dunmanus Bay. Mahon spent several days with the Longleys during which time he also saw a psychiatrist at the Shaftsbury Clinic and reported "nine months of unbroken sobriety".[60] (It was not true, but he was hoping he would be able to make it true in the coming months.) The circumstances of Farrell's death were not entirely clear—some suspected self-harm— but Mahon insisted on describing his death as a tragic accident in the obituary he wrote for the *New Statesman*. Farrell, it seems, had been fishing from a rock when he had been swept into the sea by the waves.

Whatever the specific circumstances, his friend's death at just 44 came as a great shock. Mahon admired greatly Farrell's depiction in his novels of the decline of Britain's imperial power, and shared Farrell's jaundiced view of contemporary society. They had been close, but, in addition to feeling that personal loss, he could not help but wonder what new work he might have gone on to produce had he lived. The Empire Trilogy was only the beginning of something larger, Mahon observed, adding, in a statement that applied to himself as well, "He measured himself ... against the giants of modern literature."[61]

Mahon was through with Northern Ireland. He had decided to return to London, even though the Observatory Gardens flat had been sublet and was not available. Instead he took a room in Walter Allen's home in Canonbury Square, just a short walk from where MacNeice had once lived, at 52 Canonbury Park South. The arrangements were temporary, and, as he explained to Patricia Moynagh, "The idea is that Doreen and the kids will come over when I've found a decent living space".[62]

Ronald Mason, the head of Radio Drama at the BBC, helped get Mahon a temporary job in the script unit. "I am Beebed for the foreseeable future", he wrote Asekoff, adding hopefully, "there may be a permanent job for me in the to-be-reconstituted Features Dept come next spring". He was spending his days at Broadcasting House and his evenings pursuing writing projects, which he hoped would be more lucrative than poetry. "Fuck poetry", he wrote Longley.[63] He considered—and later thought better of—a radio play set in a hospital ward, which would draw upon his own recent experiences. He also considered writing a play based on Thomas de Quincey's *The Opium Eater*, or an adaptation of Brian Moore's *Fergus*. He was looking forward to the publication of *Poems 1962–1978*, and searching for a more permanent residence—one that would help persuade Doreen to return. Housing prices in London were high, however, and, on top of that, "I have to disguise my accent when making inquiries of estate agents, in case they think I was the one who killed Lord Mountbatten".[64]

Mahon and Patricia Moynagh went together to the memorial service for J.G. Farrell at St Bride's in Fleet Street, and a couple of weeks later Mahon pitched the idea of a feature on his friend to the BBC radio producer Piers Plowright.[65] His *New Statesman* piece had been hurried, and he wanted to do a proper feature, one that would include interviews with Farrell's wide circle of friends.

In November *The Sea in Winter* appeared in a limited edition of 300 copies.[66] Peter Fallon had done his best with the book. Aware of the importance Mahon placed on his forthcoming OUP volume, Fallon rushed to beat that book into print, thus giving Mahon his first hardcover publication and avoiding the complications of royalties that might have been due to Oxford had *The Sea in Winter* followed publication of the poem there. Mahon had begun a long epistolary poem addressed to O'Grady years before, but the poem had developed rapidly during his time at Coleraine, where it is set and from which it draws much local colour. "October 1977–September 1978, Portstewart—Portrush", Mahon fixes the place and time in its first published form.

The poem would shrink from its original 22 stanzas to a mere 12 in later reprintings, but in its first, more expansive form it offers an intimate

Derek Mahon, c. 1944. (*Emory*)

"A first rate chorister": Derek Mahon in St Peter's Church choir robe, c. 1954. (*Emory*)

Derek Mahon with his father, Norman Mahon, and mother, Maisie Harrison Mahon, 7 Glenwell Park, Newtownabbey, Co. Antrim, c. 1961. (*Emory*)

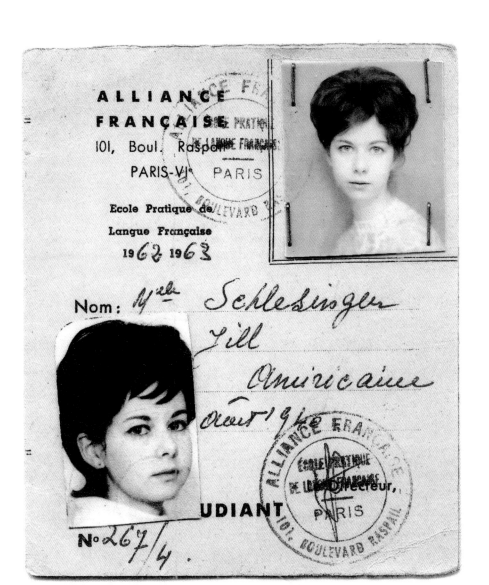

Alliance Française identity card for Jill Schlesinger, 1962–3. (*Courtesy of Jill Schlesinger*)

Peter Alscher, Ruth Grene and
Derek Mahon, Co. Wicklow,
c. 1964. (*Courtesy of Ruth Grene*)

Derek Mahon as best man
at the wedding of Michael
and Edna Longley, Dalkey,
Co. Dublin, 30 December
1964. (*Courtesy of Michael
and Edna Longley*)

"The Less Deceived": Derek Mahon and Michael Longley pose for a publicity photograph after sharing the Eric Gregory Award in March 1965. (*Emory*)

"The Poets Lie Where They Fell": Derek Mahon in Toronto, 1967. (*Courtesy of Paul Jackel*)

Derek Mahon, c. 1968. (*Courtesy of Gay O'Halloran*)

Derek Mahon reading at the Morden Tower, Newcastle upon Tyne, December 1970. (*Jeremy James/Morden Tower*)

Doreen Douglas, by A. Gascoigne, c. 1971. (*Emory*)

Derek and Doreen's wedding at St Mary Abbots Parish Church, Kensington, London, 30 September 1972. (*Courtesy of Glyn Hughes*)

Michael Longley,
Seamus Heaney and
Derek Mahon at Marie
Heaney's parents' home
in Ardboe, Co. Tyrone,
1977. (*Emory*)

Derek Mahon with Seamus
Heaney, *In Their Element*
reading tour, 1977. (*Emory*)

Craigvara House, Portrush, Co. Antrim. "That was the year of the black nights and clear mornings …" (*Emory*)

Derek Mahon (*centre rear*) on the set of *Summer Lightning* starring Paul Scofield, October 1984. (*RTÉ Stills Library*)

Derek Mahon with Cathal Ó Searcaigh and Pat King at Wake Forest University, North Carolina, 1984. (*Courtesy of Rachel Brown*)

Derek Mahon and Dillon Johnston at Wake Forest University, 1984. (*Courtesy of Rachel Brown*)

Derek Mahon with his son, Rory, and daughter Katie outside Doheny & Nesbitt in Baggot Street, Dublin, c. summer 1990, by Tony Gavin. (*Emory*)

Derek Mahon, c. 1995, by Bill Doyle. (*Emory*)

view of Mahon's time in Coleraine and a glimpse of his own state of mind
during that troubled period:

> When I returned one year ago
> I felt like Tonio Kröger—slow
> To come to terms with my own past
> Yet knowing I could never cast
> Aside the things that made me what,
> For better or worse, I am. The upshot?
> Chaos and instability,
> The cool gaze of the RUC.
>
> Also the prodigal son in *Ghosts,*
> Back on the grim, arthritic coasts
> Of the cold north, where I found myself
> Unnerved, my talents on the shelf,
> Slumped in a deckchair, full of pills,
> While light died in the choral hills—
> On antabuse and mogadon
> Recovering, crying out for the sun.

Mahon was reaching for literary models for his own recent experience,
in this instance Mann's *Tonio Kröger* and the mad son in Ibsen's *Ghosts.*

He also used the poem as an occasion to give vent to his doubts about
the value of poetry itself. Compiling the first selected edition of his poems
over recent months had reminded him how inconsequential an activity it
all was. "All farts in a biscuit tin", he calls it in early versions. Yet *The Sea
in Winter* makes a powerful counter argument. The poem as a whole has a
shape and a dramatic movement towards a state of restoration. From the
beginning that movement has been towards an ideal future:

> the day the Dying Gaul revives,
> the day the girl among the trees
> strides through our wrecked technologies,
> the stones speak out, the rainbow ends,
> the wine goes round among the friends,
> the lost are found, the parted lovers
> lie at peace beneath the covers.

By the end of the long poem, this future—this condition—is achieved by poetic force alone.

Mahon received advance copies of *Poems 1962–1978* in early November. He made a weekend trip to Portballintrae to present Doreen with a copy of the book, only to find her sick with the flu. He had dedicated the collection to her and to Rory and Katie. More than any other, this was Doreen's book. The cover featured a detail from Botticelli's *Abundance* in which a young mother walks towards the viewer, leading her children. Mahon was asking his wife to return to him. He was back in London to read from the new collection at the Poetry Society a few days later. Writing in the PBS *Bulletin*, he described the book as "the work of a young man who thought he knew quite a lot about one thing and another … and discovered that he knew, in fact, nothing of importance".

Chapter 10

| THE SCRIPTWRITER

In December Seamus Heaney chose Thomas Kinsella's *One and Other Poems*, Tom Flanagan's *The Year of the French*, and *The Complete Prose of Osip Mandelstam* for a "Books of the Year" feature in the *Sunday Times*.[1] A few days later Mahon confided to Peter Fallon, "I don't expect *Poems* to make much of a splash over here, since I've been lying low and a lot of people probably think I'm dead". He went on to take exception to a recent review that had remarked on his intelligence. "My intelligence is not, I hope, in question; but, as I need hardly point out, this is only one aspect, and not necessarily the most important, of the artistic enterprise". He added, "I will go largely unreviewed, which suits me fine, for they would only say that I was intelligent and go into the usual Marx Bros routine about the Northern Poets, i.e. the Ulster Poets. But none of this matters: I have other fish to fry".[2] A few weeks later he wrote Dillon Johnston that "the new Mahon book is out, but the country is strangely quiet. Can it be that nobody noticed?"[3]

In fact, *Poems 1962–1978* was widely reviewed over the coming months. Among the earliest was Brendan Kennelly's notice in *The Irish Times* in which he praised Mahon's lyric wit and called the collection "the best book of poems I have read for years".[4] Jack Holland praised the formalism of Mahon's poems, what he called his poise, scrupulousness and reserve.[5] A number of reviewers singled out "A Disused Shed in Co. Wexford";

Andrew Motion called it Mahon's "masterpiece", while Blake Morrison wrote it deserved its reputation "as one of the finest British poems of the past decade". Peter Porter even went so far as to use his review as an occasion to atone for an earlier editorial lapse: "As a literary editor, I once rejected this poem", he admitted apologetically in the pages of *The Observer*.[6]

The one negative note sounded was over Mahon's reworking of earlier poems. Simmons, always one to take a patronising tone with his fellow poets, noted "a few unhappy alterations".[7] Peter Porter expressed his dismay at finding "a poet under 40 devoting more time to tidying the drawers of his wardrobe than to adding new garments to it",[8] and Blake Morrison, after cataloguing a litany of Mahon's changes, added, "Whether these revisions are generally for the good is not at all clear".[9]

A secondary theme of the reviews was Mahon's conflicted relationship with Ireland. Andrew Motion noted his preoccupation with escape, an issue he suggested "has shown no sign of being resolved".[10] Blake Morrison, putting it differently, placed Mahon "in the community" of Northern Irish poets, despite being "the least locally attached". When Radio 3 devoted a Critics' Forum to a discussion of Mahon's poetry in mid-January, Frank Kermode, Claire Tomalin and Benedict Nightingale took up the inevitable subject of Mahon's treatment of the Troubles. Nightingale disagreed with the moderator's suggestion that Mahon had avoided the subject.

> I don't think he exactly avoids them, I don't think he is temperamentally perhaps equipped to cope with them ... he tends to wince away from them but he winces away in effect into a sort of philosophy that actually is his own, a philosophy of stoicism, renunciation, withdrawal, and I think he investigates the implications of opting out of society with some integrity and indeed with a great deal of interest.[11]

Nightingale argued that Mahon cast the Troubles in the context of a much longer and more extended view of human history. "I think he has long ago left the Irish Troubles behind him".

Mahon was back in Northern Ireland for Christmas and again saw Doreen and the children. He was still living at Walter Allen's home and working at Broadcasting House, which he was calling "the Ministry of Truth".[12] He was trying to give up drinking and struggling to break the repetitive cycle of craving, relapse and remorse. An unpublished and abandoned poem, "Bad Time", likely dates from these months. While he never allowed the poem to be published, a surviving draft offers a raw view of his emotional state during his separation from his wife and children.

It comes to most, sooner or later, the season
Of pain, perhaps of prolonged solitude,
When we are lost as in a dark wood,
Uncertain of our direction, and we spend
Days in circular thought, nights in despair.
How did it happen, how did we get there?
We hold on by instinct and unreason,
Not knowing when or if it will ever end.

It is hard then not to remember the good times—
The children laughing under a spring sky,
Relish in love and work, the casual dreams
Dreamt in the expectation of fulfilment;
The clamorous friends, gleeful activity,
A kind of life for which we knew ourselves
Intended, strange to this predicament
With the clocks thundering on silent shelves.

There are ups and downs, dictated not so much
By hopes and fears as by rhythms of which
We have no knowledge, therefore no control.
If this should be the dark night of the soul,
And perhaps it is, can we place our trust
In the dawn that follows the darkest hour?
Or will it simply get darker and darker,
A cold knife lodged forever in the cold breast?

Mahon was lost in Dante's dark wood and from this condition of despondency he offered a glimpse of his own strategies of coping:

We may take our rueful precautions as if this
Will indeed be the case, adopt a course

Of stoic reading, learn a bleak routine
Whose consolations fall somewhere between
Those of philosophy and those of art;
Have done with living, close the heart,
Wrap up in shrouds, lie down in a black box
And wait for the long night where no day breaks.[13]

In February London was the site of a six-week celebration of Irish arts and culture, A Sense of Ireland, which featured visual arts, music, theatre, dance, film, fiction and poetry. Most of Ireland's leading artists, Northern and southern, descended on the city for exhibitions and performances. Peter Fallon and Andrew Carpenter organised the readings, and among those whom they lined up were Eavan Boland, Seamus Deane, Paul Durcan, Seamus Heaney, John Hewitt, Aidan Higgins, Jennifer Johnston, Michael Longley, John Montague, Paul Muldoon, Richard Murphy, Desmond O'Grady and James Simmons.

Mahon dubbed the extravaganza "the feast of Ireland" but declined Fallon's invitation to take part. He planned, however, to attend some of the readings, telling Dillon Johnston he foresaw "great swilling of Perrier".[14] Heaney opened the literary programme with a reading at the Round House in Camden Town on 3 February. The following week there was a dramatic reading with music of John Montague's *The Rough Field*, and later a performance of Richard Murphy's *The Battle of Aughrim*.[15]

While the programme was a celebration of Irish art, the organisers were mindful of events across the Irish Sea. As one reporter put it, the festival organisers hoped "to pour art on troubled waters",[16] and another suggested the aim was to counter the stereotypical image of the Irish, "gun in one hand and rosary beads in the other".[17] The Irish ambassador noted blandly that the festival was an opportunity "to increase understanding and friendship between the people of these islands".[18] While Mahon would have been all for that, vapid though the statement was, he also would have taken a cynical view of the use of art for such ends. He found the treatment of art as a kind of news report on the state of the Troubles to be a limiting one, and he had skipped similar events when he thought the arts were being politicised.

Mahon was not alone in taking a dim view of the proceedings. A writer for the *TLS* noted:

Among the participants in this extraordinary marathon—I have heard it described in Dublin as a jamboree—are political scientists, historians, sociologists and economists who will be able to shed light on what Irishness, being Irish, or having a sense of Ireland mean. There will be so many of those that one hopes that the noisy arguments to which they will inevitably give rise will not drown out the voices of those equally distinguished literary men whose function appears confined to introducing each other and reading from their own recent output.[19]

In the end Mahon's decision not to participate was a personal one. He had only just returned to London after a disastrous two years in Coleraine, and the last thing he cared to do was to publicly celebrate his Irishness. While he was getting control of his drinking, he remained separated from his wife and children in an emotionally fragile state. He had returned to London vowing never to live in the North again. "Sorry I wouldn't read for you", he wrote to Peter Fallon, "but I'm a quirky bastard".[20]

Doreen visited for a week in early February, during the jamboree, and she and Derek were working at a reconciliation. One of Doreen's conditions for returning was that he get "a salaried job", and Mahon was making inquiries at a number of London publishers.[21] At the end of the week, after Doreen returned to Northern Ireland, Mahon took up the children's story he had begun during his recent time in America, "The Boy Who Fell in Love with a Bridge". The story tells of a young boy whose walks take him over a bridge until, one day, a storm sweeps it away. The story is a metaphor for his and Doreen's separation. The boy cries by the stream where the bridge once stood until a tall man comes along and helps rebuild it. "It won't be as good as the old one, of course, but at least it will be a bridge", he tells the child.[22] As he often does in his writing for children, Mahon adopts the persona of a young boy confronting for the first time life's cruelty. He sent a copy of the story to Patricia Moynagh, hoping to interest her in illustrating it as a children's book, but these plans never came to fruition.[23] The story meant more to him than it did to her.

More promising was his work for radio and television. At the end of February he did a Radio 3 feature on Heaney, and was interviewing contributors for programmes on J.G. Farrell and Olivia Manning. He and Piers Plowright would meet in the listening room at Broadcasting House to edit tapes and record Mahon's narration. Manning was in her seventies at the time, and the interview Mahon conducted with her was the last she gave before her death just a few months later. She used the occasion to warn about the ecological destruction of the planet and, more particularly, the threat to animal life. In the broadcast, Mahon called her "an ecology freak before ecology was fashionable".[24] What he most admired in Manning was the way her novels—like those of J.G. Farrell—traced civilisation's decline, whether expressed in the decline of empire or the destructiveness of a global world war. Her own experience of the war had, in fact, brought out the very best in her work. In her novels "historical fortunes and personal fortunes are intertwined", and her account of hers and her husband's experiences in Bucharest, Athens and Cairo at the start of war offers a kind of "chronicle of the age". Mahon's comments about her work are revealing for what they say about the artist's relationship to history. In writing her personal story, Manning gave artistic expression to the age, and it was that convergence of the personal and the historical that made the Balkan Trilogy such a fine achievement, he noted.[25]

In March Mahon's adaptation of Jennifer Johnston's *Shadows on Our Skin* aired on the BBC 1 television programme "Play for Today". Richard Hoggart, writing in *The Listener*, called it "the only British television play so far which seriously examines the experience of an ordinary Roman Catholic family in Northern Ireland during the conflict of the last 12 years".[26] Clive James called it the best play about Northern Ireland since Stewart Parker's *I'm a Dreamer, Montreal*. "Nobody but an Irish playwright would dare to paint his countrymen in such harsh colours", he noted appreciatively in *The Observer*.[27]

With the Manning and Farrell programmes completed, Mahon's BBC contract came to an end, and in April he moved back into Observatory Gardens, which he hoped to ready for Doreen's eventual return. On the success of *Shadows*, he took up an adaptation of Johnston's *How Many Miles to Babylon?*, or "Ballymoney", he joked with Longley.[28] He was reviewing for *The Observer*, the *London Review of Books* and the *TLS*, and working on new poems. In April he mailed Longley his Coleraine poem, "North Wind", and three new ones: "Brighton Poems", "Songs of Praise" and the anthropomorphic "Table Talk".

The version of "Brighton Poems" he sent Longley differs from "Brighton Beach" in an important respect. Dedicated to his Belfast friend Paul Smyth, then living in Brighton, the first part of the poem contrasts his and his friend's shared experiences as young men with their present circumstances,

Remember those awful parties
In dreary Belfast flats,
The rough sectarian banter
Of Lavery's back bar,
The boisterous take-aways
And moonlight on wet slates?

In the fourth stanza Mahon abruptly shifts to their present lives:

Now, pushing forty, we roam
At ease along the prom,
Grass-widowers to be sure
But grown sober and wise.
The sea shuffles ashore
Beneath pale mackerel skies.[29]

Mahon would later drop this reference to himself as a grass-widower, which could connote either a wife's seasonal absence from home or a spouse's sexual wandering. More often read impersonally as a poem about the decline of empire,[30] "Brighton Beach" was, in its original form, a deeply personal poem about Mahon's marital state at mid-life. He extended the meteorological action of "North Wind" into the letter that enclosed these poems, confiding to Longley, "the sun shines on Kensington Gardens, but I miss my wife and children".[31]

Over the summer Mahon reoccupied Observatory Gardens and began getting the flat in order in anticipation of a "family reunion in August".[32] "It will be a *House and Garden* dream of the good life, except there's no garden", he told Douglas Dunn.[33] Doreen and the children returned in time for the start of school for five-year-old Rory, and Mahon began sharing the good news with close friends. He marked his wife's return with a poem that takes a backward look at their time together in rural Surrey.

Two years we spent
down there, in a quaint
outbuilding bright with recent paint.

A green retreat,
secluded and sedate,
part of a once great estate,

it watched our old
bone-shaker as it growled
with guests and groceries through heat and cold,

and heard you tocsin
meal-times with a spoon
while I sat working in the sun.

He notes "a disused garden shed / where gas-masks from the war decayed", and, in Longley-esque manner, catalogues a scene of natural abundance—apples, chestnuts, ragwort, ladysmock, foxgloves and wood-anemones—before adding: "But how could we survive indefinitely so far from the city and the sea?"[34] Mahon had resolved the question posed by "A Departure" some years before, and, in fact, had never belonged in that rural idyll so far from city or sea. Following his family reunion, Mahon asked Dunn to return the manuscript of "Bad Time". That was all behind him, and he no longer wished to see the poem in print.[35]

Mahon and Doreen were together when Brian Moore and his wife, Jean, visited London in early September 1980. Mahon had admired Moore's writing for years—he had lectured on his novels at the Yeats Summer School a few years before—and now, as he contemplated television work, Moore was at the top of his list of those whose work he would like to adapt. Both men came from Belfast and a later television proposal for *The Temptation of Eileen Hughes* would draw the connections tightly: "Brian Moore was brought up as a Catholic though his ancestry was Protestant, while Derek Mahon was brought up a Protestant though his ancestry was Catholic".[36] Mahon rejected the conventional labels and saw in Moore a counterpart to himself and his own internal contradictions. The couples arranged to meet for lunch, and Derek and Doreen brought along three-year-old Katie. Mahon was hoping to get Moore's permission to adapt one of his novels for television. While supportive of the idea, Moore was being advised not to sell television rights for *The Temptation of Eileen Hughes* until he knew if it would be optioned for film, something he wouldn't know for some months. He was encouraging of Mahon's proposal, however, and he wrote afterwards to say how much he and Jean had enjoyed meeting.

The publication of Heaney's selected prose in the autumn offered Mahon an opportunity to speak about the poet's relationship to Ireland and to his broader contemporary world. In his review of his friend's book in *The Observer*, he noted that Heaney was at a mid-point of his career, "barely past 40". (No doubt he was thinking of his own approaching 40th birthday.) Heaney's discovery of his poetic voice, he recognised, was linked to his rootedness in the local and the particular. Heaney maps the parochial with sacramental care, denying the call of a "metropolitan" world beyond. As he had done in "The Woods", Mahon contrasted the rural and the metropolitan, another way of expressing his and Heaney's own contrasting—but complementary—orientations. Even though Mahon had resolved never to live in Northern Ireland again, he admired the uses Heaney had made of the provincial and the parochial.[37] "I was moved and—yes—proud to read your piece yesterday", Heaney wrote the following day, thanking him for "the laying on of hands".[38]

A couple of weeks later Mahon reviewed together Paul Muldoon's *Why Brownlee Left* and James Simmons's *Constantly Singing* for the *London Review of Books*. Simmons had recently written an epistolary poem to Mahon that painted a harsh portrait of him during his Coleraine time. "Dear tormented poet / we remember your presence here / gratefully in the cold austere North...." Simmons notes those features of Coleraine that Mahon describes in his poems: the wind and rain, echoing streets, a Chinese restaurant and run-down hotels where one can drink until morning. He does so in a lighthearted way, suggesting Mahon's depiction of the North had had the opposite effect and proved "more an attraction than a warning".[39] The town it seems has been inundated with newcomers seeking just such experiences. Mahon had often been the object of Simmons's criticism before, and in his *London Review of Books* review he returned the favour, charging that Simmons's poems "aspire to the condition of Tin Pan Alley". He "treats language like an out-of-tune piano", he noted, commenting on Simmons's fondness for plain speech. "He makes a terrible din", Mahon continued, "but the zest is undeniable".[40] When Simmons wrote to express his dismay at the review, Mahon replied, "if you actually read it, you will see that it praises both book and author; don't be so bloody touchy".[41] That was hardly the case, and Mahon certainly knew it. Simmons was hurt as well by the fact that

Mahon's criticism stood in such sharp contrast to the praise he accorded Muldoon's *Why Brownlee Left*. In fact he opened the review with an extended reading of the 29-year-old's new collection, relegating the more senior Simmons to secondary position.

Muldoon's collection, Mahon noted, constituted "a private poetry of departure", a memorable phrase that one could apply to a number of Mahon's own recent poems. Mahon himself had recently left London for rural Surrey, left Surrey for Coleraine, left Coleraine for London again. More to the point, he and Doreen had been living apart for most of the past two years and had wondered at times if the separation was permanent. Muldoon and his first wife, Anne-Marie Conway, had recently divorced, and that event casts a long shadow over Muldoon's collection. Mahon notes Muldoon's poems perform a series of "disappearing acts", all part of "the time-honoured Irish instinct to get out". The collection as a whole is pitched towards an imagined but still unrealised future, reflected best in the two idle horses of the title poem, "like man and wife, / Shifting their weight from foot to foot / And gazing into the future".[42]

When Longley visited the reunited Mahons in Observatory Gardens in November, Mahon was anxious about the visit, his fragile family situation and how Doreen would behave. She blamed Longley for contributing to her husband's drinking problem, and the risk of a relapse was ever present. Longley reported to Montague, however, that he and Doreen had been able "to resolve the tensions and misunderstandings which were bound to accumulate when Derek was in the pit".[43] Nevertheless Mahon felt the visit a strain and wrote a note of apology for his glum mood, to which Longley answered that he had witnessed only "the normal deportment of a father of two children who are composed of energy!" As for Doreen, he added, she "couldn't have been more welcoming".[44]

Despite his anxiety about his marriage, Mahon was working well, and that autumn he proposed publishing a chapbook of his latest work with The Gallery Press. Among the new poems were "The Hunt by Night" and "Girls on the Bridge", both of which he had finished in September. The two poems were based on paintings, as was the title poem for the collection *Courtyards in Delft*, and were written in the same stanzaic form. He delivered the manuscript in early December, noting that it "represents pretty much all I've finished since *Poems 1962–1978*".[45]

Mahon was hoping the bad times were over, and he confided to Dillon Johnston that he thought he had beaten drink: "all that behind me, I think, in so far as things ever can be". He was "enfamilied in Kensington" he added, writing occasional reviews, freelancing for the BBC and exploring possible adaptations for television or film.[46] Or, as he put it to Asekoff, "I journalize, telerize, & hopefully screenwrite".[47] In late January the Montagues visited for 10 days, during which time he and John worked on a radio feature Mahon was doing on him called "A Grafted Tongue". Montague gave a reading at the Poetry Society, which turned into a late-night affair. The barman finally left Derek and John to lock up the building after themselves, causing a bit of a scene when the police were summoned to investigate.[48]

OUP was insisting that the forthcoming Gallery collection include no more than 15 poems so as not to compete with Mahon's next Oxford collection. In the end *Courtyards in Delft* contained 14. A remarkably high percentage of them (eleven) would survive later pruning and eventually take their place in his *Collected Poems*. He sent Dillon Johnston a revised version of "The Globe in North Carolina" early in the new year, which in typescript carried an epigraph from Andrei Voznesensky: "There are no religions, no revelations; there are women". It was a Gravesian acknowledgment of Doreen's importance in his life, of her role in his recovery, and of her role as a muse for his poetry.

Mahon was back in Dublin in March for the launch of the collection, but, short of cash, had had to ask Peter Fallon to send him a plane ticket.[49] Seamus Deane had arranged a reading for him at University College, Dublin and he proceeded from Dublin to Cork for another that Montague had set up. He had not found salaried employment as he had hoped to, but was keeping busy pursuing multiple projects at once. He learned in April that Jennifer Johnston's *The Old Jest* was unavailable for adaptation; her agent wanted to hold onto it for a possible run on the New York stage.[50] In the meantime, however, he and Philip Haas had completed a treatment for a film called "Gillespie", based on the life of a Paisley-like evangelist from Northern Ireland,[51] and in April they submitted a proposal to the Irish Film Board for possible funding.[52]

That same spring Irish Republican prisoners at the Maze prison, led by Bobby Sands, began a hunger strike as a protest against their loss of special prisoner status. The media followed the protest closely but events took on an entirely new dimension when Sands was elected to the Westminster parliament in early April. In this atmosphere Mahon made a rare appearance at a political demonstration, not one related to the hunger strikers or Northern Ireland's Troubles, but a "Poets Against the Bomb" reading organised as a protest against the Thatcher government's plans to deploy American-made cruise missiles in Britain. Here was an issue he could approach with moral clarity. When it came to nuclear war, there was no ambiguity about where one should stand.

With the arrival of summer, Doreen and the children left for a holiday in Majorca. Mahon stayed behind in London to continue work on his writing projects. He told Louis Asekoff he was "versing unstoppably",[53] and in early June he wrote Jacky Simms to let her know "that I'll be sending you a new collection of 50–60 pages, provisionally titled *The Hunt by Night* in September".[54] While on holiday Doreen and the children called on the aging Robert Graves in Deià. Mahon had embraced Graves's theory of artistic creativity, and in his recent work had taken pains to represent Doreen as a muse figure. She no doubt called on the elderly poet on her husband's behalf, to determine if he would make a suitable interviewee for a radio feature, should Mahon get the BBC to agree to the idea. In the end the elderly Graves seemed hardly aware of her and the children, and stared vacantly out of the window.[55] If Mahon had been considering a radio feature on the great man, Doreen's report ruled that out.

Mahon was casting about for other ideas, and he applied for an Arts Council bursary "to write a book-length poem based on the life and work of Ovid, the Roman bloke".[56] He and Heaney had talked about the project in London a few weeks before, and Heaney had agreed to help by writing a supporting letter. To make the chore as easy as possible, Mahon wrote his own statement of support and sent it to Heaney for him to adapt. "I know him to have been in unsettled financial circumstances since the expiry of a temporary BBC contract last year", Mahon wrote of himself in Heaney's voice. "He works hard at distracting tasks of a secondary nature, and an Arts Council Bursary would enable him to devote himself, for a sustained period, to work of lasting value". As for the project itself, he added, still channelling Heaney, "I think the Ovid idea an excellent one. Ovid has been surprisingly overlooked by English poets and translators in recent years and Mr. Mahon's intended 'ventriloquial' approach should result in an original and striking contribution to contemporary poetry". Mahon listed his annual income at only £4,000, explaining to Heaney that the figure was not entirely accurate, "but one must be seen to have inked-in the holes in one's socks".[57]

London was preparing for the wedding of Prince Charles and Lady Diana Spencer that July, and Mahon's parents chose the time to make a rare visit to see their son and his family. "I've got my Paisleyite parents staying just now, which means free speech is severely curtailed", he complained to Asekoff. "They are convinced I'm an IRA bomber, and it is not possible to watch the TV news at the same time in case somebody breathes a provocative remark. Their sympathy is reserved for the 'poor policemen' who get it in the neck when they go swaggering into Republican areas".[58] For all his embellishment of the scene, his description offers a rare glimpse of one of the points of friction in his relationship with his parents. Ireland's sectarian conflict had disturbed a personal fault line running through his own family. While he found political certainties inherently suspect, he identified personally with Northern Ireland's Catholic community, as his and Haas's film proposal for *Gillespie* makes clear.

The proposal takes direct aim at the pathology of hate that was gripping the North. His character sketch describes Gillespie as a "Northern Irish ultra-Protestant evangelist turned anti-Catholic demagogue and maverick politician".[59] He is "a ferocious Protestant bigot ... an appalling but irresistible figure". It was not an entirely impersonal subject, and the contradictions in Mahon's character sketch resemble those he expressed in his own early poem "Ecclesiastes". Mahon and Haas traced Gillespie's origins as an "anti-Catholic demagogue on the country-town circuit". Like Paisley, Gillespie exploits the prejudices and bigotry of his followers to launch his political career, the chief plank of which is condemnation of "the betrayal of British interests into the hands of foreign Papists". He is helped in all this by an American public relations man, further underscoring the hollowness of his convictions. Mahon and Haas describe Gillespie's growing rise in power, his hunger for "absolute power in the North", and the machinations and betrayals of his inner circle. At times the film proposal reads more like a documentary than fiction, and that may have contributed to the script not being funded. Whether or not Gillespie is a bigot, the newly established Irish Film Board hardly cared to inaugurate its new funding scheme with an assault on one of the North's leading political figures.

In the meantime, OUP had decided to push back publication of his next collection until the new year, and Mahon was growing increasingly dissatisfied with how his publisher's New York office was handling his books in America. Farrar, Straus & Giroux had done far better by Heaney, who had been able to parlay his growing US reputation into a distinguished Harvard appointment.[60] Heaney was sympathetic to his situation, and offered to show the manuscript of *The Hunt by Night* to his new publishers to gauge their interest in the book. He also wrote an appreciative statement about the collection for Mahon to use as he saw fit. Portions of this statement would be mined for a later jacket blurb—"there is a copiousness and excitement about these poems found only in work of the highest order"—one that Mahon's publishers would continue to make use of for many years. "Mr. Mahon does not shore fragments against ruin", Heaney wrote; "his homage to painters, his versions of classical and modern poets, the gravity and insouciance of his mastery of form proclaim his trust in the continuing possibilities of art that is true and beautiful". Heaney acknowledged obliquely Derek's personal trials, and suggested they were a potent source of power in his latest work:

> … some creative tremor has given him deepening access to his sources of power; it is as if the very modernity of his intelligence has goaded a primitive stamina in his imagination. Something untrammelled, rebelliously alive and in love, sustains this art and allows it to slip free of its own censorious ironies. The vision here is hard won but not hard-bitten.[61]

Mahon wrote at the bottom of this letter, "Damned right, sir!"[62] Despite Heaney's efforts, Farrar, Straus declined the new collection. Mahon's agent persuaded him to try Athenaeum, but when they passed as well, Mahon was free to join Wake Forest's Irish list.

That autumn Derek and Doreen met Mary Kenny and her husband, Richard West, both journalists who had moved to nearby Holland Park. Their son, Patrick, was the only Irish student in Rory's class at the Fox Primary School. Kenny wrote for the *Sunday Telegraph* and the *Irish Independent*, and the two couples found that, in addition to school-age children, they had much in common. In the 1970s Kenny had achieved some notoriety for taking part in the contraceptive train, an organised protest by a group of women who travelled from Dublin to Belfast to buy condoms, which were then illegal in Ireland. She had once walked out of a church service when Archbishop John Charles McQuaid spoke from the pulpit against the use of contraceptives, and she followed that with a provocative letter to *The Irish Times* in which she said Ian Paisley had been right: "Home Rule is Rome Rule".

In October Mahon finally got the salaried position he had been seeking when he replaced Craig Raine as poetry editor of the *New Statesman*. He hoped to give poetry more prominence in the weekly and minimise the use of short poems as column-fillers. He immediately began soliciting poems from friends, especially "longer poems, groups of poems, short sequences".[63] One of his first tasks, however, was clearing out work that had already been accepted but which he did not care to publish, among them poems by Richard Murphy and Frank Ormsby, which he now returned.[64] His changes were apparent in the 30 October 1981 issue where four sonnets by Tony Harrison occupied three-quarters of a page. Similar groupings, or pairs of poems, followed in the coming weeks, including pairs of poems by Tom Paulin and Medbh McGuckian.

In early November Mahon learned that his application to the Arts Council had been successful, and he was to receive £6,000 to pursue the Ovid project he had proposed in the early summer. Among the judges acting favourably on his proposal was Philip Larkin. On top of that good news, he also learned he had won the annual AIB Award from the Irish Academy. "My bank manager was seen drinking champagne in his golf club last Saturday morning", he joked in a letter to Dillon Johnston.[65] His television work was also going well. The BBC had been the primary producer of new television drama, but by the early 1980s the "Film on Four" series on Channel 4 was offering another outlet for new work. Paul Joyce had proposed an adaptation of Turgenev's novella *First Love*, and Mahon had been enlisted to give the production an Irish dimension. The film was to be co-produced by Channel 4 and RTÉ.[66] Mahon began referring to it as the "Turgenev-in-Sligo project", and joked that a Solzhenitsyn story set in the H-Block would be next.[67]

He was also at work on a translation of Gérard de Nerval's sonnet sequence *Les Chimères*, which provided a mythic pattern for his own personal concerns. Fallon had at first wavered on publishing the collection, but when Arts Council funding came through, he was suddenly in a position to publish. "This *folie de grandeur*, deriving from the munificence of certain public bodies, may be short-lived, so best take advantage while you can", Mahon wrote Fallon on hearing the good news.[68] As for payment, "I honestly forget what we did the last time; but this time let's agree on some modest sum, and if … you find even that difficult, consider money irrelevant".[69]

Mahon attended the *New Statesman* holiday party just before Christmas, and for the end-of-the-year issue he published, on a single page, poems by Carol Rumens, Osip Mandelstam, John Mole and Anthony Thwaite. He was enjoying his role as poetry editor, and he boasted to Asekoff, "I can pin a rejection slip to a sheaf of shit quicker'n you can say *The New York Review of Books*".[70] Early in the new year, he devoted full pages to poems by Hugo Williams, Glyn Hughes and Douglas Dunn. The 29 January issue featured two poems by Heaney, "Among the Whins" and "Chekhov on Sakhalin", marking Heaney's own foray into Russian literature.

When the American novelist Mary Gordon submitted a poem, "Reading Auden while nursing my daughter", she discovered just how far Mahon would take his editorial role. He accepted the poem but asked her to change a reference to Auden pushing an old woman downstairs. "I know you are only attributing the story to Gossip", he wrote Gordon, "but I feel the suggestion remains that there is substance in the charge".[71] He asked Gordon to rewrite the offending line, a request she acceded to after "a few days' anguish". "What would you think of changing 'pushed an old lady downstairs' to 'pissed in your sink till it stank?'" she offered. It is "a vulgarism, but not one that Auden would have disapproved of".[72] The poem appealed to Mahon, who had been the object of similar gossip over his own drunken behaviour. Gordon's poem concludes,

> Wherever you are, grant my child
> the gift of a philosophy,
> the knack of the general statement,
> the luck of a useless wit,
> the honour to be praised and, yes, defended
> by a few friends who remember
> that the measure of a man
> cannot be taken wholly by his manners.[73]

Mahon was in fact coming to Auden's defence in just the way the poem describes.

Mahon was invited by BBC Radio 3 to contribute a poem for the upcoming centenary of Joyce's birth. The producer wanted to pair Catholic and Protestant voices, and Mahon's "Joycecentenary Ode", composed for the occasion, was accompanied by two shorter poems by Heaney, "Gravities" and "The Wool Trade". Mahon and Heaney had participated in other joint commemorations going all the way back to their visit to MacNeice's grave and their attendance at Patrick Kavanagh's funeral. The two friends were often paired together in a public show of liberal tolerance and inclusiveness, but, for his part, Mahon resented the notion that he somehow represented a Protestant point of view. In his television work—and increasingly, in his own poems—he was in fact exploring a Catholic literary tradition.

He was looking further ahead to the upcoming 20th anniversary of MacNeice's death, for which he proposed a television documentary. While this project never came to pass, the proposal shows he hoped to offer a corrective to those readings of MacNeice as an "English" poet and to highlight instead the "life-long influence of his Irish background and childhood". In his proposal Mahon argued that the key to MacNeice's "poetic personality" was to be found in "childhood traumas", a statement one could apply to Mahon himself.[74] While he meant by this the death of MacNeice's mother at a young age, Mahon also points to a deep-seated ambiguity over his own cultural identity. "The Anglo-Irish dilemma into which he was born was inescapable, and he could never quite think of himself as an 'English' poet, while his English education and career seemed to preclude the title of 'Irish' poet". The terms Mahon uses to describe MacNeice underscore the way the older poet served as a poetic double for Mahon himself.

In March the *TLS* published "A Garage in Co. Cork". As he would later explain at readings, the poem had been prompted by a postcard image of a derelict garage he came across in a London bookshop.[75] Mahon was moved by the image to imaginatively evoke something of the absent owners' lives through the things they left behind.

Surely you paused at this roadside oasis
In your nomadic youth, and saw the mound
Of never-used cement, the curious faces,
The soft-drink ads and the uneven ground
Rainbowed with oily puddles, where a snail
Had scrawled its slimy, phosphorescent trail.

Like a frontier store-front in an old western
It might have nothing behind it but thin air,
Building materials, fruit-boxes, scrap iron,

Dust-laden shrubs and coils of rusty wire,
A cabbage-white fluttering in the sodden
Silence of an untended kitchen garden—

Nirvana! But the cracked panes reveal a dark
Interior echoing with the cries of children.
Here in this quiet corner of Co. Cork
A family ate, slept, and watched the rain
Dance clean and cobalt the exhausted grit
So that the mind shrank from the glare of it.

Where did they go? South Boston? Cricklewood?
Somebody somewhere thinks of this as home,
Remembering the old pumps where they stood,
Antique now, squirting juice into a cream
Lagonda or a dung-caked tractor while
A cloud swam on a cloud-reflecting tile.[76]

His evocation of this absent family alludes to other displacements and diasporas both personal and historical. The poem is reminiscent of "A Disused Shed", but Mahon draws these figures more lovingly than the more distant "Lost people of Treblinka and Pompeii". In fact, Mahon is himself one of the displaced Irish resettled, in a place not unlike Cricklewood, and the "you" at the poem's opening is a self-referential one to his own days bicycling Ireland's rural roads. The poem springs from much the same impulse as his early poem "In Belfast" (later "Spring in Belfast"): "One part of my mind must learn to know its place. / The things that happen in the kitchen houses / And echoing back streets of this desperate city / Should engage more than my casual interest, / Exact more interest than my casual pity". "A Garage in Co. Cork" is the fulfilment of that early ambition, and it would become a standard selection in future readings.

As summer approached, Mahon and Paul Joyce were meeting regularly, often at the Chelsea Arts Club, to wrap up a first draft of the script of Turgenev's *First Love*. It turned out Turgenev's title had already been taken by a popular television series, so for a time the two collaborators considered the more fatalistic sounding "Last Summer" before in the end settling on "Summer Lightning". Joyce was interested in introducing a

Freudian element into the script, while Mahon approached the project as another opportunity for creative self-projection.[77] The young Robert (Vladimir in Turgenev's original) is an aspiring poet, and the action is set in Wicklow and Dublin, settings that took Mahon back to his own student days. Familiar sites—among them Trinity's Front Gate, the Campanile and The Brazen Head—all make appearances in the script. Dolly St Léger (Princess Zasyekina) is a widow whose husband served in the merchant marine but drowned at sea under less-than-clear circumstances. The script hints that his drowning may have been suicide, a detail that evokes both Doreen's father's death and Mahon's own attempt to end his own life in 1962. When Robert falls in love with Dolly's beautiful daughter, Louise (Zinaida), both mother and daughter are invited to dinner with Robert's family. Over dinner the mother recounts hers and her daughter's past lives in Dublin, London and Paris. "Come now, mama, we never lived in Paris!" Louise interrupts her mother. "Well, no, that's trew [sic] we never actually *lived* in Paris. But we *nearly* did one time". Her Parisian past is reminiscent of Mahon's own claims to have once studied at the Sorbonne. He *nearly* did.

In still other ways Turgenev's story of a tragic and unfulfilled first love re-enacts and renews old traumas. At the end of Joyce's and Mahon's script, after many years have passed, we learn that Louise has died in childbirth at the age of only 23. Robert visits the morgue at the Sisters of Mercy Hospital in Dublin's North Frederick Street where he looks on Louise's dead body. For Mahon, as for Edgar Allan Poe, the death of a beautiful woman was a powerful poetic image.

With the script completed, Mahon, Doreen and the children travelled to Greece, where they spent most of June. Mahon and Doreen were joined on Paros by "the touring Montagues", who stayed with them for several days.[78] There they renewed their friendship with Gisèle d'Ailly and other island friends. Desmond O'Grady arrived near the end of the month but overlapped with them only briefly. He was a heavy drinker and Mahon was worried about an alcoholic relapse. All his previous visits had been drunken affairs, and too much time around O'Grady would be risky, he explained to Heaney.[79] Mahon returned to London on 1 July, having safely negotiated those dangers and with "a notebook full of random possibilities".[80]

He and Doreen were back home in time to hear his radio play of Brian Moore's *I Am Mary Dunne* air on the "Afternoon Theatre" on Radio 4, and they were in London when the IRA set off bombs in Hyde Park and Regent's Park on 20 July. Eleven soldiers were killed in the coordinated attacks and more than fifty bystanders wounded. Not long after, Mahon's profile of Montague, *The Grafted Tongue*, aired on BBC Radio 3. He had interviewed Heaney, Martin Dodsworth and Christopher Ricks for the programme, and the participants discussed Montague's poetry and his grafting of European idioms onto a native Gaelic stock. While there was precedent for his work in the poetry of Patrick Kavanagh, Montague was also writing within "a line of descent from Joyce and Beckett". Mahon was singling out for praise this combination of traditional and European sources. "There is no flight into pastoral nostalgia", he noted, "but neither is there a renunciation of it". He was expressing something of his own poetic values.

As the summer drew to a close, the *New Statesman* moved its offices from Holborn into a new "open plan" office in Clerkenwell, crowded with word-processors. Mahon made a nod to his and Doreen's Greek vacation when he published Glyn Hughes's "Greek sketches" in the magazine, and he accepted a poem by the Russian poet Eugene Dubnov, whom he had met earlier in the year at a Poetry Society reading. As was his practice, he suggested a number of changes to the English translation, and these were of such an extent that later reprintings would carry the note "Translated from the Russian by the author and Derek Mahon".[81] He continued to wield his editor's pen with gusto, not merely accepting work as submitted but suggesting considerable revisions. When Glyn Hughes submitted a sheaf of new work, Mahon asked for a series of changes to his poem "Full Moon". "Do we need the fishermen?" he asked; "I think not". "'Dark' better than 'blackened'", and other substitutions.[82] In the end Hughes acquiesced.

In September, Mahon heard from Jacky Simms that OUP wanted to accelerate the publication schedule for *The Hunt by Night* after all, and issue it before Christmas, unbeknownst to him, to avoid appearing at the same time as Heaney's *Sweeney Astray*. Heaney had been working on the version of the Irish medieval tale *Buile Shuibhne* off and on for ten years, and, as he confided to Mahon, "I'll have to get rid of it soon, if only to pretend to some 'achievement' before I return to the gilded young in Massachusetts".[83] *Sweeney Astray* would be published by Field Day in the new year, and Simms was advising her colleagues at OUP to "Avoid S.H.'s next book".[84]

Mahon recycled part of Heaney's Arts Council recommendation of some months before for a jacket blurb for the new book. "A few lines of entirely justified encomiasm", he called it when he sent it along to Jacky Simms. As he explained, "I feel the need to re-introduce myself to the gawking public with a deft stroke or two, or perhaps merely introduce myself to a public too busy reading Heaney and Craig Raine to pay any attention to the presence of comparable, if less televisual, figures like myself".[85] Heaney's endorsement would be quoted in full when the book first appeared in print, though in future years it would be trimmed:

This is Derek Mahon's most exuberant and authoritative single volume to date. Some creative tremor has given him deepening access to his sources of power; it is as if the very modernity of his intelligence has goaded him a primitive stamina in his imagination. There is a copiousness and excitement about these poems that is to be found only in work of the highest order.[86]

Mahon was continuing to pursue multiple film projects, and he received an expression of interest from Grafton Productions for a film treatment of Brian Moore's *The Temptation of Eileen Hughes*. On the strength of that, he and Moore began investigating possible filming locations. Moore wrote to him with his thoughts:

The hotel I had in mind was called the Goring. It's near Buckhouse [Buckingham Palace], but perhaps not posh enough. It does have a garden court and is peculiarly unattractive in that British manner. I would make it generic and ask the director to go upmarket a bit on the Goring as it must look posh to Eileen. The less trendy pub I used is called The Antelope, I think, and is just off Sloane Square in Belgravia.[87]

Mahon visited each site and reported he "was even shown a maid's room with a glimpse of the Palace".[88]

In October he made a quick trip to Dublin for a reading at Trinity and stayed with the Heaneys for the weekend. Gallery had published his version of Gérard de Nerval's *The Chimeras*, and *The Hunt by Night* was due out in days. He was not drinking, and in fact was feeling well enough to try and help Desmond O'Grady get into treatment when he passed through London en route to Ireland. He was afraid that "if he gets as far as Ireland there'll be no stopping him".[89] Mahon continued to associate his own recent alcoholic crisis with place, as if Ireland itself were at fault. He urged O'Grady "to consider yourself a Scott-Fitzgeraldian romantic invalid for about a year, lead a quiet life, re-make the soul, remain in the province of Munster, and cheer yourself up with the thought that everyone is expressing wonder and admiration at your strength of character, spiritual re-birth, etc".[90]

Mahon received his author's copies of *The Hunt by Night* in late October, and dispatched copies to close friends, including O'Grady, Jennifer Johnston and Brian Moore. Moore wrote to thank him for the new collection, noting he liked best those poems about "our past", by which he meant "North Wind" and "Rathlin Island". Indeed, the two friends shared many similar experiences, and Moore understood in a personal way the uncertainty Mahon was turning over in his mind at the time, essentially the uncertainty of "whether the future lies before us or behind".[91] When the book was selected as a Poetry Book Society Choice, Mahon contributed a prose note to the *Bulletin* in which he alludes to the major theme and preoccupation of the collection as a whole. He singles out for attention his poem of crisis "The Globe in Carolina" as being related directly to the theme of the title poem "The Hunt by Night". "I won't try to describe the sequence of events for which the title also serves as a euphemism", he writes; "had I done so in verse, I might have produced a more interesting volume. More probably I'd have been criticized for spending too much time among life studies and dream songs".[92] There is a strong confessional streak in Mahon's poems, and one of the points of tension in his work lies along that line of negotiation between self-revelation and self-concealment.

By mid-November Mahon had finished the screenplay of *The Temptation of Eileen Hughes*. In the end it would go unproduced, but he had gotten great pleasure from the project and had enjoyed retracing the characters' steps around London, "locking into place every incident and remark", as he put it to Moore.[93]

Derek and Doreen spent Christmas 1982 apart. Doreen and the children returned to north Antrim to spend the holiday with her mother, but Mahon had no desire to return to the North. He stayed in London and put together the end-of-the-year holiday issue of the *New Statesman*, which included Heaney's "Ulster Twilight" (a reworking of "Christmas

Eve"). He spent Christmas day at the home of Mary Kenny and Richard West. It was a forlorn occasion, Mary recalls. "All the guests around the table seemed to be going through some personal crisis or other". Two were in the midst of painful divorces; another had recently been diagnosed with cancer and kept bursting into tears. As for Mahon, he remained "emotionally detached", a form of withdrawal he had long ago developed in times of stress.[94]

Chapter 11

| *THE DEATH OF THE HEART*

One's sentiments — call them that — one's fidelities
are so instinctive that one hardly knows they exist: only
when they are betrayed or, worse still, when one betrays
them does one realize their power.

Elizabeth Bowen, *The Death of the Heart*

Despite the temporary relief from money worries, Derek and Doreen's marriage remained strained. Friends noticed they were quarrelling more often and increasingly contradicting one another in front of others. Privately Doreen admitted to being unhappy in her marriage. Mary Kenny saw the relationship following a familiar pattern. Doreen had been a beautiful young woman with a career in television. Marriage to a young poet had seemed tremendously exciting, but the persistent lack of money, the responsibility for two young children (now eight and six) and an "emotionally absent" husband fed her unhappiness.[1] Both she and her husband were at mid-life, and, while the Coleraine crisis was behind them, that period of separation had introduced them both to the idea of independent lives apart from one another.

Following the Divorce Reform Act of 1971 divorce rates across Britain had soared. Derek and Doreen had watched as numerous friends took that step: John and Madeleine Montague, Paul and Anne-Marie Muldoon, James and Laura Simmons. Robert Lowell had famously mined the break-up of his marriage for poetic subject matter in *For Lizzie & Harriet* and *The Dolphin*. "It was the divorce generation", Glyn Hughes later noted matter-of-factly.

For his part, Mahon too was chafing under the obligations and constraints of family life, and he sometimes felt Doreen was the one who had emotionally withdrawn from the marriage. They were more and more frequently choosing to spend holidays apart, as they did in the summers of 1984 and 1985. An unpublished poem, "House Husband", captures something of Mahon's feelings at the time: "No doubt I should be scaling peaks / Or bouncing about in space. / Instead I climb the stairs to make the beds / Or hoover the carpet in circles / Like a lunar geologist.... I tell myself and others that I am resting / Like an actor between parts. / When I go to fetch the children / The other mothers look at me / With dwindling curiosity / As I study with interest / The clouds in flight above the enclosed playground".[2]

Mahon refers to "that celestial hoover" again in "One of These Nights", which he published in the TLS in March. At a reading a few months later he introduced "Courtyards in Delft" by explaining it was "about the relationship between and excessive concern for order and the life-denying instinct".[3] He was resisting a life of middle-aged domesticity and missing his bohemian youth. If complaint was making it into his poems, one can be sure it was making its way into his and Doreen's marriage as well. When Mahon learned that Louis Asekoff and his wife, Mimi, were breaking up, he wrote his friend that it was just "the sort of damnable crisis we all seem to go in for". He was either referring to his previous separation from Doreen or anticipating another break-up still to come.

Early in the year the BBC agreed to cover Mahon's expenses for a trip to America to conduct interviews for the Lowell documentary. The American edition of *The Hunt by Night* was to be published by Wake Forest in February, and he organised the trip as a reading tour ("a wake for *Hunt*").[4] He flew first to Boston, where he stayed with Heaney, who was back at Harvard for the spring semester. Heaney helped get him a reading at nearby Northeastern University, and Mahon interviewed a number of Lowell's former colleagues and friends: William Alfred, Blair Clark, Richard Tillinghast, Helen Vendler and Heaney himself. From Boston he travelled to Asekoff's place in New York, and from there made side trips to Yale, Vassar and Brooklyn College. His instructions to Dillon Johnston were that he was not to be introduced as an "Ulster" poet (a reference to Johnston's recent *Hollins Critic* piece that called him just that). "Irish, please", he said. Nor did he want to hear himself described as "2nd in line only to Seamus Heaney".[5] In a later television documentary he explained that he, Longley and Heaney reached a point at which they lost patience with the constricting label "Ulster poet". Each had a broader world view, and, as he explained, they didn't want to be stuck with this cliché.[6]

The Hunt by Night was receiving good reviews, though the collection also elicited a letter of complaint to the *TLS* from one reader who objected to Mahon's borrowings from Brecht. There was a brief dust-up in the letters column when another reader suggested it would have been wiser to avoid rushing into print with "the news that a poem titled 'Brecht in Svendborg' derives from Brecht's *Svendborg Poems*".[7] It was just the kind of literary grumbling the *TLS* loved to publish.

In the audience at Mahon's Brooklyn reading was an attractive middle-aged woman who was an arts administrator for a school of traditional Irish music on Achill Island off the coast of County Mayo. Patricia King, "Pat", had been born in Ireland on St Patrick's Day 1939, and her parents had christened her after Ireland's patron saint. As a young woman she had emigrated to America and attended Marymount College in Tarrytown, New York, before going to Notre Dame for a masters degree in theology. Following her studies she taught theology at Rosary Hill College and later at Sacred Heart University, but dropped theological studies in order to take a second masters in English at the University of Connecticut. She married and started a family in America, though she always maintained her close ties to Ireland. In the early seventies she had helped establish the Irish Arts Center in New York City, and when Mahon met her she was managing the Curraun House Project on Achill.[8] Mahon was immediately attracted to her, and to her life story, which included nearly as many crossings and new beginnings as he himself had made.

Back in London he resumed his duties at the *New Statesman*, spending three days a week in the office and the rest of his time working on screenplays. He was trying to persuade OUP to add O'Grady to their poetry list, and that spring he took a train to Cambridge to read with Michael Longley and Eddie Linden. He skipped a reading by Medbh McGuckian, however, and, by way of apology for having done so, invited her to send him some poems for the *New Statesman*.[9] O'Grady had written a companion poem to Mahon's "The Sea in Winter", called "These Fields in Springtime", and Mahon, who felt some sense of ownership of O'Grady's poem, took it upon himself to rewrite it in a spirit of artistic collaboration.

In July the Mahon family rented a seaside cottage in Union Hall, County Cork, during which they saw a good bit of Montague and his second wife, Evelyn. The vogue for all things Russian was showing no sign of abating, as evidenced by Brian Friel's recent success with his adaptation of Chekhov's *Three Sisters*; Mahon read Gogol's *Dead Souls* while on holiday and was considering adapting it for television. Instead he took up Montague's short story "The Cry", about sectarian violence in the North. The choice was a highly personal one. Montague's story tells of a young man, Peter Douglas, who has left Northern Ireland to become a reporter in London. During a visit home, Peter witnesses the beating of a local boy by the B-Specials. When Peter expresses shock at what he has seen, his father gives vent to his own anger at the situation and reveals a breach between the generations. "Well, what are you going to do about it?", the father challenges his son, before mockingly suggesting he fight back with his typewriter. In that exchange Montague exposes both the North's ingrained bigotry and the resentment of the older generation over the new choices available to the young. Peter imagines for a time that he can do just that—fight back with an article in his London newspaper—but in the end silence falls over the community and Protestants and Catholics alike are unwilling to speak out for fear of retribution.

Mahon had come a long way from those days when he and his cousin would open the wardrobe that held his Uncle Murphy's B-Specials uniform and would take out and hold his pistol. In one revealing scene, Montague has Peter read a portion of the article he is writing:

One must distinguish between the Royal Ulster Constabulary and the familiar English 'bobby'. The Ulster police are the only ordinary police, in these islands, to carry revolvers; in times of Emergency, they are also armed with Sten guns. In addition to the RUC there are the B Specials, 12,000 over-armed and under trained auxiliaries drawn exclusively from the ranks of the Protestant majority. In fact you have all the elements of a police state ... not in Spain or South Africa, but in the British Isles.[10]

Mahon's wish to adapt Montague's story signals the distance he had travelled from his own Ulster Protestant beginnings. He takes a young Catholic man's resistance to Protestant bigotry as his subject, and in so doing reaches back to his own family past, before his ancestors "took the soup" during Famine times.

While on holiday Mahon began a new poem prompted by the picturesque Squince Harbour. One day he and Doreen went with the Montagues to visit the cottage where Jim Farrell had been living when he was tragically swept into the sea and drowned four years earlier.[11] When they arrived at the cottage, Doreen called out their friend's name as if Farrell might answer.[12] The house had been left as it had been when Farrell was still living, and Mahon took note of Japanese dictionaries and Buddhist texts which "seemed to indicate the way his thoughts were tending during his last year". As he later put it in the introduction to *The Singapore Grip*, Farrell's "early brush with death and subsequent singularity had developed in him a mystical strain, one which expressed itself in impatience with London and withdrawal to the silence of West Cork—there, in an old phrase, to make his soul".[13]

With Farrell in mind, Mahon was having thoughts about leaving London and withdrawing to a quieter life in Ireland, or, alternatively, a comfortable teaching post in America. These thoughts coincided with Heaney's public proclamation of his Irishness in *An Open Letter*, published that September by the Field Day Theatre Company. "My passport's green / No glass of ours was ever raised / To toast the Queen", Heaney stated defiantly. It was a familiar complaint. Mahon had noted in a review of the *Everyman's Book of English Verse* two years earlier, "They still call it English verse, despite the many Paddies, Jocks and Taffies".[14] Heaney wrote to Mahon soon after publication of the pamphlet to confess he had worked himself into a bit of a problem with British and Irish anthologies, one that "will have to be resolved by withdrawal (crude but logical) or inaction (hang-dog but maybe too easy)".[15]

Field Day had been established in 1980, as Brian Friel expressed it, to be "a forum where a more generous and noble notion of Irishness than the narrow inherited one can be discussed". The directors hoped their work might contribute to the emergence of a "fifth province" in Ireland, "a province of the mind", that would transcend the harsh and rigid lines of sectarian rhetoric. If this new province is to mean anything, Friel said in an *Irish Times* interview, it must first be "articulated, spoken, written, painted, sung".[16] The company made its debut with a well-received production of Friel's *Translations*. It followed that success with his adaptation of Chekhov's *Three Sisters* (1981), *The Communication Cord* (1982) and Athol Fugard's *Boesman and Lena* (1983). Friel wrote at the end of the month to invite Mahon to translate a Molière play for the new company. It is important, he wrote, to cast the play in accessible language. "The reason I suggest Molière is that I think your artistic pulse and pitch are similar to his in many ways".[17] Mahon was happy to participate in the new venture, and he quickly settled on *L'École des Maris* (*The School for Husbands*), though it was not immediately obvious how Molière's generational comedy would serve Field Day's cultural and political ends.

Mahon took a three-month leave of absence from the *New Statesman* in order to devote more time to his new writing projects, chief among them "the Robert Lowell Show". He used the time to take a week-long trip to Paris, where he had arranged a meeting with Samuel Beckett. On the day of his departure, he and Doreen attended the wedding of their friends Michael Heffernan and Margaret Windham at the Church of the Immaculate Conception near Berkeley Square. The Catholic service made him uncomfortable, and, as he later noted, "Doreen and I sing earnestly, kneel devoutly, and remember the Boyne". Afterwards he retrieved his bag and headed to the Green Park tube station, only to find himself caught in the midst of a Campaign for Nuclear Disarmament march. Dressed in his seersucker suit, he struggled to press through the marchers, wishing he could shout "I'm on your side."[18]

In Paris, Mahon stayed with friends who had a flat in the rue Tiquetonne, near Les Halles. The morning after he arrived he set out on foot to reacquaint himself with the city. It was a cool, crisp day, and Mahon crossed the Île de la Cité and strolled up the Boulevard Saint-Michel to the Luxembourg Gardens, where he paused at Baudelaire's statue. Later he lingered over the newspapers and enjoyed a lemonade at Le Select in the Boulevard du Montparnasse.[19] He was working on a poem about Camus and was hoping the sights and sounds of Paris would stimulate the new work, as indeed they did. While in the city he visited the Church of St Eustace, where he admired Rubens' painting of *The Disciples at Emmaus*, a detail he would incorporate into the new poem. He was familiar with *The Vision of Saint Eustace* by the Italian Renaissance master Pisanello, which he had seen in London, and his reflections on the Catholic saint's conversion made their way into "St. Eustace", published in *The Observer* on his return.

Beckett had suggested they meet for coffee at the Hôtel Saint Jacques in the Latin Quarter, a "souless, Hiltonesque place" with piped-in Muzak.[20] The two men had a mutual friend in Con Leventhal, Mahon's former tutor, and they reminisced about him and about Trinity. Mahon had admired Beckett's work ever since his undergraduate days, and the meeting was filled with a sense of occasion for him. He later tried to capture the meeting in a new poem, but in the end it would remain unfinished. The surviving manuscript draft describes the hotel music, the gleam of Beckett's eyeglasses, and the aging Beckett misquoting his own poetry.[21] When Mahon asked him if he still played the piano, Beckett held up his gnarled fingers and said there was no more piano playing for him. As he recounted the conversation later, Beckett then grew wistful about the benefits of growing old: the loss of memory, the inability to recall words. "It's great", Beckett said; "I've been looking forward to it all my life".[22] It was a meaningful meeting for Mahon, who returned to his flat, made notes on their conversation and worked further on his Camus poem.[23] In the coming months he would write an extended essay on Beckett's poetry in which he would praise the poetic qualities of Beckett's minimalist speech. He shared Beckett's view that silence could be the most appropriate response to much of what life offers us.

In the meantime Mahon's screenplay for *The Cry* was moving towards production with uncharacteristic speed, and plans were being made for filming to get underway in the coming weeks. The BBC began shooting in Belfast on location at Aquinas Hall, on the Malone Road, where Louis MacNeice had once lived. The house had a large bay window where MacNeice was said to have composed "Snow". The film crew moved onward to the village of Staid in County Antrim, where tensions soon erupted. It seems a copy of the script had circulated in the town in advance of shooting, and former members of the B-Specials objected to their portrayal and turned out to intimidate the crew. One member of the group stepped in front of the camera to stop the filming.[24] The Ulster Special Constabulary Association was also threatening the BBC with legal action, and the film crew was forced to abandon Staid and relocate to nearby Cushendall.[25] Mahon was not present for these events, but news of them reconfirmed his dim view of the North.

While Mahon remained on leave from the *New Statesman*, Heaney sent him a new poem for the magazine, "A Hazel Stick for Catherine Anne". "A bit strict don't you think?" Mahon shot back. Mahon quit his editorial post just before Christmas, but not before he selected Gogol's *Dead Souls* for the end-of-the-year holiday round-up of recommended reading.[26] It was an incongruous choice, appearing as it did among the other contributors' more seasonal suggestions. Christmas had always been a stressful time for him, but in the first days of the new year he reported to Dillon Johnston that he had successfully negotiated another nativity and was bracing for "another New Year chock-full of as yet unsuspected kicks in the teeth".[27]

Early in the new year Mahon and O'Grady visited Gisèle d'Ailly at her studio near Hampstead Heath. Gisèle was spending several months in London, and O'Grady was passing through the city en route to Italy. Mahon was moody and withdrawn during the visit, which he later attributed to being under considerable strain. "I do find it hard to say anything intelligent, or even merely gracious, about pictures unless they have overt literary content", he wrote Gisèle by way of apology.[28] He was taking a respite from any more picture poems himself, but looking back at the ones he had recently completed, it is hard to recognise particularly literary content to the works. Painting served instead as the basis for his own creative appropriation: Pieter de Hooch's "The Courtyard of a House in Delft" becomes Mahon's childhood home in Belfast, Paolo Uccello's "The Hunt in the Forest" alludes to an unnamed and unspecified longing within the poet himself.

In February Mahon was completing the final recordings for the Lowell programme. He had worked hard on shaping the interviews into a workable script, and it had grown to an unmanageable length, as his producer, Margaret Windham, warned him.[29] He was also anticipating the publication of *A Kensington Notebook*, his tribute poem to Ezra Pound, based on his London years living in Church Walk. Mahon approached place much as he did painting. He read the urban landscape for its literary associations, which gave him licence to make it his subject while offering a stock of images upon which to draw. Mahon received his copies of the chapbook in mid-March and promptly posted one to Beckett. He was also working on the Molière script, and he delivered a first draft of *High Time*, as he was calling it, to Friel, who responded with enthusiasm. The script had "dramatic flow and movement and both literary and visual wit", Friel wrote after reading it for the first time.[30] Mahon had decided to set the play in Dublin, at the time of the 1968 student demonstrations in Paris, with the young people all cast as hippies, but any revolutionary agenda he may have been entertaining was confined to fashion. Mahon's version was a comic romp he had got "a great kick" out of writing, as he reported it to Longley.[31]

In April Mahon made a trip to Amsterdam, where he stayed at the home of Gisèle d'Ailly while she was in London. Gisèle had sheltered several young Jewish men in her home during the war, and two of them, Manuel Goldschmidt and Claus Bock, were still living there when Mahon visited.[32] Their presence and Gisèle's stand during the war may have helped turn Mahon's thoughts to his Camus poem, "Death and the Sun", and Camus's own role in the resistance movement. On his return from Amsterdam, he mailed Longley a draft of the new poem. "It's all out of the novels, of course—Outsider, Plague and Fall, especially Fall—also the autobiographical writings", he wrote. "The idea is that Camus was a kind of Algerian Belfastman, Protestant as it were (though of course he was 'Catholic')".[33]

Mahon had been thinking about the poem for some time. As he had done with other similar literary appropriations, he incorporated into the poem details of his own life. The opening stanza juxtaposes Camus's death in an automobile accident in 1960 with Mahon's own Belfast childhood:

When the car spun from the road and your neck broke
I was hearing rain on the school bicycle shed
Or tracing the squeaky enumerations of chalk;
And later, while you lay in the *mairie,*
I pedaled home from Bab-el-Oued
To my mother silently making tea,
Bent to my homework in the firelight
Or watched an old film on television—
Gun-confrontations under a blinding sun,
Bogartian urgencies in the cold Irish night.

As the poem progresses, however, Mahon erases this distance and expresses a closer and closer identification with the plague-stricken Camus.

We too knew 'them', the minarets, the blaze
Of headlights on the coast road, the cicadas
Chattering like watches in our sodden hedges;
Yet never imagined the plague to come,
So long had it crouched there in the dark—
Rats on the pavement, rats in the mind,
'St. James Infirmary' playing to the plague wind.[34]

For Camus, the plague to come was the historical nightmare of the war and the extermination of the Jews. Jean-Baptiste Clamence notes in *The Fall* that he is living "on the site of one of the greatest crimes in history". Camus draws a link between this historical crime and Clamence himself when his protagonist comes upon a young woman drowning in a canal and makes no effort to save her. Mahon's allusion to the lyrics of the blues song "St. James Infirmary" reinforces the notion of tragic death and, if not guilt, mental anguish. The song tells the story of a man who goes to the hospital to see his dead girl "Stretched out on a cold white table, / So sweet, so cold, so fair". The blues song concludes, "Now that you've heard my story, / pour me one more shot of booze; / And if anyone comes askin' about me, / Tell 'em I got St. James Infirmary Blues".

Mahon's original title, "Death and the Sun", is a reference to François La Rochefoucauld's maxim that one cannot look long at either death or the sun. Hugh Haughton suggests it is "the 'plague wind' of the Troubles" that forms the basis for Mahon's identification with Camus. If so, the death of a nameless woman in *The Fall* and the dead girl of the blues song give particular form to a more generalised sense of guilt over Northern Ireland's historical rupture. Mahon's poem draws much of its power from the cumulative impact of these allusions. The version of the poem Mahon sent to Longley differed significantly from the version later published in *Antarctica*, including a different penultimate stanza:

> One cannot gaze directly at death or the sun.
> It is human to flinch, to seek anonymity
> By the cold canals of a strange city;
> But the stylish goalie on the run
> From history finds it lying in wait
> In a limbo of neutral angels. Redemption,
> The kingdom, lies in those dark waters.
> It is never too late, never too late!
> Forget the saints and martyrs,
> Consider the thieves and traitors[35]

In Camus' novel the concentric canals of Amsterdam evoke "the circles of hell", and Mahon exploits these multi-layered associations in order to probe man's fallen state.

Ever since the "Fire-King" and his move from Ireland to London, Mahon had been accused of being on the run from history. "Death and the Sun" makes clear there is no running away, and the only release may be the final one: dark water closing over the head of a man or a woman. Mahon later said the idea for the poem had been with him for several years. "Death and the Sun" would become one of the most heavily reworked poems in his canon. He gave it a place of importance as the concluding poem of both *Antarctica* and his *Selected Poems*; however, when he later republished it under the title "Camus in Ulster" in his *Collected Poems*, he pruned it to a single bare and enigmatic stanza.

In May Mahon returned to Wake Forest for the annual meeting of the American Conference for Irish Studies which Heaney, Carson and Paulin all attended. He spent much of the time with "Big Seamus" and talking with Pat King, "the elegant ex-nun" whom he had met at his Brooklyn reading some months before.[36] Rory, "the Heir Apparent", accompanied him on the trip, and by all accounts the visit was a success, without any alcoholic relapse.[37] On his return, he paused briefly in London before travelling onward to a festival of French and English poetry in Paris. He was back in London in time to attend the launch party for Montague's *The Dead Kingdom*, hosted by Richard Ryan at his home in Montpelier Square. Ryan had recently been posted to London where he was now the chief political officer at the Irish Embassy and deeply involved in discussions of a hoped-for political reconciliation in the North. The Ryan and Mahon children were close in age, and the two families would often meet in nearby Kensington Park.

With the arrival of summer Doreen and the children departed for a holiday in north Antrim. She and the children spent part of July at the cottage of the artist Gordon Woods in Castlerock, which they were thinking of buying before the builder's report made clear how unwise that would be. Mahon stayed in London and worked on his screenplays of Turgenev's *First Love* and Brian Moore's *The Feast of Lupercal*. Sidney Glazier, who had produced a successful television drama of Moore's *Catholics* in 1973, had invited Mahon to adapt Moore's novel, but was concerned with the script he submitted in June. To make matters worse, RTÉ ran into trouble financing the production and abruptly pulled out of the project, leaving Glazier to seek another studio.[38]

While these events were unfolding, Mahon's television adaptation of *The Cry* aired on the BBC programme "Play for Today" at the end of

July. The production received favourable reviews from the London critics and, in equal measure, condemnation from the more strident Unionist community. When the *Sunday Independent* asked Mahon how he felt dealing with material so close to his own family background, he replied, "If everybody acted in accordance with the political inhibitions they have always felt, nothing would ever get written—or done. I would like to see traditional loyalties broken up and diffused.... And in any case, I happen to be in favour of a United Ireland".[39]

High Time was also moving closer to production, and the directors Mark Long and Emil Wolk had decided to shift the setting from 1968 to the present, and to play up the free-wheeling boisterousness of the story. It was their idea to bring it "right bang up to the minute". The play was paired with Tom Paulin's version of *Antigone*, with a shared cast, and the two plays opened together in back-to-back performances at the Guildhall, Derry on 19 September before travelling to Dublin and an extended 15-city-tour, both north and south. Paulin adapted *Antigone* to make a comment on political action, with direct implications for the present, while Mahon followed Molière's French text closely, including preserving the verse form. Mahon sent his parents tickets to the Belfast performance and travelled to Dublin for the opening at the Gate Theatre, followed by a party at "the Heanery".

On seeing his play for the first time, Mahon was shocked. "I'd no idea they'd do with it what they did", he told Ciaran Carty of the *Sunday Independent*. "They took it way over the top."[40] Mahon had hoped to tease out an analogy between parental authority and political authority, playing off of Heaney's notion of Ireland as female and England as male. Instead, the directors had transformed his script into what one reviewer called a "Hellzapoppin'—Monty Python style romp".[41] Despite his initial shock, the double billing received generally positive reviews. "Enormously successful", *Theatre Ireland* called the combined performances, though the reviewer added, "there is an extent to which the two adaptations cancel each other out". Fallon, who would issue the text in a Gallery edition in the coming year, wrote Mahon that he thought the production had gone off "like a firecracker", and Eamon Grennan dubbed him the "punk playwright".[42]

While in Dublin for the *High Time* performance, Mahon visited the set where shooting was underway for his and Paul Joyce's television adaptation of Turgenev's *Summer Lightning*. His role had ended with the studio's acceptance of the script, but, following *High Time*, he took a heightened interest in the filming. He stood by and watched attentively as the actor Paul Scofield, playing Vladimir Petrovich, reflected on his lost youth. The co-production between RTÉ and Channel 4 had been plagued by difficulties and cost overruns, and it was a relief to see the work coming to fruition at all.

In August Mahon shared with Will Sulkin, his editor at OUP, the news that he anticipated having a new collection, to include "A Kensington Notebook" and "Death and the Sun", ready by January. OUP was putting limits on its poetry list, however, and Sulkin replied that the press could publish no more than six collections of poems a year and that he had already made commitments to James Berry, D.J. Enright, Roy Fisher, Zbigniew Herbert, Anne Stevenson, Chris Wallace-Crabbe, Hugo Williams and Charles Tomlinson. "How flexible are you willing to be?" he asked, and proposed delaying publication until March 1986.[43] Mahon was not pleased with this response, but a few days later he heard from Sulkin again: "I can't help thinking that I made a mistake in pushing you from October '85 to March '86", he wrote by way of apology; "the March slot is available to you if you want it".[44]

For some months Mahon had been negotiating a possible teaching appointment—"visiting resider", he called it—at Rutgers University in Camden, New Jersey, across the Delaware River from Philadelphia.[45] The city had a lot to recommend it, including "the second highest crime rate of any comparable community in USA", he joked to Asekoff.[46] In October he visited the campus to explore that possibility further. He made side-trips to read at Swarthmore, Villanova and Princeton, and Pat King travelled from New York for the Villanova reading, their third meeting in recent months. Mahon was increasingly attracted to this smart and elegant woman who was interested in his own work, and on his return to London he and Pat continued to exchange letters. In order to avoid discovery, he recorded her details in his address book under her husband's name, Tom King.[47] He wrote to her of his upcoming plans to visit Paris, and Pat wrote that she would be on Achill in late spring where she hoped to get some work done on the dissertation she had begun on his own poetry. She returned often to Ireland where her two children were attending boarding school.[48] Mahon was noting every detail of her travels and looking for opportunities to see her again.

Over the autumn he was also exchanging letters with Paul Durcan, who had recently divorced his wife, Nessa, and taken a place near the waterfront in Dublin's Ringsend. Durcan was living alone, and he confided that a week might pass without him speaking to a single person. "The Republic is not kind to people whose marriages have floundered", he explained.[49] A depressive personality at the best of times, Durcan was blaming himself for the break-up of his marriage. Mahon took careful note of his friend's experience with a mixture of envy and fear. In November, just days after Margaret Thatcher and Garret FitzGerald had held an Anglo-Irish Summit meeting at Chequers, Durcan was in London to interview Mahon for a profile he was writing for *Magill* magazine. They met at the Chelsea Arts Club, one of Mahon's regular meeting places, and a couple of weeks later the Christmas number of *Magill* featured an admiring profile describing Mahon's early life, his Trinity years and his later career as a poet and scriptwriter. In the interview, Mahon offered one of his most direct statements to date on the political situation in the North:

The Protestants are the problem, not the Brits. The Brits, for all their bluster, will go when they have to. But the Protestants are a terrified people; terrified and maimed. Most societies are pretty sick, but Northern Ireland is sick unto death, perhaps because at a deep level it knows it shouldn't exist.

He then shifted from the collective to the individual, casting the conflict in deeply personal, even psychological, terms. "The Ulster Protestant must be saved from himself; he will have to rethink himself or quit".[50] It is a revealing comment, one that casts light on his own embrace of a Catholic literary tradition that included writers like Montague and Moore. The day after their interview, Mahon was on a plane to Paris, where he gave readings at the British Institute and the Sorbonne. Neither reading paid much, and he economised by staying at George Whitman's bookshop, Shakespeare & Company, across the river from Nôtre Dame. It was on this second visit to Paris that year that he met, through Montague, the art critic Ann Cremin with whom he would become friends.

He was back in London a few days later when he received a distressed call from his mother letting him know his father was gravely ill. He made a hurried trip to Belfast to see his father for the last time, and two weeks later, on New Year's Eve 1984, he received word that Norman Mahon was dead. A service was held a few days later at the Roselawn Crematorium, where one of the mourners vented his anger at Mahon for his harsh portrayal of the B-Specials in *The Cry*.[51] Writing to Longley afterwards, Mahon confessed, "I myself would have much preferred the rattle of soil on the coffin lid at Carnmoney, ecclesiastical vestments flapping in the wind, eyes streaming with the cold, muck on the boots". Instead, "it had to be Auschwitz with muzak".[52] Mahon had been estranged from his father for years, and even on this occasion the tears that he evokes in his letter are from the wind and cold rather than from any wellspring of grief.

Over the winter Mahon was working on the screenplay of Elizabeth Bowen's novel *The Death of the Heart*. "Four weeks' work, off and on", he described it to Longley.[53] Bowen's novel of betrayal probes the basis of human relationships and examines one young girl's discovery of their inherent unreliability and fragility. Bowen's protagonist, Portia Quayne, has been raised in hotels, without a permanent place to call home. After her mother's death she is alone in the world, and out of necessity goes to live with her half-brother and his wife, who are locked in a sterile marriage. Portia is deceived by an insincere cad named Eddie, who says he loves her, but when he betrays her trust, Portia is left even more devastatingly alone than before. While the novel offers a picture of male arrogance and cruelty, Mahon, in his loneliness, sympathised with Portia. His own marriage seemed increasingly false, and his and Doreen's future together uncertain.

Mahon had reviewed the *Selected Letters of Robert Graves* the previous autumn, and Graves and the muse were still much on his mind when he took up Longley's *Poems 1963–1983* to review early in the new year. The function of poetry, he wrote, is the invocation of the muse. "This was once a warning to man that he must keep in harmony with the family of living creatures among which he was born, by obedience to the wishes of the lady of the house". One cannot read the review without seeing it as a statement about his own strained marriage. He gets back to the subject at hand, calling his friend "a love poet and a nature poet, a celebrant of the female principle".[54] But even as Mahon engages in a Gravesian celebration of women, it is uncertain whether the muse he idealises is still Doreen. Mahon sent Longley a copy of the review with his congratulations on the book. As for new poems of his own, he confessed there was "no sign". Quoting Rilke, he added an injunction for himself, "You must <u>change your life</u>".[55]

His short poem "Dejection", inspired by Coleridge's ode, was published in *The Irish Times* in early February.[56] The four-line poem is, like Coleridge's "Dejection: An Ode", a poem about the inability to write a poem. "Must I stand out in thunderstorms again / Who have twice come in from the cold?" In his own working copy of *Antarctica*, Mahon later noted in the margin Randal Jarrell's observation that "a good poet is someone who [manages] in a lifetime of standing out in thunderstorms, to be struck by lightning five or six times; a dozen or two dozen times and he is great!"[57] By the time he came to write that, however, the lightning strike was something to be sought after and even hoped for. In February 1985 Mahon was anticipating being forced out of doors. In his mind, his ability to write and the stability of his home life were in fact deeply connected.

When Mahon saw Will Sulkin at the Oxford Poetry Festival, he learned that *The Hunt by Night* had gone out of print. Despite that, Oxford was delaying his new collection since they still held a sizeable stock of *Poems 1962–1978*. It didn't seem to matter that Mahon had come to dislike that collection and was eager to see it superseded.[58] These frustrations were all the encouragement he needed to explore interest elsewhere, and he raised the prospect of a *Collected Poems* with Paul Keegan of Penguin a few weeks later.[59] While he remained contractually obligated to OUP, Penguin opened a door by initially undertaking to publish his translation work. Keegan approached Jaccottet's French publisher, Gallimard, about the prospect of a Penguin Jaccottet.[60] In fact, Mahon was exploring multiple changes in his life, and, as he had done before, he imagined that change required a move from one place to another—even, it seems, from one country to another.

Rory Brennan, of Poetry Ireland, helped organise a series of readings in Dublin, Cork and Galway in March, and Mahon spent the trip looking for suitable housing where his family might live. Hedli MacNeice had recently moved to Paris, and he was particularly attracted to the idea of moving into her former house in Kinsale. He had recently read Alannah Hopkin's novel *The Out-Haul*, which is set in a small west Cork village, and when he and Doreen met her and became friends, she too encouraged the Kinsale idea.[61] He asked O'Grady to keep his eye out for suitable options, saying he would settle for any "comfortable family house in reasonable nick". Their plan was to keep the Observatory Gardens flat in London "for pied-à-terre purposes" and "make our rehibernicisation a gradual process".[62]

Mahon was encouraged in this decision by the Arts Council's new programme of subsidies for Irish artists. He had been elected to membership in Aosdána shortly after its founding, but there was a residency requirement in order to qualify for the annual *cnuas* stipend. While the money was by no means extravagant, moving to Ireland did hold out the promise of some degree of financial stability which Mahon could always supplement with royalties, reading fees and other occasional income. He was now calling Ireland his "spiritual home".[63]

Mahon paused in Dublin en route to Kinsale, where he was interviewed by Terence Brown, who asked him if he would ever return to Ireland to live and write there. "I hope to", he said. When Brown reminded him of his harsh statements about the sterility of Irish poetry he had made when he left Dublin 15 years earlier, Mahon did his best to explain that ill temper. "You have to bear in mind that in 1970 I'd been living in Ireland for several years, I'd been living in Dublin, and I remember quite distinctly that I was in a state of intense exasperation with Ireland, especially since the troubles had started up".[64]

When Brown asked him about his personal beliefs—whether in myth, magic or religious faith—Mahon explained that he felt no need to follow either Eliot or Yeats in embracing a system of faith or in making a spiritual world of his own as Yeats had done. "I don't feel the need to impose an order where none too obviously exists. I suppose to use what is an old-fashioned term, I'm an existentialist with a small 'e'".[65] Mahon had his Camus poem, "Death and the Sun", still fresh in his mind. That evening he gave a reading at Buswells Hotel before travelling on to Montague's home in Cork the next day, from which he made a house-hunting trip to Kinsale.

Mahon planned to return to Kinsale with Doreen to show her some of the places he had seen, but once back in London he wrote O'Grady to report a change of plan owing to "a certain continuing coolness from the Muse".[66] A few days later, however, he was reporting that they had discussed the Kinsale idea further and "pretty much decided to be serious about it".[67] He was already committed to the move, and these plans had grown in his mind and taken definite shape, but Doreen did not share her husband's enthusiasm.[68] A few weeks later Doreen made her own weekend trip to Kinsale to see the town for herself. He reported that she had returned "wildly enthusiastic", and told O'Grady, "the reconnaissance done, we are both committed to the Kinsale idea".[69]

The town satisfied several of Mahon's requirements for a desirable place to live. The streets drop down from the surrounding hills into the town centre, which wraps around a tidal harbour at a bend near the mouth of the Bandon River. The protected harbour had made it a desirable settlement since medieval times, but Kinsale is remembered most as the site of the defeat of the Irish in the Battle of Kinsale in 1601. Also of interest to Mahon was the wreck of the *Lusitania* 11 miles offshore (in "The Seasons" he would take note of "old shipwrecks visible from the air"). Kinsale also had MacNeice associations, through Hedli, and there were friends nearby. Desmond O'Grady was just across the harbour—or "the lagoon", as O'Grady preferred to call it—Montague not far away in Cork City, Alannah Hopkin had family connections in Kinsale and still made the town home for part of the year. The plan was to keep looking for a house over the summer, but to put money down on one before the end of the year.

When *Summer Lightning* aired on RTÉ in April, the reviewer for the *Irish Independent* took exception to the English-Irish production arrangements. "Could the fault really be the involvement of Channel 4, and that the feeling for unrequited love in pre-Famine Ireland by the programme's British-based writer/director Paul Joyce might understandably be limited".[70] Anglo-Irish cooperation was a particularly delicate matter (never mind that the greater cultural crossing the film made was from Turgenev's nineteenth-century Russia). The Irish and British governments were moving towards the signing of the Anglo-Irish Agreement later in the year, giving the Republic a role in Northern Ireland's political process for the first time. Mahon was sceptical, however, of the upcoming summit which he expected would produce only a decision to hold yet another summit.[71]

Derek and Doreen discussed spending the summer holiday with the Ryans on the Isle of Rhé, off the west coast of France, but, as with their house-hunting, husband and wife were of two minds. In the end Doreen took the children and returned to Greece, while her husband travelled to Achill to be near Pat, who was spending the summer there. Doreen was under considerable stress when she arrived at Glyn and Roya Hughes's home in Athens. Her temper flared when the conversation turned to politics and Roya drew a comparison between Ireland's Troubles and Greek-Turkish relations. Doreen couldn't let the remark pass. She turned to Glyn and snapped how long are you going to go on living with this?

In fact, Glyn and Roya were experiencing strains in their own marriage, and Glyn later looked back on the blow-up as a turning point in his relationship with his wife.[72]

The summer started equally badly for Mahon, who on arrival found Achill rainy and depressing. He was reading Thomas Kinsella's anthology of Irish poetry, *An Duanaire*, and a poem he wrote that summer opens with an epigraph in Irish which he translated as "a desolate waif scarce seeing the light of day". "That's how I felt (at first) in rainy Achill last month, thinking of Doreen and the kids in Greece", he wrote Peter Fallon.[73] "*At first*" because he and Pat King had coordinated their summer schedules, and she soon arrived for a two-week summer school. Derek and Pat had been attracted to one another from their first meeting, and their intimacy had deepened during his Wake Forest visit. Pat was not prepared to leave her husband, however, nor could Mahon urge such a step when he had not taken it himself. They were instead looking for ways to spend time with one another while they wondered what the future might hold.

While on Achill, Mahon's "Death and the Sun" appeared in the TLS, altered now from the version first sent to Longley. Before returning to London, he detoured through Kinsale to continue house-hunting but still without success. A note to Desmond O'Grady captures something of his melancholy mood: "Starting guns in the bay for a yacht race as I take the low road into town; driving rain, clear skies, driving rain, but what the hell it's home".[74] He was still set on moving to the seaside town, but whether he would do this with or without Doreen was not yet clear.

Sidney Glazier had continued to seek a studio for Mahon's screenplay of *The Feast of Lupercal*, now entitled *A Moment of Love*, and had offered the script to the BBC, which optioned it for possible production at a later time. Also that autumn, Mahon received a letter from his friend Nicholas Grene, suggesting he apply for a newly established writing fellowship at Trinity College. The duties of the post were light: conduct a creative writing workshop, give occasional lectures or readings and be available to consult with students.[75] At his friend's urging, he applied, and while he awaited word on the outcome he travelled to Leuven, Belgium, for the European Festival of Poetry organised by the Leuven Institute for Ireland in Europe. He received his author's copies of *Antarctica* on his return to London in early November, and dashed off a thank-you note to Peter Fallon, in which he confessed he was bracing for reviews "pronouncing me all washed up ... as if I didn't know".[76] Relations with Doreen had been strained even before his departure, but, on his return from Belgium, she sensed a change in her husband's behaviour. When she confronted him with her suspicions, he confessed that he was seeing someone else— not Pat King, but a woman he had met at the Leuven conference named Jenneke.

Mahon acted out this betrayal by defacing the copy of *Poems 1962– 1978* which he had taken with him to Belgium. He struck through the dedication and soaked the book in water, whether in a tub or a toilet is not clear.[77] It seems he was acting out his anger and frustration with a figurative drowning of the book he so closely linked to Doreen, but the action too brings to mind his own near drowning many years before.

Despite his and Doreen's history of separation and more recent estrangement, the admission of infidelity came as an utter shock. Drink had been the great test of their marriage, Doreen had thought, not adultery. When someone once commented on her husband's alcoholism, Doreen had replied, "Yes, but he's *my* alcoholic". That dependency had offered a measure of security that was now shattered.[78]

In this moment of crisis Mahon turned to the Ryans, who took him in while trying not to pick sides in the break-up. Doreen turned to her friend Sandra Leitch for support before taking the children and travelling to her mother's home in Portballintrae. Back in the Observatory Gardens flat, alone, Mahon tried to capture in verse the creative possibilities of this moment of metamorphosis:

> After you left I spent
> an hour cloud-gazing
> at the back window,
> imagining the flight
>
> and slow descent
> through rain-cloud
> to your private
> kingdom by the sea
>
> and thinking, 'take out
> pen and paper,
> this is the time
> to get it down!'

He had always viewed moments of intense feeling as sources for poetry, "places where a thought might grow".

> That night I slept
> in a thick forest,
> its dead trees
> covered with hoar-frost,
>
> There sat the midnight court,
> its only function
> to hear the evidence
> I brought against myself.
>
> A stream crashed in the bracken,
> a rosy moon
> droned its faint
> blues for the earth.
>
> Waking at six I thought
> of wartime and looked to see
> a flickering vapour trail
> high above the dawn sea,
>
> that rising pin of light
> a new star in the east
> promising a way back
> to origins, a clean start.

While he had imagined this moment for many months, it did not come without enormous feelings of guilt and self-reproach. As he had often done in the past, he projected his inner psychological state onto the inanimate objects he found around him:

> Now sunlight on a quilt,
> on an empty dress
> over a chair,
> on books and furniture

A discarded line references "a Greek rug" and "paperbacks".

> Frankly, I'd looked forward
> to being alone
> for a while and getting
> some writing done;
>
> to recreating the ideal
> conditions of student days—
> the silent rooms,
> the mirror and the lamp;
>
> but in your absence
> I hear, not the cries
> of involuntary memory
> or the music of the spheres
>
> but a fly buzzing
> furiously at the window,
> heartbroken by the baffling
> brightness and hardness,
>
> and at night, my own
> self-terror, remorseless
> as a drum roll
> splitting the dark.
>
> There is no silence
> as restful as your wit;
> come back now and
> give me peace to write!

The poem, "Night and Day", would become the provisional title for a new collection, but in the end the poem remained unpublished, as would a larger collection of the same title. However, Mahon would mine this poem for images and tropes that would re-emerge in his later poems for years to come, among them: woman as muse, a fly at the window and a cry for reunion and reconciliation.

His appointment as Writer Fellow at Trinity could not have come at a more opportune time. He set aside his plans to move to Kinsale, and made arrangements instead to be in Dublin for the upcoming term. He was there for the joint launch of *Antarctica* and *High Time*, and just before Christmas his film treatment of Elizabeth Bowen's *The Death of the Heart* was broadcast on ITV. That novel of human failing and betrayal offered an ironic counterpoint to the events of the past months. Sandra Leitch visited Doreen and the children on Christmas day, following their return, and found the Observatory Gardens flat heavy with gloom. Mahon had published no new poems in recent months, nothing at all since his single summer poem "Achill". Asked to contribute to an anthology in support of famine relief in Africa, he sent two old poems: "The Facts of Life", with its confessional line, "Nothing came out as I intended", and the more hopeful "Everything Is Going To Be All Right". In fact, the break-up of his and Doreen's marriage marked the beginning of a long period of creative sterility. As he had foreseen in his review of Longley's poems some months before, creativity was linked to a stable home life and the approval of the muse. There had been cries for help over the past year, his "Dejection" ode, his appeals to friends. But at the end of 1985, Mahon left his wife, the consequences of which would stifle his creativity for close to ten years and reverberate through the late poems when he eventually began to write again.

Chapter 12

| THE ABSENT MUSE

M ahon arrived in Dublin in early January to take up his duties
as Trinity College's first Writer Fellow. "Derek Mahon is back
in Ireland for good", the college announced with satisfaction.[1]
The appointment came with a modest monthly stipend and rooms in
college, but in anticipation of Jenneke's arrival he took a flat in Anglesea
Road, Ballsbridge. He had been eager to move out of college rooms as
an undergraduate, and was not inclined at this late date to relive that
aspect of his college experience. Jenneke had left her husband to join
him in Dublin, and in the first flush of their new lives they were talking
hopefully of some permanent arrangement. More than one of his Dublin
friends was taken aback when he introduced Jenneke matter-of-factly as
his "common-law wife".[2] The future, however, was far from clear. Jenneke
thought she might start a business supplying specialty foods and pâté to
local shops and restaurants, and when Doreen learned of these plans, she
contemptuously dubbed her rival "the goose-stuffer".[3]

Mahon did not tell his mother of his and Doreen's separation, or
of Jenneke, perhaps because of some uncertainty about whether the
separation was indeed permanent. Instead, he let his mother think he
and Doreen were living apart temporarily, for the duration of the Trinity
fellowship. He was sending what money he could to Doreen and the

children, leaving himself little to live on, and in that emergency he turned to friends for help. Jennifer Johnston gave him £1,000 and Peter Fallon sent him a small advance for *The School for Wives*, which he was hoping the Abbey would produce (an "unfortunate title in the circumstances").[4] Josephine Hart, who had been through a painful divorce and recently remarried, loaned him £4,000.[5] He needed something more permanent than one-time advances or loans, however, and applied for a *cnuas*, the annual stipend for artists administered by Aosdána, and began reviewing books on a regular basis for *The Irish Times*. Reviewing, he told Dillon Johnston, was now "a permanent feature of my working life".[6] Though he had not contributed to *Vogue* in nearly a decade, the magazine paid well, and he dashed off a quick piece of job work for them, a survey of contemporary British poetry.[7]

Mahon had agreed to conduct one creative writing class and one on writing for television. He was surprised when 38 students showed up on the first day. It seems flyers announcing the class had been posted on campus bulletin boards for days, and quite a few students came expecting to enrol. Mahon was annoyed at this development and instructed the students brusquely to submit a poem about a particular place and return in a week. The following week he returned all but four of the poems he had received and wrote the remaining four on the chalkboard. The class discussed the poems, and at the end of the hour he dismissed everyone except the four students whose poems he had selected, among them the poet Sara Berkeley, the journalist Rosita Boland and the playwright Deirdre Hines. "It was a mess, really", Boland later recalled.[8]

The reduced class met on Tuesdays at 11 a.m. in his office in the School of English. Mahon, in his seersucker suit, began by asking them to give him an "autobiography in less than twenty-four lines", along with a prose account of themselves. In each subsequent week he picked a new theme; one week he had them write ekphrastic poems. He emphasised the importance of form, and assigned exercises writing sonnets and villanelles.[9] When Sara Berkeley read a poem, "The Glass Bubble", with its lines, "How much do you weigh? / Half an ounce? / A sheet of paper", he listened with particular interest. Balancing a sheet of paper on his open hand, he declared that one could write about anything one liked, but "one *must become* the thing one writes about".[10] The statement brings to mind his own habit of imbuing inanimate objects with thought and feeling: a table, a chair, a kettle.

Despite the awkward beginning, Mahon was taking teaching seriously, and he was still hoping for a comfortable sinecure at some American university. Towards that end, he consented to an interview with a journalist from *Newsweek* magazine which had a large international distribution. The reporter took the familiar journalistic line and linked Northern Ireland's creative flowering to the Troubles, a limiting view that Mahon found personally abhorrent. When the piece came out, "Famous Seamus" (at 47 Heaney was already being called that) was flanked by photos of Mahon and McGuckian. "Utter banality" Mahon scribbled on his copy of the magazine.[11]

As a faculty member, Mahon had access to Trinity's Senior Common Room, where he could often be found lounging and reading the papers. "The Poets Lie Where They Fell" was taking on a new meaning entirely. Among those Mahon renewed friendships with on his return to Dublin was Paul Durcan, whose poems he was rereading. In a review essay for the *Irish Review* he called Durcan's most recent collection, *The Berlin Wall Café*, a hymn to a broken marriage. He was studying his friend's work closely for the poetic uses he had made of his recent experience, and insisted that Durcan, in an interesting reversal, had come through it all "more of a feminist than ever". His poems avoid any hint of self-pity, Mahon wrote, and instead cast his former wife as a heroic figure with mythical precedents in the story of Orpheus and Eurydice.[12] In the aftermath of his separation from Doreen, Mahon was redefining a feminist position that might even allow room for a husband fleeing a failed marriage. His comments anticipate the mythologising of his own marriage that he would undertake when he began to write again. Those poems were still some way off, and the drafts dating from these months would all remain unfinished and unpublished.

In the spring of 1986 Mahon attended a Trinity garden party and suggested (apparently in earnest) that the provost introduce peacocks onto the grounds of the college, an idea which, for some unexplained reason, was not taken up. His and Jenneke's initial excitement at their liberation from their respective marriages began to give way to familiarity and even tedium, and when she learned her husband had overdosed on Nembutal, she decided it was time to return to him. Mahon admitted to Dillon Johnston that it had been a relief to see her go. "It wasn't working out at all and the lady's foolishness was beginning to irritate me", he wrote him.[13] Another factor, however, was that he and Pat King were making plans to meet that summer. Pat arrived in Dublin in early June, just as Mahon was finishing his teaching duties. As they negotiated these adjustments in their personal lives, Ireland was debating the removal of the ban on divorce. The referendum to overturn the ban came to a vote in late June, only to be overwhelmingly defeated by 63 per cent of the popular vote.

Mahon delivered his script of *School for Wives* to Christopher Fitz-Simon at the Abbey at the end of the month, and posted to Penguin the translations of Philippe Jaccottet's poems he had been working on for some months. He also began a translation of Raphaële Billetdoux's novel *Mes Nuits Sont Plus Belles Que Vos Jours* (Penguin would publish the novel the following year as *Night Without Day*). He had entered a period of ventriloquism. Translation offered him alternative voices with which to speak about his own experience. Billetdoux's "stylish piece of novelistic sex'n'violence", as Mahon described it to Dillon Johnston, recounts a spontaneous and reckless love affair set in Paris, which ends tragically with the lovers drowned at sea.[14] Death by drowning still exerted a powerful pull on Mahon's imagination, and Billetdoux's novel combines sexual liberation and death in a Freudian tangle of self-annihilation. The final events of the novel unfold in the presence of a fly buzzing in the room, like the fly Mahon introduced into his unfinished poem about the break-up of his marriage, "Night and Day".

In his rush to put Trinity behind him in 1965, some twenty years before, Mahon had never properly entered his name for commencement, nor had he requested to receive his degree in absentia. As a result, he had never actually taken his undergraduate degree. As the spring term drew to a close, he decided to remedy that and "commence" with the graduating class of 1986. When the day came, Seamus and Marie Heaney were on hand to lend moral support, and Mahon marked this rite of passage by posing for pictures in the fur-lined gown he had escaped 20 years before. It was as if he was turning the clock hands back and beginning his life over again.

Derek and Pat arrived in Kinsale in late June and moved into Desmond O'Grady's cottage while he was away in Greece. Mahon had agreed to look after Desmond's dog, Ogham, and, in consideration of that, paid only a modest rent. Rincurran Cottage, as it was called, was located in Scilly, just off the High Road, between Kinsale and the Charles Fort. From behind the house one could look out over the harbour to the open sea in the distance. Pat's two boys were in boarding school in Cork City, so she had a pretext for future visits, but she was in agony about her marriage and neither she nor Mahon knew what the future might hold. Pat had made plans to return to America via London, and at the end of July Mahon accompanied her to London. He saw Doreen during the week and reported a "bad scene" with her. She had begun seeing the journalist Stan Gebler Davies, who, by coincidence, spent part of each year in Kinsale. Mahon confided to Asekoff that "Doreen is definitely over now".[15] As for Pat, "where we go next is an open question. My own feelings are deeply engaged; but familial prudence might count with her. Hard to say: she's capable of anything, really".[16]

From Rincurran Cottage it was only a ten-minute walk into town, past Desmond's local, "The Spaniard". Mahon was sticking to his discipline of sober living, his only indulgence being cigarettes. As he later described these months in an abandoned poem draft called "Rincurran Cottage", only "books and turf and Mick McQuaid / might keep a man from going mad".[17] Mahon had begun drawing a *cnuas*, but he was sending the money to Doreen and, as a result, was unable to begin repaying the loans he had received at the start of the year. Peter and Jean Fallon visited him in Kinsale during these weeks of solitude, after Pat's departure, as did the poet J.D. McClatchy, who offered to try and line up readings for him at Princeton and Yale. If Heaney could arrange another at Harvard, he could put together a reading tour, all part of his effort to see Pat again.

In anticipation of O'Grady's return at the end of the summer, Mahon took a flat in a large house on Compass Hill owned by Dr William Fitzgerald, a first cousin of Jennifer Johnston.[18] The house had originally been built as accommodation for married officers from the Charles Fort but in more recent years had been rented as holiday flats.[19] It was large and spacious, with a harbour view, and was only a short walk into town. "The Grove" would become Mahon's most reliable home, off and on, for the next 25 years. It was there, in early November, where he received a letter from his mother:

I asked Doreen for your address. It has been evident to me for a long time that you are not living with her and the children. This is probably the reason that neither of you write to me, nor do Rory or Katie, although I have written to and phoned them. I feel cut off from my little family; no one seems to want to tell me anything.[20]

After the death of his father, his mother had sold the house in Newtownabbey and moved into a small flat in Bangor, County Down. The move had all been for the best, she said, but, in an acknowledgment of her own advancing years and declining health, she closed, "I keep wondering if I will ever see you again". Her letter elicited no reply from her son, and she followed it up with another, just before his 45th birthday. "Not having heard from you for a long time I was wondering if you are still in Kinsale and hope you will receive this letter". She shared news of the recent John Hewitt celebration at the Queen's Festival—"all the well known poets took part"—as well as news of family members before closing "perhaps you will write before too long".[21]

Mahon was translating Samuel Beckett's "Mirlitonnades" (from *mirliton*, a crude flute or kazoo) under the working title "Some Squeals". He sent a number of these translations to Beckett, who replied that he didn't think they were completely successful, but offered to go over them with Mahon when he was next in Paris.[22] They missed each other, however, when Mahon visited for the *Semaine du Livre* conference that autumn. In the meantime, McClatchy, following up on his and Mahon's recent conversation about teaching opportunities, shared the news that Muldoon had already "slipped between the sheets" and secured an appointment at Princeton.[23] It was bad timing. Mahon was planning to read there in just a few weeks.

Early in the new year Mahon flew to America for his reading tour, including, in addition to Princeton, a reading at Seton Hall. In New York he saw Eamon Grennan, who couldn't resist making a quip about the publication of his "School for Significant Others".[24] Mahon was making useful contacts, among them Henri Cole of the Academy of American Poets, who invited him to return the following year. He also met on this trip a New York physician, Kevin Cahill, who would later render great service when Mahon moved to New York a few years later.

On his return to Kinsale he received author's copies of new editions of *The Hunt by Night* and *Poems 1962–1978*. "Many thanks for the reissued POEMS and HUNT", he wrote Jacky Simms. "I now have a difficult letter to write…. I would like at this point to be released from all contractual obligations with OUP so that I may publish in [the] future with Gallery Press, Dublin, director Peter Fallon". He had been considering this step for some months and Fallon had offered helpful advice on how to make the break even before his American reading tour. "Let's begin with what

I take to be a shared hope", Fallon had written him, "In 1990 (?) The Gallery Press will publish a *Collected Poems* of Derek Mahon (which we hope Penguin will accept afterward), and, before or after this, Gallery will publish individual Mahon collections. In other words, Mahon will move from Oxford to Gallery". Fallon advised him to ask for release from all contractual obligations, to have rights in existing books revert to the author and that those books be allowed to go out of print. He thought OUP would be more likely to release Mahon to a smaller publisher with only limited distribution in the UK market, and therefore he added, "I shouldn't mention Penguin".[25]

The decision to break his 20-year relationship with Oxford University Press was a deeply personal one, and Jacky Simms's pleadings with him sometimes take on the tone of a lover's quarrel: "I've been writing to you in my head, and in my heart, ever since your letter arrived", she wrote on receiving his letter.[26] "I'm not really able just to tear up the past", she added in another; "it isn't sensible to expect OUP to jettison our commitment and loyalty as if it had never been".[27] While the split had been a long time in coming, the reissue of *Poems 1962–1978* had been the deciding factor. More than any other, it had been Doreen's book, and it was now linked in his mind to a former life he felt he had to move past. He was looking ahead to a new collection that would include *Antarctica* and, with luck, some new poems. Simms tried to downplay the significance of the reprinted editions. The print runs had been small and the reissue was meant only "to tide over the gap, as we agreed, until you revised some of the poems for your *Collected*".[28] But Mahon saw the reissuing of the two books in a different light altogether.

As he struggled to explain his decision, his explanations took on broader cultural dimensions. "The point is that I want to be published from Ireland henceforth", he told Simms. It seems he had been in earnest when he had spoken of Ireland as his spiritual home. His *cnuas*, his affiliation with *The Irish Times*, his hopes for living in the country permanently, all contributed to a new identification with Ireland. His breach with OUP marked the end of his London life and signalled a new beginning of the kind to which his poems so often aspire.

Disentangling himself from his OUP contract, however, proved more difficult than he had imagined, and the issue dragged on, without resolution, for many months. He pleaded with Simms to let him go, but in the interim, while he waited for a final resolution to the issue, he found it impossible to write new poems. "This interval of discussion and negotiation has created an atmosphere, for me, inimical to new work.... Your reluctance to grant my request is creating a block. I need to feel free to envisage a new book my way, or nothing will get done. Will you please help me, or at least not hinder me?"[29] Fallon had no more luck forcing OUP's hand, but in the face of this impasse, he did persuade Mahon to co-edit with him a new Penguin anthology of contemporary Irish poetry. While the rights to Mahon's own poems remained entangled with OUP, nothing stood in the way of Mahon producing an anthology of the kind Fallon had been urging.

With the approach of summer, Mahon was growing increasingly impatient at the lack of progress. At the end of May, he wrote Simms what he hoped would be his final word on the matter: "You ask if there is a hurry to decide. Yes, from my point of view, there is. You say you hoped we might wait until my next book is ready; but there will be no next book if we go on like this. Certainly we can, as you propose, meet in London, but I'm not planning to be there until the autumn, and don't want to spin out our pointless negotiations until then or I'll have wasted a potentially fruitful summer. So please, Jacky, let's get on with it. I hate to seem harsh, but this is really my last word".[30] OUP reluctantly accepted his decision that the imprint would no longer be his "principal publisher"; however, they also noted that the Press "will wish to keep your titles available so long as they can publish and sell them effectively". The notion that *Poems 1962–1978* would continue to be reissued indefinitely only perpetuated the original offence. "I am dismayed by the thought that OUP might go on reprinting that awful Brown Book every two years in perpetuity".[31]

When Fallon visited Kinsale in the last week of May to talk over their publishing projects, Mahon warned him that Pat would be there and asked him not to show any surprise. "She is merely another person staying in the house. It's daft, I know; but the dear girl thinks she is invisible, and proceeds on that assumption, so let's not disabuse her".[32] Pat planned to spend most of the summer in Ireland, and the following week she and Mahon embarked on a driving tour, stopping first at the grave of Elizabeth Bowen at St Colman's Church in nearby Farahy. Mahon's adaptation of Bowen's *The Death of the Heart* had aired on Masterpiece Theatre in America a few weeks earlier, and it seemed a fitting time to pay homage. From there they drove to the Tyrone Guthrie Centre near Newbliss, County Monaghan, at the invitation of Bernard Loughlin.

Guthrie's former home and surrounding grounds had been made into an artists' retreat just a few years earlier. It rained for much of the visit, but, in a break in the weather, Mahon and Pat went rowing on Annaghmakerrig Lake. He wrote Fallon from there that he was "writing at last, if slowly". He was hoping to have enough poems for an "*Antarctica*-sized book" in the spring, to be followed by the new selected poems which he wanted to replace his OUP selection.[33]

Mahon learned in May that he had been chosen to receive a $10,000 award from the American-Ireland Fund. As welcome as the windfall was, it was only temporary relief from financial worries. "All it will do is clear two overdrafts and put me in the black for the first time in years", he told Fallon; "I give myself till Christmas to get back in the red where I belong".[34] The chairman of the prize committee had expected Mahon to accept the award at a dinner in Belfast in June, but Mahon had no interest in returning to Belfast and, in the end, the chairman mailed a cheque to him at the Tyrone Guthrie Centre.[35] While he and Pat were away, Trinity College awarded him a master's degree in absentia. As a graduate in good standing, he was eligible for the degree on payment of a modest fee. No further coursework was required, and the degree would enhance Mahon's qualifications for the kind of university appointment he was seeking.

Over the summer, *Night Without Day* was moving closer to publication, and Mahon was reading proofs for his selected Jaccottet for Penguin. His plan was that Gallery would handle sales of his poetry in Ireland, and Viking Penguin would do so in Britain and America. His Billetdoux and Jaccottet translations were not bound by any OUP contract and, as a result, were the first steps in this larger plan. He and Pat spent most of July back in Kinsale before setting out again for the annual Yeats Summer School, where Declan Kiberd had invited him to read and conduct a poetry workshop. They combined the trip with stops at the Galway Arts Festival and the Kilkenny Arts Week where he had requested a room for himself and his "wife".

Among the unfinished drafts dating from the summer is one Mahon conceived of as a companion poem to "Derry Morning", called "Driving in Ulster". The poem revisits numerous sites of Mahon's early life, including the Derry coast ("nearly the death of me"), County Antrim and Belfast. While he never completed the poem, the surviving fragments offer a glimpse of his and Pat's summer driving tour: "A red sun watched ~~our~~ your Citroën / Rise and descend from glen to glen".[36] His self-correction, that substitution of "your" for "our", conveys a great deal about his own uncertainty over his and Pat's relationship. Were they a couple, or was he merely a passenger in her car? It remained far from clear what the future held.

After Pat returned to Connecticut, Mahon shared with Louis Asekoff details of his travels, adding another important development: "During the summer I started, very tentatively, taking a drink again, and find I can do so without difficulty. Whether seven years' abstinence has built up a resistance, or whether the original crisis was 'situational', I don't know; but am now drinking in moderation and feeling and looking none the worse for it". Mahon was happy at his imagined recovery—another sign of the new beginning he was making in other parts of his life—and he shared the good news with more close friends. "Since I don't get drunk (careful not to) the question arises, why bother? Well, it got kinda boring being bone-dry; besides, it might help me recapture some lost poetry". Mahon was concerned about how his friends would take the news, and advised them not to say "Mahon [is] on the booze again", but rather, "Mahon can drink after all".[37]

That autumn Mahon helped organise the first Kinsale Arts Week celebrations, which included readings by the Kinsale coterie: O'Grady, Aidan Higgins and himself. He also invited Montague and Nuala Ní Dhomhnaill, whose poems he was translating as part of his continuing exploration of his own Irish origins. He was working from literal cribs which Ní Dhomhnaill sent him and, from them, creating essentially new poems. He was struggling, however, to write any original work of his own, and he blamed the distraction of reviewing and television work. He confessed to feeling "a special hatred of the TV rubbish, which puts one in a bind since it pays, sort of".[38] Pat returned for a lengthy visit in November and Mahon gave his now-customary warning to Peter Fallon. She would be around until the end of the month, "pretending, as usual, to be invisible; so please respect her wishes. Ring by all means, but remember she 'isn't here'. Jesus".[39]

As he struggled to overcome his writer's block, Mahon returned to some unfinished poems, among them "April in Moscow", which he had first begun following his Coleraine crisis. He would later re-entitle that poem "White Night" and pair it with "The Earth", but in the aftermath of his move to Kinsale he was thinking of the poem as part of a larger sequence. He planned to insert a new poem, "Autumn", between the two parts, making this a three-part poem sequence. The abandoned "Autumn" addresses most directly his personal circumstances at the time:

> I have split up with my family,
> My loved ones are far away;
> Now a familiar solitude
> Lies on the silent forest.

The first-person speaker, however, is not entirely alone:

> Yet here we are in a cottage
> Where nobody ever comes;
> As in the famous poem,
> The paths are overgrown.

> The window-frames stare down at us,
> Anxious about our future.
> We made no promises,
> We shall meet our fate head-on.

Another unfinished draft gives us a glimpse of Mahon's living arrangements at the time:

> You shed your clothes impatiently
> As the wood sheds its leaves;
> Desire roars like a storm
> In the crackling autumn forest.

> God-sent, you are the one good gift
> On the high road to disaster;
> The sick grief everywhere
> Serves only to draw us together.

OUP was still refusing to let *Poems 1962–1978* go out of print, and during the continuing impasse Peter Fallon proposed that Gallery publish an entirely new selection to replace the offending volume.

Through his agent Stephen Durbridge, Mahon learned that the BBC wished him to write a screenplay of Moore's *The Temptation of Eileen*

Hughes. The only difficulty was the script was already under contract with another studio. Durbridge warned him, "you will have to be exceedingly careful that the script which you write is different from your previous screenplay and that you must not use either scenes or dialogue from the earlier version".[40] While Mahon was negotiating these difficulties, Brian Friel suggested he undertake a stage adaptation of Molière's *Tartuffe.*

With nowhere to go for the approaching holiday, he wrote to Mount Melleray Abbey outside Cappoquin, County Waterford to ask if he might spend Christmas there. He received a note from the abbot saying he would be welcome.[41] Christmas had always been an emotionally treacherous time for him, and he was hoping the Abbey would offer a refuge from holiday revellers and an alcoholic relapse. His stay began badly, however, when he arrived with a bottle of Hennessy. If he had brought the bottle to nurse during his stay, he had a change of heart and presented it to the surprised abbot, who said he would save it for the bishop.[42] Something of Mahon's experience there shows up in another unpublished poem draft:

Plainsong in a dripping Cistercian
monastery in mist-shrouded hills,
golden light through a rose window;
a crucifix above the bed
a cloud of unknowing.[43]

He had planned to spend a fortnight at the abbey but left after a week. As he later recalled, "Soon as I got to town I drank a large gin and felt better at once".[44]

He and Peter Fallon had hoped to deliver the manuscript of their anthology of Irish poetry to Paul Keegan, at Penguin, by the end of the year, but that deadline came and went. In the first week of January Mahon travelled to France for a symposium on "Louis MacNeice and his Successors", organised by Professor Jacqueline Genet at the University of Caen. Michael and Edna Longley came over for the event, as did Hedli MacNeice, while he and "Mrs. Mahon" stayed at the Hôtel Le Dauphin near the university.

Mahon was briefly back in Kinsale before departing again for America. Henri Cole had invited him to deliver the annual Biddle Lecture to the Academy of American Poets, and Mahon flew to New York for the occasion and stayed at Asekoff's apartment, near Columbia University.

The lecture was held the following Tuesday evening at the Guggenheim Museum. After being introduced by the critic M.L. Rosenthal, Mahon took the stage and proceeded to speak more directly than was usual of the position of the contemporary poet caught between "a heart-breaking reversion to atavistic violence" and "cheering new prospects of long-overdue change". What the poet living in such times can offer, he argued, was "a new imaginative and historical mutation" that subsumes "all sects, denominations and inherited assumptions under what Wolfe Tone called 'the common name of Irishman'".[45] The talk is among Mahon's most direct statements on the role of the artist in a time of political crisis.

When he had begun drinking again the previous summer, he had done so cautiously, but he was drinking heavily during his New York visit. Asekoff was concerned about his friend and later blamed himself: "one of the sorrows of my life was that he fell off the wagon while staying with me in NY after about five or six years of being sober".[46] Mahon was still feeling blocked creatively, and Asekoff stressed the importance of writing every day, even if it were only a single line. It was during this trip that Mahon met the poet Samuel Menashe, who wrote spare, tightly compressed poems, whose style seemed to offer him a way forward.

After leaving New York, Mahon and Pat visited Toronto, where he read at the Harbourfront Centre, before going to St Paul, Minnesota for a reading arranged by the editor and writer Thomas Dillon Redshaw, and another at nearby Carleton College. On the ride into Minneapolis, his host pointed out the spot where John Berryman jumped to his death from the Washington Avenue Bridge. He was back in an icy New York a few days later where he and Paul Muldoon read at the Manhattan Theatre Club. As he spoke that night, "going through the usual old rubbish", he was telling himself "never again".[47] Drinking and the rigours of travel made it an exhausting trip, made worse when he threw his back out on the way to the airport. Back in Kinsale, he wrote to thank Asekoff for his hospitality and to swear off any more such trips: "No more readings/ lectures ill-paid, starting late, followed by hostile persons with harsh moustaches demanding that I sign books when all I want to do is relax and talk to my friends".[48] He also enclosed a short new poem:

Somewhere my son,
His vigour, his laughter;
Somewhere my daughter.[49]

On his return, he wrote to Sara Berkeley as well and for his address replaced "The Grove" with "The Grave".[50] Mahon and Peter Fallon met in Kinsale to go over the typescript of their anthology in late May, but when Fallon arrived for the weekend he found Mahon drinking and in no state to work. Mahon apologised a few days later for his "general inadequacy" and for making Peter "come all this way to so little purpose". He closed that note with the assurance "I am not turning into O'Grady".[51]

When word of his drinking reached Doreen, she threatened to cut off access to the children, now 12 and 10. She refused to allow them to visit their father in Kinsale. Adding to his worries, he remained unsure of his and Pat's future. "We've had one or two rather inconclusive phone talks since I got back and seem to be leaving things in mid-air for the moment", he told Asekoff.[52] In the meantime he found himself unable to write, and was wondering whether his poetry would ever come back.[53]

Redshaw had nominated Mahon for the O'Shaughnessy Poetry Award, given by the Irish American Cultural Institute, and in late summer he learned he was to receive the $2,500 prize at a luncheon at the Shelbourne Hotel in early September. When the day arrived, however, Mahon was in London for the launch of his translations of Philippe Jaccottet's *Selected Poems*. He and Jaccottet gave a joint reading at the Poetry Society, attended by Joseph Brodsky and Yehuda Amichai.[54] That same month, he received the Denis Devlin Award for *Antarctica*, though the collection was more than two years old. While he maintained the appearance of a writing life through occasional readings, he had produced little in the way of new poems.

While in London Mahon saw Rory and Katie. Doreen and the children had recently moved out of the Observatory Gardens flat into a house in Shepherd's Bush. Katie was going to a new school and learning to play the piano, and Rory had taken up skateboarding, which had left him with a leg in a plaster cast. When he met Doreen on this visit, he was shocked to see that her hair had begun to turn grey. He later confided to Mary Leland that he felt as if it was a scar he had inflicted.[55]

In November Mahon moved into an upper-floor flat in a ramshackle house in Cork Street, in Kinsale, called the "Dutch House" after its Dutch gable. The house had been occupied at one time or another by a series of friends, including Aidan Higgins and Alannah Hopkin. As was his custom, he took the attic flat which had a single back window from which one could see the harbour. He and Peter Fallon were finalising the contents of their anthology, and both were eager to put it behind them, "Then all we'll have to worry about are the attacks, turned backs, letter bombs".[56]

Mahon was still publishing no new poems, only his reviews for *The Irish Times*. In the spring he proposed to Brian Friel that he write an adaptation of Heinrich Von Kleist's *The Broken Jug*. The play, with its themes of lost innocence and secret guilt, suited Mahon's purposes perfectly, and Friel, Stephen Rea and Tom Kilroy, the last of whom had recently joined the Field Day board, were enthusiastic. He received a small advance to begin work on the script, which Field Day hoped to produce the following year.[57]

Mahon left Kinsale before the seasonal influx of summer visitors and returned to Dublin, where he had found a flat at 58 Fitzwilliam Square. It was the smallest of Dublin's Georgian squares, just south of Merrion Square where he and Longley had once lived. He was still hoping to move to America and in June he applied for a residency at the Yaddo artists' retreat, in Saratoga Springs, New York. He noted on his application that his *Selected Poems* would soon be published and he had the outline of "a new slim volume". He proposed using his time at Yaddo to finalise the new collection and work on a new version of *The Bacchae*, which had been commissioned by the Dublin Theatre Festival. He continued to review books, while Peter Fallon negotiated the joint Gallery and Viking Penguin publication of his *Selected Poems*.

In the summer Mahon received the welcome news that he had won the Scott Moncrieff Prize for his translation of Philippe Jaccottet's *Selected Poems* almost two years after its first publication. As usual, he was in financial straits, and he asked that the prize money be sent directly to his bank manager's attention at the Bank of Ireland. When an upper floor flat became available at 45 Fitzwilliam Square, he moved again. From his window he had a view of the square and its private garden. He later noted it was precisely "four and a half minutes from these steps to Doheny & Nesbitt's. Eight minutes to the Shelbourne Bar".[58]

That autumn the Dublin Theatre Festival produced Mahon's *School for Wives* to poor reviews. The comedic elements failed to come off successfully, and the reviewer for *The Irish Press* noted that the performance he attended "barely raised a forced chuckle".[59] In the meantime, Fallon was urging Keegan to set an earlier publication date for Mahon's *Selected*. "He's suffered such a block, so few poems since *Antarctica*, such a sense of being held and hobbled by OUP that I suspect he hopes or likes to believe that the appearance of the book in editions which will please him, i.e. Penguin's/Gallery's, might open the door for him, release him, as it were".[60] As the year drew to a close, Mahon was again losing his battle with drink, and shortly before Christmas he was admitted to St Patrick's Hospital. He would memorialise the time in a new poem, "Dawn at St. Patrick's":

> … the real
> hospital is a cheerful
> modern extension at the back
> hung with restful reproductions of Dufy, Klee and Braque.
> Television, Russian fiction, snooker with the staff,
> a snifter of Lucozade, a paragraph
> of *Newsweek* or the *Daily Mail*
>
> are my daily routine
> during the festive season.
> They don't lock the razors here
> as in Bowditch Hall. We have remained upright—
> though, to be frank, the Christmas dinner scene,
> with grown men in their festive gear,
> was a sobering sight.
>
> I watch the last
> planes of the year go past,
> silently climbing a cloud-lit sky.
> Earth-bound, soon I'll be taking a train to Cork
> and trying to get back to work
> at my sea-lit, fort-view desk
> in the turf-smoky dusk.
>
> Meanwhile,
> next door, a visiting priest
> intones to a faithful dormitory.
> I sit on my Protestant bed, a make-believe existentialist
> and stare at the clouds of unknowing. We style
> as best we may, our private destiny;
> or so it seems to me

as I chew my thumb
and try to figure out
what brought me to my present state—
an 'educated man', a man of consequence, no bum
but one who has hardly grasped what life is about,
if anything. My children, far away,
don't know where I am today

in a Dublin asylum
with a paper whistle and a mince pie,
my bits and pieces making a home from home.[61]

Chapter 13

| A DARK WOOD

I am entrenched
Against the snow,
Visor lowered
To blunt its blow

I am where I go

Samuel Menashe, "Winter"[1]

When Mahon learned that his application to Yaddo had been accepted, he began making plans to spend the spring of 1990 in America. He was covering Brendan Kennelly's classes at Trinity while Kennelly was on leave, but was drinking uncontrollably. At Terence Brown's urging he again agreed to seek treatment, and Terence drove him to St Patrick's, where there was an outstanding bill from his previous stay. The hospital would not readmit him until his account was settled, and Terence promptly took care of the bill.[2]

Even in this state, he was still writing regularly for *The Irish Times*, and before leaving Dublin the paper ran his review of Richard Holmes's biography of Coleridge, in which Mahon makes clear his identification with the Romantic poet. He noted Coleridge's struggle with opium addiction, his devotion to his muse, Sara Hutchinson, and observed that he was "generally thought to have been an atrocious husband". He praised the major poems, singling out "Dejection: An Ode" which he noted in a self-referential aside "reads like the work of a man of forty-nine not twenty-nine".[3] He saw something of himself in these biographical details, and Coleridge would figure prominently in the long poem he would soon begin.

Mahon flew to New York in late March, and from there took a train to Albany to meet John Montague, who was teaching at the university there. He spent a night with Adrian and Alison Frazier in nearby Schenectady, and the following morning, Monday, Alison drove him to Yaddo. They passed the Saratoga Race Course before turning off the road into the wooded estate. "Thick woodland stretched to left and right; squirrels bounced from the road; two lakes came into view, darkly silent, still fringed with ice that would melt before the month was out", Mahon later wrote of his arrival there.[4] He was given a room in West House with a view over the green lawn. His immediate neighbour was a composer, Gloria Coates, whom he nicknamed "Gloria in Excelsis". Heaney had informed friends Bob and Peg Boyers of his arrival, and the couple met him early in his stay and later in the month organised a reading at Skidmore College. Mahon was hoping the change of setting and enforced solitude would prove restorative, but a week into his stay he reported to Peter Fallon there were still "no poems yet".[5] Instead he was working on his *Bacchae* script and writing letters inquiring about possible teaching jobs in America.

Some time during his stay, however, he began a new verse letter, addressed to his two children. The poem that would emerge is related to his earlier epistolary poems, "Beyond Howth Head" and "The Sea in Winter", but while those poems spanned a wide range of social and historical subjects, "The Yaddo Letter" was deeply personal. The scope of the new poem was his family, and in its autobiographical directness and tone it resembles "Dawn at St. Patrick's", the poem with which it would be paired when first published.

> Here among silent lakes and dripping pines
> off Route 9P, I write you guys these lines
> to ask you what you're up to and what not.

He recalls their time together in London:

> I try to imagine you asleep, at work,
> or walking with your mother in Hyde Park
> where once we walked each Sunday, hand in hand,
> to feed the daffy ducks on the Round Pond,
> chucking crumbs to the ones we liked the best,
> comical, tufted yellow-eyes, ignoring all the rest.

Remember birthday parties, rockets at Hallowe'en,
bus-rides to Covent Garden to see Eugene?
The day we drove to Brighton? Maybe not.
Summer and winter I would rise and trot
my fingers up your backs like a mad mouse
to wake you chuckling. Now I wake in a silent
house in a dark wood....[6]

The poem recounts the break-up of his and Doreen's marriage, his move to County Cork, and itemises his losses along the way: "What I lost was a wife, a life, and you". It is a raw poem, one that tries to order the disorder of his own life and establish that "continuity with the past" which he insists is one of the keys to happiness. Even as he offers this fatherly wisdom, however, he admits such insight cannot protect one from hurt.

Children of light, may your researches be
reflections on this old anomaly;
may you remember, as the years go by
and you grow slowly towards maturity,
that life consists in the receipt of life,
its fun and games, its boredom and its grief;
that no one, sons or daughters, fathers, wives,
escapes the rough stuff that makes up our lives.[7]

Once he began the poem, it came quickly. Alice Quinn turned it down for *The New Yorker* in June, saying apologetically that she thought it too personal to serve as his debut in the magazine.[8]

At the end of his stay at Yaddo he travelled to Boston for a reading in Cambridge with Medbh McGuckian and Paul Durcan. From there it was back to New York for more "Irish hooliganism", as he put it.[9] The 92nd Street Y had organised an Irish Literature Festival, to be kicked off by readings from Heaney, Montague and Ní Dhomhnaill on the 14th, followed two nights later by Mahon, Durcan and Muldoon. Eamon Grennan introduced the speakers that evening, calling Mahon a "scrupulous philosopher of boundaries". Mahon acknowledged Dillon Johnston's support as publisher of his work in America and read a selection of poems picked for the occasion—poems for his New York friends Samuel Menashe and Philip Haas, and another, "How to Live", for "a woman friend". It was an appreciative audience, laughing at the right moments and hanging on his words at others. The one discordant note came when he introduced "Craigvara House". "The least said about that the better", he told the crowd, before launching into a disturbing imitation of Robert Lowell's hesitant and stuttering manner of speaking: "I went through … a k-k-kind of mental … emotional crisis … and this poem is about that.… It's about a-a-a psy-psy-psychic trauma and its resolution".[10] The audience was bewildered by the role-playing and relieved when Mahon switched back into his own voice and proceeded with the reading.

His role-playing betrayed a self-consciousness about his own alcoholism and its repetitive nature. Despite his recent hospitalisation, he was still drinking, often heavily, and it was only a few nights after the Y reading that he and Montague spent a drunken evening together at the aptly named Kinsale Tavern on the Upper East Side. That night, Mahon insisted on making a chivalric show of drinking champagne out of a woman's slipper, at which point Montague helpfully ordered the necessary champagne. Later that evening Montague had to help him back to Richard Ryan's apartment where he was staying, only to have Mahon lash out at him angrily in a torrent of verbal abuse.[11] Alcohol had made him emotionally erratic, and it was the kind of outburst that was becoming increasingly common.

Dr Kevin Cahill, whom Mahon had met on one of his previous visits to New York, was serving at the time as director of the American Irish Historical Society. When he learned of Mahon's condition, he intervened and arranged for his admission to the Lenox Hill Hospital to dry out. Dr Cahill's son, Chris, knew Mahon's poetry and went to visit him there. He found him looking perfectly fine and waiting calmly to check out. They chatted about mutual acquaintances without Mahon betraying any sign of his recent alcoholic crisis. Chris was shocked to learn two days later that he was in extremis again.[12] This scenario repeated itself a number of times. He would be released from hospital, and "within an hour would be in a bar drinking … there seemed to be no stopping the destruction".[13]

Mahon returned to Dublin for the summer, and he was back at Fitzwilliam Square in time for the launch of his and Fallon's *Penguin Book of Contemporary Irish Poetry* on 6 June. The book had been a direct response, if a delayed one, to Muldoon's 1986 *Faber Book of Contemporary Irish Poetry*, which had included only ten poets. Muldoon's selection had not been representative, Mahon felt, and it displayed a Northern bias he and Fallon hoped to remedy.[14] "If the present anthology can be said to have any polemical purpose, that purpose would be to correct imbalances created over the years by editors, publishers and critics, and to dispel the illusion that Irish poetry has been written exclusively by persons of Northern provenance", they wrote in their introduction.[15] They aimed to present an "unpartitioned intellect", to use Montague's memorable phrase, composed of both Northern and southern writers. The night following the launch party, four of the anthology's contributors—Ní Dhomhnaill, Michael Hartnett, Longley and Durcan—read selections in Dublin. Meanwhile, Mahon's *Selected Poems* was moving closer to publication, and Fallon was doing his best to represent Mahon's interests with OUP and Viking.

Rory and Katie visited their father in Dublin over the summer. Doreen was appealing to him for money, and warned him she could not continue to provide for herself and the children without more reliable support.[16] She had instructed her solicitor to move forward with divorce proceedings, and was hoping to formalise an annual maintenance agreement as part of the settlement. Mahon had been directing £9,000 pounds a year to her and the children, but the timing of the payments had often been unpredictable. He replied through his own solicitor that he was "broadly speaking prepared to consent to the Divorce being sought", but could not afford to have the papers executed in London. As his solicitor put it, speaking on his behalf, "he is not in a position at present to instruct English Solicitors to accept service of any Divorce proceedings.... It might be possible for you to arrange service of the documents on our client in Ireland".[17]

These pressures contributed to Mahon's anxiety and to his alcohol abuse, which friends were watching helplessly. "I long to see him", Longley confided to Heaney, "and yet dread a re-run of certain scenes from the past".[18] Mahon had agreed to read at Emory University in Atlanta in September, but when Van Morrison invited Montague, Seamus Deane and him to Luggala in County Wicklow to collaborate on a possible album, Mahon abruptly cancelled the reading. He drank heavily that weekend, and in the end, the artistic collaboration came to nothing.[19]

Towards the end of the summer Mahon was offered a teaching appointment at Villanova University, outside Philadelphia, and he began planning to spend a month in New York over the Christmas holiday before taking up the new job in January. He had copies of his *Selected*

Poems in hand by the end of the year, when he signed copies for New York friends. Even in the absence of any new poems, Fallon was keeping Mahon's work in print and before the reading public, but it was unclear when, or if, he would break free of his writer's block. When he sent "Dawn at St. Patrick's" and "The Yaddo Letter" to the *American Poetry Review* in January 1991, he wrote in the accompanying letter "this is the last time I submit anything anywhere".[20]

At Villanova, Mahon was provided an apartment close to campus. It was an unsettled time, however, and he spent most weekends back in New York. He was making inquiries among friends about places to live in the city, and he was also casting about for another teaching post to follow the four-month Villanova appointment. It was around this time that he met and became friends with Barry Murphy, a cabinet-maker who lived in the Village and frequented the Lion's Head, a bar in Christopher Street that was popular with journalists and writers. The novelist David Markson was another regular, and he would sometimes join Mahon and Murphy there. "The Head", as they called it, had a heavy-drinking, Irish American clientele and it remained one of the few Village bars without a television. The familiar joke was that the patrons were not writers with drinking problems, but drinkers with writing problems. It became Mahon's New York social centre, a place where he could get a meal and count on joining in barroom banter. Pat was nearby in Connecticut and continuing to work on her dissertation. A particularly memorable occasion in this otherwise unsettled time was celebrating her birthday and watching the annual St Patrick's Day parade from the window of the American Irish Historical Society.

Towards the end of the term, Mahon read at a number of nearby colleges and universities, all part of his effort to secure a new teaching post. He lectured on contemporary Irish poetry at a New York Institute for the Humanities luncheon, followed by a reading at Princeton at the invitation of Muldoon. The following week he read at Immaculata College, then Bryn Mawr, and a week later at Swarthmore with Heaney and Muldoon. Lester Conner was nearby at Chestnut Hill College, and he drove Mahon to some of these events.[21] From Swarthmore he went on to Emory University for the rescheduled reading he had skipped some months before. His host, Professor Ron Schuchard, ensured an appreciative group of students were on hand for the reading, which was followed by a late-night party at his home near the campus.

When in New York Mahon stayed in a borrowed faculty apartment at NYU which faced the Washington Square arch, but it was a temporary arrangement. His friend Murphy thought he was suffering from "transient situational stress", a clinical-sounding diagnosis for having no home to call his own.[22] He was living there, in Washington Square, when an offer came to join the English Department at Queens College as Associate Professor. This was something different from the short-term, temporary posts he had held up to then. It was a tenure track position that paid nearly $50,000 a year. Queens, part of the City University of New York system, was located in Flushing, just off the Long Island Expressway. Like many urban colleges, Queens struggled to create a campus community for students and faculty alike. A colleague who was there at the time recalls there was little in the way of departmental life. Most faculty took the train to the campus to teach and scattered immediately afterwards. While the appointment was welcome, Mahon was very much on his own there.

He attended a joint reading by Medbh McGuckian and Eavan Boland at the National Arts Club in Gramercy Square on 6 November and, a week later, the launch party for the *Field Day Anthology of Irish Writing* at the New York Public Library. He was drinking on both occasions, and when Heaney expressed concern at the Field Day party, Mahon snapped, as he had with Montague, "What fucking business is it of yours?"[23] Heaney had brought with him a copy of the American edition of *Seeing Things*, which was dedicated to Mahon, but rather than give it to him then, he mailed it to him after the event. "Each time we met in New York", he wrote afterwards, "I had this book on the premises with me, but didn't find the right opportunity to hand it to you". He added, expressing something of their shared fatigue, "we are a bedraggled platoon by now … worn out by rhetoric and finger food".[24]

There was something self-destructive in Mahon's behaviour, and a colleague at Queens recalls an occasion early in the semester when he became quite upset after giving a taxi driver all the money he had (several hundred dollars, he recalls) to drive him to campus. On another occasion the department chair had to be called to intervene when he showed up at the English Department office intoxicated.[25] One evening Mahon phoned David Markson demanding, "If you don't come here with a quart of whiskey, you will be responsible for my death". Markson told him, "Derek, I'm doing this *once*, and that's it".[26] He was missing classes with some frequency, and just a few weeks into the term had to be put on disability leave after being admitted to St Vincent's Hospital, the same hospital where Dylan Thomas had famously died after drinking 18 straight whiskeys. Professor Fred Buell, an Auden specialist, stepped in to cover his classes in this latest emergency, and Mahon observed his 50th birthday in a New York City hospital.

On being discharged, he returned briefly to his Washington Square apartment before moving to another sublet on West 12th Street. The new apartment was even closer to the Lion's Head which, along with McKenna's and The White Horse, were regular stops in Mahon's perambulations around the West Village. Muldoon would note the importance of each of the bars in his description of Mahon in *The Prince of the Quotidian*: "That man with the belly like a poisoned pup / was once a strange child with a taste for verse: / now everything turns on a pub; / The Lion's Head, McKenna's, The White Horse".[27] Mahon's drinking was often a progressive affair. He would begin in one bar and over the course of the evening might move to several others. When he was "86'd" (refused service), as he sometimes was, he would simply go on to the next.[28] Late at night, towards morning, he would often make his way to the restaurant Florent in Gansevoort Street, which at the time was surrounded by meatpacking warehouses and hardcore gay bars. There were discussions among his Queens colleagues about cancelling his teaching contract, but when he began seeking help, a decision was made to try and support him through that difficult time. The therapist he began seeing, Eileen Simpson, had once been married to John Berryman and had considerable experience with poets and drink.

In the meantime Peter Fallon was moving ahead with plans to publish *The Yaddo Letter* in a limited edition. That winter, while living on West 12th Street, Mahon tentatively began a new poem that was, like *Yaddo*, based on his present circumstances. The original title, "The 12th Street Letter", and the opening reference to living in a borrowed apartment two blocks from the river places the poem quite specifically in January 1992. In later readings Mahon would often explain that he had been looking for a way to write about New York for some time, and that it had been Pat who had suggested he write about the homeless, in all their literal and figurative forms.[29] The long poem that would eventually emerge would take a wide view of that theme, incorporating the homeless, exiles far from home, estranged couples, and the displaced in many guises.

His attention to place in the early drafts anticipates a recurring preoccupation of the poem. Physical movement—in this case, two circular walks through lower Manhattan—provides a narrative structure for the poem, but at its inception, Mahon had not yet been able to marshal his resources for any forward movement whatsoever. Instead, the earliest draft is dominated by an overpowering stasis. He describes waking on a winter morning to a kind of Keatsian despondency:

> A January morning, frost, two blocks from the river,
> and what of the kick-start that should be there?
> One part of me would like to lie in bed for ever
> just reaching out for the occasional snort
> of Absolut ...[30]

In its original form the kick start was not a visit from the muse but a bottle of vodka next to the bed.[31] Elsewhere in the poem Mahon references this time of crisis, describing how he once "would lurch at 3:00 a.m. through drifting snow / to the Lion's Head, McKenna's, the White Horse".[32] The early draft is a meditation on the destructiveness of drink, the failure of the poet's voice, the absence of love, and, in the final handwritten lines, the temptation of suicide or "a dark solution", as it is described there. A note at the top of the page suggests that the early theme of the poem would be "the fatal connection between booze & writing", and in the earliest drafts death seems near. In a passage later cut from the published poem, he recalls the following scene:

> —last night
> I sat up talking to a young Jesuit.
> Suicide was the theme we hit upon
> a dark solution to make everything clear
> that weighted drop from, say, Morton St. pier?[33]

Like *The Yaddo Letter* before it, *The Hudson Letter* was conceived in a dark wood. That darkness is deepest in the early drafts of the poem which Mahon set aside soon after having begun to develop the theme.

In the spring he travelled to Washington to read at the Library of Congress at the invitation of Joseph Brodsky, then Poet Laureate of the United States. Brodsky and Mahon were neighbours in New

York (Brodsky lived on Morton Street), and he gave Mahon a warm introduction, describing him as "a poet of elegiac poise". The reading proved a remarkably personal one, a panegyric to his scattered family. He began with "Katie at the Pool" before giving his customary explanation to American audiences of his peculiar Ulster Protestant background. As he put it on the occasion, "I am politically at sea". He moved from his opening poem for his daughter to "An Old Lady" (his poem about his mother-in-law, Greta Douglas). He read "The Woods", evoking his and Doreen's time in rural Surrey, and "Girls on the Bridge", explaining that his wife was one of three sisters. But the most personally revealing selection was a slight two-line poem for Doreen: "Some sunny day we'll meet again in a new world, / the best 'till when".[34] Just what this new world was—America, some indefinite future, a spiritual afterlife—he did not say. He concluded with his poem of willed recovery "Everything Is Going To Be All Right".

Mahon was attending Alcoholics Anonymous and continuing to see Eileen Simpson, and these sessions had encouraged him to look for the origin of his self-destructive behaviour in his own family relationships and in the break-up of his marriage. He was suffering enormous feelings of guilt and doubting the value of poetry and even of his own life. It was in that vulnerable state that he phoned his department chair, Charles Molesworth, and read to him over the phone a positive review of his *Selected Poems*.[35] He gave a reading at Queens in April, and before the programme he and Molesworth sat down for his annual review. They discussed his absenteeism over the autumn and spring, and Molesworth stressed how important it was that he begin fulfilling his teaching commitments. His colleagues were counting on him to pull himself together.

It was only a few days after the Queens reading that a young woman he had recently met named Adrianna took matters into her own hands and organised an intervention. She had seen advertisements on television for a private alcoholic treatment centre called the Seafield Center, and had made inquiries there on his behalf. At her urging, Mahon agreed to go, though, in truth, on the day he was picked up, he was in no condition to resist. He was taken to the Westhampton Beach facility on Long Island where he was admitted. He had been in bad shape in the days running up to the intervention. "I thought I was talking to a 4 year old", Adrianna wrote, explaining herself, in the days after he was admitted: "I know I sounded horribly brutish with you but you know what? I'd do it all over again. You were totally fucked up".[36]

It was likely at the Seafield Center (though possibly another hospitalisation the same year) that Mahon began working on a new poem:

> There is no lonely anguish here
> but a sedated equanimity
> and a diet of old movies on TV.
> The mild psychiatrist,
> a 'social drinker', nods qualified praise.
> Relieved, we gaze
> at dripping woods to the west;
> at thunder-clouds; at a haemhorrage [sic]
> of sky the red-gold of some golden age
> where the fit fought, drank and shone
> and the rest
> died in oblivion.[37]

He was looking for a mythic pattern to his predicament, and he tried out Theseus in a labyrinth before abandoning the draft as "too Lowellian".[38] In the use he makes of his own personal history, and in tone and voice, the unfinished fragment bears a striking resemblance to *The Hudson Letter*. It was another false start on the poem sequence he had begun the previous January.

Mahon was still hospitalised when it was time to submit the final report on what use he had made of his Lannan Fellowship funds, and Fallon and Heaney both wrote reports to the foundation on his behalf, noting what a "godsend" the award had been.[39] On his release from the Seafield Center, Mahon soon found himself in extremis again. Friends were discussing among themselves what could be done, and Muldoon helped organise a ticket for his return to Ireland. Louis Asekoff recalls, "He was poured into a plane" for the flight to Dublin, but "no one expected him to live".[40]

On his return he saw the doctor Eoin O'Brien, who presented him with a stark choice: "You either lie down and the inevitable will happen soon, or you rise up and overcome this demon".[41] Just days after that, Fred Lowe, Bill McCormack and Jodi Randolph, an American academic who happened to be in Dublin at the time, arranged to have Mahon admitted to St Patrick's Hospital. They went to collect him at his Fitzwilliam Square flat, where they found him compliant and cooperative. McCormack descended the stairs ahead of him to catch him if he fell, while Lowe followed behind. Meanwhile, Randolph organised a taxi. At the hospital Mahon worried about who was going to pay. He was admitted, however, and to the great relief of his friends, spent the next nine weeks undergoing treatment. Coincidently, "Dawn at St. Patrick's", based on his 1989 hospitalisation, had only just been published.

He was in St Patrick's when word reached him that his *Selected Poems* had won *The Irish Times*/Aer Lingus Literature Prize for Poetry, having been chosen over new collections by Paula Meehan and Medbh McGuckian. Eavan Boland had chaired the panel of judges, and the choice was both a recognition of his life's work to date and a personal plea from an old friend that he save himself.

Under the circumstances Mahon's medical leave from Queens was extended through the end of the semester, and on his release from St Patrick's in October he returned to his Fitzwilliam Square flat for several weeks. The award ceremony was held at the Royal Dublin Society on 20 November, three days before his birthday. In making the presentation, President Mary Robinson quoted lines from "A Disused Shed" about the lost people of Treblinka and Pompeii. In the audience, keeping watch on Mahon during the evening, was his psychiatrist Dr Anthony Clare, who was Medical Director of St Patrick's at the time. The award came with £10,000, but, under the circumstances, arrangements were made for the prize money to go to the Arts Council, which had covered Mahon's hospital bills on his behalf.

Mahon returned to New York in mid-December, though he did not need to take up teaching duties for several weeks. He spent that Christmas with Eamon Grennan and his wife, Rachel, in Poughkeepsie, but he was back in New York City when the Modern Language Association met there between Christmas and New Year's Day. That week Emory's Ron Schuchard met Mahon to collect a group of his papers, which he was placing at the university's library on a regular basis. The purchase had been arranged by Linda Matthews, Head of Special Collections at the library, who had responded sympathetically to Mahon's letter seeking financial help in his latest emergency. The acquisition was an important validation of his work, and in the coming years this subsidy would prove a reliable and steady source of income.

Mahon was getting his life back on a steadier footing once again, and it helped when he found an apartment on Perry Street, a block from where Hart Crane had once lived. It was there during a winter blizzard that he again took up the "12th Street Letter", which he had started and set aside the previous year. He was also working at the time on poems about Niobe and Pygmalion for a collection based on Ovid's *Metamorphoses*. Given all he had been through in recent months, the subject appealed to him greatly, and the notion of metamorphosis would be one of the major themes of the new poem, which he was now calling "The Hudson Letter". As he explained to Fallon, the poem was to be a companion piece to *The Yaddo Letter*, "the pair serving as book-ends to a notional and as yet untitled new volume which would include Kinsale poems, translations from Ovid, Laforgue, Pasolini and Ní Dhomnhaill and choruses from *The Bacchae*".[42] It had been eight years since *Antarctica*, a devastating period which, at times, it had seemed he might not survive. But he had come through it, and in the winter he began to write again.

He reported to Fallon that he had been reconnecting with New York friends and seemed to be rehabilitated "despite my madness in the spring".[43] Back at Queens he was asked to conduct a poetry workshop for the college's life-long learning programme. This was a distance-learning programme for non-traditional students, one of whom was a disabled adult student. Their workshop sessions were conducted entirely by telephone. Tom Clark had been a schoolteacher until the onset of progressive spinal muscular atrophy confined him to a wheelchair. A naturally friendly and outgoing man, he and Mahon spoke once a week during the semester. Despite his disability, Tom exuded gratitude for life, and these weekly conversations were a tonic for Mahon, who was still struggling to establish hopeful footing in his own life.

In addition to working on "The Hudson Letter" and the Ovid project, Mahon agreed to write a regular column for John Banville at *The Irish Times*. Over the coming months his "Letter from New York" ranged widely over the high and low culture of the city, including columns on being African American in America, the poetry scene, Irish-Americans and Greenwich Village. Every few weeks he would fax the latest column to Banville from the copy shop on Bleecker Street. These columns were something different from book reviews, and the form offered him numerous opportunities for self-portrayal. He wrote about his own days in Greenwich Village, visiting the White Horse, sitting in Washington

Square, attending a reading at the 92nd Street Y. In one self-referential aside he compared Village poetry readings to AA meetings. "They have much in common", he noted, "location, grunge, open meetings, instant coffee, familiar faces, an atmosphere of 'sharing'".[44]

Despite the effort Mahon was making to stay sober, Queens chose not to renew his teaching contract for the new year. He and Molesworth discussed the matter frankly and Mahon not only agreed with the decision but urged it himself as the best course of action.[45] He had no immediate prospect of other employment, however, and, faced with that loss of income, he wrote to the college president to appeal the decision:

> My 1992 collapse (for that is what it was) had a great deal to do with difficult and disorienting life circumstances including the protracted failure to find suitable accommodation in New York City—a problem I've now solved. I'm very happily settled at the above address, where I hope to remain for the foreseeable future, and have taken up my writing projects where I left off.[46]

While he had indeed found a new apartment, that was the least of the disorienting life circumstances to which he alluded. He added,

> … since my hospitalization last fall … I have had no further alcohol or drug problems: that is to say, I've been entirely substance-free.... Moreover, although one can never be absolutely certain about these things, I feel confident that the duration and intensity of my 1993 [sic][47] hospitalization, together with the success of my ongoing recovery program, will ensure against any future recurrence.[48]

When the president declined his appeal, Mahon asked Banville to update his biographical note: "For the contributors' box, I no longer teach at CUNY, I'm happy to say: just mention the *Irish Times* Prize".[49] Despite the brave face, Mahon was left once again in uncertain financial circumstances. He was struggling to cover his children's school fees: a final payment to the Latymer Upper School for Rory and fees for Katie to attend Queen's College Preparatory School in London. Equally worrying was that without a job his visa might not be renewed.

As if that were not enough, Mahon's "Letter from New York" on 5 June thrust him into controversy when, commenting on the female poets writing in New York, he stated, "not one can sing".[50] Unfortunately, his column followed close on the heels of Field Day's debacle over the underrepresentation of women in the *Field Day Anthology of Irish Writing*. Mahon phoned John Banville at *The Irish Times* and tried to withdraw the column, only to be told that the paper had already gone to press.[51] In the following days a number of women took Mahon to task in a series of letters to the editor of *The Irish Times*, but his friend Alannah Hopkin came to his defence, pointing out that his statement had been less about women than it had been about single-issue poetry. The accusation of misogyny was misplaced, she insisted.[52] In fact, there was a measure of truth in her defence. Mahon had been objecting to didactic, issue-oriented poetry, in his words poetry that is "*about*" something "instead of being that thing itself".[53] It was in this context that he wrote his most overtly feminist work to date, "Sappho in 'Judith's Room'", so named for the bookstore on nearby Washington Street.[54] Mahon was building "The Hudson Letter" around his walks through lower Manhattan, drawing heavily on the literary associations of the city to create a richly allusive intertextual palimpsest. As he had put it in an earlier "Letter from New York", it was as if the city itself were a text, "every block a quotation".[55]

In "Sappho in 'Judith's Room'", he imagines stepping into the feminist bookstore, which sets off a chain of associations. Upon seeing Sappho's books on a shelf, he remarks on the survival of her work ("miraculously, I hold here in my hands / stanzas exhumed from the Egyptian sands"). That sense of persistence runs counter to Mahon's more characteristic reflections on art's impermanence, as seen in such poems as "Heraclitus on Rivers", "The Sea in Winter" or indeed, early sections of *The Hudson Letter* itself. His preoccupation with history's circular patterning and the reincarnation of the self in new forms is replaced by the notion of regeneration through art. Sappho herself is subsumed into her art and lives on within a literary tradition continuously remaking itself. Mahon imagines Sappho surveying with satisfaction the shelves of the bookstore:

I'm happiest here in a place like Judith's Room
with Djuna, Janis, Gloria, Brooke, and Kim.
Girls all, be with me now and keep me warm—
didn't I say we'd live again in another form?"

The self-doubts and the questioning that had plagued Mahon when he first began the "12th Street Letter" have been dispelled, and he alludes here to one of his earliest poems, "Girls in their Seasons". "Girls all, be with me now and keep me warm", he had first written 30 years before, under different circumstances entirely.

Mahon and Pat spent July and part of August 1993 together in Ireland, where they visited James Simmons's Poets' House on Islandmagee, attended the John Hewitt Summer School in County Antrim, and saw Richard Ryan in County Mayo. Though he was without a teaching post, he returned to New York and his Perry Street apartment at the end of the summer. Having previously let down his American publisher, he agreed to a series of readings in Boston, New York and Washington to promote the Penguin edition of his *Selected Poems*. Without any regular employment, however, it was not clear that he would be able to remain in the United States. He needed a job in order renew his visa. Dr Kevin Cahill appealed to a friend at Cedar Crest College, in Allentown, Pennsylvania, but the college was unable to create a position on such short notice and was also wary of overstating its financial commitment. In the end Chris Cahill offered him a position as Poetry Editor of *The Recorder*, the journal of the American Irish Historical Society. It was all a bit of a sham. Mahon drafted his own job offer, and, as Cahill recalls, it was promptly retracted the very next day, having served its purpose of documenting his phantom employment.

Through all this "The Hudson Letter" was continuing to expand, and Mahon was now calling it "the Long Poem". He was finding the discursive form and the use of his own personal experience liberating. When Eamon Grennan visited him at his Greenwich Village apartment to interview him for *The Paris Review*, Mahon spoke quite openly about this new development in his writing. He explained, in a passage later omitted from the published interview, that he had overcome his hesitation about putting Doreen and the children into poems. "I think that you have to take certain things by the horns and proceed with apparent confidence", he told him. "Yes, I had the private life, and the argument with alcohol, [but] I seem to be one of those writers for whom it is important to be able to talk somehow about myself and about the conditions of my life".[56]

Without regular employment, Mahon again turned to the theatre. Fallon was continuing to pitch *The Bacchae* to anyone he thought might take an interest in producing the play. Mahon had begun an adaptation of Oscar Wilde's *The Picture of Dorian Gray*, and in March Anne Clark at the Gate Theatre commissioned him to write an adaptation of Racine's *Phaedra*. That same month he travelled to California to take part in the Lannan Foundation's reading series. He flew into Ontario, California, and first gave a reading at Claremont McKenna College before attending the Lannan event the following night. While in southern California his host drove him down Sunset Boulevard through Bel Air and Beverly Hills, and he also visited Brian and Jean Moore in nearby Malibu.[57] The following evening he read from his *Selected Poems* at the Lannan Foundation in Los Angeles. Among the poems he read that evening was one new one, "Pygmalion", which had only just been published in the *London Review of Books*. "He lived alone / without a wife to call his own", Mahon begins his retelling of the myth, before describing Pygmalion fashioning a lover out of ivory. In Mahon's treatment, it is a poem about the transformative power of art.

He had planned to read at Berkeley, but when those plans fell through on short notice, he found himself in San Francisco without a place to stay. His friend Elgy Gillespie, the former *Irish Times* journalist, was living in the city, and she came to his rescue and put him up at her place. She was sharing a house with two gay men at the time, one of whom had AIDS, and during his stay Mahon was quite worried that he not spread a cold he was fighting.[58] While in San Francisco, he called and arranged to meet Thom Gunn. Gunn's recent collection of poems, *The Man with Night Sweats*, offers a series of reflections on the AIDS epidemic and the healing power of art. Mahon was reading his literary surroundings closely and turning over in his mind what would be incorporated into his own long poem. His trip to the west coast prompted a series of thoughts about the American west which helped to shape "Albums" (later re-entitled "The Travel Section") which he submitted to *The New Yorker* on his return to New York.

As had become his pattern, he returned to Ireland for July and August. Pat was working at Ireland House and hoping to finish her dissertation, so did not accompany him this time. His mother had been in poor health and writing heart-rending letters to her son, but despite her appeals, he did not get to Bangor during the summer. As usual, money was extremely tight, and Katie's school fees were again past due. He was continuing to seek a teaching position for the autumn, but had had a disastrous interview for a post at Sarah Lawrence College, and the hoped-for job offer never materialised. In the end, he pieced together part-time appointments at Barnard College and NYU.

Part of the difficulty was that his heart had never been in teaching. He saw teaching as a necessary expediency, a way of subsidising his writing. By his own admission, there were few actual teaching hours involved.[59] His Barnard class had no syllabus; instead, he conducted the class as an extended conversation. "I really learned absolutely nothing about poetry", one student complained at the end of term.[60] Mahon would himself acknowledge what a sham it all was in *The Hudson Letter*, in which he substitutes Columbia for Barnard:

> Sometimes, as I sit in the Knickerbocker or stand up there
> in Columbia University like Philby in Red Square,
> I blush like a traitor; but what kind of a traitor?[61]

Nor did he embrace other forms of academic service. Towards the end of term, he agreed to speak at a colleague's Irish Studies class, but, when the appointed time came, he had a change of heart and abruptly walked out of the seminar without delivering his talk.

It was a relief from the tedium of teaching when Aidan Higgins and Alannah Hopkin visited for a week in October. Mahon had arranged a reading for Higgins at Ireland House, where Pat was now working, off Washington Square. On the night of the reading, the university bookstore had been unable to obtain copies of any of Higgins's books, and in his brief introductory remarks, Mahon noted the irony of books being unobtainable for "the finest Irish novelist since Beckett".[62] That lack was more than made up for, however, by the appreciative audience. Over the course of the week, Mahon pointed out to his friends the places that would appear in *The Hudson Letter*, including the 10th Street pier where Annie Moore gazes across the water at the Statue of Liberty.

Fallon was hoping to follow the publication of Mahon's *Selected Poems* with a *Selected Prose*, and Terence Brown had been enlisted to help track down the scattered journalistic pieces. Over the autumn, however, Mahon became increasingly uneasy at the thought of such a book. I'm not sure we should really go ahead with it, he told Fallon by phone in mid-October.[63] As he explained, he had no feel for a unifying "prose purpose" to what would essentially be a selection of occasional reviews and essays.[64] Longley had just published a collection of autobiographical pieces, *Tuppenny Stung*, and Mahon briefly considered recasting his book as a memoir as well. In the end, he had doubts about that approach.

With the arrival of spring, Mahon was teaching poetry at the Cooper Union. Alice Quinn published two sections of the forthcoming *Hudson Letter* in *The New Yorker*, even as Mahon was making final changes to the manuscript, including the addition of dates at the end of the poem, suggesting a nine-month period of gestation from winter to summer 1995. In fact, he had begun the poem three years earlier, before abandoning it in a time of crisis, and resuming it again in the winter of 1993. The poem had grown over the past two years, and he was continuing to add details to bring it up to the very moment.

He noted his friend Eugene Lambe's death: "friends and contemporaries begin to go / —Nina Gilliam, Eugene Lambe, and others too".[65] Like Auden, Mahon saw art as a means of "breaking bread with the dead". When a winter storm collapsed the aviary at the Bronx Zoo in early February he incorporated into section six references to those "toughs of the air" and their fight for survival in the city. He read from his own Ovid translation at the 92nd Street Y in February, another autobiographical detail he worked into the finished poem.

In his interview with Eamon Grennan, he had spoken quite directly about the break-up of his marriage and had alluded to his and Pat's relationship. "I think that most people, perhaps everyone, live somewhere on the scale", he had explained, "and the most married are actually very unmarried in many ways, and among the unmarried are some very married souls".[66] While still married to Doreen, he was counting himself among the unmarried, but that did not prevent him from viewing his relationship with Pat as a kind of marriage. He would acknowledge something of his feeling for her in the dedication of the book and in the late addition of "Domnei" where love of woman is directly linked to the personal recovery the poem has been working towards:

> but when the earth renews itself in spring
> and whitethorn flowers to hear the blackbird sing
> I too sing, although she whom I admire
> finds little to her taste in what I write.
> I praise not only her clear skin and fine eyes
> but also her frank speech and distinguished air;
> so dumbstruck am I on her visiting days

I can find no words to speak of my desire
yet, when she leaves me, my composure flees.
No one I know can hold a candle to her
and when the world dims, as it does tonight,
I see the house she goes to blaze with light.[67]

Mahon had decided to return to Ireland at the end of June, but before doing so he and Pat took a holiday in Key West, arriving just a day after Hurricane Allison swept the Keys. As he had done throughout *The Hudson Letter*, he worked details of this climatic devastation into the poem, changing the name of the storm to Hurricane Angie. His account of their June holiday, "Key West", follows "Domnei" in the published poem sequence.

Mahon had always drawn upon his own life experience for source material for his poems, but never before had he done so in such an extended form. *The Hudson Letter* expressed what he wanted to say about New York City and dramatised his struggle to recover from a near-fatal alcoholic crisis. Many years later he would describe the period living in Manhattan as a "terrific time". It was an extraordinary rewriting of history. He returned to Ireland, he would insist, only when he feared turning into an American. The statement was an acknowledgment of all those Irish who had come before who never did return.[68] But, in fact, *The Hudson Letter* had been bending towards Ireland from the beginning. As his friend Aidan Higgins put it, "one has to go far from home to write so touchingly of it".[69]

Chapter 14

| ITHACA

Mahon was back in Fitzwilliam Square in time to attend the July commencement ceremony at Trinity, where he was awarded an honorary Doctor of Letters. It was a gratifying development after the emotional crises of recent years, and for one who had struggled so long for academic position and recognition. It had been ten years since Mahon had published a major new collection of poems, but *The Hudson Letter* was in press at last. Numerous friends had stood by him through the bad time. Peter Fallon had kept his work in print, and had conceived new projects to keep him working and to generate earnings; Heaney had done his best to secure teaching posts and bursaries; Linda Matthews and Ron Schuchard had established the Mahon archive at Emory University. Friends had taken him into their homes, got him treatment and continued to believe in him, even when he had given up believing in himself.

Fallon had advance copies of *The Hudson Letter* in hand in early October, and planned to give Mahon his author's copies at the launch of Montague's *Collected Poems*, which was also being published that month. That same week, news broke that Heaney had won the Nobel Prize for Literature. He had been rumoured to be under consideration for years, but the announcement was no less stunning for that. "It is a great day for Seamus Heaney, for Irish literature, and for Ireland",

The Irish Times announced on its editorial page, though some of his fellow writers might have felt otherwise.[1] Montague's and Mahon's new collections were suddenly cast into shadow, a point Mahon would later demonstrate literally when he insisted on being photographed in silhouette for a collection of interviews with Irish writers.[2] The news of Heaney's Nobel reverberated in other ways, too. Montague was quoted in *The Irish Times* saying he himself had earned "twice over" the recognition of "some of the younger Northern poets".[3] While Montague did not name the poets he had in mind, Heaney's Nobel had only heightened the competitiveness among the friends and rivals. "I'm black in the face with envy", Mahon had written Longley years before, when Heaney was the first into print. Those feelings were still there, and Mahon would use the forthcoming publication of his selected journalism to put some space between himself and Heaney. He was no longer a "Northern Irish poet", he insisted in an *Irish Times* interview. In the days following the Nobel announcement, that seemed the wrong pool to swim in. All he would concede was that he was *from* Northern Ireland, something else entirely.

On 9 November Mahon read from *The Hudson Letter* for a standing-room-only audience at Waterstone's bookshop in Dawson Street, Dublin. He had taken an unusual degree of interest in the sales of the new collection, and he noted in a letter to Fallon just how disappointing these had been. He attributed it all to a "Heaney-induced sales glitch" and suggested it might be time to make a particular push before Heaney's *The Spirit Level* was published in the spring.

As usual, he did not care to be in Dublin during the holidays, and he slipped away to Kinsale, where he spent Christmas day with his friends Aidan and Alannah. A few weeks later he boarded a plane for America for a short, three-city *Hudson Letter* tour to New York, Washington and Atlanta. He opened the tour at Ireland House, which appears in *The Hudson Letter* as "No. 1, 5th Avenue", the home of Bridget Moore's employer in the centre of Manhattan. From there he travelled to Washington DC for a reading at Georgetown University. A major Vermeer retrospective was on view at the National Gallery of Art, and Mahon hoped to see it while visiting. When his host, George O'Brien, explained that tickets had sold out weeks before, Mahon would have none of it. He insisted they drive to the Irish Embassy, where he presented himself to a helpless foreign service officer, who did his best to relay the same disappointing news. Still not satisfied, Mahon insisted they drive next to the British Embassy, where the scene repeated itself. In the end, he got no further than the museum postcard shop (so much for the benefits of dual citizenship).[4] In Atlanta he read a selection from the new collection before ending with his customary closing poem, "A Garage in Co. Cork". While in the city, now the site of his own archive, he visited the home of Margaret Mitchell, whose *Gone with the Wind* recounts the experience of another Irish immigrant in America.

Mahon was back in Dublin in the first week of February, in time for the opening of his adaptation of *Phaedra* at the Gate Theatre. He told a newspaper reporter he had followed Racine's original closely: "It's a faithful rendering, line by line, into contemporary idiom". He had enjoyed the work, and, in the same interview, he described the play's theme as "the guilt of existence".[5] The actress Dearbhla Molloy had been cast as the lead, and she gave a strong performance to positive reviews. Mahon would offer his own tribute to her portrayal of "articulate terror" in his poem "At the Gate Theatre", in which he lifts a key passage, the emotional centre of the play, from his own script:

> … Ah, what new pain must I now undergo?
> What monstrous torture have I yet to know?
> All I've endured, the madness and the fear,
> self-pity, rage, humiliation, self-hate,
> the insult of rejection, even, were mere
> ripples of the approaching storm …[6]

Despite good notices, the play closed after only a few weeks, but the short run was more a reflection on Dublin audiences than on Mahon's translation, *The Irish Times* suggested.[7] By all accounts it was a critical success, and, on the strength of the production, Patrick Mason and Judy Friel invited him to undertake an adaptation of *Cyrano de Bergerac* for the Abbey. It would be years before he would act on the suggestion.

Through his translation work Mahon was positioning himself within a European tradition, and over the following months he made trips to Paris and Prague for readings and festivals. He read with Montague and Seamus Deane as part of a six-month celebration of Irish arts across France dubbed *L'Imaginaire Irlandais*. His friend, the art critic and translator Ann Cremin, wrote a biting attack on the whole proceedings, which she likened to "intellectual terrorism", a point of view Mahon would have shared.[8] Government-sponsored arts initiatives might be handsomely funded, but they resulted in uneasy alliances of which Mahon was wary. In August Peter Fallon brought out Mahon's selected prose under the title *Journalism*. Mahon still had his doubts about whether the collection of occasional pieces made up a successful book, and the plain and rather deflating title had been his idea. He returned to the continent again for the Frankfurt Book Fair, which, on the heels of Heaney's Nobel, had chosen the theme "Ireland and its Diaspora", a subject Mahon knew well.

Mahon had resolved once again to forego further reviewing, and instead he was assembling a new collection of poems in the style of *The Hudson Letter*. His Gate Theatre poem would eventually appear in the new volume, as well as a poem set "At the Shelbourne" which had become the centre, though a dry one, of his Dublin social circle. Like "To Mrs. Moore at Inishannon" and "Sappho in 'Judith's Room'", the poem is another in which he adopts the voice of a female persona, in this case Elizabeth Bowen, who spent part of the war years living in a service flat in Kildare Street, near the Shelbourne Hotel, and reporting on Irish attitudes to the war to Britain's Secretary of State for Dominion Affairs.[9] Mahon intertwines her wartime experiences with those of his own family, referring at one point to "a darkened convoy strung out in moonlight" like those for which his uncles had provided escort. The more important point of connection, however, is the revulsion he shares with Bowen at the deceitfulness of political speech. He incorporates into the poem her comment to Virginia Woolf on the "deep, rather futile talks. It is hard afterwards / to remember the drift, though I remember words, / that smoke-screen use of words!" Mahon was compressing historical epochs and making an indirect comment on the ceasefire negotiations that were continuing over the summer.

Mahon had agreed to advise on a Claddagh Records project to produce spoken word recordings of Irish poets reading their work, but when he and Montague met with Richard Ryan to discuss the project in September, differences of opinion had emerged. Later, in the Shelbourne Bar, he was already in an irritable mood when Montague made a careless remark about an upcoming trip to predominantly Protestant Bangor for a literary festival in a few days time. Montague's comments touched a nerve with Mahon, and, when Montague pressed him on why he was not going too, Mahon grew furious and abruptly flounced out of the bar. His mother was living in Bangor at the time, and his feelings for the North and his family ties there had always been complicated. To make matters worse, he had rebuffed his mother's appeals and had not been able to bring himself to visit her in some time. Montague's joking, fuelled by too many whiskeys, led to a breach between the two friends, and afterwards Mahon began going to great lengths to avoid him. They had been close friends for almost thirty years, and Montague had come to his aid in many ways during that time. Mahon's sudden renunciation of their friendship hurt him, and left him baffled.

Just a few days after that incident, Mahon learned that his mother had died. Their relationship had always been a distant one, and he had only become more intent on keeping that distance in the years following his and Doreen's separation. His mother's letters had been few—his even fewer—and those he did receive, formulaic: news of her health, pleas that he write and best wishes on his birthday. She always sent a birthday card with her love. Something of his disdain for the North and its bigotry could be traced to his own upbringing and his relationship with his parents (it was this nerve Montague had inadvertently touched), and only in death could he bring himself to acknowledge any feelings for his mother at all. "Death in Bangor" notes her obsessive tidiness and thrift, and, above all, the narrowness of her life. The poem, written from a first-person perspective, opens on a cold hillside in County Down with Mahon staring "at an open grave or out to sea" (the two were much the same in his mind). The key movement of the poem, however, is the conceit that she too is a kind of artist, "a rage-for-order-freak", which binds mother and son to one another.

> ... Little soul, the body's guest and companion,
> this is a cold epitaph from your only son,
> the wish genuine if the tone ambiguous.
> Oh, I can love you now that you're dead and gone
> to the many mansions in your mother's house;
> all artifice stripped away, we give you back to nature
> but something of you, perhaps the incurable ache
> of art, goes with me as I travel south
> past misty drumlins, shining lanes to the shore,
> above the Mournes a final helicopter,
> sun-showers and rainbows all the way through Louth,
> cottages buried deep in ivy and rhododendron,
> ranch houses, dusty palms, blue skies of the republic ...[10]

It is a highly unusual elegy, and Mahon achieves a measure of feeling in its closing lines he had not been able to express in life.

In time Mahon would include the elegy in his new collection, which he was calling *The Yellow Book* in reference to a previous *fin de siècle*. He continued to find the discursive style of the new poems liberating, though it invited, at times, a harsh tone, as in "The Idiocy of Human Aspiration". Anthony Cronin would later suggest *The Hudson Letter* and *The Yellow Book* be regarded as one, and in fact a postscript to *The Hudson Letter*, "America Deserta", provides a direct link between the two volumes.[11] In personal terms, the poem was a way of prolonging his ongoing conversation with Pat King begun in the previous collection:

> I valued above all our restful evening walks
> to the West Side pierheads and the desolate docks
> under a sunset close-encounter blaze
> to watch the future form from the heat-haze
> in the garbage-mouth of the Hudson ...[12]

Looking back on his New York years, he acknowledges he was "an alien among aliens", and, like Elizabeth Bowen before him, a spy for the old world in the new. The poem is in part a nostalgic look at favourite places and moments, and in part a critique of a debased contemporary culture. Whatever forms his culture's sickness takes, his subject is the condition of the soul that registers these experiences. Against a setting of urban disease, he reminds us of human affection, and in that way the poem is also a personal letter to friends like Samuel Menashe, Pat King and Eugene Lambe, to whom the volume as a whole would be dedicated.

> I think of diner mornings in ice and thaw,
> the Lion's Head, renamed the Monkey's Paw,
> and moments on the Hudson River Line;
> you wildly decadent in forbidden furs
> in the shadow of the Bobst or the Twin Towers,
> the skyline at your back, the pearl-rope bridges
> and a nation singing its heart out in the business pages.[13]

It would prove to be a remarkably prescient forecast of the economic crisis to come a decade later: "the great money scam begins its long decline / to pot-holed roads and unfinished construction sites".

At the same time he was writing derisively of the global boom economy, he found himself the beneficiary of an unexpected inheritance. His mother, it turned out, had indeed been frugal all her life, and her savings had grown along with the rising economy. As he was concluding *The Yellow Book,* Mahon found himself the holder of an investment portfolio for the first time in his life.

He delivered the completed manuscript of *The Yellow Book* to Peter Fallon in July, and having turned the new collection over travelled to Greece at the invitation of his friend Stella Lubsen, whom he and Doreen had first met there years before. Stella and her husband divided their time between Switzerland and Paros, and it was there, on Paros, watching Stella's 18-year-old daughter and her friends cavort in the pool, he composed "Aphrodite's Pool". The poem describes a moment of stillness between actions. The girls' wet footprints dry in the sun, while a somnolent Mahon dozes on an inflatable raft, listening to the cicadas and the wind on the water. The poem is situated in a half-waking space between actions, between two states of consciousness, but its subject is that perennial one for Mahon, "the mythic moment of metamorphosis".[14]

On his return to Dublin, he sent Fallon the new poem as a late addition to *The Yellow Book.* He had copies of the collection in hand by early October, and in the days following publication, he was once again telling friends he was through with poetry. He was withdrawing in other ways, too. When Montague and his partner, Elizabeth Wassell, came to Dublin for the dedication of the new Oscar Wilde statue in Merrion Square, Mahon stayed away and went to great lengths to avoid the Shelbourne or other familiar haunts where their paths might cross. His recovery was holding, however, and he was living a carefully regulated life. He instructed waiters that no alcohol was to be used in the preparation of his meals. That autumn his close friends Aidan and Alannah, whom he had been responsible for introducing, were married at a small civil proceeding in the Registry Office in Molesworth Street. Mahon served as best man, and following the brief exchange of vows the friends went across the street to Buswells to celebrate late love with champagne and mineral water.

As had become his pattern, Mahon again spent Christmas in Kinsale. He was there when *The Irish Times* reviewed *The Yellow Book,* welcoming it as a powerful indictment of contemporary culture. Gerald Dawe noted the misanthropic tone of the collection as a whole but praised the work for refusing to lapse into "the requisite consolations of so much contemporary poetry".[15] It was a veiled reference to Heaney, who was increasingly being met with a post-Nobel backlash from Dublin's independent-minded literary community. Other reviewers followed suit, similarly comparing and contrasting the two friends. Seán O'Brien noted: "while Heaney is a gregarious poet, responsible at bottom to an idea of community, Mahon is a solitary, a latter-day *poète maudit*, for whom Baudelaire and Nerval are something more than literary exemplars".[16] William Scammell suggested Mahon was carving out a position on the periphery of our culture and praised the collection as "his best book since *Hunt by Night*".[17] Anthony Cronin, writing in the *Sunday Independent*, called it "one of the finest English-language poetic achievements of recent years".[18]

Though Mahon was turning down invitations to read in Ireland, he accepted an invitation to visit the Princess Grace Library in Monaco. There he read selections from *The Hudson Letter* and *The Yellow Book*, closing with the forward-looking "Kinsale" and "A Garage in Co. Cork". He went from there to Switzerland, where he saw Stella and her husband at their home in Vufflens-le-Château on the northern side of Lake Geneva. Mahon was becoming something of a literary tourist, and while visiting them he made a day trip to Rilke's gravesite in Raron, stopping in Montreux to see the Palace Hotel, where Nabokov had lived for many years.

He was back in Dublin when the Good Friday Agreement was signed, which set in motion a referendum on the political future of Northern Ireland. Its passage would lead to dramatic decline in the levels of bloodshed and violence that had plagued the country for most of Mahon's adult life. His attention, however, was increasingly abroad, and he was back on the continent later in the spring when he travelled to Venice, once again, to meet up with Stella. Free of money worries (thanks to his mother's life-long frugality), he was able to indulge himself, and he and Stella had high tea at the Grand Hôtel des Bains on the Lido and enjoyed the view of Venice across the lagoon. Thomas Mann had once lived in the hotel and the setting had been the inspiration for his novel *Death in Venice*. He and Stella visited the graves of Ezra Pound and Olga Rudge on nearby San Michele, and sought out as well that of Joseph Brodsky, who had only recently been interred there.

From Venice Mahon proceeded to Florence, where he visited the Uffizi Gallery and strolled among the Renaissance paintings. He was reading a biography of the art historian and forger Bernard Berenson and thinking about the relationship of originality, authenticity and beauty, which he had explored in his poem "The Forger" years before. He had once posed the question whether a forgery could ever be a work of art in a true sense. "It depends what you mean by art, I suppose. Large questions of 'soul' and 'vision' arise: and who is to say that 'soul' is not a mysterious felicity of technique in the same way that, in Mann's phrase, 'love is a noble selectiveness of sexuality'". These questions were on his mind again in the spring of 1998.[19]

As he did in any new city, he sought out places with literary associations, in this instance the Café Giubbe Rosse which had once been frequented by Eugenio Montale and later Dylan Thomas. A selection of Mahon's poems had been published by a small Italian press in Milan, and he was exploring further publication possibilities. Mahon returned to Dublin for the summer where he saw his children, but was making plans to return to Italy as soon as he could. While in Dublin he learned from Peter Fallon *The Yellow Book* had been shortlisted for the Forward Prize (in the end, the award went to Ted Hughes for his collection *Birthday Letters*).

In August Mahon received funding from the Lannan Foundation to support the completion of his *Collected Poems*. He used the grant to cover a return trip to Italy with Pat the following October. One catches glimpses of Pat and himself in a number of self-referential asides in *Roman Script*, the new poem sequence inspired by his travels. They are like characters in an Italian farce, he suggests; he an "amorous bad-boy" and she a "glamorous nun", as indeed she once had been.[20] The poem opens at dawn, that time of renewal and new possibility:

> Rain in the night; now cock-crow and engine-hum
> wake us at first light on the Janiculum
> and we open the shutters to extravagant mists
> behind which an autumn sun hotly insists;
> poplar and pine, low dove and glistening drop,
> bright lemon, jonquil, jasmine and heliotrope—
> the Respighi moment, life mimicking art again
> as when the fiddles provoke line-dancing rain.[21]

Increasingly Mahon was reflecting on his own advancing years, the approaching millennium, and what, if anything, would survive him to mark his time on earth. He and Pat explored Rome, visiting churches, basilicas and the Forum, which further contributed to his ruminations on the transience of human love and its persistence in art, a theme he evokes in *Roman Script* when he pauses to admire a marble statue of Persephone.

Roman Script juxtaposes Mahon's experience of Rome's history and art with the coarser side of the modern city. He is distracted at one point by the noise of prisoners in the exercise yard of the nearby Regina Coeli. The prison had once been a convent, which suited Mahon's purposes perfectly. Indeed, the whole poem sequence is a meditation on our figurative imprisonment in our mortal bodies and the role art might play in ensuring that some record of our time on earth survives. He found a model for the artistic life in the Italian poet and film director Pier Paolo Pasolini, to whom he gives homage in the closing stanza of the poem:

> His is the true direction we have lost
> since his corpse showed up on the beach at Ostia
> and life as we know it evolved into imagery,
> production values, packaged history,
> the genocidal corporate imperative
> and the bright garbage on the incoming wave
> best seen at the morning rush-hour in driving rain:
> 'in the refuse of the world a new world is born'.[22]

Mahon had been working towards this criticism of the commercialisation of art from the beginning, and towards this expression of hope for some purer art to follow.

Though his *cnuas* had been renewed on the condition that he remain resident in Ireland, he was in fact spending extended periods abroad, and, after wintering in Italy, he and Pat returned again in the new year. He enrolled in an Italian class at the British Institute in Rome, and was sharpening his language skills further by translating Italian poetry. He was considering publishing a selection of his translations under the title *An Italian Anthology: From Petrarch to Pasolini*. There is a sense in which this work, and his immersion in Italian culture generally, entailed an erasure of self, as if the label "Ulster poet" had finally been put to rest. When he received a letter from a reference book publisher asking that he update his biographical entry, he wrote back, "I would be grateful if you would omit me altogether from the new edition of *Who's Who in Ireland*".[23]

Over the summer and autumn of 1999 Mahon's *Collected Poems* moved closer to publication: final selections were made and the book moved into production. In a wilful rejection of the poetry business, however, Mahon instructed Peter Fallon that no review copies were to be distributed. As a result, when the book representing his life's work appeared just after his birthday, in late November, there was no notice of it whatsoever. He was writing for a private audience. The limited edition chapbooks *Roman Script*, *Seaside Cemetery* and *Resistance Days* were each private productions as well: an account of his and Pat's time in Italy, a translation of Paul Valéry's *Le Cimetière marin* published in an edition of only 175 copies the year Mahon turned 60, and a poem addressed to his friend John Minihan. When Colm Tóibín selected his *Collected Poems* for mention in a Books of the Year feature in *The Irish Times* at the end of the year, the newspaper had to explain why the volume had not yet been reviewed by the paper: "A phone call to Gallery revealed that Mahon has taken the highly unusual step of issuing instructions to his publishers not to send out any review copies, and will not be offering any reasons why".[24]

In all these ways, Mahon was positioning himself as an outsider, on the margins of society, and from that vantage-point was continuing what Hugh Haughton has called "a continuous protest against modern culture".[25] While his poems were taking an increasingly strong environmental stance, the sickness of the planet in poems like "Lapis Lazuli" is always a symptom of a larger debasement of values in the culture at large. When Pat was diagnosed with cancer and began chemotherapy in 2000, her illness, too, seemed emblematic of a more widespread and pervasive disease.

Following the publication of his *Collected Poems*, and "in flight from corporate Christendom", Mahon visited Morocco, where he retraced Beckett's footsteps and saw in the new millennium.[26] Back in Dublin, he received a letter from Britain's ambassador to Ireland, Ivor Roberts, asking if Tony Blair might put his name forward to the Queen for consideration for an OBE, Officer of the Order of the British Empire. Mahon spoke to Ambassador Roberts by phone to decline the honour.[27] He spent the following months in Dublin where he attended the opening of his friend John Minihan's exhibition at the National Photographic Archive in Temple Bar. Minihan had once been a press photographer, a member of the Fleet Street paparazzi, before turning his back on that way of life and withdrawing with his family to west Cork. It was just the kind of gesture of renunciation that Mahon found deeply appealing.

In the autumn he was in Paris where he took a room at the Hôtel La Louisiane in the rue de Seine for an extended stay. Most days he read the papers at the café *Les Deux Magots* and strolled the city streets, "a *flâneur* in the dense galaxies of text".[28] It was there he began a verse letter to Minihan. Like other verse letters before, *Resistance Days* opens with Mahon establishing his location: "I write this from the Louisiane, rm. 14—". As Hugh Haughton has noted, Mahon is among our most mindful poets of place.[29] He was rereading Bonnefoy and Eluard and recalling his student days in the city 40 years before. His memories are intertwined with the city's literary associations in an intertextual swirl: "Old existentialists, old beats, old punks / sat here of old; some dedicated drunks / still sing in the marketplace, and out back / there's an old guy who knew Jack Kerouac". He recounts his impressions of Tangier and the sights and sounds of Paris before turning to a series of reflections on the nature of art and its necessary opposition to "the murderous tedium / of business culture". It is that resistance to society's commercial culture that he admires in Minihan (a quality he had admired, too, in J.G. Farrell).[30]

It was this sense of the artist as outsider that led Mahon to edit an edition of the poems of Patrick MacDonogh for Gallery. MacDonogh had been a contemporary of MacNeice and Kavanagh, but his work had been overshadowed by his more famous fellow poets. While MacDonogh enjoyed a "cult following", his reputation had not kept pace with either of his contemporaries. He produced "a distinguished though not extensive body of work, one rendered even more exiguous by a self-critical severity which led him to discard, select, and refine from volume to volume until ... he arrived at an almost final text".[31] Mahon might as well have been writing about himself. He was cultivating his obscurity, and that spring he declined the Queen's Gold Medal for poetry, after Andrew Motion wrote letting him know that he was the choice of the selection committee.[32] These events were unfolding while Mahon was making a selection of MacDonogh's poems and writing his introduction to the volume. Mahon, who had so recently strolled the ruins in Rome, found in his predecessor's work another demonstration of the inherent fragility of art and the fickleness of what survives.

Mahon was back in Paris that autumn for another extended stay at the Hôtel La Louisiane, and early in the new year, was making plans for a return visit to the United States. Richard Ryan offered him use of his ambassador's residence in New York and from there he made shorter trips to see friends in other parts of the country. He had all but given up public readings, but he flew to Atlanta for a reading at the Georgian Terrace Hotel. From there he flew to New Orleans for several days, then Savannah, where the artist Anthony Paliser began Mahon's portrait.

———

Mahon was back in Fitzwilliam Square for the summer but he resumed his itinerant life again that autumn when he flew to London and borrowed a Soho flat while the owner was away. He had joined the Groucho Club in nearby Dean Street which, along with the Greek restaurants in the neighbourhood, became his new base for meeting friends. Over the winter he began seeing Jane Desmarais, a lecturer in the English Department at Goldsmith's College. Jane was a student of Wilde and had recently published a study of Aubrey Beardsley. They had a mutual friend in Bill McCormack, from whom she had recently separated.

Jane had wanted to have a child for some time, but it is not clear that she shared these hopes with Mahon. When he learned she was pregnant, the news came as a shock, and he was deeply worried how Pat would take it and how his grown children would react on learning that they were to have a new sibling. In the midst of these worries, he lost his lease on his Fitzwilliam Square flat, the one fixed address he had maintained during his recent travels. He returned to Dublin in January to clean out the flat. Once again the familiar pattern repeated itself; once again he found himself without a home to call his own.

Back in London Mahon gave a reading with the actor Peter Marinker at John Calder's bookshop in Waterloo. Calder was in his mid-seventies at the time, but was remembered as an early publisher of Samuel Beckett. Mahon read in the back room of his bookshop surrounded by friends, including Jane, Minihan and his former Penguin editor Paul Keegan. It was an intimate occasion and the kind of gathering of friends for which he would still appear.

Jane was living near Hampstead Cemetery at the time, and, using her home as a base, Mahon explored the nearby heath, visited the Keats House and took note of Coleridge's former home in Highgate. He had reviewed Richard Holmes's biography of Coleridge years before, but under the influence of these associations he took up that review again and expanded the review into a longer essay on the Romantic poet he most admired. As was his tendency, he drew from Coleridge's life story those details that most closely paralleled his own. Coleridge had moved to the area "to recover his shattered health", he noted, and also perhaps "to escape the shadow of Wordsworth". While Coleridge never completely recovered from his opium addiction, he reached a point where he was able to manage it. His best work, however, was behind him, and his move to "The Grove" on Highgate Hill was, in Coleridge's own words, his "destined harbour".[33]

Mahon was looking for just such a harbour himself, and the publication of a new long poem in the *TLS*, "Calypso", offers a poetic treatment of that theme. What if Homer had it wrong, Mahon muses; perhaps Odysseus never did make it home but was instead lulled ashore by the Sirens' song where he found his way into a lover's arms. In his reimagining of the myth, years pass and Odysseus settles into a life of ease on his island, amid parsley, cows and goats. But sometimes, when the wind blows a certain way, he might catch a scent of his former home:

> Ithaca, 'home', not far now as the kite flew,
> he sniffed those evenings when a sea-wind blew
> but lingered in that cool cave behind the dunes
> enchanted now by hazel and sea-grey eyes,
> the star-flow of the hair, the skittish tones,
> sand-quivering foam, long leisure, lip and gland
> in the early-morning light, the sun ablaze
> through leaves and linen, through her open hand,
> briar and cumuli; so the years unwound
> to a whisper of spring water and kitchen noise.

In his reimagining of the *Iliad* Mahon found a mythic pattern for his own long journey far from home. That myth also offered him a glimpse of how the story might end:

> Bemused with his straw hat and driftwood stick,
> unmoved by the new wars and the new ships,
> he died there, fame and vigour in eclipse,
> listening to voices echo, decks and crates
> creak in the harbour like tectonic plates—
> or was he sharp still in this blithe disgrace,
> deliberate pilot of his own foggy shipwreck?
> Homer was wrong, he never made it back; or,
> if he did, spent many a curious night hour
> still questioning that strange, oracular face.[34]

Mahon stayed with Jane in the final weeks of her pregnancy, but they had no plans to establish a home together. The baby had been unexpected, and he had no desire to relive his years of early fatherhood. By the time his new daughter was born in November 2003, Mahon had come to embrace the idea of late fatherhood and they named the baby Maisie, after his mother.

In the end Mahon found his own destined harbour in Kinsale where he and Doreen had once planned to live many years before. He took a flat in the aptly named house The Grove on Compass Hill, where he had sometimes stayed on earlier visits. All life was indeed a series of repetitions. He had always had a fondness for this southern coast where his friend J.G. Farrell had spent the final months of his life. Aidan Higgins and Alannah Hopkin were living in the town, and Minihan was not far away. "Will the long voyage end here among friends", he asked in a new poem, "Harbour Lights", written soon after his return to Ireland. That poem anticipates that final erasure of self when each of us will return to our elemental origins. It is a poem not of dawn but of dusk:

> A buoy nods faintly in the harbour mouth
> as I slope down to the front for a last walk
> and watch trawlers disgorging at the dock
> in the loud work-glow of a Romanian freighter,
> dark oil-drums and fish boxes on the quay,
> winches and ropes, intestines of the sea
> alive with the stench of pre-historic water.[35]

AFTERWORD

Omissions are not accidents.

Marianne Moore, *The Complete Poems*

Mahon's move to Kinsale proved to be the beginning of a remarkably creative time. He published three new collections of poems in six years: *Harbour Lights* in 2005, *Life on Earth* in 2008, and *An Autumn Wind* in 2010. He also undertook the re-editing of his life's work: a selection of his translations, *Raw Material*, was published in 2011; and, in the same year, he reissued an expanded volume of his collected poems, now called *New Collected Poems*. There were prizes and late recognition for a lifetime devotion to his craft. His two oldest children established lives of their own. Rory married, and Katie became a mother, making him into some shade of the grandfather he had once written about in his own youth. Maisie learned simpler life lessons. Life was indeed a repetition of familiar patterns, but among these events were also painful blows. Doreen died of cancer in the summer of 2010. They never had managed to finalise their divorce.

As this account of his life neared completion, Mahon became increasingly anxious about the story it would tell. While he had always drawn upon his own life experience as subject matter for poems, poetry had allowed for some reassuring distance between his real and fictive lives. He had tried to write such an account himself in the 1990s, but only a fragment of that had ever been published after he concluded "there's too much to be ashamed of". He later agreed to participate in a documentary film, but, after the fact, had to admit it was really something of "a cover-up job". It contained nothing about his children or his parents, nothing about the bad times "of which there were many". "I spent five years in New York", he noted, but there was "nothing, or almost nothing, about New York".[1] When he and I saw one another in Kinsale in February 2012, he spoke of his recently published *New Collected Poems*, *Selected Prose* and the forthcoming collected drama as constituting a kind of autobiography. Indeed, Mahon has been writing such an autobiography from the very beginning, and his poems, prose and dramatic writing offer the most intimate glimpse of a soul in the making.

As I was nearing the end of this biography, he wrote to ask if he would be able to read the manuscript before publication.[2] We had met many times over the years—in New York, Dublin, London and Kinsale—and he had made himself available to answer questions about many aspects of his life. But these were not interviews in any formal sense; he only consented to a tape recorder on one occasion. Instead he spoke about his life in a series of conversations, often over a meal, in the Shelbourne Bar or on walks around Dublin, Dún Laoghaire or the narrow streets of Soho. He would often correct errors of one kind or another. As the book developed, however, he was increasingly unable to limit himself to corrections of fact. There had always been people and events which he did not care to discuss, but he began naming people who should not be mentioned in the book. Do not contact Doreen, Stella or Jane. "Sorry about Pat, but there you are", he wrote to me on one occasion. "Perhaps you could write about her, if at all, as an abstract Muse who just happens to bear her name".[3]

I had read his reviews of literary biographies over the years—his writing on Coleridge's life was the most instructive—and had looked closely for what qualities he singled out for praise. I replied to his letter by saying I was not confident, if he were to read the manuscript, that he would be able to limit himself to corrections of fact. On some level, I believe he understood my position, but this decision to go our separate ways only contributed to his anxiety over the book. "I have to tell you in all honesty that for some time now the prospect of our Book has been disturbing my peace of mind", he wrote to me a few weeks later. "Ungracious as it may seem, I'm finding it necessary to try to banish all thought of it & pretend it isn't happening".[4] Before he had received my reply, he wrote again, just days later, to add that we should not meet in Kinsale in the summer as we had discussed. "Sorry, & sorry that K'sale won't be such a good idea this summer after all. (God, I feel awful.)"[5]

———

Derek Mahon's anxiety at the approaching publication of this book is reminiscent of other moments of crisis in his life. The first of these, and the most profound, was the breakdown in his second year at Trinity culminating in his attempted suicide. The outbreak of the Troubles in 1968 came as a different kind of shock, one that rent the North apart and also left him, literally, without a home. These crises were followed by others: an alcoholic collapse, hospitalisation and the first separation from his wife and children when he served as Writer in Residence at the New University of Ulster. He experienced a similar breakdown again following the collapse of his marriage. His greatest point of extremity occurred in New York when it was unclear if he would even survive.

These moments of crisis are what he had in mind when he spoke in 2009 of his shameful past, but from the beginning poetry served as a means to confront and even transcend personal failures. "Take out pen and paper, this is the time to get it down!" he wrote in the first hours after separation from his wife. "After the Titanic" is the key poem for accessing the early trauma during his time as a student. "A Chinese Restaurant in Portrush" does so for the Coleraine years. In "Dawn at St. Patrick's" we see him hospitalised in Dublin in the late 1980s, while *The Yaddo Letter* and *The Hudson Letter* chronicle the bad times in New York in painful detail.

What is clear is that the origin of Mahon's art lies in suffering. Poetry offered him forms with which to seek some peace with the world, some state of wholeness that often eluded him in life. "Let me in, let me in", he cries in *The Hudson Letter*, because the original injury was a displacement from home, and the story of his life has been the story of his attempts to find his way there again. In the end Mahon made Kinsale that fictive home. It was a provisional one at best, another temporary address, a rented flat on a high hill and a writing desk at the window overlooking the harbour below. The setting brings to mind the flotsam left at the shore in a number of his most memorable poems. From the beginning he has been taking an inventory of these losses: seaweed, wrack, broken toys, hatboxes, pieces of wood, a boot, discarded tins and a thousand limpets left by the ebb-tide.

These are primal images in Mahon's poetry of loss, signs of our own insignificance in the face of nature's more insistent patterns. As a poet Mahon found consolation in poetic forms, in rhyme, which he once called "the pre-linguistic drumbeat".[6] In the heavens the planets spin in their orbits, the tide washes over a muddy beach, and even in the depth of winter spring cannot be far away. In an abandoned garden shed mushrooms bend towards light; somewhere a shirt-hanger makes an unexpected sound; and sunlight gleams off a rain-soaked hubcap. In the end, the losses he records are not his alone but ours also.

REFERENCES

Preface (pp 1–5)

1. Mahon, *Night-Crossing*, James O'Halloran collection.
2. Jon Stallworthy to Mahon, 29 July 1968, Oxford University Press archive.
3. Tim Pat Coogan, *The Troubles* (London: Arrow, 1996), 71–2.
4. Eavan Boland, "The Northern Writer's [*sic*] Crisis of Conscience: Community", *Irish Times* (12 August 1970), 12.
5. Eavan Boland, "The Northern writers' crisis of conscience: Crisis", *Irish Times* (13 August 1970), 12.
6. Boland, ibid., 12.
7. Eavan Boland, "The Northern writers' crisis of conscience: Creativity", *Irish Times* (14 August 1970).
8. "Derek Mahon: The Art of Poetry, LXXXIIII", interviewed by Eamon Grennan, *Paris Review* (Spring 2000), 164.
9. Edna Longley, "An Ironic Conscience at One Minute to Midnight", *Fortnight* (17 December 1984), 17.
10. Hugh Haughton, *The Poetry of Derek Mahon* (Oxford: OUP, 2007), 7.
11. Fran Brearton, "Dancing Unto Death: Perceptions of the Somme, the Titanic and Ulster Protestantism", *The Irish Review* (Winter–Spring 1997), 98.
12. Mahon, "After the Titanic", *Collected Poems* (Oldcastle: Gallery Press, 1999), 30.
13. "Drowning and rescue in Liffey", *Irish Press* (23 January 1962), 1.
14. Mahon, "Jail Journal", *Collected Poems* (Oldcastle: Gallery Press, 1999), 31.
15. Michael Longley, "A Poet of Power", *Irish Times*, 1 October 1968.

Chapter 1 (pp 7–17)

1. John Blake, *Northern Ireland in the Second World War* (Belfast: Blackstaff Press, 2000), 226–35.
2. Blake, ibid.
3. Mahon, "Autobiographies", *Collected Poems* (Oldcastle: Gallery Press, 1999), 91.
4. Roy Harrison and Kathleen McDowell interview, Bangor, 14 April 2003.
5. Mahon, *Huts and Sheds* (Oldcastle: Gallery Press, 2011), [1].
6. "Q. and A. with Derek Mahon", *Irish Literary Supplement* (Fall 1991), 27.
7. Mahon, "The Poetry Nonsense", *Selected Prose* (Oldcastle: Gallery Press, 2012), 27.

8. "Derek Mahon Interviewed", *Poetry Review* (Summer 1991), 4.

9. "Q. and A. with Derek Mahon", *Irish Literary Supplement* (Fall 1991), 27.

10. Mahon to the author, 14 July 2010.

11. Spenser recounts details of the tenth-century King Mahon of Munster in *A View of the Present State of Ireland.* One of Archbishop Thomas Becket's murderers is named Reginald Firtzurse, as told in Eliot's *Murder in the Cathedral,* and an old seaman named Mahon in Joseph Conrad's *Youth* insists that his name be pronounced "Mann".

12. "Q. and A. with Derek Mahon", *Irish Literary Supplement* (Fall 1991), 27.

13. "The Art of Poetry", *Paris Review* (Spring 2000), 155.

14. Interview with the author, London, 30 November 2002.

15. Interview with the author, London, 30 November 2002.

16. Mahon, "A Refusal to Mourn", *Collected Poems* (Oldcastle: Gallery Press, 1999), 87–8.

17. "The Art of Poetry", *Paris Review* (Spring 2000), 155.

18. Mahon, "A Bangor Requiem", *Collected Poems* (Oldcastle: Gallery Press, 1999), 260.

19. Mahon, "A Bangor Requiem", *Collected Poems* (Oldcastle: Gallery Press, 1999), 261.

20. Roy Harrison and Kathleen McDowell interview, Bangor, 14 April 2003.

21. Mahon, "Aunt Louise", typescript, n.d., James O'Halloran collection.

22. Mahon, "A View from the Long Grass", typescript, Mahon papers, Emory.

23. Mahon, "Courtyards in Delft", *Collected Poems* (Oldcastle: Gallery Press, 1999), 105.

24. Paul Durcan, "World of Derek Mahon", *Magill* (Christmas 1984), 43.

25. Mahon, "A View from the Long Grass", typescript, Mahon papers, Emory.

26. Mahon, ibid.

27. Mahon, interview by John Brown, *In the Chair* (Cliffs of Moher: Salmon, 2002), 113.

28. Mahon, "A View from the Long Grass", typescript, Mahon papers, Emory.

29. Mahon, ibid.

30. "The Art of Poetry", *Paris Review* (Spring 2000), 156.

31. Mahon, "Nostalgias", *Collected Poems* (Oldcastle: Gallery Press, 1999), 75.

32. "The Art of Poetry", *Paris Review* (Spring 2000), 156.

33. "Q. and A. with Derek Mahon", *Irish Literary Supplement* (Fall 1991), 27.

34. Mahon, "A Cavehill Childhood Memory", *Fortnight* (September 1984), 18.

35. Ibid., 18.

36. Ibid., 18.

37. Mahon, "A View from the Long Grass", typescript, Mahon papers, Emory.

38. Mahon, "A View from the Long Grass", typescript, Mahon papers, Emory.

39. Ibid.

Chapter 2 (pp 18–27)

1. Mahon, "Lupercal", *T.C.D.: A College Miscellany* (3 November 1961), 8–9.

2. Derek Mahon interview, London, 30 November 2002.

3. Mahon, *Dreams of a Summer Night* (Oldcastle: Gallery Press, 2010), [7].

4. John Jamieson, *The History of the Royal Belfast Academical Institution, 1810–1960* (Belfast: William Mullan, 1959), xv.

5. Derek Mahon student file, Royal Belfast Academical Institution (RBAI).

6. RBAI to N. Mahon, 19 May 1953, student file, Royal Belfast Academical Institution.

7. Brian Annesley, email to the author, 18 October 2012.

8. Roy Harrison and Kathleen McDowell interview, Bangor, 14 April 2003.

9. *School News* (Midsummer 1954), 28.

10. Progress Report, Royal School of Church Music, 20–24 April 1954, James O'Halloran collection.

11. Harold Jackson reports that the poem was printed as a Christmas card by the Church of St Peter's sometime in the 1950s. Molly Breene, the daughter of the Rector of St Peter's at the time, confirms it was her father's practice to produce such a card every Christmas and that the cards often included an illustration. Mahon, however, remembers it being printed as an insert in the Church's *Parish Notes*. In either case, no copies of this first published poem have been located.

12. *School News* (Midsummer 1956), 15.

13. Roy Harrison and Kathleen McDowell interview, Bangor, 14 April 2003.

14. "The Art of Poetry", *Paris Review* (Spring 2000), 158.

15. "The Art of Poetry", *Paris Review* (Spring 2000), 159–60.

16. Mahon, "I have been to England", *School News* (Easter 1955), 11–12.

17. "The Last Resort", *Collected Poems* (Oldcastle: Gallery Press, 1999), 93.

18. Mahon, *Dreams of a Summer Night* (Oldcastle: Gallery Press, 2010), [1].

19. Mahon, "Cushendun in Winter", *Art Notes* (Oldcastle: Gallery Press, 2006), [10].

20. *School News* (Easter 1955), 29.

21. *School News* (Midsummer 1956), 24.

22. Mahon, "Junior Debating Society", *School News* (Christmas 1956), 36.

23. W.L.P., "France", *School News* (Christmas 1956), 31–3.

24. *True as a Turtle* was directed by Wendy Toye and starred John Gregson and Cecil Parker.

25. "Literary Society", *School News* (Easter 1958), 25–6.

26. "The School Players", *School News* (Easter 1957), 9–12.

27. Derek Mahon interview, London, 29 November 2002.

28. Derek Mahon interview, London, 29 November 2002.

29. Mahon, "Art of Poetry", *Paris Review* (Spring 2000), 157.

30. "Q. and A. with Derek Mahon", *Irish Literary Supplement* (Fall 1991), 27.

31. Brian Annesley, email to the author, 11 October 2012.

32. Paul Durcan, "World of Derek Mahon", *Magill* (Christmas 1984), 45.

33. Durcan, ibid., 45.

34. Kate Olivier, email to the author, 15 October 2003.

35. "The Forrest Reid Memorial Prize", *School News* (Christmas 1958), 28.

36. "Q. and A. with Derek Mahon", *Irish Literary Supplement* (Fall 1991), 27.

37. Mahon, "Children at Prayer", *School News* (Easter 1959), 19–20.

38. Stanley Spencer painted a series of resurrection paintings. Mahon is probably referring in his poem to the most famous of the series, *The Resurrection, Cookham.*

39. Mahon, "Resurrection", *School News* (Easter 1959), 20.

40. "Debating Society", *School News* (Midsummer 1959), 30.

41. Derek Mahon interview, London, 29 November 2002.

42. Mahon, "Memoir, 1941–1980", typescript, Derek Mahon papers, Emory.

43. "Q. and A. with Derek Mahon", *Irish Literary Supplement* (Fall 1991), 27.

Chapter 3 (pp 28–48)

1. Derek Mahon, "Yeats and the Lights of Dublin", *The Dublin Review* (Autumn 2002), 73.

2. Mahon, "The Art of Poetry", *Paris Review* (Spring 2000), 160.

3. John Houston, email to the author, 24 January 2010.

4. The year before Mahon's arrival, 43 per cent of students came from the Republic, 26 per cent from Britain, 17 per cent from abroad and 14 per cent from Northern Ireland. See J.V. Luce, *Trinity College Dublin: The First 200 Years* (Dublin: Trinity College, 1992), 153.

5. Jeremy Lewis, "First Impressions", in Sebastian Balfour et al (eds), *Trinity Tales* (Dublin: Lilliput, 2009), 113.

6. John Houston, email to the author, 20 January 2010.

7. *The Architect's Journal* noted at the time "the main quad is neither an asphalt desert nor a sacrosanct lawn, but a vivid mixture of setts, turf, and baby Fiats" (15 June 1961).

8. Jeremy Lewis, "First Impressions", in Sebastian Balfour et al (eds), *Trinity Tales* (Dublin: Lilliput, 2009), 112.

9. Thomas Murtagh interview, Dublin, 19 February 2003.

10. Young Northern Poet, "Blood Sports" (letter to the editor), *Trinity News* (1 June 1961), 3.

11. Michael Longley, *Tuppenny Stung* (Belfast: Lagan Press, 1994), 33.

12. Jeremy Lewis, *Playing for Time* (London: Collins, 1987), 208.

13. Mahon, "A Ghostly Rumble Among the Drums", typescript, Longley papers, Emory.

14. Deborah de Vere White, "Turning Cartwheels", in Sebastian Balfour et al (eds), *Trinity Tales* (Dublin: Lilliput, 2009), 118.

15. Mahon, "Daedalus [*sic*] to Icarus" (letter to the editor), *Irish Times*, 12 October 1995, 15.

16. Mahon, "Yeats and the Lights of Dublin", *The Dublin Review* (Autumn 2002), 73. See also "Alec Reid", *T.C.D.: A College Miscellany* (10 March 1961), 11; and "Alec Reid—Critic Wit Friend", *Trinity News* (6 June 1963), 2.

17. The action was explained as a disciplinary action against the Literary and Historical Society for its role in publishing a sordid short story in a college magazine. As Skeffington's wife writes in her life of her husband, however, "Hardly a doubt remained as to the actual target of the ban". See Andrée Sheehy Skeffington, *Skeff: The Life of Owen Sheehy Skeffington, 1909–1970* (Dublin: Lilliput, 1991), 202.

18. Andrée Sheehy Skeffington to Mahon, 23 July 1986, James O'Halloran collection.

19. Michael Longley, *Tuppenny Stung* (Belfast: Lagan Press, 1994), 34.

20. Derek Mahon, "A Way of Happening, A Mouth," *Trinity News*, 18 May 1961, 3.

21. Mahon, "The Poet Speaks: Derek Mahon and Peter Orr" (C144, tape no. 1859), 31 January 1973, National Sound Archive.

22. Mahon, "A Ghostly Rumble Among the Drums", typescript, Longley papers, Emory.

23. Derek Mahon interview, London, 29 November 2002.

24. Mahon's Uncle Roy recalls a cottage was located somewhere near the Westland Road, not far from young Derek's childhood home. Interview with Roy Harrison, Bangor, 14 April 2003.

25. Mahon, "Lupercal", *T.C.D.* (3 November 1961), 8–9.

26. Diarmuid Kennedy, "Key of Hell: the Literature of Cave Hill", www.blackcity.co.uk.

27. Derek Mahon interview, London, 27 November 2002.

28. Philip Larkin, "Annus Mirabilis", *Collected Poems* (NY: Farrar, Straus and Giroux, 1988), 146.

29. Mahon, "Autobiographies", *Collected Poems* (Oldcastle: Gallery Press, 1999), 92–3.

30. Mahon, "Ghostly Rumble Among the Drums", typescript, Longley papers, Emory.

31. Letty Mooring, interview with the author, London, 15 January 2003.

32. Derek Mahon interview, London, 29 November 2002.

33. Mahon, "Eclogues between the Truculent", *Castles on the Air* (n.p.: BBC, n.d.), 48–9.

34. Letty Mooring interview, London, 15 January 2003.

35. Mahon to W.R. Rodgers [30 April 1961], Rodgers papers, Public Record Office of Northern Ireland.

36. Mahon to W.R. Rodgers, ibid.

37. Longley, "Glimpses of Louis MacNeice", *Castles on the Air* (n.p.: BBC, n.d.), 55.

38. Mahon to W.R. Rodgers [late November 1961], Rodgers papers, Public Record Office of Northern Ireland.

39. Mahon, interview with the author, London, 29 November 2002.

40. "Mod. Lang. Revival", *Trinity News* (23 November 1961), 1.

41. Longley, *Tuppenny Stung* (Belfast: Lagan Press, 1994), 37.

42. Mahon, "The Titanic", *Icarus* (June 1961), 19.

43. Mahon, "Un Beau Pays, Mal Habite", *Magill* (February 1979), 19–21.

44. Thomas Murtagh interview with the author, Dublin, 19 February 2003.

45. Michael Longley interview with the author, London, 4 November 2002.

46. "Man Killed in Liffey Fall", *Irish Times* (23 January 1962), 1.

47. "Drowning and rescue in Liffey", *Irish Press* (23 January 1962), 1.

48. Michael Longley interview with the author, London, 4 November 2002.

49. Mahon, "A Bender", unpublished typescript, Richard Rooke collection. Mahon would later rework some lines from this abandoned poem into a new poem titled "Resurrection", but it too would remain unpublished.

50. Mahon, "Brahms Trio", *The Dubliner* (Winter 1964), 34.

51. Mahon, "Second Childhood", unpublished typescript, Richard Rooke collection.

52. Mahon, "Never Otherwise", *Icarus* [March 1962], 12.

53. Longley, "The Flying Fish", *Irish Times* (10 February 1962), 8.

54. Untitled [profile of Terence de Vere White], *T.C.D.* vol. 67, no. 2009, n.d., 4.

55. Mahon, "From Le Poète Contumace", *Review No.* 4 (February 1962), 16–17; and "Ballad of the Hanged", *Review No.* 5 [May 1963], n.p.

56. Mahon, "Poète Maudit", *Icarus* [June 1962], 37.

57. Alec Reid, "Icarus: A Post Mortum", *Trinity News*, 7 December 1961.

58. "Andrew Stone" was the pseudonym of Ian Blake. See Blake, "All the Golden Oldies", in Sebastian Balfour et al (eds), *Trinity Tales* (Dublin: Lilliput, 2009), 70.

59. Andrew Stone, "And Another Muse", *T.C.D.: A College Miscellany* (23 November 1962), 11.

60. Interview with Louis Asekoff, 10 January 2005.

61. Jeremy Lewis, *Playing for Time* (London: Collins, 1987), 45.

62. John Boyle, Foreword, *Threshold* (Autumn/Winter 1961/62), 5.

63. MacNeice, "Under the Sugar Loaf", *New Statesman* (29 June 1962), 948.

64. Longley, "Glimpses of MacNeice", *Castles on the Air* (n.p.: BBC, n.d.), 55.

65. Mahon, "Eclogues between the Truculent", in *Castles on the Air* (n.p.: BBC Northern Ireland, [2007]), 48–9.

66. Mahon to W.R. Rodgers [Summer 1962], Rodgers papers, Public Record Office of Northern Ireland.

67. Mahon to W.R. Rodgers [8 October 1962], Rodgers papers, Public Record Office of Northern Ireland.

68. Mahon had encountered the poetry of the Dom Moraes when he reviewed *Penguin Modern Poets* for *Icarus* a few months before. See "Penguin Modern Poets", *Icarus* (June 1962), 56–7.

69. [Derek Mahon], "Editorial", *Icarus* (December 1962), 1–4.

70. Michael Longley, *Tuppenny Stung* (Belfast: Lagan Press, 1994), 38.

71. Longley, ibid., 37.

72. Longley, ibid., 38.

73. Derek Mahon, "Brahms Trio", *The Dubliner* (Winter 1964), 35.

74. Her husband, Grattan Puxon, was a contributor to *Icarus* and a campaigner on behalf of the Travelling community.

75. "Poets honoured", *Trinity News* (30 May 1963), 1.

76. Mahon, interview with the author, London, 29 November 2002.

77. Mahon, "A Ghostly Rumble Among the Drums", typescript, James O'Halloran collection.

Chapter 4 (pp 49–64)

1. Mahon to Louis Asekoff, 10 June [1963], Asekoff letters, Emory.

2. Interview with Jill Schlesinger, 4 October 2011.

3. Mahon to Asekoff, 10 June [1963], Asekoff letters, Emory.

4. Mahon to Jill Schlesinger, Newtownabbey, [Winter 1963], collection of the author.

5. Mahon, "Bird Sanctuary", *Irish Times* (4 April 1964), 8.

6. Stallworthy to Mahon, 9 August 1963, Oxford University Press archive.

7. "Girls in their Seasons", *The Dubliner* (Summer 1963), 18–20.

8. Jill Schlesinger interview, 4 October 2011.

9. Jon Stallworthy, *Louis MacNeice* (London: Norton, 1995), 474–82.

10.   Mahon, "Renovations—Euston Road", typescript, James O'Halloran collection.

11.   Mahon, "La Condition Ouvrière", *Icarus* [June 1964], 3.

12.   Mahon, "An Irishman in London", autograph manuscript, Richard Rooke collection.

13.   Mahon to Louis Asekoff, [25 May 1964], Asekoff letters, Emory.

14.   Mahon, "True Romance", unpublished typescript, Richard Rooke collection.

15.   Derek Mahon interview, London, 29 November 2002.

16.   Heaney, *Stepping Stones* (London: Faber, 2008), 74.

17.   Philip Edwards, "Icarus", *T.C.D.* (30 November 1962), 10.

18.   Mahon, "In Memory", *Irish Times* (4 January 1964), 8.

19.   Mahon to Jill Schlesinger, Newtownabbey, [Winter 1963], collection of the author.

20.   Stallworthy to Mahon, 29 January 1964, Oxford University Press archive.

21.   Eavan Boland, "Compact and Compromise: Derek Mahon as a Young Poet", *Irish University Review* (Spring/Summer 1994), 61.

22.   Michael Longley interview, London, 4 November 2002.

23.   Mahon, "Young Eavan and Early Boland", *Irish University Review* (Spring 1993), 23.

24.   Mahon, "Young Eavan & Early Boland", manuscript draft, Mahon papers, Emory.

25.   Mahon, "Young Eavan & Early Boland", ibid.

26.   Mahon, "Young Eavan & Early Boland", ibid.

27.   Eavan Boland, "Compact and Compromise: Derek Mahon as a Young Poet", *Irish University Review* (Spring/Summer 1994), 63.

28.   Mahon to "Kiddo" [Louis Asekoff], Dublin, n.d. [24 May 1964], Asekoff letters, Emory.

29.   Ted Hughes, "Gregory Award Poets: 1964", Ted Hughes papers, Emory.

30.   Jeremy Lewis, *Playing for Time* (London: Collins, 1987), 223.

31.   Interview with Edna Longley, Belfast, 15 April 2003.

32.   Mahon to Asekoff [7 June 1964], Asekoff letters, Emory.

33.   Mahon to Asekoff, ibid.

34.   Mahon to [Louis Asekoff], Dublin, [7 June 1964], Asekoff letters, Emory.

35.   Boland to Edna Longley, n.d. [1964], Longley papers, Emory.

36.   Eavan Boland, "Belfast vs. Dublin", *New Territory* (Dublin: Figgis, 1967), 16.

37.   Interview with Thomas Murtagh, Dublin, 19 February 2003.

38.   Cathal McCabe, *The Poetry of Derek Mahon*, DPhil thesis, Jesus College, 2002, 18.

39.   Mahon to Longley, n.d. [October 1964], Longley papers, Emory.

40.   Mahon to Longley, ibid.

41.   Mahon, "Negroes on the Right Bank", typescript, Richard Rooke collection.

42. Eavan Boland, email to the author, 11 January 2014.

43. Cathal McCabe, *The Poetry of Derek Mahon*, DPhil thesis, Jesus College, 2002, 18.

44. Mahon to Asekoff [16 December 1964], Asekoff letters, Emory.

45. Nicholas Grene, "Sleepwalking through the Sixties", *Trinity Tales* (Dublin: Lilliput, 2009), 219.

46. Mahon to Michael and Edna Longley, n.d. [Spring 1965], Longley papers, Emory.

47. *T.C.D.* (February 1965), 10.

48. A later title for "November Notes in Brittany", which at the time was a three-part poem including "Still Life", "Night-Owl" and "Dawn". Only "Dawn" would merit being retained in the revised sequence "Breton Walks", where it appears as "Morning".

49. Mahon to Stallworthy, Dublin, 21 January 1965, Oxford University Press archive.

50. Eavan Boland, "Compact and Compromise", Irish University Review (Spring/Summer 1994), 61.

51. Mahon to Longleys, Dublin, n.d. [early 1965], Longley papers, Emory.

52. Boland, "Compact and Compromise", *Irish University Review* (Spring/Summer 1994), 61.

53. Mahon, "Glengormley", *Collected Poems* (Oldcastle: Gallery Press, 1999), 14.

54. Boland, "Compact and Compromise", *Irish University Review* (Spring/Summer 1994), 63.

55. Mahon to Edna Longley, n.d. [Spring 1965], Longley papers, Emory.

56. In "The Poetry Nonsense" Mahon placed this visit in March 1964, but the poem was first published in April 1965 and it is unlikely he would have held it back from publication a full year. He also enclosed the poem in a June 1965 letter to Louis Asekoff in which he describes it as his "latest" (see Mahon to Asekoff, Newtownabbey, [23 June 1965], Asekoff Letters, Emory).

57. Interview with Michael Longley in *Reading the Future* (Dublin: Lilliput, 2000), 123.

58. Heaney, *Stepping Stones* (London: Faber, 2008), 77–8.

59. "Derek Mahon Interviewed", *Poetry Review* (Summer 1991), 5.

60. Philip Hobsbaum, email to the author, 21 December 1998.

61. Derek Mahon, "Poetry in Northern Ireland", *20th Century Studies* (November 1970), 91.

62. In the Longley papers there is a set of poems by Mahon that resembles a Group sheet; however, a number of the poems present on the sheet were not written until after Mahon had left Belfast for Canada ("Canadian Pacific", "As God is My Judge" and "The Poets Lie Where They Fell"). He would not have been able

to present these poems before Hobsbaum left Belfast for Glasgow early in the spring of 1966. It is likely Longley took it upon himself to prepare a Group sheet of Mahon's poems that he presented in his place at a later Group meeting, when the sessions were being conducted by Seamus Heaney.

63. Mahon to Stallworthy, Belfast, 24 March [1965], Oxford University Press archive.

64. Stallworthy to Mahon, 12 May 1965, Oxford University Press archive.

65. Interview with the author, London, 29 November 2002.

66. "Derek Mahon", *Trinity News* (18 February 1965), 6.

67. Eavan Boland, "Belfast vs. Dublin", *New Territory* (Dublin: Figgis, 1967), 16.

68. Mahon, "A Ghostly Rumble Among the Drums", Derek Mahon papers, Emory.

69. Mahon, "Dublin Evening", *Icarus* [June 1965], 43.

Chapter 5 (pp 65–79)

1. Mahon, "Recalling Aran", *The Dublin Magazine* (Spring 1966), 68.

2. Mahon to Michael and Edna Longley, London, Ontario [12 September 1965], Longley papers, Emory.

3. Mahon to Longley, London, Ontario [September 1965], Longley papers, Emory.

4. Richard Rooke, email to the author, 18 December 2011.

5. Mahon to Longley, London, Ontario [September 1965], Longley papers, Emory.

6. Mahon, "Malcolm Lowry: The Road to Parián", Icarus, no. 43 [June 1964], 20–24.

7. Mahon to Longley, London, Ontario [November 1965], Longley papers, Emory.

8. Mahon to Michael and Edna Longley [October 1965], Longley papers, Emory.

9. Mahon, "Exit Molloy", *The Island* (March 1966), 22.

10. Mahon to Longley, London, Ontario [November 1965], Longley papers, Emory.

11. Mahon to Longley, London, Ontario [early December 1965], Longley papers, Emory.

12. Mahon to Jill Schlesinger, London, Ontario [25 November 1965], collection of the author.

13. Mahon to Michael and Edna Longley, London, Ontario [early December 1965], Longley papers, Emory.

14. Mahon, "Spring Letter in Winter", *The Dublin Magazine* (Spring 1966), 68.

15. Eavan Boland, rev. of *Twelve Poems*, Icarus, no. 47 (December 1965), 42–3.

16. Mahon to Michael and Edna Longley [December 1965], Longley papers, Emory.

17. Mahon to Michael and Edna Longley, ibid.

18. Jack Sweeney to Michael Longley, (19 February 1966), Longley papers, Emory.

19. Mahon to Michael and Edna Longley, [December 1965], Longley papers, Emory.

20. Mahon to Michael and Edna Longley, [January 1966], Longley papers, Emory.

21. Mahon to Michael and Edna Longley, Cambridge, [January 1966], Longley papers, Emory.

22. Interview with Eamon Grennan, 22 September 2004.

23. Mahon to Jill Schlesinger, Cambridge, Mass. [10 February 1966], collection of the author.

24. Mahon to Michael and Edna Longley, Cambridge [January 1966], Longley papers, Emory.

25. Mahon to Longley, Lee, Mass. [early 1966], Longley papers, Emory.

26. Mahon to Longley, Cambridge [January 1966], Longley papers, Emory.

27. Mahon to Michael and Edna Longley, Cambridge [January 1966], Longley papers, Emory.

28. Mahon to Michael and Edna Longley, ibid.

29. Cathal McCabe, *The Poetry of Derek Mahon*, DPhil, Jesus College (2002), 24.

30. Mahon to Michael and Edna Longley, Cambridge [Summer 1966], Longley papers, Emory.

31. Mahon to Michael and Edna Longley, Toronto [Autumn 1966], Longley papers, Emory.

32. Mary M. Morrissey, email to the author, 29 April 2013.

33. Interview with Eamon Grennan, 22 September 2004.

34. Mahon to Edna Longley, [Toronto], [January 1967], Longley papers, Emory.

35. Interview with Eamon Grennan, 22 September 2004.

36. Mahon to Asekoff, Toronto [Autumn 1967], Asekoff letters, Emory.

37. "Michael Longley in Conversation with Jody Allen Randolph", *Poetry Ireland*, no. 79 (2004), 78.

38. Mahon to Michael and Edna Longley, Cambridge [May 1966], Longley papers, Emory.

39. Mahon to Michael and Edna Longley, Cambridge [May 1966], Longley papers, Emory.

40. Mahon to Longley, Toronto [early 1967], Longley papers, Emory.

41. Interview with Paul Jackel, New York, 23 January 2004.

42. Mahon to Michael and Edna Longley, Toronto, [Fall 1966] Longley papers, Emory.

43. Mahon to Longleys, Toronto [Fall 1966], Longley papers, Emory.

44. Mahon to Longley, Toronto [late November 1966], Longley papers, Emory.

45. Mahon to Michael and Edna Longley, Toronto [Fall 1966], Longley papers, Emory.

46. Mahon to Longley, Toronto, [late November 1966], Longley papers, Emory.

47. Mahon to Longley, ibid.

48. Mahon to Longley, Toronto, [5 December 1966], Longley papers, Emory.

49. Mahon to Longley, Toronto, [late November 1966], Longley papers, Emory.

50. Mahon to Longley, Toronto, [5 December 1966], Longley papers, Emory.
51. Mahon to Michael and Edna Longley, Toronto [January 1967], Longley papers, Emory.
52. Mahon to Michael and Edna Longley [January 1967], Longley papers, Emory.
53. Mahon to Jim Randall, Toronto [9 February 1967], Univ. of Rhode Island.
54. Mahon to Longley, Montreal [March 1967], Longley papers, Emory.
55. Mahon, "Cultural thaw in the acres of snow", *Belfast Telegraph* (25 March 1967).
56. Harry Chambers, "Festival Poetry Pamphlets", *Phoenix*, no. 1 (March 1967), 50–55.
57. Mahon to Michael and Edna Longley, Toronto [April 1967], Longley papers, Emory.
58. Mahon to Michael and Edna Longley, Toronto [early 1967], Longley papers, Emory.
59. Mahon to Michael and Edna Longley, Toronto [April 1967], Longley papers, Emory.

Chapter 6 (pp 80–100)

1. "April on Toronto Island", *The Dublin Magazine* (Summer 1967), 29.
2. Michael Longley interview with the author, London, 4 November 2002.
3. Mahon, "In the Aran Islands", *Irish Press* (4 April 1969), 7.
4. Mahon, "Aran", *Collected Poems* (Oldcastle: Gallery Press, 1999), 37.
5. Mahon to Jill Schlesinger, Newtownabbey [21 August 1967], collection of the author.
6. Mahon to Jill Schlesinger, ibid.
7. Stallworthy to Mahon, n.p., (4 July 1967), Oxford University Press archive.
8. Stallworthy to "JHP", n.p., (7 August 1967), Oxford University Press archive.
9. Stallworthy to Mahon, n.p., (30 October 1967), Oxford University Press archive.
10. Stallworthy to Mahon, ibid.
11. Mahon to Stallworthy, Belfast, (5 November [1967]), Oxford University Press archive.
12. James Simmons to Tony Harrison, Castlerock, (5 December 1967), Simmons Papers, Emory.
13. Heaney, "Explorations II: Poet: Seamus Heaney", radio script (Spring 1978), collection of the author.
14. Mahon, "Patrick Kavanagh", *Dublin Magazine* (Spring 1968), 6–8.
15. Mahon, "Patrick Kavanagh: An Epitaph", *Dublin Magazine* (Spring 1968), 12.
16. Mahon, "Patrick Kavanagh", *Dublin Magazine* (Spring 1968), 6–8.
17. Mahon, "Pilgrim Poet", typescript, Paul Durcan papers, National Library of Ireland.

18. Derek Mahon, "Ecclesiastes", *Ecclesiastes* (Manchester: Phoenix, 1970), 13.

19. Quoted in Cathal McCabe, *The Poetry of Derek Mahon*, DPhil thesis, Jesus College, 27.

20. Alan Hayes, email to the author, 8 April 2004.

21. "Teaching in February", *The Dublin Magazine* (Spring 1968), 64.

22. Mahon to Jill Schlesinger, Belfast [October 1967], collection of the author.

23. Mahon to Jill Schlesinger, Belfast, ibid.

24. Mahon to Jill Schlesinger, Belfast [25 March 1968], collection of the author.

25. Mahon to Jill Schlesinger, Belfast, 26 March [1968], collection of the author.

26. Mahon to Jill Schlesinger, Newtownabbey [21 August [1968], collection of the author.

27. Mahon to Jon Stallworthy, Newtownabbey [early August 1968], Oxford University Press archive.

28. "Derek Mahon writes", *Poetry Book Society Bulletin*, no. 58, Autumn 1968.

29. "Derek Mahon writes", ibid.

30. Michael Longley, "A Poet of Power", *Irish Times*, 1 October 1968.

31. "In Their Element", 23 May 1977, BBC Northern Ireland Sound Archive.

32. Walter Allen to John Hewitt, Coleraine (17 September 1968), John Hewitt papers, Public Record Office of Northern Ireland.

33. Suzanne Lowry, "Poetry: Who Writes It?" *Belfast Telegraph*, 21 November 1968.

34. Mahon to Asekoff, Monkstown, 12 January 1969, Asekoff letters, Emory.

35. Mahon, untitled typescript ("The Wind that blows these words to you"), Robin Skelton collection, Univ. of Victoria.

36. Interview with W.J. McCormack, Dublin, 30 November 2007.

37. Mahon to Seamus and Marie Heaney, Monkstown [1969], Heaney papers, Emory.

38. Hugh Haughton, *The Poetry of Derek Mahon* (Oxford: Oxford, 2007), 62.

39. "Introducing Derek Mahon", *Trinity News* (30 October 1969), 6.

40. Ibid., 6.

41. Mahon, "Excerpt from a play", *Threshold* (Summer 1970), 7–9.

42. Quoted in Patricia King, *Places Where a Thought Might Grow*, PhD Dissertation (City University of New York, 1995), 186.

43. John Hewitt to Jack Sweeney, 5 July 1969, Jack Sweeney papers, UCD archives.

44. W.J. McCormack, *Battle of the Books* (Dublin: Lilliput, 1986), 9.

45. Interview with W.J. McCormack, Dublin, 30 November 2007.

46. "Editorial", *Atlantis*, no. 1 (March 1970), 5.

47. Seamus Deane, email to the author, 6 December 2004.

48. Mahon, "An Image from Beckett", *The Listener*, 30 October 1969.

49. Conor Cruise O'Brien, "Burke and Machiavelli", *Atlantis*, no. 1 (March 1970), 11.

50. Seamus Deane, email to the author, 6 December 2004.

51. Brian Friel, "Derry Appeal", *Irish Press* (6 November 1969), 11.

52. "Derry's other ghetto", *Irish Press* (8 November 1969), 3.

53. Seamus Heaney, "Christmas, 1971", reprinted in *Finders Keepers: Selected Prose, 1971–2001* (London: Faber, 2002), 41.

54. Longley, "Strife and the Ulster Poet", *Hibernia* (7 November 1969).

55. Longley, "An Exploded View, notes & tables of contents", Longley papers, Emory.

56. Mahon to BBC, 9 December 1969, BBC Written Archives Centre.

57. "Books, Plays, Poems: Home and Heroes", script, BBC Written Archives Centre.

58. "Books, Plays, Poems", radio scripts, Michael Longley papers, Emory.

59. Letter to the Editor, *Irish Times* (7 January 1970), 9.

60. Mahon, "Poetry in Northern Ireland", *20th Century Studies* (November 1970), 91.

61. Editorial, *Atlantis* (March 1970), 5.

62. Mahon to Jeremy Lewis [ca. March 1970], courtesy of Jeremy Lewis.

63. Mahon, *Beyond Howth Head* (Dublin: Dolmen Press, 1970), 8.

64. Mahon, ibid.

65. Mahon, ibid.

66. Mahon, ibid.

67. Mahon, ibid.

68. Mahon, "Straight Lines Breaking Becoming Circles", *Phoenix*, no. 5 (Summer 1969), 12.

69. Mahon, *Beyond Howth Head* (Dublin: Dolmen Press, 1970), 10.

70. Anthony Glavin, "The Hot World", *Hibernia* (25 September–8 October 1970), 11.

71. Mahon, *Beyond Howth Head* (Dublin: Dolmen Press, 1970), 11.

72. Mahon, ibid.

73. Mahon, ibid., 12.

74. Mahon, "Beyond Howth Head", *Collected Poems* (Oldcastle: Gallery Press, 1999), 57.

75. Mahon, "Art of Fiction CLVIII", corrected typescript, Mahon papers, Emory.

Chapter 7 (pp 101–17)

1. Derek Mahon, "Poetry in Northern Ireland", *20th Century Studies* (November 1970), 90.

2. Unpublished interview by Mary Hilker, typescript (11 March 1987), James O'Halloran collection.

3. Ibid.

4. "Harriet Cooke Talks to the Poet Derek Mahon", *Irish Times*, 17 January 1973.

5. Mahon to Asekoff, 29 June [1971], Louis Asekoff letters, Emory.

6. Michael Hartnett, "The New British Poets", Irish Press (25 September 1971), 12.

7. Derek Mahon, "This Dump, This Dump", review of *A Pagan Place*, by Edna O'Brien. *The Listener* (23 April 1970), 556–7.

8. Jeremy Lewis interview, London, 25 February 2003.

9. Quoted in *The Poetry Nonsense*, directed by Roger Greene, Caranna Productions, 2010.

10. In 1976 Bernard Stone lost his lease on the Kensington Church Walk property, and Turret Books moved to Floral Street in Covent Garden where Mahon continued to frequent the shop in its new location.

11. Quoted in *The Poetry Nonsense*, directed by Roger Greene, Caranna Productions, 2010.

12. Maurice Leitch, "Ward's Irish House, London, 1971", *Eddie's Own Aquarius*. ed. by Constance Short and Tony Carroll (Galway: Cahermee, 2005), 136.

13. Jeremy Lewis, "The platonic pub", *New Statesman* (4 October 1985), 35–6.

14. Mahon, "This Dump, This Dump", rev. of *A Pagan Place*, by Edna O'Brien. *The Listener* (23 April 1970), 556–7.

15. Mahon, "The Shandeleer", rev. of *The Vivisector*, by Patrick White. *The Listener* (5 November 1970), 635.

16. "Dan Gerou's Bend", review of *Wonders of Ireland*, by Eric Newby and Diane Petry. *The Listener* (25 December 1969), 900.

17. Derek Mahon, "Poetry in Northern Ireland", *20th Century Studies* (November 1970), 90.

18. Desmond Egan and Michael Hartnett, *Choice: An Anthology of Irish Poetry Selected by the Poets Themselves with a Comment on their Choice* (Curragh: Goldsmith Press, 1973), 80.

19. Mahon, *Ecclesiastes* (Manchester: Phoenix Pamphlet Poets, no. 9, 1970), [4].

20. Mahon, ibid., 5.

21. Mahon, "The Major waits for war in the Majestic", *The Times* (8 October 1970), 14.

22. Mahon, letter to author, Kinsale, 10 September [2009].

23. Mahon Permissions file, BBC Written Archives Centre, Caversham.

24. Mahon to Stallworthy, May [1971], OUP archive.

25. Stallworthy, OUP memorandum, [Summer 1971], OUP archive.

26. Mahon, "Rage for Order", *The Listener* (6 May 1971), 585.

27. Sandra Leitch interview, London, 12 September 2010.

28. Mahon to Michael Longley [Summer 1971], Longley papers.

29. In *The Ulster Renaissance* (Oxford 2006), Heather Clark compresses this chronology and treats the exchange of verse letters in 1969 and 1971 as part of a single sequence. In fact, Mahon declined to participate a second time, and Longley's poem was a one-sided verse letter.

30. Mahon to Longley, n.d. [1971], Longley papers, Emory.

31. Michael Longley, "Two Letters", *New Statesman* (3 December 1971), 786.

32. Longley, ibid.

33. Mahon to Longley, [December 1971], Longley papers, Emory.

34. Mahon, "Two Letters", *New Statesman* (10 December 1971), 821.

35. Longley, "To Derek Mahon", in *An Exploded View* (London: Victor Gollancz, 1973), 36.

36. Longley, "My Protestant Education", *New Statesman* (16 August 1974), 220.

37. Mahon to Asekoff, [Jan 1973], courtesy of Louis Asekoff.

38. Heaney interview with Robert McCrum, *Observer* (19 July 2009), 16.

39. Mahon to Lady Dufferin (14 February [1972]), ICA archive, Tate Library and Archive.

40. "Poetry International", by Richard Holmes. *The Times* (22 June 1972), 10.

41. Mahon, "Fire King", holograph manuscript, 31 March 1972, courtesy of Glyn Hughes.

42. Mahon, Introduction, *Sphere Book of Modern Irish Poetry* (London: Sphere Books, 1972), 11.

43. Mahon included poems by Eiléan Ní Chuilleanáin and Eavan Boland in the Sphere anthology, but he made no effort to place their work in relation to the tradition he describes in his introduction.

44. Mahon, Introduction, *Sphere Book of Modern Irish Poetry* (London: Sphere Books, 1972), 14.

45. Mahon, sleeve note for *Ravenswood Poems: Read by the Poet* by Richard Ryan.

46. Mahon, ibid.

47. Mahon to John Hewitt, 20 April [1972], Hewitt papers, Public Record Office of Northern Ireland.

48. Fallon to Mahon, n.d., Peter Fallon/Gallery Press collection, Emory.

49. Oxford memorandum, 10 April 1972, Oxford University Press archive.

50. Philobiblion to Mahon, 13 June 1972. University of Victoria Archives and Special Collections.

51. *A Picture of Dorian Gray*, script, Robin Skelton papers, University of Victoria.

52. Sandra Leitch, interview with the author, London, 12 September 2010.

53. Glyn Hughes, email to the author, 12 August 2009.

54. Mahon, "Runes", typescript, courtesy of Glyn Hughes.

55. Douglas Dunn to the author, 7 June 2010.

56. Douglas Dunn, "Realisms", in *Love or Nothing* (London: Faber, 1974), 19–21.

57. Douglas Dunn to Michael Longley, 25 July 1972, Michael Longley papers, Emory.

58. Longley to Douglas Dunn, 27 July 1972, Douglas Dunn papers, St Andrews.

59. Longley to Douglas Dunn, ibid.

60. James Simmons, "Living in London", *Fortnight* (8 June 1972), 16.

61. Douglas Dunn to Michael Longley, 25 July 1972, Michael Longley papers, Emory.

62. Mahon, "A good companion", *The Times*, 12 April 1973, 15.

63. Mahon to Douglas Dunn, postcard, Trets, 18 July 1972, Douglas Dunn papers, St Andrews.

64. Kate Olivier diary, courtesy of Kate Olivier.

65. Glyn Hughes, email to the author, 1 April 2010.

66. Mahon to Asekoff, [January 1973], courtesy of Louis Asekoff.

Chapter 8 (pp 118–38)

1. Mahon to Louis Asekoff, [January 1973], Asekoff collection, Emory.

2. Mahon to Robin Skelton, 5 February [1973], Skelton papers, University of Victoria.

3. "The Poet Speaks: Derek Mahon and Peter Orr", 31 January 1973, National Sound Archive (C144, tape no. 1859).

4. Mahon, "A Disused Shed in Co. Wexford", typescript, 10 January 1973, Longley Papers, Emory.

5. Seamus Heaney, "Place and Displacement: Recent Poetry from Northern Ireland", *Finders Keepers* (London: Faber, 2003), 119.

6. J.G. Farrell, *The Lung* (London: Hutchinson, 1965), 33.

7. Mahon, "A Disused Shed in Co. Wexford", *Collected Poems* (Oldcastle: Gallery Press, 1999), 89–90.

8. Mahon to Robin Skelton, 5 February [1973], Skelton papers, University of Victoria.

9. Elsa Pomeroy to Douglas Dunn, 3 January 1973, Douglas Dunn papers, St Andrews.

10. Doreen Mahon to John Hewitt, 28 March 1973, John Hewitt papers, Public Record Office of Northern Ireland.

11. Mahon to Robin Skelton, 26 March [1973], Skelton papers, University of Victoria.

12. Mahon, "The Snow Party", *Encounter* (April 1973), 10.

13. Mahon, review of *The Rough Field*, *Malahat Review* (July 1973), 132–7.

14. Mahon to Serge Fauchereau, London, 19 July 1973, courtesy of Serge Fauchereau.

15. Mahon to D.E.S. Maxwell, London, 30 July 1973, D.E.S. Maxwell correspondence, National Library of Ireland.

16. Lester Conner to the author, n.d. [2003].

17. "Booker winner bites the hand", *Evening Standard* (29 November 1973), 20.

18. Mahon to W.J. McCormack, London, [Autumn 1973], Hugh Maxton correspondence, Leeds.

19. Mahon to Longley, London, 15 November [1973], Longley papers, Emory.

20. Mahon to Longley, ibid.

21. Mahon to Longley, ibid.

22. Maurice Leitch, telephone interview with author, 30 December 2009.

23. Derek Mahon and John Montague, CAIS conference, audiotape, 1974, collection of the author.

24. Mahon to Louis Asekoff, [Spring 1974], Louis Asekoff letters, Emory.

25. Lavinia Greacen, *J.G. Farrell: The Making of a Writer* (London: Bloomsbury, 1999), 310.

26. "J.G. Farrell", *Vogue* [British edition], (June 1974), 138–9.

27. Mahon to Douglas Dunn, 3 June [1974], Douglas Dunn papers, St Andrews.

28. Mahon, "Spotlight on Poets", *Vogue* [British edition], (15 September 1974), 94.

29. Mahon, ibid., 90.

30. James Simmons, "Flight of the Earls Now Leaving", *Irish Times* (4 June 1974), 10.

31. Edna Longley, "Derek Mahon", *Honest Ulsterman* (March/July 1974), 30.

32. Mahon, "Afterlives", *New Statesman*, (20 September 1974), 387.

33. Mahon to Simmons, [Autumn 1974], James Simmons papers, Emory.

34. Mahon to Douglas Dunn, postcard [August 1974], Douglas Dunn papers, St Andrews.

35. Philip Haas telephone interview, 30 June 2009.

36. Stella Lubsen, email to the author, 3 October 2010.

37. Doreen Mahon to Moynagh, postcard, [18 July 1974], courtesy of Patricia Moynagh.

38. Mahon, "C.P. Cavafy's Alexandria", *New Review* (January 1975), 63.

39. Mahon to O'Grady, London, 7 September [1974], O'Grady papers, Emory.

40. Mahon to D.E.S. Maxwell, 4 November 1974. D.E.S. Maxwell correspondence, National Library of Ireland.

41. Mahon, "The Woods", *Times Literary Supplement* (31 July 1981), 880.

42. Mahon to Douglas Dunn, 24 November [1975], Douglas Dunn papers, St Andrews.

43. Mahon to Longley, [Autumn 1974], Longley papers, Emory.

44. Mahon to Longley, ibid.

45. Mahon to Longley, ibid.

46. Patricia Moynagh, letter to the author, London, 21 January 2013.

47. Mahon, "Each Poem for me is a New Beginning", *Cork Review* (June 1981), 11.

48. Mahon to Desmond O'Grady, London, 1 January 1975, O'Grady papers, Emory.

49. Mahon to Asekoff, 18 March 1975, Louis Asekoff letters, Emory.

50. Mahon, "Ford Manor", *Literary Review* (Winter 1979), 231.

51. Interview with the author, 30 December 2009.

52. Mahon to Longley, Lingfield [Spring 1975], Longley papers, Emory.

53. Andrew Waterman, email to the author, 17 March 2009.

54. Mahon to Desmond O'Grady, Lingfield, 7 June [1975], O'Grady papers, Emory.

55. Mahon to Louis Asekoff, postcard [10 July 1975], Louis Asekoff letters, Emory.

56. Mahon to Louis Asekoff, Lingfield, 30 June [1975], Louis Asekoff letters, Emory.

57. Edna Longley, "Snow-Parties", *Irish Times* (26 August 1975), 8.

58. Edna Longley, ibid.

59. Edna Longley, ibid.

60. Edna Longley, "Fire and Air", *Honest Ulsterman* (Winter 1975), 182.

61. Ciaran Carson, "Escaped from the Massacre", *Honest Ulsterman* (Winter 1975), 183.

62. *Letters of Robert Lowell*, ed. by Saskia Hamilton (New York: Farrar, Straus & Giroux, 2005).

63. Mahon, letter to author, Kinsale, 10 September [2009].

64. Elgy Gillespie, email to the author, 15 August 2009.

65. Gillespie, ibid.

66. Elgy Gillespie, "Robert Lowell in Kilkenny", typescript, Robert Lowell papers, Harry Ransom Center.

67. Mahon to Douglas Dunn, Lingfield, 24 November [1975], Douglas Dunn papers, St Andrews.

68. Longley to Ted Little, 29 October 1975, ICA archive, Tate Library and Archive, 955/8/23.

69. Longley to Ted Little, ibid.

70. Longley to Ted Little, 6 February 1976, ICA archive, Tate Library and Archive. 955/8/23.

71. "Festival of Ulster Poetry" press release, ICA archive, Tate Library and Archive.

72. Maurice Leitch, interview with the author, 30 December 2009.

73. John Montague to Seamus Heaney, May 1976, Heaney papers, Emory.

74. Louis Asekoff, interview with the author, New York, 10 January 2005.

75. Sandra Leitch, interview with author, London, 12 September 2010.

76. Mahon to Longley, Lingfield [Spring 1975], Longley papers, Emory.

77. Mahon to Ormsby, Lingfield, 7 October [1976], Ormsby papers, Emory.

78. Mahon to Ormsby, ibid.

79. Mahon to Michael and Edna Longley, postcard, 14 February [1977], Longley papers, Emory.

80. Mahon to Michael Longley, Epsom, Surrey, 9 March 1977, Longley papers, Emory.

81. Mahon to James Simmons, 24 February [1977], James Simmons papers, Emory.

82. Mahon to Douglas Dunn, 26 February [1977], Douglas Dunn papers, St Andrews.

83. Mahon to Jon Stallworthy, Lingfield, 29 March [1977], OUP archive.

84. Mahon, "The Living Poet", corrected typescript, Mahon papers, Emory.

Chapter 9 (pp 139–58)

1. "Poetry to link the two communities", *Irish Press* (7 December 1970), 13.

2. Michael Longley, "Poetry", in *Causeway: The Arts in Ulster*, Michael Longley (ed.), (Belfast: Arts Council of Northern Ireland, 1971), 107. Edna Longley expanded on the analogy in her 1975 review of *The Snow Party*. See Longley, "Fire and Air", *Honest Ulsterman* (Winter 1975), 179–83.

3. Longley to Mahon, 23 May 1975, Michael Longley papers, Emory.

4. Longley to Heaney, 5 May 1975, Longley papers, Emory.

5. Mahon, letter to the author, Kinsale, 10 September [2009].

6. Mahon, "In Their Element", 23 May 1977, BBC Northern Ireland Sound Archive.

7. Longley to Heaney, 5 May 1977, Longley papers, Emory.

8. Mahon to Fallon, 1 August [1977] and 8 August [1977], Fallon/Gallery Press collection, Emory.

9. Mahon, "Going Home", *Collected Poems* (Oldcastle: Gallery Press, 1999), 95.

10. Mahon, "Dry Hill", *The Literary Review* (Winter 1978), 235.

11. Mahon to Richard Ryan, 11 December 1985, James O'Halloran collection.

12. Doreen Mahon to Patricia Moynagh, 30 January 1978, courtesy of Patricia Moynagh.

13. Interview with Maurice and Sandra Leitch, 16 January 2010.

14. Mahon, "The Chinese Restaurant in Portrush", *Collected Poems* (Oldcastle: Gallery Press, 1999), 97.

15. Andrew Waterman to the author, 17 March 2009.

16. Mahon to Steve Regan, 6 May [1978]; courtesy of Steve Regan.

17. Andrew Waterman, "On the Mend", *Encounter* (June 1979), 42.

18. "The Old Snaps", enclosed with Mahon to Longley, 23 May [1978], Longley Papers, Emory.

19. Mahon, "The Old Snaps", *Poems 1962–1978* (Oxford, 1979), 102.

20. Jennifer Johnston to the author, 2 August [2010].

21. Mahon to Longley, 23 May [1978], Longley papers, Emory.

22. Mahon to D.E.S. Maxwell, Coleraine, 19 May [1978]. Maxwell papers, National Library of Ireland.

23. Mahon, "Have a Heart", *New Statesman* (23 June 1978), 852.

24. Mahon to D.E.S. Maxwell, 19 May [1978], Maxwell papers, National Library of Ireland.

25. Mahon to Douglas Dunn, Cork, 12 July [1978], Dunn papers, St Andrews.

26. Mahon to Desmond O'Grady, [Dublin], 8 June [1978], O'Grady papers, Emory.

27. Eamon Grennan diary, June 1978, Grennan papers, Emory.

28. Interview with Eamon Grennan, Atlanta, 22 September 2004.

29. Mary Leland, "Passing the Curragh", *The Little Galloway Girls* (London: Hamish Hamilton, 1987), 134–5.

30. Mary Leland, telephone interview with the author, 13 May 2011.

31. Evelyn Montague to John Montague, Cork, 27 July 1978, Montague papers, National Library of Ireland.

32. Mahon to John and Evelyn Montague, Coleraine, 8 September 1978, Montague papers, National Library of Ireland.

33. Maurice and Sandra Leitch telephone interview, 16 January 2010.

34. Mahon, "Craigvara House", *Poetry Ireland Review* (Autumn 1985), 8–10.

35. Mahon to Peter Fallon, Coleraine, 24 October [1978], Fallon/Gallery Press collection, Emory.

36. Mahon to Jacqueline Simms, 20 September [1978], Oxford University Press archive.

37. James Raimes to Jacqueline Simms, 8 December 1978, Oxford University Press archive.

38. Jacqueline Simms to James Raimes, 2 January 1979, OUP archive.

39. Jacqueline Simms to James Raimes, ibid.

40. Elgy Gillespie, email to the author, 15 August 2009.

41. Elgy Gillespie, "Derek Mahon: The Saturday Profile", *Irish Times* (2 December 1978), 14.

42. Gillespie, ibid., 14.

43. Mahon to Asekoff, 13 November [1978], Louis Asekoff letters, Emory.

44. Mahon, "Derry Morning", typescript, enclosed with Mahon to Peter Fallon, 22 December [1980], Peter Fallon/Gallery Press collection, Emory.

45. Mahon, "Derry Morning: an interlude", *New Statesman* (10 April 1981), 23.

46. Mahon, "North Wind", *Honest Ulsterman* (July/October 1980), 3–4.

47. Mahon to Peter Fallon, Coleraine, 8 March [1979], Fallon/Gallery Press collection, Emory.

48. Mahon to Simms, 3 May [1979], Oxford University Press archive.

49. Simms to Mahon, 3 May 1979, Oxford University Press archive.

50. Mahon to Simms, 17 May [1979], Oxford University Press archive.

51. Interview with Edna Longley, Belfast, 15 April 2003.

52. Mahon to Louis Asekoff, 30 April [1979], Louis Asekoff letters, Emory.

53. Mahon to Simms, 2 July [1979], Oxford University Press archive.

54. Natalie Wexler, "Irish Poet: Even His Looks Contradictory", *Winston-Salem Journal* (29 July 1979), B1.

55. Kendall Reid, email to the author, 6 May 2009.

56. Mahon, "The Living Poet", corrected typescript, Mahon papers, Emory.

57. Mahon to Dillon Johnston, 22 July 1981, Mahon papers, Emory.

58. Mahon, "The Globe in Carolina", *Collected Poems* (Oldcastle: Gallery Press, 1999), 141–2.

59. Mahon, "Astronomy in North Carolina", *Aquarius*, no. 12 (1980), 51–2.

60. Michael Longley to Seamus Heaney, 3 September 1979, Heaney papers, Emory.

61. Mahon, "J.G. Farrell, 1935–1979 ", *New Statesman* (31 August 1979), 313.

62. Mahon to Patricia Moynagh, London, 22 September 1979; courtesy of Patricia Moynagh.

63. Mahon to Longley, London [late Nov. 1979], Longley papers, Emory.

64. Mahon to Dillon Johnston, London, 3 October [1979], Mahon papers, Emory.

65. Piers Plowright, email to the author, 23 June 2009.

66. Mahon to Peter Fallon, London, 1 November [1979]. Fallon/Gallery Press collection, Emory.

Chapter 10 (pp 159–81)

1. Seamus Heaney, "Books of the Year", *Sunday Times* (9 December 1979).

2. Mahon to Peter Fallon, 16 December [1979], Peter Fallon/Gallery Press collection, Emory.

3. Mahon to Dillon Johnston, 4 January [1980], Mahon papers, Emory.

4. Brendan Kennelly, "Lyric Wit", *Irish Times* (22 December 1979).

5. Jack Holland, "A Searing Objectivity", *The Nation* (20 September 1980), 260.

6. Peter Porter, "Voices from Ulster", *The Observer* (27 January 1980).

7. James Simmons, "Two talented friends", *Books Ireland* (Jan–Feb 1980), 21.

8. Peter Porter, "Voices from Ulster", *The Observer* (27 January 1980).

9. Blake Morrison, "An expropriated mycologist", *Times Literary Supplement* (15 February 1980), 168.

10. Andrew Motion, "Alien Eyes", *New Statesman* (14 December 1979).

11. "Critics Forum", BBC transcript, 12 January 1980, Mahon papers, Emory.

12. Mahon to Brian Friel, 6 February 1980, Brian Friel papers, National Library of Ireland.

13. Mahon, "Bad Time", typescript, James O'Halloran collection.

14. Mahon to Dillon Johnston, 4 January [1980], Mahon papers, Emory.

15. *A Sense of Ireland* [programme] (London: A Sense of Ireland, 1980).

16. W.L. Webb, "The pen is alive and well and flowing in the Emerald Isle", *The Guardian* (1 February 1980), 10.

17. Ivan Gibbons, "Home Thoughts from Abroad", *Fortnight*, no. 175 (March 1980), 13.

18. *A Sense of Ireland* [programme], (London: A Sense of Ireland, 1980), [iv].

19. Leon Ó Broin, "A Sense of Ireland", *Times Literary Supplement* (15 February 1980), 172.

20. Mahon to Peter Fallon, postcard, 29 March [1980], Peter Fallon/Gallery Press collection, Emory.

21. Mahon to Michael Longley, 21 April [1980], Longley papers, Emory.

22. Mahon, "The Boy Who Fell in Love with a Bridge", typescript, courtesy of Patricia Moynagh.

23. Interview with Patricia Moynagh, London, 28 March 2009.

24. "Never a Day Without a Line", sound recording, collection of the author.

25. "Never a Day Without a Line", ibid.

26. Richard Hoggart, "Ulster: a 'switch-off' TV subject?" *The Listener* (28 February 1980), 261.

27. Clive James, "Shadows in Ulster", *The Observer* (23 March 1980), 20.

28. Mahon to Longley, London, April 21, [1980], Longley papers, Emory.

29. Mahon, "Brighton Poems", enclosed with Mahon to Longley, London, April 21, [1980], Longley papers, Emory.

30. See Hugh Haughton, *Poetry of Derek Mahon* (Oxford: Oxford University Press, 2007), 194–5.

31. Mahon to Michael Longley, 21 April [1980], Longley papers, Emory.

32. Mahon to Glyn Hughes, postcard, [Summer] 1980, Mahon papers, Emory.

33. Mahon to Douglas Dunn, London, 5 June [1980], Douglas Dunn papers, St Andrews.

34. Mahon, "The Woods", *TLS* (31 July 1981), 880.

35. Mahon to Douglas Dunn, postcard, 23 January 1981, Douglas Dunn papers, St Andrews.

36. "Temptation of Eileen Hughes" [film proposal], n.d., Mahon papers, Emory.

37. Mahon, "Poet's Voice", *The Observer* (2 November 1980), 28.

38. Heaney to Mahon, 3 November 1980, Mahon papers, Emory.

39. James Simmons, "For Derek Mahon", typescript, November 1980, Mahon papers, Emory.

40. Mahon, "Long Goodbye", *London Review of Books* (20 November–4 December 1980), 6.

41. Mahon to James Simmons, postcard, (10 December 1980), Simmons papers, Emory.

42. Mahon, "Long Goodbye", *London Review of Books*, (20 November–4 December 1980), 6.

43. Longley to Montague, n.p., 24 November 1980, Montague papers, National Library of Ireland.

44. Longley to Mahon, 18 November 1980, Mahon papers, Emory.

45. Mahon to Peter Fallon, London, 8 December [1980], Fallon/Gallery Press collection, Emory.

46. Mahon to Dillon Johnston, London, 16 January [1981], Mahon papers, Emory.

47. Mahon to Louis Asekoff, postcard, 17 March 1981, Mahon papers, Emory.

48. Brian Mitchell to John Montague, London, 28 January 1981, Montague papers, National Library of Ireland.

49. Mahon to Peter Fallon, postcard, 3 February 1981, Fallon/Gallery Press collection, Emory.

50. Jennifer Johnston to Mahon, postcard, 27 April 1981, Mahon papers, Emory.

51. Philip Haas telephone interview, 30 June 2009.

52. Mahon to Sheamus Smith, 28 April [1981], O'Halloran collection.

53. Mahon to Louis Asekoff, Mahon: Letters to Louis Asekoff, Emory.

54. Mahon to Jacqueline Simms, postcard, 12 June 1981, Oxford University Press archive.

55. Mahon to Louis Asekoff, 24 June [1981], Mahon papers, Emory.

56. Mahon to Jacqueline Simms, 17 June [1981], Oxford University Press archive.

57. Mahon to Seamus Heaney, 5 June [1981], Heaney papers, Emory.

58. Mahon to Louis Asekoff, 17 August [1981], Mahon papers, Emory.

59. "Notes on the Characters", *Gillespie* typescript, James O'Halloran collection.

60. Heaney accepted the offer of a temporary teaching appointment early in 1981, and he took up his duties at Harvard the following year.

61. Heaney to Mahon, Dublin, 22 September 1981, Mahon papers, Emory.

62. Heaney to Mahon, ibid.

63. Mahon to Douglas Dunn, London, 9 October [1981], Douglas Dunn papers, St Andrews.

64. Mahon to Richard Murphy, 20 November [1981], Murphy papers, Tulsa; and Mahon to Frank Ormsby, 15 October [1981], Ormsby papers, Emory.

65. Mahon to Dillon Johnston, 5 November [1981], Mahon papers, Emory.

66. Paul Joyce, email to the author, 12 December 2010.

67. Mahon to Peter Fallon, London, n.d. [Autumn 1981], Peter Fallon/Gallery Press collection.

68. Mahon to Peter Fallon, [Autumn 1981], Fallon/Gallery Press collection, Emory.
69. Mahon to Fallon, ibid.
70. Mahon to Louis Asekoff, 19 January [1982], Mahon papers, Emory.
71. Mahon to Mary Gordon, 11 February 1982, Mahon papers, Emory.
72. Mary Gordon to Mahon, 26 February 1982, Mahon papers, Emory.
73. Mary Gordon, "Reading Auden", *New Statesman* (18 June 1982).
74. "Come Back Early Or Never Come" [film proposal], Derek Mahon papers, Emory.
75. "A Garage in Co. Cork" was originally titled "Kavanagh's Garage" in manuscript. The specific postcard that prompted the poem was of "McGrotty's Garage".
76. Mahon, "A Garage in Co. Cork", *TLS* (14 May 1982), 541.
77. Mahon and Paul Joyce, *Last Summer* [*Summer Lightning*], script, 10 June 1982, Mahon papers, Emory.
78. Mahon to Peter Fallon, 14 August [1982], Fallon Press collection, Emory.
79. Mahon to Seamus Heaney, 16 April [1982], Heaney papers, Emory.
80. Mahon to Peter Fallon, 14 August [1982], Fallon papers, Emory.
81. Eugene Dubnov, email to the author, 28 February 2011.
82. Mahon to Glyn Hughes, 4 January [1983], Mahon papers, Emory.
83. Seamus Heaney to Mahon, 7 September 1982, Mahon papers, Emory.
84. Mahon to Jacqueline Simms, 25 September, [1982], Oxford University Press archive.
85. Mahon to Jacqueline Simms, ibid.
86. Mahon to Jacqueline Simms, ibid.
87. Brian Moore to Mahon, 8 October 1982, Mahon papers, Emory.
88. Mahon to Brian Moore, 15 November [1982], Moore papers, Texas.
89. Mahon to Louis Asekoff, 26 October [1982], Mahon: Letters to Louis Asekoff, Emory.
90. Mahon to Desmond O'Grady, 8 February [1983], O'Grady papers, Emory.
91. Brian Moore to Mahon, 11 November [1982], Mahon papers, Emory.
92. Mahon, "Derek Mahon writes…" *Poetry Book Society Bulletin* (Winter 1982), 1.
93. Mahon to Brian Moore, 15 November [1982], Brian Moore papers, Texas.
94. Mary Kenny, email to the author, 27 April 2009.

Chapter 11 (pp 182–204)

1. Mary Kenny, email to the author, 27 April 2009.
2. Mahon, "House Husband", n.d., James O'Halloran collection.
3. Mahon, "The Living Poet", corrected typescript, November, 1982, Mahon papers, Emory.
4. Mahon to Dillon Johnston, postcard, 14 January [1983], Mahon papers, Emory.
5. Mahon to Louis Asekoff, 26 October [1982], Mahon papers, Emory.

6. Quoted in *The Poetry Nonsense*, directed by Roger Greene, Caranna Productions, 2010.

7. "The Hunt by Night" [letter to the editor], *TLS* (17 June 1983), 632.

8. Patricia King to Ms Robinson, 1 March 1993, Mahon papers, Emory.

9. Mahon to Medbh McGuckian, postcard, 24 May [1983], Medbh McGuckian papers, Emory.

10. Derek Mahon, "The Cry" [rehearsal script], Mahon papers, Emory.

11. Mahon mistakenly places this visit in 1981 in his Introduction to J.G. Farrell's *The Singapore Grip* (ix).

12. John Montague, email to the author, 4 March 2012.

13. Mahon, Introduction, *The Singapore Grip* (New York: New York Review Books, 1999), ix–x.

14. Mahon, "A Bed of Roses", *Irish Times* (16 May 1981), 5.

15. Seamus Heaney to Mahon, postcard [23 October 1983], Mahon papers, Emory.

16. "Field Day's New Double Bill", *Irish Times*, 18 September 1984.

17. Brian Friel to Mahon, 31 October 1983, Mahon papers, Emory.

18. Mahon, Paris diary, Mahon papers, Emory.

19. Mahon, ibid.

20. Mahon, "Enigma of the Western World", *The Observer* (13 April 1986), 21.

21. Mahon, "Louis & Sam", typescript, Mahon papers, Emory.

22. Mahon, "Enigma of the Western World", *The Observer* (13 April 1986), 21.

23. Derek Mahon, "A Parisian October Notebook", *Fortnight* (December 1983), 29.

24. "TV film stirs anger in village", *Belfast Telegraph* (2 December 1983).

25. "BBC stops 'B' Specials filming in Straid", *Belfast Telegraph* (3 December 1983).

26. "The Pleasures of Reading", *New Statesman* (16/23 December 1983), 40.

27. Mahon to Dillon Johnston, 26 December [1983], Mahon papers, Emory.

28. Mahon to Gisèle d'Ailly, 12 February [1984], the Gisèle d'Ailly archive, Castrum Peregrini.

29. Margaret Windham to Mahon, 6 February 1984, Mahon papers, Emory.

30. Brian Friel to Mahon, 14 March 1984, Mahon papers, Emory.

31. Mahon to Longley, 18 April [1984], Longley papers, Emory.

32. Stella Lubsen, email to the author, 20 October 2010.

33. Mahon to Michael Longley, 18 April [1984], Longley papers, Emory.

34. "Death and the Sun", typescript, enclosed with Mahon to Longley, 18 April [1984], Longley papers, Emory.

35. "Death and the Sun", typescript enclosed with Mahon to Longley, 18 April [1984], Longley papers, Emory.

36. Mahon to Louis Asekoff, 25 May [1984], Mahon papers, Emory.

37. Mahon to Dillon Johnston, 11 May [1984], Mahon papers, Emory.

38. Sidney Glazier to Brian Moore, 25 June 1984, Brian Moore papers, Texas.
39. "Critics praise Ulster play", *Sunday Independent* (12 August 1984), 12.
40. "The right Mahon for a farce", *Sunday Independent* (30 September 1984), 13.
41. Ray Rosenfield, *The Stage* (11 October 1984).
42. Eamon Grennan to Mahon, postcard, 7 November 1984, O'Halloran collection.
43. Will Sulkin to Mahon, 28 August 1984, O'Halloran collection.
44. Will Sulkin to Mahon, 19 September 1984, O'Halloran collection.
45. Mahon to Louis Asekoff, 30 April [1984], Mahon papers, Emory.
46. Mahon to Louis Asekoff, 25 May [1984], Mahon papers, Emory.
47. Mahon, address book, n.d., Mahon papers, Emory.
48. Patricia King to Mahon, 6 December 1984, Mahon papers, Emory.
49. Paul Durcan to Mahon, 6 October 1984, O'Halloran collection.
50. Paul Durcan, "The World of Derek Mahon", *Magill* (25 December 1984).
51. Mahon, "Bowen on the Box", *Selected Prose* (Oldcastle: Gallery Press, 2012), 92.
52. Mahon to Longley, 14 January [1985], Longley papers, Emory.
53. Mahon to Longley, ibid.
54. Mahon, "An Enormous Yes", review of *Poems 1963–1983*, by Michael Longley, *Literary Review* (February 1985), 55.
55. Mahon to Longley, 14 January [1985], Longley papers, Emory.
56. Mahon, "Dejection", *Irish Times* (2 February 1985), 11.
57. The statement is a quotation from Randall Jarrell's *Poetry and the Age*. See Mahon's note in his personal copy of *Antarctica*, Emory.
58. Will Sulkin to Mahon, 25 February 1985, Oxford University Press archive.
59. Paul Keegan to Mahon, 4 March 1985, Mahon papers, Emory.
60. Mahon to Peter Jay, 13 May [1985], Anvil Press archive, Harry Ransom Center.
61. Alannah Hopkin, email to the author, 5 August 2011.
62. Mahon to Desmond O'Grady, "St. Patrick's Day" [1985], O'Grady papers, Emory.
63. Paul Durcan, "The World of Derek Mahon", *Magill* (December 1984), 46.
64. "An Interview with Derek Mahon", *Poetry Ireland Review* (Autumn 1985), 11.
65. "An Interview with Derek Mahon", ibid., 15.
66. Mahon to Desmond O'Grady, 12 March [1985], O'Grady papers, Emory.
67. Mahon to O'Grady, "St. Patrick's Day" [1985], O'Grady papers, Emory.
68. Sandra Leitch interview, 12 September 2010.
69. Mahon to Desmond O'Grady, 26 May [1985], O'Grady papers, Emory.
70. Stephen Dixon, "Russian Love in a Mist", *Guardian* (30 May 1985).
71. Mahon to Peter Fallon, 2 November [1985], Fallon/Gallery Press collection, Emory.
72. Glyn Hughes, email to the author, 16 December 2010.
73. Mahon to Peter Fallon, 15 August [1985], Fallon/Gallery Press collection, Emory.

74. Mahon to Desmond O'Grady, 4 August [1985], O'Grady papers, Emory.
75. Nicholas Grene to Mahon, November 1985, Mahon papers, Boston College.
76. Mahon to Peter Fallon, 2 November [1985], Fallon/Gallery Press collection, Emory.
77. Mahon's copy of *Poems 1962–1978* from the collection of James O'Halloran.
78. Sandra Leitch, interview with author, London, 12 September 2010.

Chapter 12 (pp 205–21)

1. "The Return of Derek Mahon", press release, 28 January 1986, Mahon papers, Emory.
2. Patricia Moynagh, interview, London, 28 March 2009.
3. Sandra Leitch interview, London, 12 September 2010.
4. Mahon to Louis Asekoff, 30 September [1986], Mahon papers, Emory.
5. Mahon to Josephine Saatchi, 14 January 1986, O'Halloran collection.
6. Mahon to Dillon Johnston, 25 July [1986], Mahon papers, Emory.
7. Mahon, "Poets: Alive and Often Well", *Vogue* (March 1986), 172 & 178.
8. Rosita Boland, interview with the author, Dublin, 22 February 2012.
9. Sara Tolchin, email to the author, 20 January 2011.
10. Rosita Boland to Mahon, 6 March 1987, O'Halloran collection.
11. "The Ulster Renaissance", *Newsweek* (12 May 1986), 52.
12. Mahon, "Orpheus Ascending: The Poetry of Paul Durcan", *Irish Review*, [Spring] 1986, 15–19.
13. Mahon to Dillon Johnston, 25 July [1986], Mahon papers, Emory.
14. Mahon to Dillon Johnston, 25 July [1986], Mahon papers, Emory.
15. Mahon to Louis Asekoff, 12 October [1986], Mahon papers, Emory.
16. Mahon to Louis Asekoff, 30 September [1986], Mahon papers, Emory.
17. Mahon, "Rincurran Cottage", Mahon papers, Emory.
18. Desmond O'Grady to Mahon, 16 July 1986, O'Halloran collection.
19. Rosita Boland, "It's a way of celebrating life", *Irish Times* (12 July 2010).
20. Maisie Mahon to Mahon, 10 November 1986, O'Halloran collection.
21. Maisie Mahon to Mahon, 17 November 1986, O'Halloran collection.
22. Samuel Beckett to Mahon, 6 October 1986, O'Halloran collection.
23. J.D. McClatchy to Mahon, 7 December 1986, O'Halloran collection.
24. Grennan to Mahon, postcard, 15 January 1987, O'Halloran collection.
25. Peter Fallon to Mahon, 29 January 1987, O'Halloran collection.
26. Jacqueline Simms to Mahon, 12 March 1987, Peter Fallon/Gallery Press collection, Emory.
27. Jacqueline Simms to Mahon, 8 April 1987, Peter Fallon/Gallery Press collection, Emory.

28. Jacqueline Simms to Mahon, ibid.

29. Mahon to Jacqueline Simms, 21 May [1987], Peter Fallon/Gallery Press collection, Emory.

30. Mahon to Jacqueline Simms, ibid.

31. Mahon to Peter Fallon, 5 June [1987], Peter Fallon/Gallery Press archive, Emory.

32. Mahon to Peter Fallon, 21 May [1987], Peter Fallon/Gallery Press archive, Emory.

33. Mahon to Peter Fallon, postcard, 23 June [1987], Peter Fallon/Gallery Press archive, Emory.

34. Mahon to Peter Fallon, 21 May [1987], Peter Fallon/Gallery Press archive, Emory.

35. William Shannon to Mahon, 2 June 1987, O'Halloran collection.

36. Mahon, "Driving in Ulster", typescript, [1987], O'Halloran collection.

37. Mahon to Louis Asekoff, 12 September [1987], Mahon papers, Emory.

38. Mahon to Louis Asekoff, ibid.

39. Mahon to Peter Fallon, 10 November [1987], Peter Fallon/Gallery Press archive, Emory.

40. Stephen Durbridge to Mahon, 30 July 1987, Mahon papers, Emory.

41. Patrick Ryan to Mahon, 19 October 1987, O'Halloran collection.

42. Mahon, *Huts and Sheds* (Oldcastle: Gallery, 2011), [6].

43. "Rincurran Cottage", n.d., O'Halloran collection.

44. Mahon, *Huts and Sheds* (Oldcastle: Gallery, 2011), [6].

45. Mahon, "Mother of Invention: Freedom and Necessity in Contemporary Irish Poetry", typescript, Mahon papers, Emory.

46. Louis Asekoff, New York, interview with the author, 10 January 2005.

47. Mahon to Sara Berkeley, Kinsale, 23 February [1988], courtesy of Sara Berkeley.

48. Mahon to Louis Asekoff, 24 February [1988], Mahon papers, Emory.

49. Mahon to Asekoff, ibid.

50. Mahon to Sara Berkeley, Kinsale, 4 March [1988], courtesy of Sara Berkeley.

51. Mahon to Peter Fallon, 24 [May] [1988], Fallon/Gallery Press collection, Emory.

52. Mahon to Louis Asekoff, 24 February [1988], Mahon papers, Emory.

53. Mary Leland, telephone interview with the author, 13 May 2011.

54. Mahon to Dillon Johnston, 16 September [1988], Mahon papers, Emory.

55. Mary Leland, telephone interview with the author, 13 May 2011.

56. Peter Fallon to Mahon, 27 November 1988, O'Halloran collection.

57. Brian Friel to Mahon, 17 May 1989, O'Halloran collection.

58. Mahon, *The Poetry Nonsense*, Caranna Productions, 2010.

59. Gerry Moriarty, "One of the rules is don't force farce", *Irish Press* (3 October 1989), 8.

60. Peter Fallon to Paul Keegan, 21 November 1989, Fallon/Gallery Press collection.

61. Mahon, "Dawn at St. Patrick's", *Collected Poems* (Oldcastle: Gallery Press, 1999), 169–70.

Chapter 13 (pp 222–41)

1. When Samuel Menashe offered to dedicate a poem to him, Mahon chose "Winter". Samuel Menashe to Mahon, 28 July 1994, Mahon papers, Emory.
2. Interview with Terence Brown, Dublin, 5 July 2013.
3. Mahon, "The Mariner sets sail", *Irish Times* (10 February 1990), 9.
4. Mahon, "A Month at Yaddo", typescript, Mahon papers, Emory.
5. Mahon to Fallon, postcard, 10 April [1990], Fallon/Gallery Press collection, Emory.
6. Mahon, "The Yaddo Letter", *Collected Poems* (Oldcastle: Gallery Press, 1999), 182–5.
7. Mahon, ibid.
8. Alice Quinn to Mahon, 6 June [1990], Mahon papers, Emory.
9. Mahon to Dillon Johnston, 25 April 1990, Mahon papers, Emory.
10. Mahon, "Irish Literature Festival", 16 May 1990, sound recording, 92nd Street Y.
11. John Montague to Mahon, n.d. [October 1997], Montague papers, National Library of Ireland.
12. Christopher Cahill, interview with the author, New York, 29 January 2010.
13. Louis Asekoff interview, New York, 10 January 2005.
14. "Penguin Book of Cont. Irish Verse", manuscript note, O'Halloran collection.
15. Introduction, *Penguin Book of Contemporary Irish Poetry* (London: Penguin, 1990), xx.
16. Doreen Mahon to Mahon, 19 September 1990, Mahon papers, Emory.
17. M.J. Horgan & Sons to Oliver O. Fischer & Company, 22 November 1990, Mahon papers, Emory.
18. Longley to Heaney, 5 November 1990, Heaney papers, Emory.
19. Interview with Gerald Dawe, Dún Laoghaire, 20 July 2013.
20. Mahon to "Sirs", 16 January [1991], American Poetry Review archive, University of Pennsylvania.
21. Lester Conner to the author, n.d. [2003].
22. Barry Murphy to Mahon, 10 March 1991, Mahon papers, Emory.
23. James O'Halloran interview, 20 January 2003.
24. Heaney to Mahon, 16 November 1991, Heaney papers, Emory.
25. Charles Molesworth, email to the author, 21 March 2010.
26. Barry Murphy interview, New York, 16 January 2013.
27. Paul Muldoon, *The Prince of the Quotidian* (Winston-Salem: Wake Forest, 1994), 25.

28. Barry Murphy interview, New York, 16 January 2013.

29. Mahon, remarks at Emory University reading, 29 January 1996.

30. Mahon, "12th St. Letter", manuscript, Mahon papers, Emory.

31. In an unpublished lecture that he delivered around this time, Mahon noted that Auden kept a bottle of vodka beside his bed. See: "Auden on St. Mark's Place", Mahon papers, Emory.

32. Mahon, *The Hudson Letter* (Oldcastle: Gallery Press, 1995), 43.

33. Mahon, "12th St. Letter", manuscript, Mahon papers, Emory.

34. Mahon, "Adam Zagajewski and Derek Mahon reading their poems", sound recording, Library of Congress.

35. Charles Molesworth, email to the author, 21 March 2010.

36. Adrianna Santos to Mahon, 16 May 1992, Mahon papers, Emory.

37. Mahon, "Drying Out", manuscript, Mahon papers, Emory.

38. Mahon, "Drying Out", Mahon papers, Emory.

39. Barbara Dalderis memorandum, 19 May 1992, Mahon papers, Emory.

40. Louis Asekoff interview, New York, 10 January 2005.

41. Eoin O'Brien, email to the author, 26 August 2012.

42. Mahon to Fallon, 5 January 1993, Fallon/Gallery Press collection, Emory.

43. Mahon to Fallon, ibid.

44. Mahon, "Poets galore", *Irish Times* (5 June 1993), 9.

45. Charles Molesworth, email to the author, 21 March 2010.

46. Mahon to Shirley Strum Kenny, 18 April 1993, Mahon papers, Emory.

47. Mahon was referring to his hospitalisation at St Patrick's Hospital from August 14th–October 20th, 1992.

48. Mahon to Shirley Strum Kenny, ibid.

49. Mahon to John Banville, June [1993], Mahon papers, Emory.

50. Mahon, "Poets galore", *Irish Times* (5 June 1993), 9.

51. Barry Murphy interview, New York, 16 January 2013.

52. Alannah Hopkin, letter to the editor, *Irish Times* (18 June 1993), 14.

53. Mahon, "Poets galore", *Irish Times* (5 June 1993), 9.

54. While the manuscript drafts are undated, the bookstore Judith's Room closed permanently just a few months later.

55. Mahon, "Writer's town", *Irish Times* (1 May 1993), 9.

56. Mahon, "Art of Fiction", typescript, Mahon papers, Emory.

57. Mahon, "In the land of cheap thrills", *Irish Times* (9 April 1994), 9.

58. Elgy Gillespie, email to the author, 15 August 2009.

59. Mahon, *The Poetry Nonsense*, Caranna Productions, 2010.

60. Barnard student evaluations, Mahon papers, Emory.

61. Mahon, *The Hudson Letter* (Oldcastle: Gallery Press, 1995), 35.

62.   Mahon, Aidan Higgins introduction, Mahon papers, Emory.

63.   Peter Fallon, phone conversation notes, 18 October 1994, Fallon/Gallery Press collection, Emory.

64.   Peter Fallon, phone conversation notes, 10 November 1994, Fallon/Gallery Press collection, Emory.

65.   Mahon, *The Hudson Letter* (Oldcastle: Gallery Press, 1995), 61.

66.   Mahon, "The Art of Fiction", typescript, Mahon papers, Emory.

67.   Mahon, "Domnei", *Collected Poems* (Oldcastle: Gallery Press, 1999), 213–14.

68.   Mahon, *The Poetry Nonsense*, Caranna Productions, 2010.

69.   Aidan Higgins to Mahon, December 1995, Mahon papers, Emory.

Chapter 14 (pp 242–56)

1.   "Heaney's Laureate", *Irish Times* (6 October 1995), 15.

2.   Cliodhna Ni Anluain (ed.), *Reading the Future: Irish Writers in Conversation with Mike Murphy* (Dublin: Lilliput Press, 2000).

3.   Katie Donovan, "Words for the speechless", *Irish Times* (18 October 1995), 12.

4.   George O'Brien interview, Washington, DC, 23 October 2009.

5.   Helen Meany, "Star wars in the human heart", *Irish Times*, 1 Feburary 1996, 10.

6.   Mahon, *The Yellow Book* (Oldcastle: Gallery Press, 1997), 30.

7.   Fintan O'Toole, "Are we all Europeans now", *Irish Times*, 5 March 1996, 10.

8.   Ann Cremin, "A Diary of the Art Year in Ireland", *Irish Arts Review*, vol. 13 (1997), 18–19.

9.   Mahon, "Dublin's Shelbourne Hotel", *Ireland of the Welcomes* (August 1996), 23.

10.   Mahon, "A Bangor Requiem", *Collected Poems* (Oldcastle: Gallery Press, 1999), 260–61.

11.   Anthony Cronin, "Heroes and drop-outs", *Sunday Independent* (25 January 1998), 8.

12.   Mahon, *The Yellow Book* (Oldcastle: Gallery Press, 1997), 46–8.

13.   Mahon, ibid.

14.   Mahon, "Aphrodite's Pool", *The Yellow Book* (Oldcastle: Gallery Press, 1997).

15.   Gerald Dawe, "Floating free of the Here and Now", *Irish Times* (22 December 1997).

16.   Sean O'Brien, "The poet as awkward customer", *Sunday Times* (25 January 1998).

17.   William Scammell, "A man's aesthetic", *The Independent* (London), (15 February, 1998), 32.

18.   Anthony Cronin, "Heroes and drop-outs", *Sunday Independent* (25 January 1998), 8.

19.   Mahon, "Felicities and Forgeries", *The Listener*, 4 February 1971, 153.

20. Mahon, *Roman Script* (Oldcastle: Gallery Press, 1999), [1].

21. Mahon, ibid.

22. Mahon, ibid.

23. Mahon to Cairnduff, 10 March 1999, Mahon papers, Emory.

24. "Not a verse for publicity", *Irish Times* (22 January 2000), Weekend.

25. Hugh Haughton, "Heraclitus of the postmodern", *TLS* (6 October 2000).

26. Mahon, *Resistance Days* (Oldcastle: Gallery Press, 2001), [6].

27. Ivor Roberts to Mahon, 29 May 2000, Mahon papers, Emory.

28. Mahon, ibid.

29. Hugh Haughton, "Heraclitus of the postmodern", *TLS* (6 October 2000).

30. Mahon, *Resistance Days* (Oldcastle: Gallery Press, 2001), [10].

31. Mahon, Introduction, *Poems*, by Patrick MacDonogh (Oldcastle: Gallery Press, 2001), 9–20.

32. Andrew Motion to Mahon, [Spring 2001], Mahon papers, Emory.

33. Mahon, "The Road to Highgate", *Selected Prose* (Oldcastle: Gallery Press, 2012), 56–63.

34. Mahon, "Calypso", *Harbour Lights* (Oldcastle: Gallery Press, 2005), 57–60.

35. Mahon, "Harbour Lights", *Harbour Lights* (Oldcastle: Gallery Press, 2005), 65.

Afterword (pp 257-60)

1. Mahon, "The Poetry Nonsense", *Selected Prose* (Oldcastle: Gallery Press, 2012), 31.

2. Mahon to the author, Kinsale, postcard, 20 April [2012].

3. Mahon to the author, Kinsale, 18 May [2011].

4. Mahon to the author, 12 May 2012.

5. Mahon to the author, 19 May 2012.

6. Mahon, "The Poetry Nonsense", *Selected Prose* (Oldcastle: Gallery Press, 2012), 31.

CHRONOLOGICAL LIST OF POEMS BY DATE OF FIRST PUBLICATION

The only exact knowledge there is, is the knowledge of the date of publication and the format of books.

Anatole France

1955   Untitled ("I have been to England"). *School News* (Easter 1955): 11–12.

1958   "Requiescat". *School News*, vol. 65, no. 209 (Midsummer 1958): 12–13.
Untitled ("The power that gives the waters breath"). *School News*, vol. 66, no. 210 (Christmas 1958): 28–30.

1959   "Children at Prayer". *School News*, vol. 66, no. 211 (Easter 1959): 19–20.
"'Resurrection'" (poem). Ibid., 20.
"Dancehall Impromptu". Ibid., 21.

1960   "Compline". *School News*, vol. 67, no. 215 (Summer 1960): 14–15.
"This Neuter Moon". Ibid., 15.
"No Love Poems". Ibid., 15–16.
"That Second Self". Ibid., 16.
"Subsidy Bungalows". *Icarus*, no. 32 (December 1960): 22.

1961   "Whatever Fall or Blow". *Icarus*, no. 33 (March 1961): 22.
"Love Poem". Ibid., 23.
"The Fall of Icarus". *Icarus*, no. 34 (June 1961): 2.
"The Titanic". Ibid., 19.
"O Where Now Is Robin". Ibid., 30.
"Endgame". Ibid., 31.
"Break of Day". *Icarus*, no. 35 (December 1961): 38.
"Among Lanterns". Ibid., 39.

1962   "from Le Poète contumace", by Tristan Corbière (translation). *Review No. 4* (Modern Languages Society, Trinity College), vol. 3, no. 1 (February 1962): 16–17.

"Never Otherwise". *Icarus*, no. 36 [March 1962]: 12.

"Tristan and Isolde". Ibid., 13.

"All Such Terrors". *The Dubliner*, no. 3 (May–June 1962): 29.

"May Day Celebrations". *T.C.D.: A College Miscellany*, vol. LXVII, no. 2006 (18 May 1962): 15.

"Out of the Depths". *Icarus*, no. 37 (June 1962): 13.

"Epitaph, from Tristan Corbiere". Ibid., 37.

"Poete Maudit". Ibid., 38.

"The Evil Eye". Ibid., 53.

"Marilyn Monroe". *The Dubliner*, no. 5 (September–October 1962): 45.

"Before Migrating". *Icarus*, no. 38 (December 1962): 16.

"An Unborn Child". Ibid., 19–20.

1963   "My Wicked Uncle". *Icarus*, no. 39 (March 1963): 16–17.

"Lovers Wake to Differences". *Arena*, no. 1 (Spring 1963): 11.

"Ballad of the Hanged". *Review No. 5* (Modern Languages Society, Trinity College), [ca. May 1963].

"Girls in their Seasons". *The Dubliner*, vol. 2, no. 2 (Summer 1963): 18–20.

"None the Worse". Ibid., 20–21.

"End of Season". *The Listener*, vol. LXX, no. 1798 (12 September 1963): 388.

"Our Tom". *T.C.D.: A College Miscellany*, no. 1231 (22 November 1963): 12.

"Poets of the Later Nineteenth Century". *T.C.D.: A College Miscellany*, no. 1232 (29 November 1963): 8.

"De Quincey at Grasmere". *Icarus*, no. 41 [December 1963]: 18.

1964   "In Memory". *The Irish Times* (4 January 1964): 8.

"Homage to Malcolm Lowry". *The Irish Times* (15 February 1964): 8.

"An Irishman in London". *Icarus*, no. 42 (March 1964): 8–10.

"In Belfast". Ibid., 31.

"Bird Sanctuary". *The Irish Times* (4 April 1964): 8.

"Memorandum in Spring". *Icarus*, no. 43 [June 1964]: 2.

"La Condition Ouvrière". Ibid., 3.

"Sisyphus". Ibid., 3.

"The Death of the Heart". *Outposts*, no. 61 (Summer 1964): 7.

"Elevation". *The Dubliner*, vol. 3, no. 2 (Summer 1964): 17.

"De Profundis Clamavi". Ibid., 19.

"That Day We Drove to Donegal". *The Dubliner*, vol. 3, no. 4 (Winter 1964): 34.

"Brahms Trio". Ibid., 35.

"The Graduate in Metal Box". *Icarus*, no. 44 [December 1964]: 15.

"To Hell with Frank Sinatra". Ibid., 43.

1965   "Man and Bird". *T.C.D.: A College Miscellany*, no. 1255 [5 March 1965]: 5.

"Kreutzer Sonata". Ibid., 5.

"The Poets". Ibid., 5.

"Man and Bird". *The Irish Times* (13 March 1965): 8.

"Suburban Walk". *Icarus*, no. 45 [March 1965]: 4.

"An Irishman in London". *The Dublin Magazine*, vol. 4, no. 1 (Spring 1965): 6–7.

"November Notes in Brittany". *Poetry Ireland*, no. 5 (Spring 1965): 2–3.

> Three-part poem: I "Still Life", II "Night Owl", and III "Dawn". Part III "Dawn" would later appear in altered form as "Morning in Brittany" in *Twelve Poems*.

"In Carrowdore Churchyard". *The Irish Times* (16–17 April 1965): 8.

"Dublin Evening". *Icarus*, no. 46 [June 1965]: 43.

"Late-Night Walk". *The Dublin Magazine*, vol. 4, no. 2 (Summer 1965): 62.

"Kreutzer sonata". *The Northern Review*, vol. 1, no. 2 [Summer 1965]: 13.

"Suburban walk". Ibid., 13. See above.

"Grandfather". Ibid., 14.

"In Carrowdore Churchyard". *Outposts*, no. 65 (Summer 1965): 1. See above.

"Day Trip to Donegal". *Poetry Review*, vol. 56, no. 3 (Autumn 1965): 132–3.

"Toronto". *Icarus*, no. 47 (December 1965): 35.

1966   "Canadian Pacific". *The Island*, no. 2 (March 1966): 22.

"Exit Molloy". Ibid., 22.

"The Charles River in January". Ibid., 23.

"Canadian Pacific". *The Dublin Magazine*, vol. 5, no. 1 (Spring 1966): 55.

"Spring Letter in Winter". Ibid., 68.

"Recalling Aran". Ibid., 68.

"Exit Molloy". *The Dublin Magazine*, vol. 5, nos. 3–4 (Autumn/Winter 1966): 38.

"Preface to a Love Poem". Ibid., 54–5.

1967   "Bird Sanctuary". *Phoenix* (New Quarterly Series), no. 1 (March 1967): 16–17.

"Boise, Idaho". Ibid., 17.

"As God is My Judge". Ibid., 18.

"Poem to the Memory of Louis-Ferdinand Céline". Ibid., 19.

"Winter Song for the Rivers of New England". Ibid., 19.

"The Poets Lie Where They Fell". *Icarus*, no. 51 ([June] 1967): 49.

"April on Toronto Island". *The Dublin Magazine*, vol. 6, no. 2 (Summer 1967): 29.

"Parapeople". Ibid., 30.

"Legacies" (translation of François Villon). *Phoenix*, no. 2 (Summer 1967): 36–40.

"In Carrowdore Churchyard". *Threshold*, no. 21 (Summer 1967): 135.

"Van Gogh Among the Miners". *The Irish Times* (2 September 1967): 10.

"The Forger". *The Dublin Magazine*, vol. 6, nos. 3–4 (Autumn/Winter 1967): 14.

1968   "Consolations of Philosophy". *Icarus*, no. 53 (Hilary Term 1968): 14.

"Body and Soul". Ibid., 15.

"Gipsies". Ibid., 24.

"Patrick Kavanagh: An Epitaph". *The Dublin Magazine*, vol. 7, no. 1 (Spring 1968): 12.

"Brian Nolan: An Epitaph". Ibid., 28.

"Teaching in February". Ibid., 64.

"Homecoming". *Broadsheet*, [no. 4], [May 1968], not paginated.

"A Dying Art". *The Honest Ulsterman*, no. 1 (May 1968): 15.

"Ecclesiastes". Ibid., 15.

"Ecclesiastes Country". *The Listener*, vol. 80, no. 2052 (25 July 1968): 110.

"Consolations of Philosophy". Ibid., 110.

"Homecoming". *The Listener*, vol. 80, no. 2061 (26 September 1968): 416.

"Tragic Hero of Our Time". *The Dublin Magazine*, vol. 7, nos. 2–4, (Autumn/Winter 1968): 48.

"1 Corinthians 13". *The Honest Ulsterman*, no. 8 (December 1968): 5.

"A Dying Art". *The Listener*, vol. 80, no. 2074 (26 December 1968): 866.

"Consolations of Philosophy". *Everyman*, no. 1 (1968): 131.

1969   "A Stone-Age Figure Far Below". *Irish Press* (4 April 1969): 7.

"In the Aran Islands". Ibid., 7.

"Fall Out". *The Dublin Magazine*, vol. 8, nos. 1–2 (Spring/Summer 1969): 40.

"Straight Lines Breaking Becoming Circles". *Phoenix*, no. 5 (Summer 1969): 12.

"A Stone-Age Figure Far Below". *Threshold*, no. 22 (Summer 1969): 49.

"An Image from Beckett". *The Listener*, vol. 82, no. 2118 (30 October 1969): 605.

"An Image from Beckett". *Hibernia* (21 November 1969): 14.

1970   "Traveller's Night-Song". *Phoenix*, nos. 6–7 (Summer 1970): 24.

"Grandfather", *Books, Plays, Poems*, BBC Radio for Schools (Summer Term 1970): 13.

"My Wicked Uncle". Ibid., 13.

"Day Trip to Donegal". Ibid., 28.

"Van Gogh Among the Miners". Ibid., 39.

"The Forger". Ibid., 40.

"On a Photograph of Edvard Munch's Room in Oslo". *The Listener*, vol. 84, no. 2177 (17 December 1970): 849.

1971   "From 'The Diary of Hans Pilatus'". *Malahat Review*, no. 17 (January 1971): 42–3.

"Deaths". *Hibernia* (30 April 1971), 20.

"Rage for Order". *The Listener*, vol. 85, no. 2197 (6 May 1971): 585.

"Death of a Film-Star". *Books, Plays, Poems*, BBC Radio for Schools (Summer Term 1971): 44.

"Night Thought while Reading Gibbon". *The Listener*, vol. 86, no. 2209 (29 July 1971): 144.

"J. P. Donleavy's Dublin". *The Honest Ulsterman*, no. 29 (July–Aug. 1971): 29.

"I am Raftery". Ibid., 29.

"Gypsies II". Ibid., 30.

"The Graduate in Metal Box". Ibid., 30.

1972   "Lives". *Hibernia* (21 January 1972): 11.

"A Tolerable Wisdom". *Irish Press* (20 May 1972): 9.

"Job's Comforter". Ibid., 9.

"A Dark Country". *Atlantis*, no. 4 (September 1972), 24.

"Rocks". Ibid., 25.

"Entropy". Ibid., 25–7.

"The Last Dane". Ibid., 27.

"Ecclesiastes". *This Week* (Dublin), vol. 3, no. 43 (24 August 1972), 43.

"Ecclesiastes". *Poetry* 1972 (Critical Quarterly Poetry Supplement), [1972]:
15.

"Edvard Munch". Ibid., 15–16.

"What Will Remain". Ibid., 16–17.

"Rocks". *Aquarius*, no. 5 (1972): 16.

"Folk Song". Ibid., 16.

1973   "From Beyond Howth Head". *Les Lettres Nouvelles* (March 1973): 196–7.

"J.P. Donleavy's Dublin". Ibid., 196–7.

"The Snow Party". *Encounter*, vol. 40, no. 4 (April 1973): 10.

"Death of a Film-Star". *Books, Plays, Poems*, BBC Radio for Schools
(Summer Term 1973): 50.

"Going Home". *Encounter*, vol. 41, no. 1 (July 1973): 92.

"Before". *Times Literary Supplement* (6 July 1973), 764.

"A Disused Shed in County Wexford". *The Listener* (27 September 1973):
412.

"After Nerval" (translation). *The Honest Ulsterman*, 40 (September/
October 1973): 3.

"After Eluard" (translation). Ibid. 3–4.

"A Fable". *Atlantis*, no. 6 (Winter 1973/74): 14–16.

"A Disused Shed in Co. Wexford". *Antaeus*, no. 12 (Winter 1973): 86–7.

1974   "In Belfast", *Community Forum*, vol. 4, no. 1 (1974): 14. See above.

"A Disused Shed in County Wexford". *Irish Press* (2 February 1974): 6.

"A Noise Like Leaves". *The Honest Ulsterman*, no. 42/43 (March/July 1974):
41–2.

"Fire-King". *The Lace Curtain*, no. 5 (Spring 1974): 80–81.

"Afterlives". *New Statesman*, vol. 88, no. 2270 (20 September 1974): 387.

"A Refusal to Mourn". *Irish Press* (30 November 1974): 6.

"The Antigone Riddle". *Broadsheet*, no. 22 (December 1974), not paginated.

"A Hermit". *Aquarius*, no. 7 (1974): 31.

1975   "C.P. Cavafy's Alexandria". *The New Review*, vol. 1, no. 10 (January 1975):
63.

"Four Versions of Cavafy" (poem sequence). Ibid., 64.

Four-part poem sequence: 1. "Voices"; 2. "A Considered Pause"; 3.
"The Souls of the Old Men"; and 4. "The Facts of Life".

"A Refusal to Mourn". *New Statesman*, vol. 89, no. 2293 (28 February 1975):
282.

"Primavera". *New Statesman* (2 May 1975): 594.

"The Antigone Riddle". *Lines Review*, No. 52/53 (May 1975): 39.

"Thammuz". Ibid., 39–40.

"The Chair Squeaks". Ibid., 40.

"The Ruined House". Ibid., 40.

"Ecclesiastes". *The Niagara Magazine*, no. 3 (Summer 1975): 33.

"The Banished Gods". *Irish Press* (26 July 1975): 6.

"After Nerval". *New Statesman* (18 July 1975): 83.

"At Penshurst". *New Statesman*, vol. 90, no. 2327 (24 October 1975): 514.

"A True Story". *The Honest Ulsterman*, no. 50 (Winter 1975): 157–9.

1976   "The Screech Owl" (translation of Philippe Jaccottet's "L'Effraie"). *New Statesman*, vol. 91, no. 2337 (2 January 1976): 18.

"The Voice" (translation of Philippe Jaccottet's "La Voix"). Ibid., 18.

"Light Music" (poem sequence). *The Emerson Review* (Spring 1976): 65–6.
> A poem sequence: "Aesthetics", "Interiors", "Please", "Midnight", "Joyce in Paris" and "What Louis Saw".

"Revelation". *Gown* (Gown Poetry Supplement), vol. 22, no. 9 (6 May 1976): [2].

"Twilight". Ibid., [3].

"from Light Music, an ongoing sequence, 1–10" (poem sequence). *Irish Press* (25 September 1976): 6.
> Includes: "Architecture", "History", "Portrush", "Donegal", "North Sea", "Twilight", "Clarte Deserte", "Magrite", "Come In" and "Revelation".

"From Light Music, an ongoing sequence" (poem sequence). *The Honest Ulsterman*, no. 53 (November–December 1976): 44–5.
> Includes: "Please", "Walking the Boy", "Aesthetics", "Mozart", "Timber", "Spring" and "Byzantium".

"Consolations of Philosophy". *Icarus*, no. 70 (1976): not paginated.

1977   "Surrey Poems". *The Irish Press* (24 September 1977): 9.
> Three-part poem: "Midsummer", "Field Bath" and "Dry Hill".

1978   "A Departure". *Quarto*, vol. 4, no. 1 (January 1978): [14].

"A Departure". *Poetry Review*, vol. 68, no. 1 (April 1978): 34–5.

"Surrey Poems". *Quarto*, vol. 4, no. 3 (May 1978): 29.
> Two-part poem sequence: "Midsummer" and "Field Bath".

"The Return". *New Statesman*, vol. 95, no. 2463 (2 June 1978): 751.

"Autobiographies" (poem sequence). *The Honest Ulsterman*, no. 60 (July/October 1978): 3–6.

> Multi-part poem sequence: "The Home Front", "The Lost Girls", "The Last Resort" and "The Bicycle".

"In a Sussex Pub". *New Statesman*, vol. 96, no. 2469 (14 July 1978): 62.

"Heraclitus on Rivers". *New Statesman*, vol. 96, no. 2482 (13 October 1978): 481.

"The Chinese Restaurant in Portrush". *New Statesman*, vol. 96, no. 2488 (24 November 1978): 718.

"The Early Anthropologists". *Stone Ferry Review*, no. 2 (Winter 1978): 5–6.

"Jet Trail and Early Moon". *Cyphers*, no. 9 (Winter 1978): 30.

> Part one of "Two Poems for John and Evelyn Montague".

"The Attic". Ibid., 30–31.

> Part two of "Two Poems for John and Evelyn Montague".

"Light Music" (poem sequence). *Exile: A Literary Quarterly*, vol. 5, nos. 3–4 (1978): 87–91.

> Multi-part poem sequence: "Architecture", "History", "Negatives", "Portrush", "Donegal", "North Sea", "Rory", "Twilight", "Mozart", "Morphology", "Come In", "October", "Elpenor", "Revelation" and "Flying".

1979 "The Early Anthropologists". *Quarto*, vol. 5, no. 1 (February 1979): 10.

"Autobiographies" (poem sequence). *New Statesman*, vol. 97, no. 2504 (16 March 1979): 367.

> Multi-part poem sequence: "The Home Front", "The Lost Girls", "The Last Resort" and "The Bicycle".

"The Poet in Residence". *Ploughshares*, vol. 5, no. 3 (Fall 1979): 25–8.

"The Poet in Residence". *Hibernia* (8 November 1979): 14.

"Ford Manor". *The Literary Review*, vol. 22, no. 2 (Winter 1979): 231.

"Goodbye to the Trees". Ibid., 231–3.

"Surrey Poems" (poem sequence). Ibid., 234–5.

> Three-part poem sequence: "Midsummer", "Field Bath" and "Dry Hill".

"Penshurst Place". Ibid., 236.

"Sole". Ibid., 236.

"Father-in-Law". *Aquarius*, no. 11 (1979): 91.

1980 "Astronomy in North Carolina". *Aquarius*, no. 12 (1980): 51–2.

"Knut Hamsun in Old Age". *Times Literary Supplement* (8 February 1980): 136.

"The World Is Everything That Is the Case'". *Ploughshares*, vol. 6, no.1 (Spring 1980): 129.

"Rathlin Island". Ibid., 130.

"Table Talk". *London Review of Books*, vol. 2, no. 13 (3–16 July 1980): 4.

"Rathlin Island". *Hibernia* (31 July 1980): 22.

"North Wind". *The Honest Ulsterman*, no. 66 (July/October 1980): 3–4.

"Brighton Poems" (two-part poem). Ibid., 5–6.

"Rathlin Island". *Poetry Review*, vol. 70, nos. 1–2 (September 1980): 8.

"The World Is Everything That Is the Case". Ibid., 10.

"Old Roscoff". *The Irish Times* (8 November 1980): 13.

"April in Moscow". Ibid., 13.

"The Hunt by Night". *Times Literary Supplement* (5 December 1980): 1290.

"Songs of Praise". *London Review of Books*, vol. 2, no. 24 (18 December 1980–21 January 1981): 11.

"Girls on the Bridge". *Times Literary Supplement* (26 December 1980): 1467.

"Astronomy in North Carolina". *Aquarius*, no. 12 (1980): 51–2.

1981   "North Wind: Portrush". *London Magazine*, vol. 20, nos. 11–12 (February/March 1981): 70–72.

"The Elephants". Ibid., 72–3.

"April in Moscow". Ibid., 73–4.

"An Old Lady". *The Irish Times* (28 March 1981), Weekend Supplement, 5.

"Derry Morning: An Interlude". *New Statesman*, vol. 101, no. 2612 (10 April 1981): 23.

"Derry Morning". *Cork Review*, vol. 2, no. 3 (June 1981): 26.

"Knut Hamsun in Old Age". Ibid., 26.

"Rock Music". *New Statesman*, vol. 102, no. 2627 (24 July 1981): 20.

"The Woods". *Times Literary Supplement* (31 July 1981): 880.

"A Postcard from Berlin". *Poetry Ireland Review*, no. 2 (Summer 1981): 11.

"From the Drunken Boat". *The Honest Ulsterman*, no. 70 (November/December 1981): 18–19.

"Another Sunday Morning". *Encounter*, vol. 57, no. 6 (December 1981): 18–19.

"Pythagorean Lines: Respectful Version". *Cyphers*, no. 16 (Winter 1981): 12.

"El Desdichado" (after Nerval). *Aquarius* nos. 13/14 (1981/82): 123.

1982   "At the Pool". *Encounter*, vol. 58, no. 1 (January 1982): 32.

"The Terminal Bar". *Times Literary Supplement* (22 January 1982): 74.

"Coca Cola". *Encounter*, vol. 58, no. 2 (February 1982): 17.

"One of These Nights". *Times Literary Supplement* (5 March 1982): 264.

"The Andean Flute". *New Edinburgh Review*, no. 57 (Spring 1982): 9.

"The Dawn Chorus". Ibid., 17.

"A Danish Refuge". *Irish Press* (1 May 1982): 9.

"To the Unborn". Ibid., 9.

"A Garage in County Cork". *Times Literary Supplement* (14 May 1982): 541.

"The Dawn Chorus". *Digraphe*, no. 27 (June 1982): 59.

"The Andean Flute". Ibid., 61.

"The Mayo Tao". Ibid., 63.

"The North African Campaign". Ibid., 65.

"Afterlives". Ibid., 66.

"A True Story". Ibid., 68–9.

"How to Live". *Hudson Review*, vol. 35, no. 2 (Summer 1982): 251.

"A Lighthouse in Maine". Ibid., 251–3.

"A Garage in County Cork". *Irish Press* (21 August 1982), 9.

1983   "Glengormley". *The Agni Review*, no. 19 [1983]: 23.

"My Wicked Uncle". Ibid., 24–5.

"April on Toronto Island". Ibid., 26.

"Poem Beginning with a Line by Cavafy". Ibid., 27.

"Courtyards in Delft". Ibid., 28–9.

"The Terminal Bar". Ibid., 30.

"A Kensington Notebook". *PN Review* 32, vol. 9, no. 6 (1983): 13–14.

"Antarctica". *Aquarius*, nos. 15–16 (1983–4): 76.

"Afternoon Sex". *PN Review* 33, vol. 10, no. 1 (1983): 41.

"On a Proposed Voyage". Ibid., 41.

> "Afternoon Sex" and "On a Proposed Voyage" appear under the collective title "Two Amores".

"Joycentenary Ode". *James Joyce Broadsheet*, no. 11 (June 1983): 3.

"Squince". *The Irish Times* (27 August 1983), Weekend Supplement, 4.

"St Eustace". *The Observer* (18 December 1983): 29.

"The Forger". *PN Review* 36, vol. 10, no. 4 [1983/84]: 21.

"An Image from Beckett". Ibid., 21.

"Consolations of Philosophy". Ibid., 22.

"Dog Days". Ibid., 22.

"The Snow Party". Ibid., 22.

"A Disused Shed in Co. Wexford". Ibid., 23.

"The Return". Ibid., 23.

"Courtyards in Delft". Ibid., 24.

"North Wind: Portrush". Ibid., 24.

"The Andean Flute". Ibid., 25.

"Tractatus". Ibid., 25.

"The Woods". Ibid., 25.

1984   "Morning Radio". *Encounter*, vol. 62, no. 4 (April 1984): 7.

1985   "Dejection". *The Irish Times* (2 February 1985), Weekend Supplement, 11.

"Mt. Gabriel". Ibid., 11.

"Death and the Sun". *Times Literary Supplement* (26 July 1985): 834.

"Achill". *Irish Times* (7 September 1985), Weekend Supplement, 13.

"Craigvara House". *Poetry Ireland Review*, no. 14 (Autumn 1985): 8–10.

"October". *Agenda*, vol. 23, nos. 3–4 (Autumn/Winter 1985–86): 28.

"Tithonus". Ibid., 29–32.

1986   "Day and Night". *The Irish Times* (12 July 1986): 10.

"Philippe Jaccottet: Two Poems" (translations). *Poetry Ireland Review*, no. 16 (Summer 1986): 7–8.

    Two untitled poems with first lines "Being a stranger in this life, I speak" and "I know now I possess nothing of my own."

"Autumn" by Eugene Dubnov (translation). *Centennial Review*, vol. 30, no. 4 (Fall 1986): 474.

"The Word Joy" (translation of Philippe Jaccottet). *Times Literary Supplement* (26 September 1986): 1069.

"Gramsci's Ashes". *The Irish Times* (25 October 1986), Weekend Supplement, 4.

"Achill". *An Gael* (NY: Irish Arts Center), vol. 3, no. 2 (Winter 1986): 14.

"Kinsale". Ibid., 15.

"An Image from Beckett". *Hermathena*, no. 141 (Winter 1986): 10–11.

"In the Steps of the Moon" (translation of Philippe Jaccottet). *Verse*, no. 6 (1986): 29.

"Patience" (translation of Philippe Jaccottet). Ibid., 29.

"Portovenere" (translation of Philippe Jaccottet). Ibid., 29.

"The Tenant" (translation of Philippe Jaccottet). Ibid., 30.

1987   "Glimpses" (translation of Philippe Jaccottet). *Agenda,* vol. 24, no. 4/vol. 25, no. 1 (Winter/Spring 1987): 14–15.

"To Henry Purcell" (translation of Philippe Jaccottet). Ibid., 16–17.

"Words in the Air" (translation of Philippe Jaccottet). *The Irish Times* (4 April 1987): 5.

"Words in the Air" (translation of Philippe Jaccottet). *Times Literary Supplement* (19 June 1987): 669.

"Night Drive". *Hudson Review,* vol. 39, no. 4 (Winter 1987): 614.

"October" (poem). Ibid., 615.

"A Garage in County Cork". *Pembroke Magazine* (Pembroke State University), no. 19 (1987): 85–6.

1988   "Patience" (translation of Philippe Jaccottet). *The Observer* (4 September 1988): 40.

"No Breathing Now" (translation of Philippe Jaccottet). Ibid., 40.

"Streams and Forests" (translation of Philippe Jaccottet). *Irish Review,* no. 3 (1988): 97–8.

1989–91   No poems.

1992   "Dawn at St. Patrick's". *American Poetry Review,* vol. 21, no. 4 (July–August 1992): 14.

"The Yaddo Letter". Ibid., 15–16.

"Canadian Pacific". *The Irish Times* (5 September 1992), Weekend Supplement, 7.

"Thinking of Inis Oirr in Cambridge". Ibid., 7.

"The Bird-Life of Kinsale". *The Irish Times* (21 November 1992), Weekend Supplement, 9.

1993   "Tractatus". *Bollettario,* nos. 10–11 (Jan.–May 1993): 13–24.

"Dawn Chorus". Ibid.

"Tithonus". Ibid.

"Snow Party". Ibid.

"Last of the Fire Kings". Ibid.

"Hunt by Night". Ibid.

"October". Ibid.

> from *Light Music* (poem sequence), nos.: 3, "Negatives"; 7, "Rory"; 10, "Midnight"; 11, "Timber"; 12, "Joyce in Paris"; 15, "Morphology"; 16, "Enter"; 27, "Loft"; and 30, "Donegal"; Ibid.

"Night Drive—St. Petersburg, 1900". *Los Angeles Times* (26 December
    1993): BR6.
"River Rhymes" (poem sequence). *Soho Square*, no. 6 [1993]: 46–9.

1994   "Pygmalion". *London Review of Books*, vol. 16, no. 2 (27 January 1994): 18.
"The Old Bath-House Inscription". *Hermathena*, no. 156 (Summer 1994):
    59.
"Burbles". Ibid., 59–60.
Untitled ["Courtyards in Delft"]. *Irish Arts Review*, vol. 10 (1994), 110.

1995   "Albums: The Wild West". *New Yorker* (9 January 1995): 63.
"To Mrs. Moore at Inishannon". *New Yorker* (20 March 1995): 75.
"River Rhymes" (poem sequence). *Notre Dame Review* (Spring 1995): 76–8.
"Burbles". *Southern Review*, vol. 31, no. 3 (Summer 1995): 515.
"Antarctica". *At Cooper Union* (Summer 1995): 15.
"Noon at St. Michael's". *Poetry Ireland Review*, no. 46 (Summer 1995):
    38–9.
"The Travel Section". *The Honest Ulsterman*, no. 100 (Autumn 1995): 68.
"Anglo-Irish Clerihews" (poem sequence). Ibid., 69–70.
"Chinatown". *Poetry*, vol. 167, nos. 1–2 (October–November 1995): 10–11.

1996   "Landscape". *Poetry Ireland Review*, no. 50 (Summer 1996): 74.
"Shiver in Your Tenement". *The Recorder*, vol. 9, no. 2 (Fall 1996): 2–3.
"XVIII The Small Rain". *Agenda*, vol. 33, nos. 3–4 (Autumn–Winter 1996):
    28–30.
"from Racine's *Phaedra* (Act IV, Scene VI)". Ibid., 31–2.
"The Attic". *Tracks*, no. 11 (1996): 66.

1997   "From Gramsci's Ashes" (translation). *The Recorder*, vol. 10, nos. 1–2
    (Spring and Fall 1997): 66–7.
"Night Thoughts". *Chicago Review*, vol. 43, no. 4 (Fall 1997): 114.
"Remembering the '90s". Ibid., 116.
"Smoke". Ibid., 119.
"Three Poems by Philippe Jaccottet" (translations). *Element*, no. 4 (1997):
    58–63.
        Translations of three poems by Philippe Jaccottet: "Comme je
        suis un étranger dans notre vie" ("Being a stranger in this life, I
        speak"), "Je sais maintenant que je ne possède rien" ("I know now
        I possess nothing of my own—") and "Portovenere".

1998 "The Idiocy of Human Aspiration". *Princeton University Library Chronicle*, vol. LIX, no. 3 (Spring 1998): 449–50.

"Autumn Day". *W.P. Journal* (Monaghan), nos. 26 & 27 (March–April 1998): 5.

1999 "After Michelangelo". *Eire-Ireland*, vol. 33, nos. 3–4 (Fall/Winter 1998) and vol. 34, no. 1 (Spring 1999): 309.

"From 'Gramsci's Ashes'". *The Irish Times* (24 April 1999), Weekend Supplement, 8.

"Ghosts". *Poetry Ireland Review*, no. 60 (Spring 1999): 18.

"A Dirge". Ibid., 19.

"Northern Starlight". Ibid., 20.

"Ghosts". *Sunday Times* (20 June 1999): 9.

"Courtyards in Delft". *The Independent* (24 October 1999): 13.

"After Michelangelo". *The Shop*, no. 1 (Autumn/Winter 1999): 4.

2000 "Gipsies". *The Independent* (31 October 2000): 11.

2001 "New Wave". *London Review of Books*, vol. 23, no. 7 (5 April 2001): 6.

"The Seaside Cemetery" (translation). *Times Literary Supplement* (7 September 2001): 23.

"The Seaside Cemetery" (translation). *The Recorder*, vol. 14, no. 2 (Fall 2001): 10–14.

2002 "Resistance Days". *London Review of Books*, vol. 24, no. 8 (25 April 2002): 29.

"Shapes and Shadows". *The Irish Times* (29 June 2002), Weekend Supplement, 5.

"Calypso". *Times Literary Supplement*, no. 5200 (29 November 2002): 13.

2003 No poems.

2004 "Red Cloud". *Agenda*, vol. 40, nos. 1–3 (Winter/Spring 2004): 254.

2005 "Lucretius on Clouds". *Times Literary Supplement*, no. 5315 (11 February 2005): 3.

"The Cloud Ceiling". *Times Literary Supplement*, no. 5319 (11 March 2005): 5.

"Jean Rhys in Kettner's". *The Guardian Review* (2 April 2005): 35.

2006   "Biographia Literaria". *Times Literary Supplement*, no. 5379 (5 May 2006): 15.

"Jardin du Luxembourg" (translation after Rilke). *Times Literary Supplement* (2 June 2006): 4.

"Borgeby-Gard" (version after Rilke). *The Irish Times* (19 August 2006), Weekend Supplement, 10.

"from 'Burbles'". *Times Literary Supplement* (3 November 2006): 13.

2007   "Brian Moore's Belfast". *An Sionnach*, vol. 3, no. 1 (Spring 2007): 9–10.

"Somewhere the Wave". *Icarus*, vol. 57 (Spring 2007): 9.

"Tara Boulevard". Ibid., 10.

"Insomnia". *Archipelago*, no. 1 (Summer 2007): 3–4.

"Somewhere the Wave". *Granta*, no. 100 (Winter 2007): 351.

2008   No poems.

2009   "A Country Kitchen". *The Irish Times* (11 April 1999), "Heaney at 70" (special supplement), 12.

"Homage to Goa". *Times Literary Supplement* (21 September 2009).

2010   "At the 'Butler Arms'". *Times Literary Supplement* (5 February 2010): 4.

"The Thunder Shower". *New Yorker* (8 March 2010): 50–51.

"Air India". *The Guardian* (20 March 2010): 19.

"Kinsale". *The Irish Times* (12 July 2010): 11.

2011   "Monochrome". *The Irish Times* (7 May 2011), 11.

"Here in Tenerife". *The Guardian* (11 June 2011): 20.

"The One-Thirty". *Poetry Ireland Review*, no. 103 (2011): 5–6.

BOOKS BY DEREK MAHON

Twelve Poems. Belfast: Queen's University, 1965.

Design for a Grecian Urn. Cambridge, Mass.: Erato, 1966.

Night-Crossing. London: Oxford University Press, 1968.

Beyond Howth Head. Dublin: Dolmen Press, 1970.

Ecclesiastes. Didsbury, Manchester: Phoenix, 1970.

Lives. London: Oxford University Press, 1972.

The Snow Party. London: Oxford University Press, 1975.

Light Music. Belfast: Ulsterman Publications, 1977.

Sea in Winter. Old Deerfield, Mass.: Deerfield & Dublin: Gallery Press, 1979.

Poems 1962–1978. Oxford: Oxford University Press, 1979.

Courtyards in Delft. Oldcastle, Co. Meath: Gallery Press, 1981.

The Chimeras. Oldcastle, Co. Meath: Gallery Press, 1982.

The Hunt by Night. London: Oxford University Press, 1982.

A Kensington Notebook. London: Anvil, 1984.

Antarctica. Dublin: Gallery Press, 1985.

High Time. Dublin: Gallery Press, 1985.

The School for Wives. Dublin: Gallery Press, 1986.

Night without Day, a translation of *Mes Nuits Sont Plus Belles Que Vos Jours*, by Raphaële Billetdoux. New York: Viking, 1987.

The Bacchae, after Euripides. Oldcastle, Co. Meath: Gallery Press, 1991.

Selected Poems. London: Oxford University Press, 1991.

The Yaddo Letter. Oldcastle, Co. Meath: Gallery Press, 1992.

The Hudson Letter. Oldcastle, Co. Meath: Gallery Press, 1995.

Racine's Phaedra. Oldcastle, Co. Meath: Gallery Press, 1996.

Journalism: Selected Prose, 1970–1995, ed. Terence Brown. Oldcastle, Co. Meath: Gallery Press, 1996.

The Yellow Book. Oldcastle, Co. Meath: Gallery Press, 1997.

Roman Script. Oldcastle, Co. Meath: Gallery Press, 1999.

Collected Poems. Oldcastle, Co. Meath: Gallery Press, 1999.

The Seaside Cemetery, a version of 'Le Cimetière marin', by Paul Valéry. Oldcastle, Co. Meath: Gallery Press, 2001.

Resistance Days. Oldcastle, Co. Meath: Gallery Press, 2001.

Birds, a version of *Oiseaux*, by Saint-John Perse. Oldcastle, Co. Meath: Gallery Press, 2002.

Cyrano de Bergerac. Oldcastle, Co. Meath: Gallery Press, 2004.

Harbour Lights. Oldcastle, Co. Meath: Gallery Press, 2005.

Adaptations. Oldcastle, Co. Meath: Gallery Press, 2006.

Art Notes. Oldcastle, Co. Meath: Gallery Press, 2006.

Somewhere the Wave. Oldcastle, Co. Meath: Gallery Press, 2007.

Homage to Gaia. Oldcastle, Co. Meath: Gallery Press, 2008.

Life on Earth. Oldcastle, Co. Meath: Gallery Press, 2009.

Sixtus and Cynthia. Oldcastle, Co. Meath: Gallery Press, 2009.

An Autumn Wind. Oldcastle, Co. Meath: Gallery Press, 2010.

Monochrome. Oldcastle, Co. Meath: Gallery Press, 2010.

Dreams of a Summer Night. Oldcastle, Co. Meath: Gallery Press, 2010.

New Collected Poems. Oldcastle, Co. Meath: Gallery Press, 2011.

Raw Material. Oldcastle, Co. Meath: Gallery Press, 2011.

Huts and Sheds. Oldcastle, Co. Meath: Gallery Press, 2011.

Selected Prose. Oldcastle, Co. Meath: Gallery Press, 2012.

Theatre. Oldcastle, Co. Meath: Gallery Press, 2013.

Echo's Grove. Oldcastle, Co. Meath: Gallery Press, 2013.

The Flying Boats. Oldcastle, Co. Meath: Gallery Press, 2014.

A NOTE ON MANUSCRIPT SOURCES

The largest collection of Derek Mahon's papers is held by Emory University's Robert W. Woodruff Library. In 1991 Linda Matthews, then Head of Special Collections, acquired an initial group of Mahon's papers dating from the 1980s. That acquisition has been augmented with regular additions to the collection from Mahon himself, covering most fully the years 1990–2006. Dillon Johnston later placed in the collection copies of Mahon's correspondence with Wake Forest University Press (1976–90), and the library acquired another group of Mahon's papers, largely 1985–8, from the collector Raymond Danowski. Mahon's own correspondence to others is found in numerous other Emory collections, including, most notably, the papers of Michael Longley, Seamus Heaney, Peter Fallon, Louis Asekoff, Paul Muldoon, Desmond O'Grady and James Simmons.

The late James O'Halloran assembled a large collection of Mahon's personal and literary papers dating largely from the mid-1980s. Within this collection, however, are manuscripts and typescripts of earlier books, including *Light Music* (1977), *The Sea in Winter* (1979), *Poems 1962–1978* (1979), *The Chimeras* (1982) and *The Hunt by Night* (1982). At the time of this writing, this collection remains in private hands.

The Burns Library of Boston College holds a small collection of Mahon's personal and literary papers spanning the years 1985–6.

Mahon's former roommate Richard Rooke saved a collection of Mahon's early manuscripts dating from the autumn of 1965. Others who have shared original letters or copies include Jill Schlesinger, Glyn Hughes, Stella Lubsen-Admiraal, Patricia Moynagh and Barry Murphy.

Oxford University Press files contain Mahon's correspondence with his publisher from the late-1960s through the mid-1980s.

These and other smaller collections of primary sources are cited in the notes.

BIBLIOGRAPHY

Balfour, Sebastian, Laurie Howes, Michael de Larrabeiti, and Anthony Weale, eds. *Trinity Tales: Trinity College Dublin in the Sixties*. Dublin: Lilliput Press, 2009.

Blake, John W. *Northern Ireland in the Second World War*. Belfast: Blackstaff Press, 2000.

Boland, Eavan. "Compact and Compromise: Derek Mahon as a Young Poet." *Irish University Review* (Spring/Summer 1994): 61.

Brearton, Fran. "Dancing Unto Death: Perceptions of the Somme, the Titanic and Ulster Protestantism." *The Irish Review* (Winter–Spring 1997), 98.

Brown, John, ed. *In the Chair: Interviews with Poets from the North of Ireland*. Cliffs of Moher: Salmon, 2002.

Brown, Terence. *Ireland: A Social and Cultural History, 1922 to the Present*. Ithaca: Cornell University Press, 1985.

Buxton, Rachel. *Robert Frost and Northern Irish Poetry*. Oxford: Oxford University Press, 2004.

Castles on the Air: The Life and Work of Poet and Broadcaster Louis MacNeice. n.p.: BBC, n.d.

Clark, Heather. *The Ulster Renaissance*. Oxford: Oxford University Press, 2006.

Coogan, Tim Pat. *The Troubles*. London: Arrow, 1996.

Dawe, Gerald and Edna Longley. *Across a Roaring Hill: The Protestant Imagination in Modern Ireland*. Belfast: Blackstaff, 1985.

Deane, Seamus. "Derek Mahon: Freedom from History" in *Celtic Revivals: Essays in Modern Irish Literature, 1880–1980*. London: Faber, 1985.

Durcan, Paul. "The World of Derek Mahon", *Magill* (Christmas 1984): 38–46.

Gillespie, Elgy, "Robert Lowell in Kilkenny", in *Changing the Times: Irish Women Journalists, 1969–1981*. Dublin: Lilliput, 2003.

Goodby, John. *Irish Poetry since 1950*. Manchester: Manchester University Press, 2000.

Greacen, Lavinia. *J.G. Farrell: The Making of a Writer*. London: Bloomsbury, 1999.

Haughton, Hugh. *The Poetry of Derek Mahon*. Oxford: Oxford University Press, 2007.

Heaney, Seamus. *Finders Keepers: Selected Prose, 1971–2001*. London: Faber, 2002.

Jamieson, John. *The History of the Royal Belfast Academical Institution, 1810–1960*. Belfast: William Mullan, 1959.

Johnston, Dillon. *Irish Poetry after Joyce*. Syracuse: Syracuse University Press, 1997.

—*The Poetic Economies of England and Ireland, 1912–2000*. Houndmills, Hampshire: Palgrave, 2001.

Kennedy-Andrews, Elmer. *The Poetry of Derek Mahon*. Gerrards Cross, Buckinghamshire: Colin Smythe, 2002.

King, Patricia. *Places Where a Thought Might Grow*. PhD Dissertation, City University of New York, 1995.

Leland, Mary. *The Little Galloway Girls*. London: Hamish Hamilton, 1987.

Lewis, Jeremy. *Playing for Time*. London: Collins, 1987.

Longley, Edna. "An Ironic Conscience at One Minute to Midnight", *Fortnight* (17 December 1984), 17.

—*The Living Stream: Literature and Revisionism in Ireland*. Newcastle: Bloodaxe, 1994.

Longley, Michael, ed. *Causeway: The Arts in Ulster*. Belfast: Arts Council of Northern Ireland, 1971.

—"Michael Longley in Conversation with Jody Allen Randolph." *Poetry Ireland*, no. 79 (2004): 78.

—*Tuppenny Stung*. Belfast: Lagan Press, 1994.

Luce, J. V. *Trinity College Dublin: The First 200 Years*. Dublin: Trinity College, 1992.

McCabe, Cathal. *The Poetry of Derek Mahon*. DPhil thesis, Jesus College, 2002.

McCormack, W. J. *Battle of the Books*. Dublin: Lilliput, 1986.

Ní Anluain, Cliodhna, ed. *Reading the Future: Irish Writers in Conversation with Mike Murphy*. Dublin: Lilliput Press, 2000.

O'Brien, Sean. *The Deregulated Muse*. Newcastle: Bloodaxe, 1998.

O'Driscoll, Dennis, ed. *Stepping Stones: Interviews with Seamus Heaney*. London: Faber, 2008.

The Poetry Nonsense, directed by Roger Greene, Caranna Productions, 2010.

Stallworthy, Jon. *Louis MacNeice: A Biography*. London: Norton, 1995.

INDEX